BERKSHIRE OUTDOORS

Hikes & Walks

Hikes & Walks

IN THE BERKSHIRE HILLS

TEXT BY LAUREN R. STEVENS

Illustrations by Alison Kolesar
Maps by Alison Kolesar and Vaughan Gray

Berkshire House Publishers
Stockbridge, Massachusetts

The text of this book was designed and composed by Jane McWhorter. The typefaces are Palatino and Helvetica. Cover photograph of Laurel Hill, Stockbridge © Apple Hill Designs by Nancy Fay Hecker. Hiking maps by Alison Kolesar are based on U.S. Geological Survey Quadrants. Vaughan Gray drew the supplementary maps. Map on p. 109 is adapted from "Pittsfield: A Self-Guided Historic Walking Tour" by Pittsfield Central.

Library of Congress Cataloging-in-Publication Data
Stevens, Lauren R. 1938-
Hikes & walks in the Berkshire Hills / text by Lauren R. Stevens : illustrations by Alison Kolesar : maps by Alison Kolesar and Vaughan Gray.
p. cm.
Includes bibliographical references.
ISBN 0-936399-03-1 : $9.95
1. Hiking — Massachusetts — Berkshire Hills — Guide-books.
2. Walking — Massachusetts — Berkshire Hills — Guide-books.
3. Berkshire Hills (Mass.) — Description and travel — Guide-books.
I. Title. II. Title: Hikes & Walks in the Berkshire Hills.
GV199.42.M42B47 1990
917.44'10443 — dc20   90-80107   CIP

Editors: David Emblidge and Virginia Rowe

Berkshire House Publishers
Box 297
Stockbridge, Massachusetts 01262

Manufactured in the United States of America

First printing September, 1990
10 9 8 7 6 5 4 3

BERKSHIRE, THE BERKSHIRES, THE BERKSHIRE HILLS

What is the name of this place, anyway? The original Berkshire is in England, south of Oxford. There it's pronounced "Bark-shuh." "Shire" refers to an Anglo-Saxon administrative district.

Purists refer to the "Berkshire Hills," meaning specifically what this book calls the southern Taconics, including peaks in New York State. The logic of calling all hills in Berkshire County the Berkshire Hills seems to be gaining acceptance.

Berkshire residents — and visitors — refer to the area variously as "Berkshire County," as simply "Berkshire," and as "the Berkshires," actually a 20th-century term created to publicize the area. This book does likewise.

To my parents

"Then all my gladsome way along . . ."
– Jonathan J. Schütz (1640–1690)

TABLE OF CONTENTS

List of Maps and Legend 11
Preface 15
Introduction 18
How to Use This Book 22
Transportation 25
Lodging and Dining 33
Safety 34
Berkshire History 38

HIKES & WALKS

SOUTH COUNTY

Mount Washington 45
    Hikes: Alander Mountain/Bash Bish Falls 46
              Mount Everett 51

Sheffield 55
    Walks: Salisbury Road 56
             Bartholomew's Cobble/Ashley House 58

Egremont 61
    Walk: Baldwin Hill Road North & South 61

New Marlborough 63
    Walks: Harmon Road 63
             Campbell Falls 66
             York Pond 66

Great Barrington 67
    Walks: Seekonk 69
             Benedict Pond 72
    Hike: Monument Mountain 73

Tyringham 76
    Walk: The Tyringham Cobble 78

Stockbridge 79
   Walks: Ice Glen 80
             Bowker's Woods 82
             Prospect Hill 83
             Glendale 84
             Gould Meadows and Bullard Woods 85

CENTRAL COUNTY

Lenox 88
   Walks: Kennedy Park 90
             Reservoirs 91
             Golden Hill 94
   Hike: Pleasant Valley / Lenox Mountain 95

Richmond 99
   Walk: East Road 99

Peru 101
   Walk: Rice Sanctuary 101

Pittsfield 104
   Walks: Downtown 106
             Canoe Meadows 110
   Hike: Berry Pond 112

Hancock 116
   Hike: Shaker Mountain 117

Dalton 122
   Walk: Wahconah Falls 123

Windsor 124
   Walk: Windsor Jambs 125
   Hike: Notchview / Judges Hill 127

NORTH COUNTY

Cheshire 131
   Walk: Hoosic River Railroad 131

Adams and Mount Greylock 135
   Walks: Overlook Trail 138
          Campground Trails:
            Stony Ledge 139
            March Cataract 139
            Deer Hill 139
          Mount Prospect from Notch Road 140
   Hikes: Cheshire Harbor Trail 141
          Bellows Pipe Trail 144
          The Hopper 148
          Stony Ledge and Roaring Brook Trail 152

Williamstown 158
   Walk: Stone Hill 159
   Hikes: Berlin Mountain 163
          Pine Cobble and Broad Brook Trails 168
          RRR Brooks 174
          The Dome 180

North Adams 183
   Walk: The Cascades 184

Florida and Savoy 186
   Walks: Borden Mountain and Tannery Falls 189
   Hike: Spruce Hill 192

Florida and Monroe: Tunnel and Turbine 195
   Hike: Spruce Mountain 197

WALKS FOR THE BLIND AND DISABLED 201

Great Barrington and Monterey
Walks: Beartown State Forest, Benedict Pond 202

Becket
Nature Trails: October Mountain State Forest,
Finerty Pond 205

Pittsfield
Nature Trails: Pittsfield State Forest 208

Washington
Walk: Warner Hill-Appalachian Trail 212

Adams
Mount Greylock State Reservation, Mount Prospect ..214

APPENDICES
Hikes & Walks by Degree of Difficulty 216
Long Hikes and Trail Systems 219
Boots, Books, Maps, Packs 222
Bibliography 223

LIST OF MAPS

County divisions, 24
Relief map, 41

Maps & Page Numbers	**U.S.Geological Survey Quadrangle**

SOUTH COUNTY

Mt. Washington
    Alander Mtn./Bash Bish Falls, 49 .... Bash Bish
    Mount Everett, 53 .... Bash Bish
Sheffield
    Salisbury Road, 57 .... Bash Bish
    Bartholomew's Cobble
      & Ashley House, 59 .... Ashley Falls
New Marlborough
    Harmon Rd., 64 .... Monterey, South Sandisfield
    Campbell Falls, 65 .... South Sandisfield
Gt. Barrington
    Seekonk, 70 .... Egremont
    Benedict Pond, 71 .... Gt. Barrington
    Monument Mountain, 75 .... Gt. Barrington
Tyringham
    Tyringham Cobble, 77 .... Monterey
Stockbridge
    Several Walks, 86 .... Stockbridge

CENTRAL COUNTY

Lenox
    Kennedy Park, 89 .... W. Pittsfield
    Reservoirs, 92 .... Stockbridge

Golden Hill, 93 .... E. Lee,
                                                        Stockbridge
        Pleasant Valley / Lenox Mountain, 97 ... Pittsfield
Peru
        Rice Sanctuary, 103 .... Peru
Pittsfield
        Downtown, 109 .... W. Pittsfield
        Canoe Meadows, 111 .... E. Pittsfield
        Berry Pond, 115 .... W. Pittsfield,
                                                        Hancock
Hancock
        Shaker Mountain, 121 .... W. Pittsfield
Dalton-Windsor
        Wahconah Falls / Windsor Jambs, 126 .. Peru, Windsor
Windsor
        Notchview / Judge's Hill, 129 .... Windsor

NORTH COUNTY

Cheshire
        Hoosic River Railroad, 133 .... Cheshire
Adams
        Mt. Greylock, 156 .... Cheshire,
                                                        Williamstown
Williamstown
        Stone Hill, 161 .... Williamstown
        Berlin Mountain, 167 .... Berlin
        Pine Cobble / Broad Brook /
            The Dome, 173 .... Pownal,
                                                        Williamstown
        RRR Brooks, 179 .... Berlin,
                                                        Williamstown
No. Adams
        The Cascades, 185 .... Williamstown
Florida & Savoy
        Borden Mountain & Tannery Falls, 191 .. Plainfield, Rowe
        Spruce Hill, 193 .... No. Adams

Florida & Monroe
    Spruce Mtn., 199 .... Rowe, No. Adams

WALKS FOR THE BLIND AND DISABLED
October Mtn. State Forest

    Finerty Pond, 207 .... E. Lee

United States Geological Survey (USGS) maps are available, by
quadrangles, as listed above. These do not conform to town
boundaries, but are named by the distinguishing feature on
each quad. The maps are available at book and sporting goods
stores (see the Appendix), or from USGS, Reston, VA 22092.

MAP LEGEND

paved road	seasonally present stream
unpaved road	rail line
trail described in text (except where it coincides with Appalachian Trail)	state line
Appalachian Trail	U.S. highway
contour lines	State highway
river or stream	Interstate highway

PREFACE

I am proud to say that the Berkshire Natural Resources Council has played a significant role in bringing this book into being. *Hikes & Walks in the Berkshire Hills* will help people to enjoy, as I do, taking a stroll in these lovely settings. Furthermore, while following these routes, walkers will be learning of the extraordinary amount of protected land in the county as well as much that should be protected.

The Berkshires are, by and large, gentle hills, and their grandeur has for a long time been more pastoral than wild. Early settlement had defined landscape patterns long before Nathaniel Hawthorne and Herman Melville arrived in Berkshire. By 1825, our roads were bordered by fields and stone walls and our village centers were places of dignity and prosperity. As a consequence, the Berkshire landscape of today (or at least the best of it) is still defined by these early settlements. I hope this guide will not only help you to discover new walks and hikes throughout Berkshire, but will also provide new vantage points from which to appreciate a landscape that has served many generations. In this way, it is intended as a loving document that celebrates our small region.

Much of Berkshire has been protected through both public land trust and private conservation groups. I doubt if there are many regions that can boast of such a vast assembly of parks and state forests and pubic reservations, not to speak of the diversity of properties and landscapes that have been saved.

The history of land preservation in Berkshire is yet to be written, but during the 1930s a process began of placing woodlots in the public trust as parks and state forests, now totaling 95,000 acres, under the Department of Environmental Management. The Department of Fisheries, Wildlife and Environmental Law Enforcement has acquired thousands of additional acres as Wildlife Management Areas. Other land has been protected as municipal watersheds. More recently, the National Park Service has been acquiring a corridor for the Appalachian Trail that runs lengthwise through the county.

Private, not-for-profit groups have also been at work. The Appalachian Trail Conference has cooperated with the Park Service in protecting and maintaining the Appalachian Trail, while the Appalachian Mtn. Club supervises trail work on Mt. Greylock, interprets the natural setting, and hosts visitors at Bascom Lodge.

The Trustees of Reservations has collected since 1891 such valuable land and historic buildings as Bartholomew's Cobble, the Col. John Ashley House, Field Farm, Goose Pond Reservation, the Mission House, Monument Mountain Reservation, Naumkeag, Notchview Reservation, and Tyringham Cobble.

The Massachusetts Audubon Society maintains Pleasant Valley and Canoe Meadows sanctuaries, and the New England Forestry Foundation owns and maintains the Rice Sanctuary for public enjoyment.

The Berkshire Natural Resources Council (BNRC) was founded in 1967 as a private agent for land protection in the county. As its director, I have worked with towns, individuals, and public officials on land-use matters; I have advocated environmental proposals with the state on behalf of the Resources Council; and I have brought land under protection on behalf of Berkshire County Land Trust and Conservation Fund, an affiliate of BNRC.

In recent years, BNRC has assisted communities in setting up local land trusts. I hope that some day every town in Berkshire County will have one. These young land trusts already have acquired significant open lands and have worked with the council to establish the Berkshire County Land Trust Alliance. This body can take advantage both of a community land trust's extraordinary responsiveness to local needs and an alliance's ability to bring massed weight to bear on crucial issues.

As a forum and news source on land use and environmental issues, *Berkshire Green*, a quarterly magazine, is published by the alliance. In 1988 BNRC published Deborah Burns' and Lauren R. Stevens' *Most Excellent Majesty:*

A History of Mt. Greylock, as a way of informing the public concerning the touch point of environmental concern in the county and the state.

Our goal, as always, is to see to it that our children have opportunities like ours, to meet the real thing: the grace, the beauty, the charm, the challenge of the Berkshire landscape. BNRC or any of the organizations I have mentioned would welcome inquiries on how to help.

George S. Wislocki, Director
Berkshire Natural Resources Council
20 Bank Row
Pittsfield, MA 01201

INTRODUCTION

Whether you want to amble in an afternoon through an azalea grove or take a strenuous day hike with sweeping vistas of five states, it's tough to beat Berkshire County. For variety and tradition, few areas in this country offer prospects as rich as those of the western end of Massachusetts. Some of the routes described in this book move you inward, toward contemplation and quiet. As Henry David Thoreau said of the Bellows Pipe, his trail to the summit of Mt. Greylock, "It seemed a road for the pilgrim to enter upon who would climb to the gates of heaven." Other routes, perhaps beside brooks dropping for hundreds of feet or along rocky ridges fringed with fir, make you want to shout with joy. And through them all you absorb the rhythms that previous generations have trod, an at-oneness with ancients known and unknown, famous and infamous.

These descriptions overflow into neighboring states and counties because Berkshire's mountainous boundaries — the Taconics, Greens, Hoosacs, and Litchfield Hills — themselves offer prime areas to get out and enjoy the out-of-doors under your own locomotion. The Berkshire region can test the limbs and meet the curiosities of daily walkers in infinite ways. This little book is content to list many of the best: 39 walks and 17 hikes, together with brief descriptions of 21 towns and cities in which they mostly take place.

A Few Definitions and Limitations

Walks are easier and less exerting than *Hikes*, not necessarily because they are shorter but because they involve less up and down. Several walks in this book are longer than some of the hikes. Although hike descriptions are more or less commensurate with hike lengths, walk descriptions are more idiosyncratic. They will all get you there, but some linger longer on the details of nature or culture.

Each description tells you the *length in miles* of the outing. Each hike description gives you *elapsed time*, on the grounds that you are more likely to wear a watch than a pedometer. A warning accompanies these figures, given in hours and minutes (1:37): you should add at least 20 minutes per hour, because minutes in the book include only travel time, not time to look at views, at historic artifacts, for the best way to ford a brook, or for an obscure blaze. Or for taking a rest. The times were measured by energetic folks, unencumbered by packs, papooses, or wandering puppies.

Most of the hikes are in the woods or on mountain ridges, as are some of the walks. Of the rest, most of the walks are primarily on gravel roads. Many pass cultural sites of significance. The text hints at some cross-country skiing and road bicycling possibilities. For more on biking, pick up Lew Cuyler's *Bike Rides in the Berkshire Hills*.

This walking book is *not* a guide to the *extended hiking trails* in and near the county, although sections that you happen to pass over while following these routes are described. For further information, see the Appendix.   The Appalachian Mtn. Club and the Taconic Hiking Club publish guides to the Appalachian Trail and Taconic Crest Trail, respectively. Christopher J. Ryan has published a guide to the Taconic Trail System. See the Bibliography for these and other pertinent guides.

The trails in this book are marked by *blazes*. A blaze is a daub of paint, at about eye level usually, directly on a tree or rock or on wood or metal attached to a tree or driven into the ground, that marks a trail. A common route for two trails may be blazed with two colors. Two blazes, one above the other, signal a sharp turn or other unusual circumstance ahead. In this county the north-south long trails are blazed white, including the Appalachian Trail; side trails to them are blazed blue; trails that don't connect to the long trails are blazed orange . . . with some local exceptions.

The purpose of this book is to pass on information on day walks and hikes accurate as of the time I explored each of these routes, to reassure you that you are indeed on the right trail, and to encourage you — because the most important thing I learned from researching this book is that even when the weather is a bit uncertain, the distance seems a little far, you've got other things to do, or you're not feeling quite 100%, going out will always make you glad.

Glad because walking is good exercise for everyone. I hope this book helps you determine which distances and degrees of difficulty are healthiest for you. Glad because the scenery varies from serene to breathtaking and there is no better way to see it than to get yourself there under your own power, true personal empowerment. Most of what you will be looking at you cannot reach by car; for the rest, driving to it is no substitute for becoming a part of it. Glad because you and I need to rediscover periodically in a civilized grandeur like Berkshire where we have come from and perhaps discover some insight into where we are going.

But you already know these things.

Thanks

Special thanks to those people who provided information and to those who have been hiking and walking companions, including county residents Robert K. Buckwalter, Henry N. Flynt, Paul Karabinos, Christopher Niebuhr, Bernice O'Brien, George Osgood, Robert J. Redington (who authored the section on guided trails for the blind), Robert Spencer, Edgar and Piri Taft, George S. Wislocki, Reinhard A. Wobus, and Alice Sedgwick Wohl.

Whit Griswold's *Berkshire Trails for Walking and Ski Touring*, now out of print, introduced me to several previously unknown venues. The publishers and I thank him for making his text available as a resource. Jonathan Sternfield's *The Berkshire Book: A Complete Guide* supplied information and maps for several sections of this book.

Several of these hikes first appeared in an earlier version in *The Advocate* newspaper in Williamstown. I spent a fine morning hiking Shaker Mtn. with John Manners, who rediscovered the site, researched its history, and lead the Boy Scouts in laying out the trail. Deborah Burns made stylistic suggestions on this manuscript. Robert D. Hatton, Jr., county trail coordinator for the Department of Environmental Management, reviewed the material. If you spot an error, blame me — and then, please, let me know about it or other improvements in care of the publisher, so we can correct the next edition.

HOW TO USE THIS BOOK

This book tries its best to be accurate and helpful. Neither the author nor the publisher can be responsible beyond that effort. Many things, both natural and manmade, are subject to change and out of the author's control. And, with the best intentions, errors are possible.

Key Terms, Important Names, Abbreviations

The word "facilities," as used here, refers to man-made structures that could be of convenience to the walker. As an example of facilities, the descriptions differentiate between flush toilets and outhouses — what the state calls pit toilets. The initials "HQ" refer to headquarters for either state-owned or privately owned properties opened to the public. The difference between *Hikes* and *Walks* is explained in the Introduction, as is the term "blazes," and how to read them.

"AMC" refers to the Appalachian Mtn. Club, the hiking and environmentally oriented not-for-profit organization that is concessionaire in Bascom Lodge on the summit of Mt. Greylock. It is related to but not the same as the Appalachian Trail Conference, the group of local organizations that maintain the Appalachian Trail ("AT"), the foot trail from Georgia to Maine. The AT passes through Berkshire County. Some of the hikes and walks in the book use parts of the footpath. While much of AT in the county runs across state land, the National Park Service has purchased stretches of land to create an AT corridor to protect the trail.

Another not-for-profit environmental organization, the Massachusetts Audubon Society, a separate entity from the National Audubon Society, owns and maintains two public sanctuaries in Berkshire, both of which are described in the text. Another major land owner is also private, the Trustees of Reservations ("TTOR"), a statewide group originally founded as analogous to a public library: a resource available to the public for beautiful and historic places. Four hikes or walks in this book take place on their land.

Yet another private group, the New England Forestry Foundation, owns the Dorothy Frances Rice Sanctuary. Hikes and walks also cross the lands of Berkshire School in Sheffield, and Buxton School and the Clark Art Institute in Williamstown. Three hikes cross land belonging to Williams College, in Williamstown. Walkers in the county owe a debt to many private landowners who willingly share the enjoyment of special places.

Walkers are indebted, as well, to numerous groups who lay out, maintain and map trails, such as the Appalachian Trail Conferences, Berkshire School, the state's Division of Forests and Parks, the Green Mtn. Club, the Williams (College) Outing Club, and the Taconic Hiking Club of New York — which is responsible for the Taconic Crest Trail (TCT).

Additional Maps

To find some of the not-so-obvious corners of the county, a supplement to regular road maps is advisable. One is *Jimapco Map C12, Berkshire County, MA,* 3rd edition, $3.25. It is available in bookstores, drugstores, and newspaper stores or from Jimapco, Box 1137, Clifton Park, NY 12065; 1-800-MAPS 123. A lovely road map is also available from the County Surveyors' Office, Bowes Building, Park Square, Pittsfield, MA 01201. Our *List of Maps* indicates the U.S. Geological Survey quadrangle(s) for each hike and walk. These maps are available at bookstores and sporting goods stores. They provide the base for virtually all county maps.

Organization

Following a generally accepted tradition, this book is organized in three parts: South, Central, and North County, as shown on the adjacent map. That should be a help in locating the hikes and walks closest to you. Here is a plug, however; try some farther removed. Differences exist, interesting in their own right and helpful in defining the characteristics of the walks with which you are most familiar.

NORTH COUNTY

Adams (Population: 9,706)
Cheshire (3,492)
Clarksburg (1,866)
Florida (735)
New Ashford (193)
North Adams (16,271)
Savoy (595)
Williamstown (8,361)

CENTRAL COUNTY

Becket (1,524)
Dalton (7, 212)
Hancock (800)
Hinsdale (2,011)
Lanesborough (3,100)
Lenox (5,557)
Peru (724)
Pittsfield (49,418)
Richmond (1,701)
Washington (602)
Windsor (638)

SOUTH COUNTY

Alford (367)
Egremont (1,052)
Great Barrington (7,014)
Lee (6,020)
Monterey (841)
Mount Washington (120)

New Marlborough (1,098)
Otis (963)
Sandisfield (735)
Sheffield (3,264)
Stockbridge (2,581)
Tyringham (365)
West Stockbridge (1,425)

TRANSPORTATION

Getting to the Berkshires

BY CAR

From Manhattan: Take the Major Deegan Expressway or the Henry Hudson Parkway to the Saw Mill River Parkway, then proceed north on the Taconic State Parkway. For the southern Berkshires, exit the Taconic at Hillsdale, Claverack, Rte. 23 and follow 23 east, towards Hillsdale and on to Gt. Barrington. For Stockbridge, Lee, and Lenox, (and all points in South and Central county) proceed up Rte. 7. For Williamstown and all of northern Berkshire, you might want to proceed farther up the Taconic and exit at Rte. 295, leading to Stephentown, then follow Rte. 43 through Hancock to Williamstown.

From New Jersey, Pennsylvania and the South: Rte. 22 north is a good choice for local color, and you can pick it up as far south as Armonk or Bedford in Westchester County, New York. From Rte. 22, farther upstate, turn right at Hillsdale on 23 east toward Gt. Barrington. For the most direct route from New Jersey, Pennsylvania and the South, take the New York Thruway to I-84 east; at the Taconic parkway go north to Rte. 23 for southern Berkshire or Rte. 295 for northern Berkshire.

From Connecticut and/or New York Metro Area: Rte. 7 is a scenic route, which can be picked up at Danbury, via I-684 and I-84. To arrive in southeastern Berkshire, Rte. 8 is a quick and scenic drive as it follows the Farmington River north.

From Boston and the East: The Massachusetts Turnpike is the quickest, easiest and one of the more scenic routes west to southern Berkshire. West of the Connecticut River, you can get off the turnpike at Exit 3 and take Rte. 202 south to Rte. 20 west and pick up Rte. 23 west at Woronoco for the best route to Otis Ridge, Butternut Basin and Catamount

BERKSHIRE ACCESS

Using Tanglewood (on the Stockbridge–Lenox line) as the Berkshire reference point, the following cities are this close.

CITY	TIME	MILES
Albany	1 hr	50
Boston	2½ hrs	135
Bridgeport	2 hrs	110
Danbury	1¾ hrs	85
Hartford	1½ hrs	70
Montreal	5 hrs	275
New Haven	2½ hrs	115
New York City	3 hrs	150
Philadelphia	4½ hrs	230
Providence	2½ hrs	125
Springfield	¾ hr	35
Waterbury	1½ hrs	75
Washington, DC	7 hrs	350
Worcester	1¾ hrs	90

Berkshire County is 56 miles south to north, from Sheffield to Williamstown. Depending on the season and the weather, it's normally a two-hour leisurely drive up Rte. 7. Because of the mountain ranges that run along this route, east-west travel across the county remains much more difficult, with all the county's east-west routes (2 in the north; 9, midcounty; and 23 in the south) being tricky drives in freezing or snowy weather.

ski areas. Most people stay on the turnpike right into Berkshire County, exiting either at Lee or West Stockbridge.

If you're coming west to the Berkshires from more northern latitudes, eastern entry to Berkshire County can be gained by driving the original Mohawk Trail, an Indian by-way. Also known as Rte. 2, this is the most direct way to Jiminy Peak and Brodie Mountain skiing .

From Hartford: The quickest route by far is I-91 north to the Massachusetts Turnpike west. Then proceed as in directions for Massachusetts Turnpike travel from Boston.

From Montreal or Albany: Leaving Canada, take I-87 (known as "the Northway") south to Albany, and exit at Rte. 7 to Rte. 2 toward Williamstown, or continue on I-87 south and I-90 east (they're the same south of Albany), connecting then to the Massachusetts Turnpike which is the continuation of I-90 east. Exit at either West Stockbridge or Lee.

BY BUS

Please note: Schedules and prices are subject to change. We advise that you call ahead to check.

From Manhattan (3.5 hours): Bonanza (800-556-3815) serves the Berkshires out of New York City's Port Authority Bus Terminal (212-564-8484) at 40th St. between 8th and 9th Aves. Tickets may be purchased at the Greyhound ticket windows (212-971-6363) near 8th Ave. Boarding is down the escalators at the center of the terminal, and then to the right, usually at Gate 13. Bonanza runs three buses daily: 8:45 a.m., 2:15 p.m., and 5:15 p.m. There is also a Friday evening bus, leaving Port Authority at 7:30. The 1993 round-trip ticket price is $46 to Gt. Barrington; one way is $23. Berkshire locales marked with an asterisk are Flag Stops, where you must wave to the bus driver in order to be picked up.

Berkshire Phone Numbers for New York Buses

Canaan, CT .... Canaan Pharmacy, Main St. 203-824-5481
Gt. Barrington .... Bill's Pharmacy, 362 Main St. 528-1590
Hillsdale, NY .... *Junction Rtes. 22 & 23 800-556-3815
Lee .... McClelland Drugs, 43 Main St. 243-0135
Lenox ..... Lenox News & Variety, 39 Housatonic St. 637-2815
New Ashford .... *Entrance to Brodie Mtn. Ski
                                                         Area, Rte. 7 800-556-3815
Pittsfield .... Bus Terminal, 57 South Church St. 442-4451
Sheffield .... *Rte. 7, First Agricultural Bank 800-556-3815
So. Egremont .... *Gaslight Store 800-556-3815
Stockbridge .... Chamber of Commerce Booth,
                                                             Main St. 298-3344
Williamstown .... Williams Inn, Main St. 458-2665

From Boston (3.5 hrs.): Bonanza and Greyhound serve the Berkshires from Boston out of the Greyhound Terminal at 10 St. James Ave. (617-423-5810). Peter Pan/Trailways runs two buses daily to Pittsfield out of the Trailways Terminal at 555 Atlantic Ave. Berkshire-bound passengers change buses at Springfield. Call 800-343-9999 for prices and schedules.

Berkshire Phone Numbers for Boston Buses

Lee .... McClelland Drugs, 43 Main St. 243-0135
Lenox ..... Lenox News & Variety, 39 Housatonic St. 637-2815
Pittsfield .... Bus Terminal, 57 South Church St. 442-4451
Williamstown .... Williams Inn, 1090 Main St. 458-9371

From Hartford (1.75 hrs.): The Greyhound Line runs two buses daily, at 11:15 a.m. and 4:20 p.m., into Pittsfield from the Greyhound Terminal at 409 Church St., Hartford (203-547-1500). Greyhound's 1993 round-trip ticket price was $42.

From Montreal (6 hrs.): Greyhound runs south to the Albany Greyhound Terminal. Connect to Pittsfield as noted below.

From Albany (1 hr.): Bonanza runs two buses daily from Albany to Pittsfield. Greyhound runs one bus daily; 1993 round-trip ticket was $13 on both lines.

BY TRAIN

From Manhattan: Amtrak (800-872-7245) can help you get to the Berkshires, but not all the way. Their turboliner from Grand Central Station runs frequently along the Hudson River. For southern Berkshire, stay aboard till Hudson; for northern Berkshire, carry on to Rensselaer. Limousine or taxi service can be arranged for the 40-mi. trip from Hudson to southern Berkshire or from Rensselaer to northern Berkshire (46 mi.).

From Hudson .... Star City Taxi 518-828-3355
From Rensselaer .... AAA Limousine 518-456-5030
                                          Diamond Limousine 518-283-8000,
                                          800-448-0844

From Boston: Amtrak runs a single train daily through the Berkshires, starting from Boston's South Station. The Pittsfield depot has no actual station; it's just a shelter. (To find the depot: take West St. westwards past the Hilton; at the first light, turn right onto Center St.; take the next right onto Depot St.; the shelter is on the left.) Anyone boarding the train in Pittsfield must purchase tickets on the train; the 1993 round-trip ticket price ranged from $26 each way to $45 round trip, depending on time of travel and seat availability. Private compartments are also available, ranging from $46.50 supplementary for a single compartment to $79 supplementary for a double compartment.

From Montreal: Amtrak runs one train daily from Montreal through Albany. The 1993 round-trip ticket price was $60, excluding holiday periods. During the Thanksgiving, Christmas, and New Year's seasons, the round-trip rate rises to $92. There is no same-day train connection from this run to the Berkshires; to get here by hired car, see information above on limousine or bus service from Albany.

From Albany: Amtrak has a single Pittsfield-bound train daily from the Albany/Rensselaer Depot on East St. (2 mi. from downtown Albany). The 1993 ticket fare was $10 one way, and ranges from $15 to $17 round trip depending on time of travel and seat availability.

BY PLANE

If you own a small airplane or decide to charter one, you can fly directly to the Berkshires, landing at Gt. Barrington, Pittsfield, or No. Adams airports.

From New York City: There are several charter air companies in the metropolitan New York Area that will fly you from La Guardia, JFK, or other airports near New York to any of the Berkshire airports. Their 1993 estimated rates ran from $400 to $2100 one way, for a twin-engine airplane (holds five plus the pilot). Airlines currently flying these routes include:

 Aircraft Charter Group 800-553-3590
 Chester Air, Chester CT 800-752-6371
 Long Island Airways 800-645-9572

and from Westchester County:

 Panorama (White Plains airport) ..... 914-328-9800 or, if
            calling from New York, 718-507-9800
 Richmor Aviation 800-331-6101

From Boston: Estimated rates for 1993 ran $325 to $690 for a twin-engine airplane (holds five plus the pilot).

 Bird Airfleet 508-372-6566
 Wiggins Airways .... 617-762-5690, Ext. 251

From Hartford: Bradley Airport in Hartford handles numerous domestic and international airlines, so you can fly to Bradley from nearly anywhere. From there, charter air service to the Berkshires is available through any of the companies listed under "From Boston" or through the Berkshire County companies listed below.

From Albany: Albany is terminus for a substantial volume of domestic jet traffic and, being under an hour from the Berkshires by car, is the closest you can get to these hills by jet. Charter connector flights from Albany to the Berkshires are available through Page Flight (518-869-0253) or through the Berkshire County companies listed below.

In Berkshire County: Three aviation companies in Berkshire County operate air taxi service to just about any other northeastern airport.

Berkshire Aviation .... Gt. Barrington Airport
                                528-1010, 528-1061
Lyon Aviation .... Pittsfield Airport
                                443-6700
Esposito Flying Service ..... Harriman & West Airport,
                                No. Adams 663-3330

These local carriers' 1993 rates for a twin-engine plane (holds five plus the pilot) averaged $165 to Albany, $485 to Boston, $235 to Hartford, $595 to La Guardia or JFK, and $495 to Teterboro, New Jersey (at the foot of the George Washington Bridge). They also have single-engine planes (holds three plus pilot) for roughly 35-40% less, but these are dependent on weather conditions.

LODGING AND DINING

Berkshire offers a host of possibilities for lodging and dining, from the humble to the luxurious. The popularity of the area as a tourist destination means that those who want to visit in the high seasons (summer and fall) must plan ahead. Lodging reservations are particularly important. We recommend two approaches to finding a place to stay and deciding where to eat. *The Berkshire Book: A Complete Guide*, by Jonathan Sternfield, from the publishers of this hiking guide, is a thoroughly researched travel book, covering not only lodging and dining, but culture, recreation, shopping and many other topics as well. *The New York Times* said its recommendations were "right on the money." It is available from bookstores throughout the United States or from the publisher (Berkshire House, Box 915, Gt. Barrington, MA 01230; $14.95). Or you can call the Berkshire Visitors Bureau (413-443-9186) to ask for their package of brochures about lodging and dining possibilities. Both *The Berkshire Book* and the Visitors Bureau provide telephone numbers for Chamber of Commerce and other lodging reservations services.

Jonathan Sternfield's *The Berkshire Book* actually reviews restaurants and food purveyors, and you might enjoy seeing whether your opinions harmonize with his. Don't forget that one of the best dining possibilities for hikers and walkers is the well-planned picnic along the trail. Berkshire offers several traditional country general stores where you can get provisions, or, if you like, elegant gourmet picnics-to-go can be ordered from many of the area's upscale grocers and caterers.

SAFETY

Walking and hiking are two of the safest and healthiest activities you might engage in. Compared to driving a car, working in the kitchen, cutting firewood . . . your chances of being injured in the slightest are extremely small. That is the way it should be: walking should be a worry-free, non-competitive, relaxing avocation. Walking doesn't even lead to pimples.

This section ought to stop right here, without borrowing trouble. Nevertheless, after wandering around the county for several decades, I have accumulated a small amount of wisdom that could, conceivably, save you an equal amount of pain.

A Few Basic Rules

I want to share with you some things you probably already know but of which you may need to be reminded. I'll do it as succinctly as possible. They are all summed up in rule number one.

1. Take a few minutes before you go out to think through what you're going to do.
2. Carry water. You can't be certain even of lovely mountain brooks.
3. Wear comfortable, stout shoes — not sneakers or running shoes.
4. Remember that it may get warmer or cooler, especially on ridges.
5. Always tell someone where you are going.
6. Signs and blazes are constructions of man and cannot always be trusted. Leave the cares of civilization behind but take along a map such as the ones in this book, a compass, and a watch.
7. Stay on the trail.
8. Do not leave any trash.

These rules and this book ought to get you where you want to go . . . and back.

A special few words for newcomers to Berkshire. Welcome! Are there any dangers lurking on the roadside or in the woods? Yes, a few. In the extreme southwestern part of the county rattlesnakes live on the rock outcroppings. This book warns you on which trails they might be encountered. *They* warn you if you are getting too near. Should you get bitten you have time to get to help from just about anywhere described here, which you should do in an unhurried but deliberate manner.

You might see a bear, which will usually run from you, especially if you make some noise. Do not try to approach a bear.

Some people are allergic to some kinds of bees. If so, they should carry a bee sting kit. In 30 years of walking in Berkshire I have never seen a rattler, a bear, or been stung by a bee (in the woods).

Poison ivy exists in openings, at lower elevations. I have asked Alison Kolesar, who drew the lovely illustrated maps for this book, to draw poison ivy leaves, so that you will know what to avoid. Ticks that carry Lyme disease are rife in Connecticut and the eastern end of Massachusetts. Perhaps over the next few years they will move out this way. Tuck your trousers into your socks and inspect yourself after outings. Because of the terrain, storms can arrive without much warning — more of a potential problem in the winter than the summer. Take along extra clothes.

Hunters

Stay out of the woods and even off gravel roads during hunting season. Check at the local town hall for the dates, because Massachusetts, Connecticut, New York, and Vermont each has different seasons and each state has a variety of seasons for different animals and weapons. In general, be on the alert from mid-November through mid-December, especially for shotgun deer season, which attracts the most two-legged participants.

Automobiles

Walk against traffic on roads. Wear reflective clothing at dusk. If you are parking your car, be certain the shoulder is firm. Lock your car. If you don't like to take your keys with you for fear of losing them, remember that losing your keys, while annoying, is ultimately less of a problem than losing your car.

Weather

Mark Twain, who ought to know because he summered in Tyringham, said of local weather, if you don't like it, wait five minutes. He exaggerated. Berkshire weather does grow less predictable as you gain elevation, however, and summer thunderstorms or winter snow squalls can come out of nowhere. Normally you would expect county weather to be affected by its proximity (less than 150 mi.) to the ocean. Because of the hills, however, this area is controlled more by the prevailing westerly wind. Thus winters are colder and summers are cooler than either east or south of Berkshire.

Average Temperature
October	49.3
January	21.2
April	44.3
July	68.3

Average precipitation
Snow	70"
Rain	36.14"
Total	43.14"

Clothing

It is not necessary to invest heavily in trendy clothing, but consider the likelihood that the weather will change on your walk. Wear layers. If that means taking a small pack, well, that pack can also carry camera, snack, small first-aid kit, extra socks, and rain gear. A pair of well-broken-in, comfortable boots or shoes is your single most important piece of equipment. These shoes are worth some extra time, applying Neatsfoot oil or waterproofing. Wear wool socks.

Trail Indicators

Most trails in the county are well marked, which means that the next blaze is generally visible from the previous one. Don't keep going if you run out of blazes. Dry creek beds look deceptively like paths — sometimes they are, but sometimes they aren't. While a blowdown can disrupt a path, forcing a temporary detour, thanks to the hard work of many volunteers the trails described in this book are kept in good shape. So if what you're on doesn't seem like a trail anymore, turn back until you find hard evidence that you're going the right way.

Useful Items in the Woods

Water, map, compass, jackknife, matches, and small flashlight. As well as providing stability and a little extra push when needed, a walking stick can check the ground ahead for dampness and fend off the blows of Little John, should you run into him while crossing the Housatonic on a log. Bring a book to read while leisurely soaking up the ambiance.

First Aid

"Off" is apparently one of the few insect repellents that really work; Avon's "Skin So Soft" is also effective, even though it was intended for other purposes. Some folks swear by Cutters' for mosquitoes and black flies. What you don't wear — such as shampoos, perfume, aftershave lotion — can also be important. If you make yourself smell like a flower, you are likely to attract bugs. Your first-aid kit should include a general purpose ointment and band-aids large enough to cover a blister on your foot.

Avoid poison ivy, bees, Lyme ticks, if there be any, rattlesnakes and bears.

After reading all this, you'll know as much as the natives.

BERKSHIRE HISTORY

Both natural history and social history in Berkshire are tales of ups and downs. Looking at both from the end of the 20th century, you may feel some past time was better than the present, but it ain't necessarily so. The county testifies that geography, for all our veneer of civilization, is still destiny. And this county, now, maintains a delicate balance of being close to but not too close to the Boston-Washington megalopolis that holds down the East Coast. It is an accessible hinterland. It has the position and the resources to rise up into the future.

Six hundred million years ago the area was down, under the ocean, which was at work forming the rocks. It was warm and wet, with sandy beaches and clear, shallow waters. The lapping waves built up beaches that turned to sandstone, which in turn metamorphosed into quartzite — the erosion-resistant backbone of many of the county's ridges. Shelled marine animals built coral reefs, which calcified into limestone. The deposits of this alkaline agent, mined on the side of Mt. Greylock in Adams, protect the area from the worst ravages of acid precipitation today. Some of that limestone was recrystalized into marble, snowy chunks of which grace the hiking trails and can be inspected at the Natural Bridge in Clarksburg. Muddy offshore sediments settled to form shales and then schists, crystalline rocks that fracture cleanly. The bands of granite that run through the southern part of the county antedate the metamorphic rock.

The continents began to shift, in response to subterranean pressure. At a speed of about an inch a year over 150 million years, the land masses that would one day be North America, Africa, and Europe moved towards each other, closing the proto-Atlantic ocean. Several arcs of offshore volcanic islands were shoved onto the continent by a series of slow but cataclysmic collisions known as the Taconic Orogeny (Taconic mountain building). The entire continental shelf was squeezed into a series of folds, the monumental forerunners of the Appalachian Range. The bases of these mountains, some Himalayan in height, must have just about filled Berkshire, when the county reached for the sky. Then the continents began to pull apart, as they are still doing.

As soon as mountains were stacked up, the process of erosion began. Rain fell, forming rivers that still drain these hills, but in those days more vigorously carving a landscape unrooted by vegetation. Not only water but wind sculpted Berkshire hills, raging unbroken by trees and shrubs. The rugged landscape was tamed, waiting only for plants to soften it.

Less than two million years ago the first of a succession of four ice sheets ground down in response to a cooling climate. These mile-high glaciers brought debris, gravel and rocks, which they deposited around the nubbins of mountains that remained. Glacial lakes covered most of north county and a good portion of the south. Because the Hoosac Valley was preglacial, once the melt set in, the Hoosic River returned to flowing across the north-south path of the ice. This and the Upper Ammonoosuc in New Hampshire are the only rivers in New England to flow from southwest to northeast. Nor were the beds of the Housatonic or Westfield much altered. The Farmington River ran up against a load of glacial trash that turned its general southerly course in Connecticut.

The ice withdrew as recently as 10,000 years ago. Vegetation and then wildlife followed its retreating edge. Perhaps a few of the earliest North American inhabitants, having boated or walked across the land bridge from Asia, were in Berkshire to bid farewell to the ice. Gradually, the evergreen forest moved north, lingering only on the tops of the highest ridges, while the broad-leaved, deciduous forest moved in, characterized in North County by sugar maple and in the south by oak, with their associated pines, ash, beech, birch and alder.

The rocky steepness of the county does not lend itself to leisurely flowing water and big lakes. With the exception of the southern reach of the Housatonic, which meanders in curlicues through Sheffield, Berkshire rivers retain little water and rush to their destinations. What lakes the county has, it owes to the efforts of 19th-century industrialists to create a head or a reservoir to provide a year-round flow of water for power or other manufacturing processes: Otis Reservoir, Cheshire Reservoir, Pontoosuc, Onota, and others.

Seen from above, the county presents the ridges that remain from the north-south running folds, the Taconics along the New York line, the lower end of the Green Mountains protruding over the Vermont line, the Hoosacs filling the northeast quadrant, the Southern Berkshire Plateau filling the southeast quadrant, and a line of river valleys, just to the left of center, made up of the Hoosic and Housatonic — albeit flowing in opposite directions — that meet in New Ashford.

The Greylock massif stands as a peninsula to the Taconics — as indeed it was when glacial Lake Bascom filled the Hoosac Valley up to the 1,300-ft. contour. Therefore it may be appropriate that the summit of Greylock lifts a War Memorial Tower, designed originally to be a lighthouse for the Charles River estuary, bearing a beacon that can be seen by people navigating most of the county. If any man-made feature is needed to unite a geographical area so well defined topographically, it would be that tower and the roads it guards (Rtes. 2, 7 and 8).

Getting in and out and around Berkshire used to be a problem. The native Americans generally thought of the area as removed from their Hudson River homes, a hunting ground to visit in the summer. The Mahicans entered from the south or north, along the river valleys. Although the Bay Colony claimed the land early on, Bay Colony residents found it tough to surmount the Berkshire barrier to the east. Early settlers found it easier to enter along the valleys, a few Dutch infiltrating through the Taconics from New York, but especially residents from the area now known as Connecticut, up the Housatonic. Thus the county was settled from the south to the north, the earliest towns in the south dating to the first quarter of the 18th century.

VERMONT

0   5   10
Miles

N
W — E
S

FRANKLIN CO.

Mount
Greylock
3491 ft.

Hoosic River Valley

HOOSAC RANGE

RANGE

NEW
YORK

Pittsfield

HAMPSHIRE CO.

TACONIC

Housatonic River Valley

SOUTHERN BERKSHIRE PLATEAU

HAMPDEN CO.

Mount
Everett
2624 ft.

CONNECTICUT

The main roads, railroads and even sewer lines now follow the valleys.

The European settlers were primarily farmers, typically working the bottom lands and, as they filled up, moving up the sides of the hills. Remains of walls, cellar holes, and orchards such as you come across in your ambles remind you that even what seem now lofty ridges were at one time home, especially for those who made their living grazing cattle or merino sheep. In Stockbridge, the English Society for the Propagation of the Gospel in Foreign Parts set up an Indian mission, which gradually acceded to the land hunger of the Europeans. By the time of the Revolution, virtually all native Americans had departed.

As a farmer installed a mill to grind his corn or saw his wood, and his neighbors came to have him do their milling, so industry followed the plough. What began as groupings to protect against French or Indian raids became trading centers. Specialty manufactures, depending on natural resources, developed, such as glass, paper, charcoal, and textiles. Even education can be seen as an industry depending on natural resources. After all, Thoreau said of Williams College's position at the foot of Greylock: "It would be no small advantage if every college were thus located at the base of a mountain, as good at least as one well-endowed professorship . . . . Some will remember, no doubt, not only that they went to college, but that they went to the mountain." In Berkshire County, three of the four colleges and many of the secondary schools are at the base of mountains.

The opening of the Erie Canal in 1825, providing a practical means for younger residents to head west where the thick topsoil had a lot fewer glacial stones than that of Berkshire, drained the county of human resources. One by one lights winked out on the sidehill farms. Whereas by the middle of the century three-quarters of the trees had been stripped for pasture land or to feed the insatiable maws of the railroad, the county has been revegetating for 150 years. In Berkshire that ratio is inverted today. The county is three-quarters wooded, which is why coyotes, bear, beaver, turkeys, and even moose are returning to join the populous deer and smaller animals.

The most important industrial event in the county's history happened in 1886, when William Stanley linked 25 shops along the main street of Great Barrington in the world's first commercial electric system. That, in turn, drew the General Electric Co. to Stanley's shop in Pittsfield. GE has been here ever since, the largest employer in the county. The second most important industrial event was the opening of the Hoosac Tunnel, at 4.75 miles the longest bore in the world in 1875, breaking through the Berkshire barrier for direct train service in the North County from Boston to Albany.

Yet even in the heady days when industry was king — the population of Pittsfield growing from 25,000 to 58,000 in the first 60 years of the 20th century — second homes, tourism, and culture were already crowned princes. In the Gilded Age that ended the 19th century, wealthy men collected great estates and built luxury palaces, known as "cottages," some 75 in Lenox and Stockbridge. Major literary figures toured the county: Emerson, Melville, Hawthorne, Holmes, Thoreau, Wharton, Twain. . . . Some settled here. Actors, musicians and artists followed, and are still following.

As the county now, somewhat painfully, recognizes that industries will never again be what they were through World War II, it is coming to rely on a service economy to which, at least, it is no stranger. Filled with fine educational institutions, public and private, with museums and musicians, with art and artifacts to grace the green walls installed infinitely earlier by nature, Berkshire's streams are cleaner and woods thicker than since farms and industry first came to these garrison hills. And the hills retain a plentiful supply of ground water, likely to become increasingly important to the future of this area.

Berkshire has now, as it has had since the ice left, an indigenous population that cares deeply for the land, witness the many towns in the county that have long had zoning, have now established land trusts and are considering land use countywide. Berkshire residents listen attentively at town meetings to discussions of protecting ridges and aquifers, saving farm land, and cleaning up hazardous waste. Little litter mars the many paths. Whether driving its roads or walking its trails, you will soon get the message that this land is cared for.

SOUTH COUNTY

MOUNT WASHINGTON

Mt. Washington, the smallest town by population in the Commonwealth of Massachusetts, has 120 residents. It contains 6,500 acres of state land — like the towns of Washington, Savoy, and New Ashford, about one-half state owned. Perched at a 2,000-ft. elevation, like Savoy and Windsor, it is a town formed by its topography. The town may have been settled first by Dutch moving east from the Hudson River as early as 1692. That would make it the oldest town in Berkshire, but the point is disputed. In any case, the mountain men who lived there about 1730 preferred to consider themselves Bay Colony residents, where individuals owned their land, rather than subject to the feudal tenure of the Hudson Valley. Hudson lord Robert Livingston sent a party onto the mountain in 1755 to extract rents deeded him by the governor of New Amsterdam. A skirmish broke out. Pioneer William Race, for whom Mt. Race and Race Brook were probably named, was killed. In 1761 Livingston's men burned six homes in Mt. Washington. In spite of the fact that the town was incorporated in 1781, the dispute continued until the New York-Massachusetts boundary was settled in 1787.

In the 1840s and '50s inhabitants earned their living by cutting trees and making charcoal; later, they farmed potatoes; now they drive down off their mountain to work at jobs elsewhere. The scenery is spectacular — a phrase not often used even in a book limited to the best of Berkshire. What a place to begin!

Camping

Part of the charm of Mt. Washington is the absence of any tourist facilities. There is a state-owned cabin on the trail between the two peaks of Alander that can be used on a first-come, first-served basis. The primitive camping area on the Alander Trail is lovely for tenting (no facilities). Camping is available at the New York end of the two-state Bash Bish Park, with facilities. A cabin is available to AMC members (reserved in advance) off East Rd. near Sages Ravine. There are camp-sites along the AT at Sages Ravine, Bear Rock Falls and Race Brook; a shelter is available just north of Mt. Everett at Glen Brook.

HIKES

ALANDER MOUNTAIN / BASH BISH FALLS

7 miles (3 hours), plus 4.5 miles to complete loop

Road approaches

Take Rte. 41 S. from So. Egremont village, but turn right just past the pond, on Mt. Washington Rd. (There is a state forest sign.) After 3 mi., the road swings southerly and begins to climb to a ridge. Signs help at the intersections, but essentially head straight to the Mt. Washington State Forest HQ, on the right 9 mi. from the village. Park there. If you choose to make this a 2-car expedition, which is recommended, take the signed road right at the church (before forest HQ) to Bash Bish Falls upper (first paved) parking lot (7.5 mi.). Leave car No. 1 there; drive No. 2 back to forest HQ.

ALANDER MOUNTAIN

The extremes of this hike, Alander Mtn. and Bash Bish Falls, are remarkable by any set of criteria. The open ridge of the mountain (2,239 ft.) has a fine view west to the Catskills and, if the weather is clear, even to the tall buildings in Albany,

New York, 50 mi. north. As you hike north from the summit, continual twists in the trail reveal new views, especially the intimate one down into an uplands farm. The waters of Bash Bish Brook plunge 200 ft. at the falls, the most spectacular in Berkshire, divided part way down by a pulpit-like granite outcropping before tumbling into a pool and thence other riffles and pools down stream. (The falls are always worth seeing, although the amount of water varies considerably: most in spring and fall.)

The Alander Trail is well marked from the Mt. Washington State Forest HQ parking lot, where you can also register to use the campground. Follow W. the triangular blue blazes the state uses to mark hiking trails, across a field, into a woods and out into another field. At this point you are on what is virtually a road, which passes an abandoned house at 9 min. Cross a brook on a bridge and continue on the road, passing the Ashley Hill Trail, also a woods road, on your left (1 mi.). Cross another bridge (17 min.).

At 22 min. you must ford a brook — you want to wear boots rather than sneakers for all hikes. Two brooks join here, with a mill foundation right. The somewhat wet trail rises moderately through hemlock forest, which gradually becomes a laurel grove, with a few birches and oaks. You pass the camping area to the left at 42 min. This oak/laurel forest is distinctly different from the northern hardwood forest you see farther upcounty, characterized by a higher percentage of sugar maples. Similar spring ephemeral flowers are visible before the leaves come on the trees, however: the mottled leaves of trout lily; hepatica with its blue-pink-white blossoms and oddly-shaped leaves; spring beauty, which has rose pink flowers with grasslike leaves; distinctive dutchman's breeches, with parsleylike leaves.

The woods road ends at a circle that you pass straight through, bearing left at a junction (both branches have blue blazes). Shortly you come to an ominous sign that says: "Last water during dry season," as the branch of the brook you are following begins to peter out. You are climbing more steeply through laurel now.

At 1:13 comes the state cabin in the notch between the south and north peaks of Alander. Just beyond is a bewildering nest of signs. Turn right, scrambling up the rocks to the western summit (3 mi. from road). Note the white blazes turning sharply N. (right) but take the time to explore the area of the old fire tower footings for the different views. The major highway on which you can see traffic is Rte. 22 in New York State. Follow along the ridge line, N., with occasional opportunities to look east as well as west, between pitch pine and thick laurel. At 1:47 you take the first of several sharp descents, following white blazes mostly painted on the rocks. Hawks sail on the warm updrafts of this ridge. The deep gorge of Bash Bish is taking shape to the right; at some point you will start to hear the roar of the falls.

After scrambling down a steep incline (2:22), a junction gives a choice of routes to the falls. The route right is shorter but involves fording Bash Bish Brook and should only be used at low water (when it hasn't rained for a while). The left fork leads past some view points and down a series of hairpin turns, through large hemlocks, into the camping area (2:49) by the shower building. Follow the white dots left, down the road to the bridge.

Massachusetts purchased the 400 acres around the falls in 1924; then, during the 1960s, 4,000 acres more to make up Mt. Washington State Forest. Since New York State owns land just downstream in Copake Falls, managing the camping area, this is the first example of these two states jointly maintaining a park (a second is planned at Petersburg Pass, west of Williamstown).

Follow the gravel road upstream from the parking lot to the falls (3:09). Stone steps lead down to the most dramatic view. As you see from the signs, swimming is not allowed. Several people trying to climb the cliffs or dive into the pools have killed themselves. Rock climbing is only allowed with permission of the park ranger. The guard rails are intended to keep you on the trails. In addition to the danger of falling, rattlesnakes have been found in the vicinity.

0   ½   1 mile   N

1800

1200

1700

Bash
Bish
Falls
camping

Lower
Parking lot

1500

Upper
Parking
lot   Falls Rd.

Bash Bish
Mtn.

1500

West

1600

Street

Cross

Road

NEW YORK
MASS.

1900

1600

1400

2000

1800

1700

1500

To
South
Egremont

camping
1800

1700

Headquarters

2239

Alander
Mtn.

Parking

East St.

cabin

Hunts
Pond

1700

1900

MT. WASHINGTON: ALANDER MTN./BASH BISH FALLS

Ten more min. take you upstream to the upper parking lot, a good place to explore the lookouts. The gorge is colonnaded with large hemlocks, some of them clinging to what appears to be nothing but rock. Like every good county cliff, Bash Bish has a myth of an Indian maiden. In this case, Bash Bish was accused of adultery and strapped into a canoe at the head of the falls as punishment. Just as the canoe was about to go over, the sun formed a halo about her head and butterflies gathered. Indians found the remains of the canoe in the pool at the bottom but not her body. You may see her image in the falls today.

This Taconic ridge on the state's border is part of the Appalachians, pushed up when the continents collided and worn down by erosion ever since. Bash Bish Brook was formed by the melting of the last glacier, 10,000 to 12,000 years ago. The quartz dike, halfway up the falls, was forced out of the earth 400 million years ago. As the sediment in the brook works in the water, it gradually destroys Bash Bish Falls.

You probably would just as soon get into No. 1 car here, as the walk by road to forest HQ is 4.5 more mi., up Falls Rd. and right on West St. A short cut, shown on old maps, along Bash Bish to the Alander Trail (3 mi. back to HQ), unfortunately crosses posted property belonging to the Mt. Washington Club. It is not blazed, signed or completely maintained. As an alternative to 2 cars, you could leave a bicycle at Bash Bish.

MOUNT EVERETT

*Sheffield and Mt. Washington 5.5 mile hike (2.75 hours),
plus 2 miles to complete the loop*

Road approaches

Although most of the hike is in the uplands of the town
of Mt. Washington, it begins at the Berkshire School, just off
Rte. 41 in Sheffield. The hike ends at a parking area about
2 mi. down the road, where the Race Brook Falls Trail comes
out. So you could use 2 cars or you could walk between the
beginning and end or, best idea, you could drop a bicycle off
at the Race Brook trailhead. The ride back to the school on a
fairly level road through lovely farm fields, looking up at
the steep sides of the mountain, would be pleasant.

To get to Berkshire School, take Berkshire School Rd.,
appropriately enough, out of Sheffield and jog N. on Rte. 41
or, from the N., take Rtes. 23 and 41 W. from Gt. Barrington.
Bear S. where 23 continues W., just after So. Egremont. The
school is 3.5 mi. S. of the junction.

MOUNT EVERETT

Mt. Everett (2,602 ft.) is the outstanding peak in Berkshire County south of the Greylock massif. Although the fire
tower is closed and off limits to the public, excellent views
extend in most directions from the generally open summit,
as well as from the Appalachian Trail (AT) to the north and
especially the south. The slopes are steep on this 5.5-mi. hike
and you want to wear good footgear, especially for climbing
over the rock outcroppings.

As an alternative, a gravel automobile road climbs very
near the summit from East St. in Mt. Washington. Call 413-
528-8928 to find out when the park is open (it depends on
road conditions). You could drive into the reservation to
picnic at Guilder Pond and walk to the summit from the
pond or from the end of the road. It would also be possible to
walk N. on the AT, to be met at Berkshire School or S. on the

AT to be met at the Race Brook trailhead, having let the car do most of the climbing.

Berkshire School (850 ft. in elevation) is most attractive, set into the side of the hills and fronted by rolling, mowed lawns. An education there comes complete with ski and hiking trails. The students maintain the Elbow Trail. You should stay on the trails, because rattlesnakes have been seen in the area.

To get to visitor parking at the school, bear right at the admissions building, past the tennis court and behind the Quonset hut. You may have to ask directions to the trailhead, but you want to walk back towards admissions. Before you get that far, follow the service road by the north end of the main building. Go past a home and straight at a hard left in the gravel road. The Elbow Trail is blazed blue, about 5 min. from parking.

The trail runs 1.2 mi. to the AT, through hemlock woods, gradually increasing in steepness. At the elbow (20 min. from the parking lot) 2 blue-blazed trails (and 1 red-blazed trail) head out. If you go generally straight on a blue, you will end up at Glen Brook. You will then have a rigorous climb, probably .25 mi., without a trail, up by steep falls until you see the red roof of the Glen Brook Shelter, right. Follow the blue blazes to the AT.

A better bet at the elbow is to take a hard right on the other blue-blazed trail, which meets the AT .5 mi. farther N. (45 min. from the parking lot). In either case, turn left (S.) on the AT, blazed white. From the Elbow Trail to summit: 1.8 mi. In 20 min. from arriving on the AT you will reach the Guilder Pond Trail, entering right; then the picnic area/ parking lot on the road to the summit.

Most of the rest of the way to the summit the trail parallels the road, until the road stops and those who drive join you on foot for the last quarter mi. Note that the AT turns left before reaching the tower, which you will do in 1:25. Over the low shrubbery, including blueberry, scrub oak and pitch pine, you catch fine views of Alander Mtn. to the west, Mt. Frissell to the south, and, if you move around, other directions as well. On a clear day, the Catskills are visible across the

MT. WASHINGTON: MT. EVERETT

Hudson River. The foundations for the old tower make a picnic site with vistas.

The descent S. from the summit provides the most exciting views of the Berkshire and Litchfield hills, and of the Housatonic River as it snakes into Connecticut. The going is moderately difficult, dropping down steeply over schist with marble outcroppings. The blue-blazed trail, left, where the brook crosses, .7 mi. from the summit (30 min.), takes you through a camping area and down Race Brook Trail to Rte. 41.

You cross a 2-log bridge, under large hemlocks, after 15 min. on Race Brook Trail, as the brook takes form in the wetlands. This interesting process gives you a graphic idea of the meaning of "watershed." At the top of the falls the trail turns left, but you may want to explore this scenic spot. The trail climbs to a lookout (55 min.) with a view into Sheffield. You cross below the upper falls — 5 falls altogether descend perhaps 1,300 ft. into the valley.

Rather than the dangerous route beside the falls, a new, 1.5-mi. trail (marked with blue blazes) works its way down the side of the ravine from the upper falls, through the laurel and large hemlocks, coming out at the paved parking area, for a total hiking time of 2.75 hrs. (not counting pausing for the views). Part-way down, a side trail leads to middle falls. At the bottom, the trail to lower falls enters from the left.

Turn left on Rte 41. There is ample shoulder to walk on. The school, remember, is on the left, a bit beyond where Berkshire School Rd. enters right.

SHEFFIELD

The southernmost town center in the county is also the generally accepted oldest (1726), no coincidence when you consider that most of the earliest settlers to Berkshire came from Connecticut. Matthew Noble arrived in 1725, alone, from Westfield, however, to make friends with the natives, clear the land, and erect a cabin. Next he fetched his daughter and returned on horseback to set up the first home in Berkshire (then still part of Hampshire County). The first struggles were not with the Indians but with the New York Dutch, who regarded western Berkshire as their own. In 1735, settlers raised the meeting house on Sheffield Plain, a mile north of the present village center.

The first county seat or shire town, when Berkshire became its own county in 1761, Sheffield watched that distinction move gradually north, from Gt. Barrington to Lenox to Pittsfield. Sheffield had its bout with industry, as is true of most Berkshire towns. Distinctively, marble from quarries in Ashley Falls adorns the custom house in Boston and the court house in New York City. Daniel Shays' Rebellion, a movement of Revolutionary War veterans who felt they had been insufficiently compensated for their services, died in battle with government troops in Sheffield in 1789. The town exported its sons.

Chester Dewey trained for four years at Williams College in the fields (literally) in which he was famous in the first half of the 19th century: botany and geology. Another son, Frederick Augustus Porter Barnard, president of Columbia University, determined that Columbia should include women. Barnard College was named for him shortly after he died in 1889.

WALKS

SALISBURY ROAD

7 miles (2.5 hours)

A most attractive stroll of a serious dimension but generally level, with mixed wooded and open landscape, begins at the junction of Salisbury and Barnum roads. It would make a fine bicycle route. Take Berkshire School Rd. or Root Lane W. from the center of town. Both shortly run into Salisbury Rd., which you should follow left. Park where Barnum, soon to become gravel, enters. Walk along Salisbury to Foley Rd., which bears left. Follow that gravel road to a tangle of roads that cross Schenob Brook. You will pass some lovely real farms and a few gentrified farms, all with distinguished vistas, particularly of Mt. Everett. To make your way through the maze, just keep turning left. You will end up on Barnum Rd. and, in another 2.0 mi., at your automobile.

SHEFFIELD: SALISBURY RD.

BARTHOLOMEW'S COBBLE AND
COL. JOHN ASHLEY HOUSE

Various trails available

These two adjacent properties of the Trustees of Reservations are south of the Sheffield town center, near the village of Ashley Falls on the Connecticut line. Turn right on Rte. 7-A, then shortly veer right over railroad tracks onto Rannappo Rd.; continue straight to Cooper Hill Rd. and turn right. The Col. John Ashley House is the oldest still-existing dwelling in Berkshire County, built in 1735. Col. Ashley led troops at the Battle of Bennington (1777). The Sheffield Declaration, written there, preceded the Declaration of Independence by three years. Theodore Sedgwick, originally of Sheffield but later of Stockbridge, successfully defended two of the Ashley slaves, Mum Bett and Brom, who sought freedom under a "born free and equal" clause in the state's constitution. That decision led to the freedom of other slaves in the state. The house is open seasonally for guided tours. A trail from it joins the Bartholomew's Cobble trails.

These can otherwise be reached by continuing straight at Cooper Hill Rd. to Weatogue Rd., just a matter of a few hundred yards, to a parking area on the left. A large map of the Trustees' property shows numerous trails. The ones around the Cobble itself, the rocky eminence between the parking lot and the Housatonic River, are shorter and steeper. These show a remarkable variety of wild flowers and shrubs growing in the rich river bottom land, which is laced with limestone. Bartholomew's Cobble is considered one of the nation's outstanding concentrations of native plants: more than 700 species, including 44 ferns and fern allies. Bird watchers have spotted 236 species here.

Trails also range across Weatogue Rd. on open fields and through wooded land. The fields are home to deer and cows, which are sometimes curious but not dangerous. The fences have British-type stiles that enable you to pass where cattle can't. It is possible to stroll about 2 mi., generally following white blazes, up the West Fence Trail to the summit of

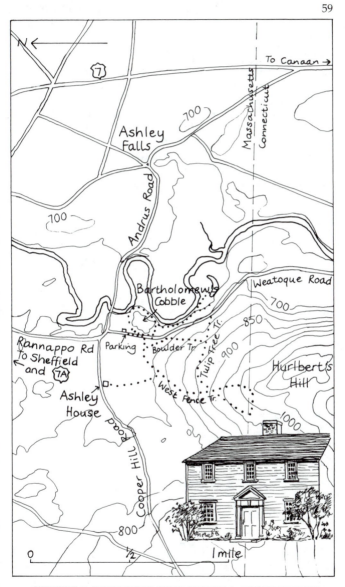

N ←

⑦

To Canaan →

Ashley
Falls

700

Andrus Road

Massachusetts
Connecticut

100

Weatoque Road

Bartholomew's
Cobble

700

850

Parking

Boulder Tr.

Tulip Tree Tr.

900

Hurlbert's
Hill

Rannappo Rd
To Sheffield
and ⑦A

West Fence Tr.

1000

Ashley
House

Cooper Hill Road

800

0   ½   1 mile

SHEFFIELD: BARTHOLOMEW'S COBBLE & ASHLEY HOUSE

Hurlbert's Hill, from which there is a lovely view centered on Mt. Everett; then return by the Tulip Tree Trail, which crosses Weatogue Rd., and returns you to the maze of trails by the river. You can cover many of the trails in 2 hours, allowing time to pause for the flora. Try to visit the Cobble in the spring, when the many ephemeral flowers — those that come out before the leaves on the trees shade them — are blossoming, but before the summer traffic hits.

TTOR charges a small fee for a tour of the Ashley house and asks for a donation to tramp the Cobble.

EGREMONT

A township that is two villages (No. and So. Egremont), the Egremonts are gently rolling, even flat, compared to upland neighboring Mt. Washington. But the walking is great here, offering extraordinarily long views for those who have neither the time nor the inclination to scale a peak. Back in the early history of Egremont, one man who wanted to remain on the plain was Gen. Henry Knox, who entered Berkshire through the Egremonts in 1776, with soldiers, 124 yoke of oxen and 58 captured cannon from Ft. Ticonderoga — all en route to Boston to help George Washington drive out the British. These days you'll find a few good shops (including a sporting goods store, open fall and winter only) and three noteworthy restaurants in So. Egremont, and one fine restaurant and a classic country general store in No. Egremont. That's it.

WALK

BALDWIN HILL ROAD NORTH AND SOUTH

6.0 miles or less (2.5 hours, round trip)

Start from either So. or No. Egremont, or station a car in each village. If you begin this round trip at the general store in No. Egremont, corner of Rte. 71 and No. Egremont-Hillsdale Rd. (at sign for Prospect Lake), go W. through a residential area for .1 mi. and turn left onto Baldwin Hill Rd. N & S (gravel), which rises gently for .6 mi. while passing by French Park on the right and through woods. The road flattens out as you begin to leave the woods; vistas appear in all directions. Pass pungent Bel Air Farm on the right and admire the vast cornfields. At 1.1 mi. (25 min.), cross the intersection of Baldwin Hill Rd. E & W. Your view includes: to the west, Catamount Ski Area; to the southwest, Mt. Everett; to the south, the Litchfield Hills in Connecticut; to the east, Monument Mt. and Warner Mt. (the latter to the east of Gt. Barrington which is hidden from view, down in a valley).

The road slopes gently downwards now toward So. Egremont. Note the airplanes rising and descending near the Gt. Barrington Airport in the valley to the east. At 2.0 mi. (50 min.), cross the intersection with Town House Hill Rd. At 2.2 mi., pass a small (private) pond left. The road is now paved and rising slightly. By 2.6 mi. it's all downhill into So. Egremont where, at Rte. 23 (3.0 mi.; 1:15 min.) you turn left and go 100 yds. to the deli or restaurant for a snack before heading back.

Alternatives include: side trips on Baldwin Hill Rd. E & W. Either way is good, although neither has any destination of note. Going E., you'll probably want to descend to just past a large white farmhouse in the pines right, then turn around and retrace your steps. Total mileage without the sidetrip is 6.0 (2.5 hrs.); with the sidetrip, 6.8.

NEW MARLBOROUGH

Benjamin Wheeler came from Marlborough, Massachusetts, in 1736, because his home town had been granted this western territory. He would have starved the first winter if some folks from Sheffield hadn't heard of his plight and struggled through the snow to his relief. But he had sufficient spirit to stick it out and invite the rest of his family to join him the next summer.

The town now has a population of 1,160, pretty well spread out. The town center is on Rte. 57, which drops south from Rte. 23 east of Gt. Barrington. Other village centers in New Marlborough township are: Hartsville, near beautiful Lake Buel, Mill River and Konkapot on the Konkapot River, Southfield, at the junction of New Marlborough and East Hill roads, Gomorrah and Clayton in the south. The town has more defined villages than any other in the county. The road signs are so thorough and numerous they virtually require you to stop the car to read them, which may be just what the citizens of New Marlborough want.

WALKS

HARMON ROAD

New Marlborough and Monterey 7 miles (2.5 hours)

A stroll begins at New Marlborough village and follows New Marlborough-Monterey Rd. (bear right at the fork) into Monterey, past the Trout Pond on Harmon Brook. You are still on the road when you turn left. Turn left again on Harmon Rd., back to the point of origin. This is a fine bike route. Rawson Brook Farm at the Monterey end sells goat cheese. the Old Inn on the Green, at the Marlborough end, is a lovely spot for a cool drink.

NEW MARLBOROUGH: HARMON RD.

NEW MARLBOROUGH: CAMPBELL FALLS

CAMPBELL FALLS

Southfield 4.5 miles (2 hours)

This walk runs through the Campbell Falls State Forest area just on the state line. Follow the Southfield Rd. S. from New Marlborough center into the village of Southfield, and the Norfolk Rd. S. from Southfield. Provisions and friendly information are available at the Southfield General Store. Park near Cookson Pond. Walk N. on Norfolk to left on Canaan Valley Rd., left on Canaan Rd. (both gravel), and left again on Campbell Falls Rd. across a bridge over Whiting Brook that might be wetter than the brook itself. A green trash can marks the short side trip to the falls (in Connecticut). A final, brief left on Norfolk Rd. should complete the tour. The road through the state forest may be a bit rough but biking is possible in season and skiing in the winter.

YORK POND

1 mile (30 min.)

South of New Marlborough, the So. Sandisfield Rd. passes the Sandisfield State Forest. Don't go by. Stop in at one of the best public swimming areas in the county, well maintained, with clean changing rooms. (This popular area is closed when 300 swimmers assemble, so you may have difficulty parking on a summer weekend.) Gasoline engines aren't allowed on the lake, so it is clean and inviting once it warms up. Efforts to keep open the walk around the lake have been thwarted by the beavers, who continually flood the trail. The supervisor is preparing 2 half-mile walks from HQ, however. One will lead to a former CCC camp and be self-guided, with numbers on foundation corresponding to numbers on a map. The other walk follows a gravel road to Josh Smith's grave, a local resident. Other lovely walks are available on gravel roads.

GREAT BARRINGTON

Gt. Barrington became the focus for southern Berkshire — the shopping center for the hilltowns that surround it, home to a registry of deeds, a court and other status symbols. Nowadays it boasts fine restaurants, theaters, bookstores, a college and numerous other amenities. Along with the center of town, on Rte. 7, there is an old mill area at Housatonic, still home to Rising Paper Co. Originally settled in 1726 at the Great Fordway on the Housatonic, which gave way to the Great Bridge, the town is also on the old Great Rd. from Boston to Albany (roughly Rte. 23 now), so it is no wonder that although named after Viscount Barrington, it magnified the name. By tradition, the Indian village that preceded the town was named Mahaiwe, or "place down stream." A venerable theater in town retains the name.

Back in the days when Americans and British were on the same side, Gen. Jeffrey Amherst, on his way to Ticonderoga, camped with his troops where the Great Rd. crossed the Green River. The town, after separating from Sheffield in 1761, became a seat of discontent with British rule. In August, 1774, a group of men seized the court house, preventing the King's Court from holding session. Thus the town claims the "first open resistance to British rule in America." Yet the town's residents included many Tories — notably leading citizen David Ingersoll, who was imprisoned in Litchfield, Connecticut, and then exiled. British General Johnny Burgoyne, marching in defeat from Saratoga on the Great Road during the Revolutionary War, was feted in Gt. Barrington; during Shays' uprising of dissident veterans the court house was once again seized.

William Cullen Bryant, this country's first native-born poet, practiced law in Gt. Barrington. A poem of his told of an unhappy Indian love affair culminating with her leap from Squaw Peak on Monument Mtn., north of the center of town. A more vivid attempt to explain the cairn or stone pile by the trail records that when the Indian maiden was hurled from the summit, she caught hold of a branch on the way down and remained suspended for two days, howling all the while, until a lightning bolt struck the tree, dropping both maiden and branch to oblivion. Her Mahican Indian relatives built the cairn in her memory, to which passers-by continue to add stones.

In a different application of electricity, William Stanley tested his theory of alternating current by providing street lighting for his home town, the first commercial use of electric current. The Housatonic Agricultural Society and its successors have held a fair at the Barrington Fairgrounds in summers ever since 1842.

Camping
The nearest campground is at Benedict Pond, Beartown State Forest, E. on Rte. 23 to forest HQ. Follow the signs along Blue Hill Rd. from there. The parking fee is modest. Lifeguards protect the swimming beach in season. At Monument Mtn., Rte. 7 N. of town, the picnic grove (910 ft. in elevation) is a lovely, shaded spot.

WALKS

SEEKONK

Gt. Barrington and Alford 3 or 6 miles (1 or 2 hours)

Road approach

Either 2 short or 1 long hike can be enjoyed on the east side of town and into Alford. Drive up Taconic St. at St. James Church, which becomes Alford Rd. after curving right. Follow Alford Rd. down hill past Simon's Rock College and then, soon, bear left on Seekonk Rd. where the walk begins.

SEEKONK

Park carefully by the small bridge. Most of these roads are gravel. Walk S. on Round Hill Rd., looking out from high farms. Turn right on Seekonk Cross Rd. and then either right on Seekonk back to the beginning or left on Green River Rd., right on No. Egremont Rd., right on Cross Rd., and right again on Seekonk Cross Rd. Left on Seekonk to the beginning. (The brook in these parts is known alternately as Alford or Seekonk.) This is a fine rolling stroll or bicycle ride with lovely panoramic views.

GREAT BARRINGTON: SEEKONK

GREAT BARRINGTON: BENEDICT POND

BENEDICT POND

5 miles (2 hours)

Another walk can be reached from Gt. Barrington's Monument Valley Rd. Coming down Rte. 7, turn left just beyond the high school. Turn left on Stony Brook Rd., which becomes Blue Hill Rd. A bicycling expedition from Monument Valley Rd. is 12 mi. Begin your walk at the Beartown State Forest HQ on Blue Hill Rd. near Rte. 23. Follow back the way you came to the gravel road to the swimming area and the camping area. Bikers will want to do a 3.5 mi. road trip around Benedict Pond. Walkers can circumambulate on a 1.5 mi. trail. This fine swimming area, presided over by lifeguards, is available, together with the changing rooms and outhouses. The pond is lovely; the woods and cliffs behind, dramatic.

The AT passes through Beartown State Forest, with a shelter S. of Mt. Wilcox, which the AT does not climb. That peak rises 2,112 ft., without much of a view because the lookout tower is closed. It is a relatively easy climb (4.0 mi. round trip) from the pond. Beartown is busy in the winter with snowmobiles and cross-country skiers.

HIKE

MONUMENT MOUNTAIN

3.0 miles (1.5 hours)

Road approaches

Monument Mtn. is a pillar of stones, unmistakable to the motorist on Rte. 7, located just north of the center of the town of Gt. Barrington, a few mi. south of Stockbridge and slightly south of Monument Mtn. Regional High School. Of the several parking lots on the west side of the road, the one at the picnic grounds (with the green Trustees of Reservations sign) is handiest for the hike described here.

MONUMENT MOUNTAIN

TTOR maintains this 503-acre reservation (and asks you to make a contribution if you hike it). This pile of stones has a largely clear ridge, giving you a good look at Beartown State Forest to the east, the Taconic Range to the west and the valleys in between. If it isn't a tradition at the regional high school below the mountain for seniors to hike to the summit, it ought to be. This is less of a wilderness hike than others in this guide. From the summit, as well as the panorama of unspoiled land, you can look directly into a landfill operation and onto the whizzing vehicles of Rte. 7 — it depends where you choose to look.

Although not lengthy, this is a steep, rugged climb. Also a storied one. In 1850, a publisher arranged an outing for several writers on this mountain: Herman Melville, Nathaniel Hawthorne and Oliver Wendell Holmes. The account of the wagon loaded with picnic goods, including champagne, and the liveried servants who accompanied them, may make you question how they made it up the trail. You will find out.

The well-trod trail, which is blazed white, leaves from the north corner of the parking lot, near a large map. It is moderately steep, passing through hemlocks, with scree (rocky rubble at the bottom of a slope) on the left. A trail enters right in 5 min. In a quarter hr., faced with a ravine, you swing left. Ignore all other trails, many of which are detours, keeping to the left. The stream on the right flows in lovely waterfalls in the spring. In places the trail is badly eroded, although the Trustees have labored hard at stone water bars, to try to deflect the freshets.

Turn left again at 22 min., on the trail to Squaw Peak. Almost immediately you pass a rock with the year the (then-called) Trustees of Public Reservations acquired the first portion of the property: 1899. The trail is quite steep, soon requiring clambering over quartzite boulders. The look-out left seems to be directly over the school. You are on the summit ridge in half an hr., but persevere, through the pitch pine, to the peak that honors an Indian maid, thought, at least by the poet, to have flung herself to her death. Pay attention to your footing, which is rough. The rocks themselves, with their lichens, are intriguing. One impending rock has the date 1888 carved in it, albeit painted over by more recent visitors.

To leave, follow back the way you came for 5 min. Then turn left just beyond the inscribed boulder. Note you are on more of a road; indeed the old carriage road up which the literary party came. Suddenly you sense something has changed. Consider. You hear more birds, not necessarily because they are louder but because you have rounded a corner of the cobble, leaving the state highway traffic noises behind you. Again, keep left as various trails enter. The going is much more gradual than on the way up. The hemlocks are larger. Even bigger are the boulders that have tumbled down the steep sides in this romantic spot.

Gradually you begin to hear the road sounds again, as you work around the south end of the mountain. A relatively newly cut trail takes you parallel with Rte. 7, N. to the picnic ground, which you reach after 1:17 walking time — not counting the time you lingered at the summit.

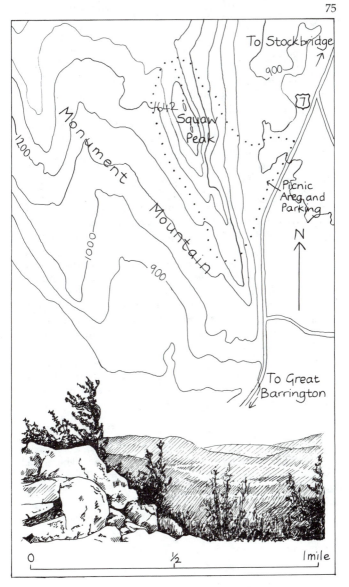

To Stockbridge

900

7

1642
Squaw
Peak

Monument Mountain

1200

1000

900

Picnic
Area and
Parking

N

To Great
Barrington

0   ½   1 mile

GREAT BARRINGTON: MONUMENT MTN.

TYRINGHAM

The Tyringham Valley remains one of the most lovely, bucolic views in Berkshire. It has stayed that way honestly. No railroad ever came through town, no interurban trolleys nor even a numbered highway. Like Williamstown, it is nearly surrounded by mountains, nestled between October Mtn. and Beartown state forests.

Settled in 1735, Tyringham has always been a farming community, although over the years it has had just a bite of many of the treats served up more extensively in other Berkshire towns. It is the only town in Massachusetts named after a woman, however: Jane Tyringham Beresford, Colonial Governor Bernard's cousin. A handful of Shakers settled here in 1792, growing to a community of 100, cultivating 1,500 acres by mid-19th century when they began to fade. Their land was purchased to build an elaborate summer colony, known as Fernside, on Hop Brook.

Industry arrived in the 19th century, especially the Steadman Rake Company. Richard Watson Gilder, editor of *Scribner's* and later *Century* magazines, arrived in 1898 to build Four Brooks Farm, which attracted the literary and artistic notables of the day, from naturalist John Burroughs to sculptor Augustus Saint-Gaudens to historian and writer Henry Adams to humorist Mark Twain — all of whom summered here.

Camping

Tyringham remains free of tourist trappings. There is a campsite, however, at Upper Goose Pond, for AT hikers, just over the line from Tyringham in Lee.

TYRINGHAM: TYRINGHAM COBBLE

WALK

THE TRYINGHAM COBBLE

2 miles (1 hour)

Road approaches

To get to Tyringham from the Lee interchange of the Massachusetts Turnpike, take the Tyringham Rd. due S. from the junction with Rte. 20, jogging briefly right on Rte. 102 W. Turn right at the town center on Jerusalem Rd. Stay right where Church St. enters. Soon you will see a TTOR sign, right, at a natural gas pipeline crossing. Park beside the road and enter the property through the stile.

THE TYRINGHAM COBBLE

Follow white blazes of the AT up an open hillside, through blackberry and juniper, bearing left on blue blazes at the junction to which you will return. The trail enters a wooded area and then comes out on a rocky outlook, the obvious picnic site. The white church and country town are picturesquely set against the wooded hillsides surrounding Goose Pond. The trail descends, through additional stiles, parallels the town's main street, and gradually swings right back to the trail junction. TTOR owns 206 acres, to which the trail provides an introduction.

STOCKBRIDGE

This 250-year-old town (incorporated in 1739) started out chartered by England's King George to "the Housatannack Tribe of Indians . . . to their use and behoof forever." The Europeans who settled there had a notion they could improve the lot of the Indians, however, which led eventually — as it often did — to the Indians being driven out.

The one-armed Rev. John Sergeant, who took the trouble to learn the Mahican language, arrived as first missionary in 1734, teaching Chiefs Konkapot and Umpachene domestic skills like agriculture and house building. His true friendship attracted Indians from many miles away. Jonathan Edwards succeeded him. While well disposed to the Native Americans, he was preoccupied with his religious writings and hectored by those Christian families sent to be worthy examples to the Indians, such as that of Ephraim Williams, Sr. This worthy sold them liquor and connived to acquire their land. So the Indian village became the center of the European town. In 1783 the natives held their last campfire here and migrated to a reservation in western New York State and thence to Wisconsin.

When Judge Theodore Sedgwick moved to Stockbridge from Sheffield in 1785, he stamped the place an important and wealthy town. By the 1860s, like Lenox, it had become the country seat for many influential eastern families. It attracted artists, like Daniel Chester French, who designed the seated Lincoln in the Lincoln Memorial, and Norman Rockwell, the magazine illustrator. It planned well, creating the Laurel Hill Association in 1835, the first village improvement organization in this country, and saving its most precious buildings and historic sites. The Laurel Hill Assoc. is still active, meeting annually, its members planting trees and maintaining trails.

Several of the early and staunch (European) families: the Sergeants, Woodbridges, Williamses, Dwights, Stoddards, Edwardses, Sedgwicks, Fields, Butlers, Choates, Parsonses, Rathbuns, Guerrieris, Burghardts, still have scions in town or nearby. Seven U.S. ambassadors have lived here: Cyrus

Field, who laid the Atlantic cable, and his equally remarkable brothers; three men educated here sat on the U.S.
Supreme Court at the same time: Henry Billings Brown,
Stephen J. Field and David Joshua Brewer. Its recent residents also include the famous and respected, such as
psychoanalyst Erik Erikson and theologian Reinhold Niebuhr.
And of course one day in the 1960s, according to the song,
Officer Obie arrested Arlo Guthrie for throwing some trash
from Alice's Restaurant by a Stockbridge roadside.

The town center, which looks like . . . well, a Norman
Rockwell *Saturday Evening Post* cover, is the most choked by
summer tourists of any Berkshire town. People park a mile
out along all the highways to visit the Indian Mission House
(the actual building, although not in its original location),
Naumkeag (the Choate mansion, now, like the Mission
House, under the care of TTOR), the many upscale shops and,
at the center of things, the Red Lion Inn. A bit farther out,
you will find Berkshire Theatre Festival, Chesterwood (the
sculptor's home), Berkshire Botanical Garden, the Norman
Rockwell Museum, and, at the north end of town, the Stockbridge Bowl, and Tanglewood (summer home of the Boston
Symphony Orchestra).

WALKS

ICE GLEN

3.5 miles or shorter (1.5 hours)

Strolls in Stockbridge are legion and lovely, not to mention the fact that summer and early fall biking or even walking is speedier than automobiling. The Laurel Hill Assoc.
publishes a *Hike and Bike Guide*, available at town hall or
library, with a useful set of maps.

Start with the Ice Glen, maintained by the Laurel Hill
Assoc. Beginning at the Red Lion Inn, walk S. half a mi. on
Rte. 7 to Ice Glen Rd., beyond the bridge. Follow this small
lane for .5 mi. Turn left. Follow the signs in what looks like

a private drive to the trail. (It is possible to leave a car here and start from the other side.) The blue-blazed trail, although short, is rough, in spite of noble efforts to ease the way over boulders and around large, prone hemlocks. It gets its name from the fact that ice lasts longer in the stony crevasse than anywhere else around. Every other Halloween the town stages a scary parade through the glen, a tradition going back 100 years.

After climbing 100 feet through the tangled glen and reading the carving in the cliff crediting David Dudley Field Jr. for donating the property to the town, you can turn right to ascend another 465 feet in elevation to Laura's Tower. The steel tower at the top, on a clear day, gives a fine view of the Berkshire Hills from Mt. Everett and Race Mtn. to Mt. Greylock. Descend from the tower as you came up, but turn right on the main trail across the Memorial Footbridge, and back to town by Park and South streets. Total mileage, starting at the Red Lion and including Laura's Tower: 3.5 mi.

To avoid the rough section through the glen and shorten the trip, start on the Memorial Footbridge side, climb to the tower, and return.

BOWKER'S WOODS

.5 mile (15 minutes)

A short trail passes near the loop in the Housatonic and across the freight line and old interurban trolley right-of-way to give you a look at Bowker's Woods. To get there, go W. on Main St. from the Red Lion Inn, continue straight at the Chime Tower, past the Indian Burial Ground on a knoll to the left, cross the river and bear right up the hill and out Glendale Rd. to a discreet opening in the stone wall, right, for the Lower Trail (1.5 mi. from the inn, not included in mileage). This is an easy and pleasant stroll, passing along a bluff by the river with lovely views. To get to the Upper Trail, which winds through some lovely pines, bear right twice after crossing the river, following Glendale North Rd. to Rte. 183. Jog right and left, just beyond a small pond, for the entrance to the trail.

PROSPECT HILL

3 miles (1 hour)

A fine route for stroll or bike takes you up Prospect Hill and back on Church St. Begin directly across Main St. from the Red Lion Inn, on Pine St. Pass the tennis courts, then bear left on Prospect Hill Rd. and continue up to Naumkeag, the Joseph H. Choate home designed in 1885 by Stanford White. Swing left on Old Meetinghouse Hill Rd., beyond, and thence by Field St. (gravel) back to Church St., getting a look at the attractive backside of Naumkeag on your way to the Chime Tower, where you turn left for the inn.

The Marian Fathers, across the road from Naumkeag, allow walkers on their extensive grounds, for an alternative route, or you can extend the trip by a mile by continuing up Prospect Hill to Larrywaug Rd. and then down N. Church St.

GLENDALE

Various options

Another set of walks and bike rides lies to the west and a bit south of Stockbridge in the village of Glendale. From the Red Lion Inn in Stockbridge follow Main St. W. by the Town Hall, Chime Tower, and the Indian Burial Ground and across the river to Glendale Rd., past the entrance to Bowker's Woods Lower Trail and S. on Castle Hill Rd. Turn left on Cherry Hill Rd. and left again on Cherry St. to the beginning (3.0 mi.). And/or venture farther out Glendale Rd., by auto perhaps, across the railroad tracks and over the river a second time to Rte. 183. Park at the Glendale Post Office and walk straight ahead up a short, steep section of Christian Hill Rd. to gravel Williamsville Rd. Turn left. Soon on your right is Chesterwood, once the home of sculptor Daniel Chester French and now a National Trust museum. Bear right at the fork to Dugway Rd., also gravel. Turn left there, along Mohawk Lake Brook to Rte. 183 and along the river, past the restored hydroelectric plant, and back to the point of origin. Although Rte. 183 winds charmingly along the Housatonic, vehicles travel too fast. Use caution or avoid Rte. 183 by retracing your footsteps.

GOULD MEADOWS AND BULLARD WOODS

Various options

Neither of these lovely properties has a trail system but both are open to the public for wandering. Both are off Hawthorne Rd., paralleling the northern side of Stockbridge Bowl (note: Hawthorne *St.*, confusingly, is perpendicular to Hawthorne *Rd.* and heads toward Lenox). There is a map at the Gould Meadows parking area, a few hundred yards down Rte. 183 from Hawthorne Rd. (you are near Tanglewood, to N., and near the site, to S., of the canoe portion of the Great Josh Billings Runaground, held annually in the fall). The higher land provides a remarkable view of the Bowl and excellent picnicking. Carry out any trash, please. You can wander down to the water if you like.

Bullard Woods is cited by state foresters as the best place in the county to see large trees. A scruffy field at the corner of Hawthorne St. and Rd. provides parking; if you look carefully you will see a sign at the edge of the field. Logging roads curve through the 50-acre stand of enormous oaks, especially along the edge of the meadow. Other large trees include sugar maples; shag bark hickory; large tulip poplar, including one about 4 feet in circumference, with a faded sign attached; and many large white pines — including one 18 feet in circumference, barred from being a record because is appears to have been formed when two trees grew together. Stumps in the woods show where chestnuts were cut in response to the blight (pre-1920).

STOCKBRIDGE: WALKS

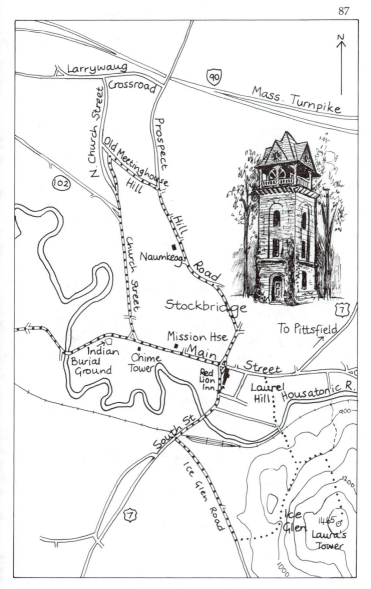

N

Larrywaug
Crossroad
90
Mass. Turnpike
N. Church Street
Prospect
Old Meetinghouse
Hill
102
Church Street
Hill Road
Naumkeag
Stockbridge
7
To Pittsfield
Indian
Burial
Ground
Chime
Tower
Mission Hse
Main
Street
Red
Lion
Inn
Laurel
Hill
Housatonic R.
900
South St
Ice Glen Road
7
Ice
Glen
1200
1465
Laura's
Tower
1000

STOCKBRIDGE: WALKS

CENTRAL COUNTY

LENOX

Lenox is not at all what you see from Rte. 7, a strip of shops and restaurants. The old center of town is on Rte. 7-A; that, too, has a touristy inclination but is recognizable as a community with a rich history.

Originally connected to the outside world only by an Indian path that followed the Housatonic River, Yokuntown was first settled in 1750 and named after Chief Yokun, a Stockbridge Indian. When the town was incorporated, in 1767, it was named for Charles Lennox, Duke of Richmond. At some time, one *n* was deemed sufficient; the opposite of the inclination that added "great" to Viscount Barrington's name. Considered a home to Tories during the Revolutionary War, by early in the 19th century its thriving industries led it to replace Gt. Barrington as the shire town: hence the court house (1816), now the Lenox Library. Pittsfield usurped the county seat in 1868.

Lenox changed utterly, however, when Charles Sedgwick moved there in 1821. Shortly thereafter, his sister, writer Catherine Sedgwick, joined him. Together they hosted the literary lights of the day and inspired other families to build great estates in town, the so-called cottages designed on the Newport, Rhode Island, model. Many well-to-do gentry from New York and Boston developed large estates in and around Lenox, tastefully tucking their enormous homes out of sight behind shrubbery. Few of these remain in private hands now. The most famous visitor at the time was the British actress Fanny Kemble, who charmed the community and to whom Longfellow addressed a sonnet. She donated the proceeds of a reading to pay for the clock in the tower of Lenox's lovely Church on the Hill.

N

1600
1400
Pleasant Valley
West Mountain Road
1300
1400
1500
Lookout Tr.
Lookout Tr.
Kennedy Park
Main Trail
Lookout Tr.
West Dugway Road
To Pittsfield
7 20
Lenox House
Parking
Main Trail
Reservoir Road
1400
Under Mountain Road
1300
1100
Cliffwood Street
Parking
To Lee
7A
Church on the Hill
Lenox
183
0   ½   1 mile

LENOX: KENNEDY PARK

WALKS

KENNEDY PARK

3-4 miles (1.5 hours)

A history of large estates — as opposed to farm land, cut-over land, or developed land — has left some of the largest trees in the county in Lenox and Stockbridge, as you can see in Bullard Woods or driving through these fashionable towns. One gorgeous glimpse of the kind of land that is not recently grown-over farm fields is Lenox's Kennedy Park. Best access is from the Church on the Hill, well within walking distance of downtown, or the lot near the junction of routes 7 and 7-A.

The area was the site of the Aspinwall Hotel, built in 1902 to accommodate the wealthy who wanted to visit their cottage-dwelling friends. The hotel burned in 1931 and its grounds became the John D. Kennedy Park in 1957. The main trail, blazed white, breeds numerous offshoots, so that you can design your own route. One possibility includes the Lookout Trail, blazed red. In combination, red and white give you an invigorating stroll.

RESERVOIRS

Lenox and Richmond 8 miles or fewer (3 hours or less)

A pleasant and lengthy walk begins outside Pleasant Valley, the Audubon wildlife sanctuary on West Mountain Rd., heading west. West Mountain Rd. becomes Reservoir Rd., passing Upper Root Reservoir (right) and then quite small Large Reservoir (left). At the fork, follow Reservoir Rd. right and then left. You are in the town of Richmond now, once a part of Yokuntown but split off when the Bay Colony sold the tracts of "Indian Land." Keep straight where Lenox Rd. enters right and bear left with it around Fairfield Pond (about 4 mi.). The next left turn will return you to Large Reservoir, whence you can follow Reservoir and West roads back to your point of departure. Some remarkable homes jut out of swiftly falling hillsides. En route you will see also wooded and pasture land. Variations are available, by taking different turns. A good bicycle route, with even more variations than for hiking, depending on ambition.

LENOX: RESERVOIRS

LEE/LENOX: GOLDEN HILL

GOLDEN HILL

Lee, Lenoxdale and Lenox 2.5 miles (1 hour)

Stride along Golden Hill Rd. in Lenox, striking agricultural fields set in the Berkshire Hills, gradually becoming residential. To get there follow Rte. 20 (from the north) to the built-up center of Lee and turn left to follow the railroad tracks to a good parking place. Then walk the tracks on the east side of the river past the narrow bridge on Golden Hill Rd. (which you will cross later on) to Willow Hill Rd. in Lenoxdale. Turn left on Willow St., at right angle up the hill (off Walker St., which continues on a diagonal) until you meet Golden Hill Rd. (which is T-shaped). Left again, on the highlands, looking into the Housatonic Valley and across it . . . behold October Mtn. State Forest. Turn left again, looking at the same view over fields of Queen Anne's lace and loosestrife. The route extends down the hill, across the narrow bridge over the river and back to the tracks, your shining path to your car, less than 2.5 mi. total. The route, without the portion on the tracks, is available, with variations, for bicycling.

HIKE

PLEASANT VALLEY / LENOX MOUNTAIN

3 miles (1.5 hours)

Road approaches

Pleasant Valley Wildlife Sanctuary is off the Lenox-Pittsfield Rd. (Rtes. 7 & 20). Turn west on W. Dugway Rd., at the sanctuary sign, N. of the junction with Rte. 7-A but S. of the junction of Holmes Rd. Follow Dugway, a black-topped road, a mile until it ends at W. Mountain Rd. Bear left on this gravel road for .8 mi. The sanctuary has parking lots on both sides of the road. It is closed on Mondays.

Restrooms are available in the barn. Maps and other interesting pamphlets are available at the window, where non-members of Massachusetts Audubon will be asked to pay a small fee for use of the sanctuary. There are no shelters or camping areas on this hike. Incidentally, no dogs are allowed on this property. Collecting of plants, of course, is not allowed; nor is it on any public lands or most private lands.

The Pleasant Valley Wildlife Sanctuary, one of two Massachusetts Audubon properties in the county, was established in 1929. Seven miles of trails wind through 1,100 acres of Berkshire uplands and beaver swamps. A trailside museum is open mid-May through October.

PLEASANT VALLEY / LENOX MOUNTAIN

This is a lovely short hike, relatively steep, with a rewarding view from the summit of Lenox Mtn. In fact, you may be able to climb the 11 flights of stairs up the Oscar R. Hutchinson Memorial Fire Tower, although the tower itself is not open. Other strategic lookouts along the trail survey the surroundings. At least in the spring, trails follow delightful brooks with sparkling waterfalls.

From the Audubon administration building follow the main trail, past the barn on the left and the Trailside

Museum on the right. From this spot you can see the destination: the tower on the ridge to the west. (In fact, you can see the tower from Rte. 7 when the foliage isn't out.) The Bluebird Trail passes through fields that are beginning to fill in with second growth. Audubon is displaying the way first weeds replace grass, bushes replace weeds, and gradually trees fill in former farm land. In this area, pines come to shield out undergrowth, and then, finally, hardwoods take over from the pines.

Follow straight ahead as two trails depart to the right. At the sanctuary all trails heading away from the administration building are blazed blue; all returning to the center are blazed yellow. Cross trails are blazed white. It is difficult to get lost.

At the bottom of the slope, cross a bridge over Yokun Brook under a stand of tall pines, leave a beaver swamp on the right, and cross a second bridge (at 8 min.), following signs to the tower at various intersections. The trail continues up the brook you just crossed. (You may want to detour on alternate trails to examine the industrious beavers' activities.)

At the 4-way intersection (12 min.), go straight. The brook is on the left. As you gain elevation, laurel, which blossoms in June, begins to fill in under hardwood trees. You pass out of the sanctuary land into Lenox watershed lands but Audubon maintains trails throughout. The trail weaves back and forth across the brook, which runs in the spring with several falls. Large hemlocks aim to the sky in the ravines and along the ledges. The schist over which the water runs contains quartz outcroppings. At 30 min. the trail begins to skirt a ledge, left. In 40 min. you come out on the summit.

The view from the summit looks down onto Richmond Pond, which seems to be very close, in spite of the 2,126 ft. of elevation. (You have climbed 786 ft. from the office.) The Catskill Mtns. rise in the southwest. The Taconic highlands to the northwest are in Pittsfield State Forest. Lake Onota lies to the west northwest. Looking east you see the high-

LENOX: PLEASANT VALLEY / LENOX MTN.

lands of October Mtn. State Forest. To the southeast you look down into the extremely pleasant valley. The tower adds some 80 ft. of *up* to the view.

Follow the Ledges Trail to the SE rather than the jeep road. Remember, returning trails are blazed yellow. In 4 min. you begin to pass over more ledges, descending and climbing along the ridge. At 1:02 from the administration building you come to a trail junction at Fairview, which gives another nice look into the sanctuary's 670 acres. Turn left on the aptly named Laurel Trail, which begins a steep descents part of which is in a stream bed. The hardwoods now include oak, birch, and beech.

At 1:15 go straight at the intersection with the Ravine Trail. At 1:19, bear right at a familiar 4 corners. You are now back on the trail you began climbing, appropriately known as Overbrook. Although you have been traversing rocky outcroppings, the valley is underlaid with limestone, buffering the effects of acid rain and affording hospitable conditions for certain ferns and other rare species. Bear right at the Y. At 1:24 cross the first bridge and at 1:30 min., pass the administration building.

The sanctuary map shows numerous other strolls and hikes, the one to the tower being the most rigorous. You could spend a full day walking through this beautifully maintained property and enjoying a picnic. Massachusetts Audubon organizes many educational activities, including cross-country skiing and snowshoeing on this property and at Canoe Meadows, the other Berkshire sanctuary, located a few miles N., off Holmes Rd. in Pittsfield.

RICHMOND

So near and yet so far. While a noisy Sunday afternoon Tanglewood traffic jam has clogged the roads through neighboring Lenox and nearby Stockbridge, just over the mountain is silent and almost forgotten Richmond, enjoying its emptiness. This is a town without a center, but it does have fine roads to walk. Here's one.

WALK

EAST ROAD

4.6 miles or less (2 hours)

Road approaches

From W. Stockbridge take Pittsfield Rd., which shortly becomes Swamp Rd., heading N. (at start in the village, be careful not to confuse Pittsfield/Swamp roads with Rte. 41). Go a little over 2 mi. to the Lenox Rd. where you turn right and then park after driving in 100 yds. or so. Park carefully: there is no official lot. East Rd. departs obliquely to left, rising.

From Tanglewood: Pass the Main Gate on Rte. 183, going S., and veer right, up the Richmond Mtn. Rd., passing Apple Tree Inn right. After climbing through several twisty turns, ignore a left turn on top of the mountain and descend toward Richmond on what, by now, is called Lenox Rd. At the bottom of the hill, pass a pond right, then curve right, leading to East Rd. Park more or less immediately, safely off the pavement, turn around and walk up.

EAST ROAD

The mountains and valley along Swamp Rd., from W. Stockbridge up through Richmond, are sparsely populated and lovely. The walk on East Rd. (mostly gravel) is a stroll from and to nowhere in particular, although if you were ambitious, you could make a loop of it as explained below. Here's a simple out and back on East Rd.: the views of enormous farm fields and the Taconic Hills to the west are interestingly different when walking in each direction. Because the mountain rises sharply on the east side of this walk, if you want sunshine, hold off until midday. Sunsets from here are dramatic.

The walk to the other end of East Rd., at Swamp Rd., is as long, short, slow or fast as you like. An estimated 2.3 mi. takes you to Swamp Rd. and so the full round trip is about 4.6 mi. The last part of East Rd. is in a woodsy residential area with some sweet country homes but no views. One highly unusual dome house can be seen about halfway out, right. You may want to walk only until the views disappear, then turn around to head back. You can picnic at roadside by the farm fields, but there are no facilities.

To make a loop: turn left on Swamp Rd. at the end of East Rd., and head S. to Lenox Rd., where you turn left again and spy your waiting car. Add 2 mi.

PERU

Peru is the highest town, in terms of elevation, in the county (and therefore the state), at 2,064 ft. It was incorporated July 4, 1771, as Partridgefield, because Oliver Partridge was one of the original purchasers of the grant. it began as a stop on a Boston to Albany stage line. The town was renamed in 1806, just two years after its western end had been lopped off to become Hinsdale, because like the country of Peru, it was in the mountains. And like the other Berkshire hilltowns, it subsisted on thin-soiled agriculture and a few mills, until young people heard of the kind of soil they grew out west. Then as now, residents went down to work in the more urban area of Pittsfield. With a population of under 700 and no shopping center, it remains one of the smallest Berkshire County towns. Few accommodations are available.

A 300-acre sanctuary near the center of town provides some excellent strolling.

WALK

RICE SANCTUARY

Various trails available

Road approaches
Take Rte. 8 to Hinsdale; turn E. on Rte. 143 to the center of town, recognizable because of the church on the left and the road junction. Turn right on South Rd. for .8 mi., then right again on Rice Rd.

DOROTHY FRANCES RICE SANCTUARY

The sign welcomes you to the Dorothy Frances Rice Sanctuary, provided you arrive during daylight hours from May 28 to October 12. Local people also ski there in the winter. The small building is a visitors' center. Nearby most of the trails come together, their arrows color coded, at a busy sign. Choose your color and follow in the direction of the arrow, because the trees are only "blazed," with colored blocks of wood, on one side. In other words, if you go the "wrong" way you won't see any blazes — although, for that matter, the trails are easy to follow, sections even mowed.

Dorothy Frances Rice died of tuberculosis shortly after graduating from Smith College, in Northampton. She loved this site of the family summer home. After her father, architect Orville Rice of New York City, died, her mother, Mary Rice, set up a trust to maintain the 300-acre property named for her daughter. The family home partly burned and was partly chewed down by voracious porcupines.

People in Peru still talk about two Smith College girls who lived in the visitors' center for one or more summers while studying the plants and animals. Eventually the trust turned the property over to the New England Forestry Foundation, together with an endowment. In season, a caretaker comes for two days a week to maintain the trails and the building. Witness 72-year-old Mel Fassell of Pittsfield, who was himself caretaker of the property for a stretch of 25 years.

Choose your color and follow your trail. Although as many as 1,500 people a year wander through the sanctuary, you probably won't see any of them. For the most part, the trails pass through old field growth laced with stone walls. The lengths of the walks vary and, of course, it is possible to connect them in different ways as they cross each other. Figure on 30 min. to an hr. — more if you want. Yes, those are bear scratches on the shed, for the Peru wilderness is alive with fauna as well as flora.

PERU: RICE SANCTUARY

PITTSFIELD

Solomon and Sarah Deming arrived from Wethersfield, Connecticut, at what's presently Elm St. and built their first home in 1752. They were Pontoosuc's first European settlers and their daughter, Dorothy, the first child of European extraction born in this wilderness. The other earliest residents were also from Connecticut, which was true in much of western Massachusetts. Settlers gathered in sufficient numbers over the next year to discuss founding a town and building a meeting house, located beside what became Park Square. They decided to name the town for William Pitt, English statesman who befriended the colonies and whose birthday was the same as the day in April, 1761 that Berkshire County split off from Hampshire County. Pittsfield was to become the shire town or county seat of Berkshire.

In 1764, Rev. Thomas Allen became the first minister, later accompanying the troops to the Battle of Bennington (1777), as the "Fighting Parson." The elm next to the first meeting house was spared in the construction of the second church, the one Charles Bulfinch designed, by the intercession of Lucretia Williams, who spent an altogether interesting few decades. Loyal to the king like her father, Israel Williams, she married the ardent patriot John Williams (no relation; every fourth person in western Massachusetts in those days was named Williams). Yet she survived and their marriage survived. At least they had plenty to talk about, and in 1783, when the peace was signed, they threw a party that, judging from contemporary accounts, may scarcely have been equaled since.

The elm, although struck by lightning, lived into the days Herman Melville spent in Pittsfield. He described scarred Capt. Ahab in terms of that tree, "greenly alive but branded." It finally had to be removed in 1864.

Poet Oliver Wendell Holmes' great-grandfather, Jacob Wendell, who originally bought the land for Pittsfield in 1736, drove a wonderful "one-hoss shay," subject of the poem "The Deacon's Masterpiece." That shay now sits in the basement of the Berkshire Museum, on South St., together with many other artifacts from the city's literary, historic, natural, and artistic past. O.W. Holmes's property is now owned by the Massachusetts Audubon Society, called as it always has been, Canoe Meadows. It is located where Pomeroy Ave. meets Holmes Rd.: Holmes Rd. being also the address of Melville's Pittsfield home, "Arrowhead" — now the headquarters of the Berkshire County Historical Society. The poet Henry Wadsworth Longfellow, of "Hiawatha" fame, stayed at the Dutch Colonial mansion built in 1781 by Henry Van Schaack, now the Pittsfield Country Club.

This building on Rte. 7, south of town, originally known as Broad Hall, was also the home for nine years of Elkanah Watson, who married science with agriculture in Berkshire. The merino sheep he imported changed the nature of farming in the county; the agricultural fairs he founded still continue in some form or other throughout western Massachusetts.

Another application of science created the modern city, which in the 19th century was smaller than its North County rival, No. Adams. In 1907 the General Electric Company established its plant in Pittsfield. A city that took 150 years to gain a population of 25,000, doubled that in the next 30 years. (And continued growing to near 58,000 in 1960. It has declined since.)

Early industries used water for paper and waterpower. As well as drawing from the Housatonic River and its tributaries, industries enlarged two lakes, Onota and Pontoosuc, as water reservoirs. Both now serve as recreational bases. Public swimming is available at Burbank Park on Onota and at the park just off Rte. 7 on Hancock Rd. for Pontoosuc. Pittsfield is refreshed by its lakes and keeps its eye on the hills that surround it.

WALKS

DOWNTOWN

8 blocks (30 minutes)

Most of the walks in this book are in the country, many on trails. Nevertheless, cities in Berkshire County, even the largest, are not far removed from landscape. In fact, the view from the top floor of the Hilton Hotel (corner of South and West streets) rivals that of many ridges. Another kind of view exists, however: that of the manmade attributes of Berkshire. This book attempts to capture some of the history of the county at all sites while walking: here in Pittsfield it's appropriate to take a downtown tour. The map of "Pittsfield: A Self-Guided Historic Walking Tour" (by Richard Silverman; published by Pittsfield Central) is available for 25 cents at the Local History Room of the Berkshire Athenaeum, the modern building at the corner of Wendell and East streets.

The Athenaeum itself, with its Local Authors' Room, Children's Room, and Herman Melville Room, should be a stop on the tour. The map suggests that you start your trip at the Berkshire Museum, on South St. just beyond Park Square. This triple-threat museum, founded in 1903 by the son of the founder of the Dalton paper mills, contains art, history, and natural history. It runs a film and lecture series in its Little Cinema and other educational programs. Here are some of the highlights of the rest of the tour.

The map takes you past a series of buildings along Park Square, including the old Athenaeum, built in "Venetian Gothic Revival" style in 1876. No longer a library, it now serves as the county district attorney's office and the mid-county registry of deeds. At the county surveyor's office on the first floor you can purchase the latest edition of the official county road map, an invaluable tool for locating the out-of-the-way, yet attractive enough to be framed.

In 1868 the then town of Pittsfield ended a 60-year struggle with Lenox about which was the appropriate town for the county seat by offering to build the Berkshire County Court House, next door. The state legislature then agreed to move the seat to the suitably gussied up building the town provided.

St. Stephen's Church, directly across the square from Wendell St., was built in 1889, and is English Gothic in style, with its sturdy proportions and rusticated stonework. Inside, the carved arches of the ceiling and stained-glass windows are worth a visit.

Across the street from St. Stephen's stands the elegant town hall, built in 1832. After years as a civic center, it is now used for bank offices. Next, to the west, the First Congregational Church, built in 1853, incorporates clock, bell, and bootscraper from a Charles Bulfinch-designed predecessor built in 1793. This substantial building serves as a reminder that from colonial days right through to mid-19th century, church and state were one in Massachusetts.

The Berkshire County Savings Bank, at the North St. corner, was built in 1894. In the warmer weather, it shares the site with its trademark, the popcorn wagon. The popper, now operated electrically, was once driven by steam. The wagon, which has stood on the corner since 1910, is on the National Register of Historic Places. The Berkshire Corner, across North St., was built in 1868 as the headquarters for Berkshire Life Insurance Co., now located in the imposing building across from the country club on South St.

Berkshire Bank and Trust building, just north of the popcorn bank, was built in 1923 in a classical revival style. The First Agricultural Bank, farther down the same side of the street, also looks just like a bank, although more distinctly Greek. The tour map notes that this is one of the few buildings on North St. that has all four sides exposed, while much of the street is a continuous wall of fronts.

The Rosa England block, just across Fenn St. and now known as the Galleria, is one of Pittsfield's Victorian buildings. Although the facade has been adapted to the 20th century, most of the elegant features were preserved. The flatiron-shaped Eagle Building at the corner of Eagle St. (1904) is as efficient a use of available space next to the railroad tracks as you could find. Although the newspaper itself has moved to larger quarters in a former mill, on So. Church St., the city is the richer for this distinctive structure and the sightly vest-pocket park that fills the tip of the triangle.

In a slight departure from the prescribed route, you might want to head E. on Eagle St. and then S. on Renne St., to pass the home of the Berkshire Artisans and take a gander at the mural that decorates the wall. The First United Methodist Church at the corner of Fenn replaces a wooden structure that partially burned in 1871. The chancel window was created by Tiffany of New York.

The city government buildings are located to the south of Fenn St. The city hall moved into the white Vermont marble, classic building in 1967. It was built as a post office in 1910. The Central Fire Station, just beyond, on the National Register of Historic Places, was built in 1895. The next year the city purchased horses to pull the heavy engines.

From here it is a short walk, continuing in the same direction, back to Park Square.

PITTSFIELD: DOWNTOWN

CANOE MEADOWS

Various trails available

This Massachusetts Audubon Sanctuary consists of 262 acres of wetlands bordering the Housatonic River. Access is from Holmes Rd. just to the N. of its junction with Pomeroy Ave. The property, with its 3 mi. of trails, is open 9 a.m. to dusk, Tuesday through Sunday. The foliage filters the sound of traffic and the sight of nearby homes, so that while in a residential area the property carries you to the open fields of an earlier Pittsfield. No rest rooms or other facilities are available. The essentially level trails across meadows and occasional bridges are skiable as long as wet areas are frozen under the snow. There is a self-guided nature tour. A donation is requested from non-members.

PITTSFIELD: CANOE MEADOWS

HIKE

BERRY POND

5 miles (2 hours)

Road approaches

From Park Square, Pittsfield, follow W. on West St., 2.5 mi.; turn right on Churchill St. for 1.25 mi.; and left at the chocolate-colored state forest sign on Cascade St. from which it is .5 mi. to the state forest entrance. There is a small fee for parking, to use the bathing beach at Lulu Pond or for camping.

From the north, turn right on Bull Hill Rd., off Rte. 7 in Lanesborough, and go .5 mi.; jog left and then right on Balance Rock Rd., which swings S. for 1.3 mi. to a Pittsfield State Forest gate. Drive in .5 mi. to see an extraordinary balanced rock, on so delicate a base you would think any breeze would blow it over. A painted rock, as well, it is covered with fools' names if not fools' faces. The rock is what is known as an erratic, carried in from the north by a glacier and deposited when the ice departed. Many trails lead to the part of the forest where you are headed, but it doesn't look wise to leave a vehicle at this parking lot. Consider Balance Rock a side trip; drive out the road and follow right to either Hancock Rd. or Causeway; turn right and then left on Churchill to Cascade; right at the State Forest sign.

Camping

Pittsfield State Forest has two campgrounds. The one at Parker Brook, to the west of the HQ, has 18 sites. The "comfort station," in state parlance, has flush toilets. The one at Berry Pond, your destination, 13 sites, with pit toilets, meaning outhouses.

BERRY POND

This is a moderately steep hike, passing the common corner of the towns of Pittsfield, Lanesborough, and Hancock — where Berry Pond is actually located in Pittsfield State Forest. You pass through some extraordinary azalea fields, which bloom in early June; by a fine overlook into New York State; and to Berry Pond, elevation 2,060 ft., the highest natural body of water in Massachusetts. (The highest, at 3,200 ft., is on Mt. Greylock, dug as water supply for Bascom Lodge.)

Because the blazing and signing of trails at Pittsfield has been erratic, you may wish to stop in at forest HQ to pick up the latest map or to inquire about the route. The problem is a bewildering excess of trails. From the state forest entrance it's .5 mi. to Lulu Pond picnic area, where you park — and where you may want to swim or at least wade at the end of the hike. Cross the road from the parking lot. Take Honwee Trail, the second below the gate, a woods road. It is blazed yellow, parallel to and only a few feet above the Lulu Brook Trail and the Berry Pond Circuit Rd. It is pleasant to look down at the brook itself as you pass through beech, maple, and birch forest, with azaleas prominent on the understory or lower foliage.

Ignore the water supply road that comes in right in a few min. and continue on a moderately rising trail — a wet, salamander heaven. It shows the marks of trail bikes in its ruts. Ignore another trail from the right at 23 min. You pass through a stand of pines. At a major intersection 15 min. later, turn left across the brook and then up Berry Pond Circuit Rd. Although the traffic can be heavy on a weekend during azalea season, the shoulders are walkable. The three towns come together just south of the road at about this point.

At 43 min. on a sharp curve to the SE, the Taconic Skyline Trail, blazed white, exits the road, right. As you follow the road left, you are walking on a section of that trail. You walk into the overlook at 52 min. The mountains before you are the Catskills. Berry Pond, surrounded by tentsites, is 3 min. ahead.

The Turner Trail, which you want to take back down the hill, is not well marked at its west end: backtrack a few hundred ft. on the Circuit Rd. to go E. via the Azalea Field Nature Trail or follow around the north side of the pond (which can be wet). Either way, you will end up on the Turner, heading SSE. It is or has been blazed red, but not consistently. At first it passes along a plateau but eventually begins to descend steeply, crossed by trails at 10, 15, and 36 min. This last you can take as a shortcut back to the up-traffic side of the Circuit Rd.

If you continue on Turner, at 40 min. turn left on a gravel road; then left again on Circuit Rd. after 5 min. In 4 more min. you will be back at the parking lot, ready for a dip.

Many other combinations of trails are possible. The route described here is skiable, as are many of the other trails and unplowed roads. One special trail at Pittsfield State Forest is wheelchair accessible, the Tranquility Trail, west of the HQ building.

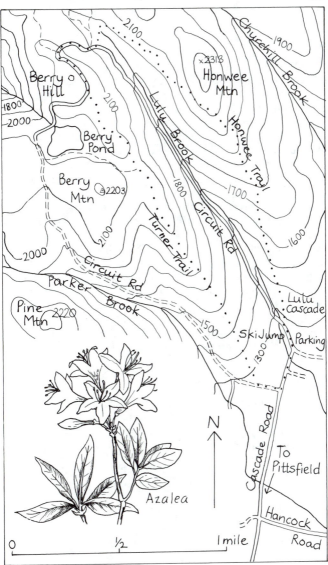

2100
1900
Chuchill Brook
×2313
Honwee Mtn
Berry Hill
1800
2000
2100
Berry Pond
Lulu Brook
Honwee Trail
1700
Berry Mtn ⊙2203
1800
Circuit Rd
1600
2100
Turner Trail
2000
Circuit Rd
Parker Brook
Lulu Cascade
Pine Mtn 2220
1500
Ski Jump
Parking
1300
N

Cascade Road

To Pittsfield

Azalea

Hancock Road

0   ½   1 mile

PITTSFIELD: BERRY POND

HANCOCK

On the map, Hancock looks like what was left over maybe when the rest of Berkshire County was laid out: a long, narrow strip along the northwestern boundary of the county and thus the state, running from Williamstown to Richmond. It is impossible to drive from one end of Hancock to the other within the town lines. Six thousand acres of mountainous Pittsfield State Forest intervene. The three sections of the town of 800: north, village, and Shaker, draw mail from different post offices, draw wires from different utilities, and pledge different loyalties.

Settled in pre-Revolutionary times, the town was originally called Jericho, because the steep slopes were likened to the walls Joshua sent tumbling. When it was incorporated in 1776, it was named for the patriot whose large signature decorates the Declaration of Independence, John Hancock. Samuel Hand, who represented the town in the state government in the 1790s, asked his fellow lawmakers for hazardous duty pay — or at least a clothing allowance — because "the mountains are so steep that one can not climb out without spoiling the knees of his pantaloons, or go back without spoiling his seat."

The biggest business by far is Jiminy Peak, once solely a ski area and now a mountain resort. The second largest business is the not-for-profit Hancock Shaker Village. Second home developments are rising. A few farms, a few stores, some bed and breakfasts and restaurants, as well as the more commercial area along Rte. 20 out of Pittsfield, make up the rest of town.

HIKE

SHAKER MOUNTAIN

6.5 miles (3 hours)

Road approaches

From Park Square in Pittsfield follow Rte. 20 W. for 5 mi. Park in the lot for Hancock Shaker Village, on your left just across the Hancock town line.

Most people taking this hike will want to tour Hancock Shaker Village first, to learn about the souls who built the industrial and holy sites you are about to visit. The Shaker religion reached its zenith in this country in the 1830s. These celibates believed that all work was an expression of God's glory; thus their furniture and craftsmanship are both simple and exquisite. A tour of 20 restored buildings, including crafts workshops and the famous round barn, takes at least 2 hrs. There is a fee. The village is open May through October, 9:30 a.m. to 5 p.m. The Visitors' Center, adjacent to the parking lot, contains rest rooms, lunch shop, information center, and museum shop. Picnic tables are available. Nearest camping is at Pittsfield State Forest.

SHAKER MOUNTAIN

'Tis a gift to be simple
'Tis a gift to be free
'Tis a gift to come down
Where you want to be. . . . — Shaker hymn

The first simple gift you will receive from the Shakers, or at least the non-profit corporation that runs their village, is the modest grounds fee for taking this hike. You will receive other gifts. Nevertheless, because the first part of it is on village property (the rest is in Pittsfield State Forest), as a courtesy tell the folks at the Visitors' Center where you are going. This remarkable hike takes you past the unrestored remains of the North Family or industrial grouping of Hancock Shakers. Included is the village's water system, mill sites, dams, the foundations of a residence, 150-year-old cart roads, charcoal-burning sites, stone walls, and hilltop holy sites of both the Hancock village and the New Lebanon (New York) Shaker Village. After that, with any luck at all, you will come down where you want to be, right where you started.

Use the crosswalk to get to the north side of Rte. 20 and to the fields behind the 1793 Meeting House, the most westerly of the village buildings. Head N. (it may be necessary to detour stock enclosures) to the logging road. The trail departs N. from a cleared log landing 2 min. from the highway. Laid out by the Boy Scouts, it is marked by green triangles with white circles. Even if these have not been kept up, you begin on an unmistakable cart road that soon follows the western side of Shaker Brook. The stone walls may have been laid up in 1845. Eight min. from the highway you arrive at the lower dam, the beginning of a sophisticated water system. The pipe fills a reservoir from which it traveled underground to the village where it first powered machinery, then supplied the wash rooms, then the stables, then the mills, and then the fields to water the cattle. Since the old bridge is washed out, find a place to hop across the brook, either at or below the dam.

As you follow down the eastern side of the stream you pass first an industrial site with a pit for a water wheel and then the cellar hole for the North Family residence. To imagine its size, compare with the Brick Dwelling in the village, although this one was made of wood. At 15 min. into the walk, not counting the time you have taken to examine the ruins, turn left up the hill, through second-growth hardwood with some shagbark hickory and hemlock, on what was probably the Shakers' original cart road to their holy site.

At 27 min. bear left where a branch of the road continues straight. This was a charcoal-burning site. At 34 min. cross under power lines that serve airplane beacon lights for the Pittsfield airport. You switch back to cross under the lines again.

At 44 min. you enter the overgrown field that was the Hancock Shaker's holy ground, which they called Mt. Sinai, now referred to as Shaker Mtn. The Shakers did not permit non-believers on this site. In 1841 or 1842, all Shaker communities were required to clear the summit of a nearby hill, focusing on a "fountain" or hexagonal fence surrounding a marble slab, about which they marched, sang, and danced in May and September. A depression in the blackberry bushes beside the trail marks the fountain; little else remains at Mt. Sinai; more artifacts are visible at Holy Mount, about a mile as the bird flies across the valley. Shakers called to each other across the chasm.

The trail follows along the ridge and then turns left, into the valley. At about 50 min., it switches back through a lovely hemlock grove. At 1:03 you come out on a lumber road. Turn left. If you wish a 1:30 min. hike, follow straight back to the village. Otherwise turn right almost immediately. This road follows to the left of a stone wall. At the end of the wall (1:18), bear left down the hill. The trail swings right, between sections of a different stone wall and across a brook (1:23). The forest in this section has not been lumbered as ruthlessly as has the forest in the valley and on Shaker Mtn. Follow up the hill to a junction of walls and trails (1:27), where you turn left, again following a stone wall.

At 1:36 pass an opening in the wall that probably admitted a cart road from the New Lebanon community to its holy ground. At 1:41 you arrive at what was a gated entrance, elevation 1,927 ft. (higher than Mt. Sinai). Follow the wall, on the inside, left to the feast ground and the foundations of the shelter (1:44). Although the Shakers planted a row of pines around each site, the CCC planted the pine trees inside, in the 1930s. If you head into the woods directly in front of the shelter, you may find the depression in the ground that marks the fountain site. There was an altar 10 yds. west of the fountain.

Downhill from the altar is a beautiful specimen of the

wall-maker's art, probably one-day's labor, 3 feet at the base and tapering to the top, 18 feet long. The brethren must have taken 350 man-days to build the wall around the sacred lot, not to mention the other walls you have seen.

Starting in front of the shelter, head W., bearing right downhill on a trail that reaches an opening in the wall (1:53). Although the path generally follows the wall to the left, it swings out in an arc before rejoining at the corner. This section of trail, which is not based on an old road and has not experienced much wear, is hard to follow even with the markers. The corner of the wall encloses a natural amphitheater (2:03), containing a spring. If you did not stop to picnic at either summit, this would be a good spot. Cross the brook below the corner and follow steeply up the hill, along the path, until it comes out on a fire road (2:20). Turn left. The brook is on your right. You pass the first of several wide spots on the road, which were charcoal-burning sites. You may find some pieces of charcoal. Follow the fire road until it turns left, up hill, while the older cart road continues straight to a brook crossing (2:29). From here follow the green triangle down the branch of the brook to take in a Shaker quarry.

At 2:41 you return to the main cart road (bear right) at the site of the high dam, which is largely washed out. It may have been constructed in 1810. Just below, the Shakers built a sawmill that bridged the stream. Logs were loaded at the retaining wall on the far side. The depressions on the near side were mill foundations. This mill, which ran on water power or steam when water wasn't sufficient, was built mid-19th century and burned in 1926.

Follow the cart road to the log landing. Total round trip is just about 3 hrs., counting only travel time. It would be possible to ski Shaker Mtn. but not Holy Mount. A ski loop, the same as for an abbreviated hike, would return via the lumber road you meet after descending Shaker Mtn.

HANCOCK: SHAKER MOUNTAIN

DALTON

A town of about 6,500 population at a junction of Rtes. 8 and 9, east of Pittsfield, Dalton has been dominated by paper manufacturing virtually since its incorporation in 1784. It is still a paper town. In 1799 Henry Wiswell, John Willard, and Zenas Crane began a mill on the Housatonic that produced the first paper made in Berkshire County. The history of the forerunners of Crane & Co. is one of rapid technological progress and spectacular fires. Local residents attributed the success of the company in part to the quality of a spring on the premises. Early on, the company made collars, bond, bank notes and parchment; now it is best known for manufacturing the paper on which the U.S. currency is printed. The Crane Paper Museum on Rte. 9, west of town, portrays the history of paper-making; additional artifacts are exhibited at the Berkshire Museum in Pittsfield.

Because the AT passes through town, Dalton is well known to through-hikers as a pleasant and friendly stop, with an array of places to eat and stay along the main street.

Wahconah Brook falls near the Windsor border. It was known to Indians but "discovered" by William Cleveland while he was looking for a beehive. He built a dam above the falls and a flume around them to drop the water on the overshot wheel of a grist mill, about 1770. His mill-stones were fashioned in France and hauled to the site by boat to Boston and oxen across the Bay Colony. About 1800 Jacob Booth added a sawmill to the site.

As is true of other county falls and cliffs, Wahconah Falls comes with an assortment of Indian traditions. In one story, Wahconah, denied a suitor from an enemy tribe, jumped into the brook. In another, Wahconah, whose father was a prominent chief, said she would marry the brave who could leap across the chasm above the falls, which was narrower in those days. Of the two who made the attempts the wrong one cleared and the right one landed in the brook. So she jumped in after him and they went over the falls together to their deaths.

WALK

WAHCONAH FALLS

A few hundred feet

The popular waterfall and gorge is located at Wahconah Falls State Park on Rte. 9 in Dalton. Coming from Dalton center, turn right at the sign, passing Dalton Tractor. About a mi. up gravel Wahconah Rd. lies the parking lot. No fee, no camping, no facilities, no lifeguard. This area has become a party spot. At last visit it had accumulated a good deal of trash. It is hard to understand why the public can't treat a beautiful resource with respect. On this 53-acre tract you will find a deep gulf, rocky ledges, large hemlocks, and a scattering of picnic grills. Trails meander through the woods on either side of the brook. The falls dive deeply over ledges below Windsor Reservoir on a tributary of the Housatonic. Deep pools below beckon the visitor who wants to cool off — strictly at your own risk, of course. (For map, see Dalton-Windsor map under "Windsor Jambs.")

WINDSOR

Once Plantation No. 4, the land making up Windsor was sold to a consortium of buyers in 1762, prototypes of today's land developers: buy a chunk of wilderness, survey it, and try to sell the lots for a good profit. The boundaries weren't exactly the same, including then part of present day Dalton and Cheshire but not the present northern part of Windsor — which was considered a section of plantation No. 5, Cummington (in Hampshire County).

As sometimes happens to developers even now, the lots moved slowly, which made it hard for the consortium to pay off its notes; furthermore, many of those who bought were also speculators rather than pioneers, so time passed before any significant settlement. Still, in 1771, residents petitioned to incorporate as Gageborough, after the pre-Revolutionary governor of the colony. In 1777 they petitioned to change the name, British Gen. Gage having fallen out of favor in 1776. By the end of that century, the area was a thriving farming community, with the usual accumulation of mills. When the sons and daughters of farmers went west and when the railroad failed to pass through town, Windsor became a byway.

By the beginning of the 20th century, Gen. Alfred E. Bates had begun accumulating former farms in the north of town, while Helen Gamwell Ely was accumulating land to the south to form her Helenscourt. In the 1920s, Elizabeth C.T. Miller bought the Bates estate. Mrs. Ely remarried Lt. Col. Arthur D. Budd, who also acquired the Miller property. Thus, the 3,000 acres of Notchview Reservation, nearly a quarter of the town, resulted from the union of two large estates, located on Rte. 9. Now owned by TTOR, Notchview borders 1,616 acres of Windsor State Forest and is nearby a similar-sized tract that is part of the state forest and part of a Wildlife Management Area, presumably fixing the character of the town for some time to come.

Camping

Camping is available for a small fee in season at Windsor Jambs State Park, part of the state forest. The area is just E. and N. of Notchview, on River Rd. (signs on Rte. 116 and Rte. 9 direct you to the park). A foot trail along Steep Bank Brook, connects the Jambs with Notchview, about 3.0 mi. to the Budd Visitors' Center. At the campground, a stream is dammed for swimming. Tourist accommodations are not available in Windsor.

WALKS

WINDSOR JAMBS

3 miles (1.5 hours)

When people talk about the Jambs, they mean the state park with its swimming area (follow the signs from Rtes. 116 or 9). Strictly speaking, however, the Jambs is (are) a nearby gorge, the name derived perhaps from the stream's narrowed route through a rock doorway. Park in the lot by park HQ. Across the road, generally bear right through the camping area for the Jambs Trail, which actually begins behind the toilet building. You can also drive to the scenic gorge on the gravel Lower Rd., but to do so would be to miss out on a 3-mi., round-trip stroll through a deep evergreen forest. The leisurely path, blazed blue, wanders in its own insouciant way through spruce, hemlock and even some pine and fir. The trail is wet and, as it runs beside the Jambs, requires sure-footedness, so wear hiking shoes. For the best effect, at the junction follow the trail to the lower Jambs, then work up along the edge, protected by the cables, to upper Jambs. The trail back leaves from the parking lot. Jambs Brook has cut deeply into slabs of rock, tumbling over many small falls, a pleasing sight even when, in midsummer, not much water passes through.

DALTON – WINDSOR: WAHCONAH FALLS / WINDSOR JAMBS

HIKE

NOTCHVIEW / JUDGE'S HILL

5.5 miles (2.25 hours)

Road approaches

Take Rte. 9 E. from Pittsfield, through Dalton. The entrance to Notchview is 1 mi. E. of the junction with Rte. 8-A. That road, recently rebuilt after years of axle bending, drops S. from Rte. 116 out of Adams, an alternate course for people setting sail from north county.

JUDGE'S HILL

The Arthur D. Budd Visitors' Center, at the parking lot, serves as an information booth and provides a place for cross-country skiers to wax and warm. Restrooms are available. There are picnic tables and there is a water source, but no camping is allowed. The Budds' former home with formal gardens is east of the center.

TTOR maintains this 3,000-acre reservation, which takes its name from the view from Lt. Col. Budd's home through a notch eastward into the hills of Cummington. Rte. 9 passes through the Notch. Budd, a World War II hero, donated the property in 1965. The Trustees charge a nominal fee to non-members for use. The property shows traces of farming the soil of these hills, known as "rock farming," and of the later era of gentlemen's estates.

The 25 mi. of trails on the property pass through trees that have grown up on former fields — and also some fields that are cut. Although you only climb 297 ft. to the summit of Judge's Hill, the highest land in Windsor, you start at an elevation of 2,000 ft. This quality of highland plateau, complete with evergreen forests, harsh climate, rocky soil, bogs, and deep stream crevasses, distinguishes Notchview. Wildlife here includes white-tail deer, bobcat, nesting hawks, and occasional bear.

You may choose any combination of a multitude of

well-marked and well-maintained trails. As a 5.5-miler, for instance, for a morning's hike (or ski), walk straight ahead from the parking area, leaving the barn on the left, and turning left on the Circuit Trail. You walk gently up through a wet, spruce area. At 12 min., turn left on Judge's Hill Trail. (All Notchview trails are blazed yellow; however, ample signs let you know which one you're on.) At first you lose elevation, crossing Shaw Rd. (gravel) and descending through mixed hardwoods and across a bridge. Then you begin to climb moderately, through an area marked by large glacial boulders.

After 31 min. you achieve the summit, marked by the stone remains of the fireplace of the Judge's "fort," laid up without mortar. Most of the surrounding growth is quite young; he must have had a marvelous view when the land was cleared. Judge James M. Barker was the most prominent member of a social and sporting group known as the Windsor Club, which held weekend hunting and fishing trips on the property. He erected the stone lunch stop, walled around and complete with stone tables and benches, about the turn of the century.

It takes 9 min. to descend to Bates Rd., a gravel surface on which you turn right. You pass between the cellar holes and stone walls of some of the 2 dozen families who at one time lived in the area. In one, a rabbit warren has been cleverly burrowed under a concrete slab. Is this the site of the Babbitt Axe Factory? Could these be the Babbitt rabbits? The Steep Bank Brook Trail, which departs left, would take you to Windsor Jambs.

Pick up the Bumpus Trail, left, through open fields to the Gen. Bates homesite. He fought Indians in Kansas and Wyoming. His cousin, Herman, was famous for the quality of the butter he produced on this highland farm, becoming known as Butter Bates. The open fields provide a nice contrast to traveling the woods, especially when the sun breaks through to warm the grass. The Bumpus trail turns abruptly right, crossing Shaw Rd. (1:14) and descending steeply into a gorge. It crosses a bridge over Shaw Brook, then climbs through evergreens. Continue straight at the Y,

WINDSOR: NOTCHVIEW / JUDGE'S HILL

9 min. later. Follow the signs towards the Visitors' Center, coming out on the open Sawmill Field, crossing it, and picking up the Circuit Trail back to the parking lot (1:55).

Among the many alternatives for walks as well as hikes is the mile-long, self-guided interpretive trail in the Hume Brook area at Notchview that explains the principles of forest land management, with an emphasis on forest aesthetics and wildlife. TTOR issues separate maps for hiking and skiing; a large map is posted by the parking lot. Bring a picnic; spend the day.

NORTH COUNTY

CHESHIRE

Cheshire in early days was called New Providence by homesick Rhode Islanders. Col. Joab Stafford led a group of his townspeople to the Battle of Bennington on August 17, 1777. A monument and a Wildlife Management Area honor him. In 1801 the town combined all its milk production for one day into a 1,255-pound cheese, which oxen dragged to a boat on the Hudson River and thence to Washington to honor newly elected President Thomas Jefferson. Most of the Cheshire lakes, the headwaters of the Hoosic River, falling within the town borders, are dammed to provide a head at low water for the former Adams Print Works. The AT crosses the river and Rte. 8 in the center of town on its way to climb into the Mt. Greylock State Reservation via Outlook Ave. Many through-hikers on the trail stop in Cheshire to pick up mail forwarded to them c/o General Delivery at the post office and to sleep at a friendly church.

WALK

HOOSIC RIVER RAILROAD

Adams and Cheshire, 4.5 miles (2 hours)

You need not worry about trains along this section of tracks, although hope soars eternal in the breasts of local railroad buffs that freight and scenic service will be restored . . . some day. In the mid-19th century the Hoosic River Railroad was an important artery. Now it is a wonderful, water level route, primarily frequented by four-legged game and waterfowl.

This walk is best enjoyed by using 2 cars. Leave auto No. 1 on the dead end of a short street just south of the Rte. 8 overpass in the south end of Adams (the idea is to have the car on the same side of the river as the tracks). Park No. 2 at the Rte. 8 roadside rest beside the reservoir or at the restaurant across from it. Take off on the tracks at the nearby grade crossing, by the reservoir dam. Cross the bridge over Kitchen Brook. You pass by some back yards with barking dogs. Play the part of the train as you cross Church St., route of the AT as well as automobiles. Soon you are removed from houses and dogs, as South Brook enters from the southeast. Stafford Hill rises northeast and the Greylock massif, northwest.

Natives call this section the Jungle, as the 10-ft.-wide Hoosic writhes through swampland. Alligators you need not worry about; however, nesting snapping turtles can be a problem in late spring. The calcareous (lime-based) wetlands west of the tracks, and marshes and shrub swamps east of the tracks, are fine habitat for a variety of water creatures. Wood duck platforms dot the wetlands, deer and muskrat tracks follow the stream. You may see snowshoe hare, pheasant, occasional fox, and some naturally reproducing brown trout as well as stocked trout. Note that although heading north, you are going downstream. Rte. 8 is close at hand, but not noticeable except for the distant sound of a truck downshifting. You see a gouged hillside of gravel pits to the left.

A brick building belonging to the town of Adams introduces the first road for 3 mi. This is the pumping station for 2 artesian wells. Around the corner appears a bridge. Although walking across is no problem, you may wonder if it is possible to ski the open trestle in winter. Yes, because skis nicely bridge the space between the ties. A snowmobiler, on the other hand, can get his runners caught in the guard rails. This is not a bicycling route, either.

Welcome to Cheshire Harbor, said to be named because it harbored runaway slaves, a lovely spot with an old swim-

CHESHIRE: HOOSIC RIVER RAILROAD

ming hole, somewhat silted in. Now the river is on the left, with Rte. 8 just the other side. You can see the stonework of a mill sluiceway. Follow the railroad under Rte. 8. On the other side you should see your car.

It would be possible to stroll from Coltsville in Pittsfield to Ashland St., No. Adams, where the Hoosic River Railroad joins the live one, coming from the Hoosac Tunnel. (Do not walk near tracks in use.) But you won't find a better stretch anywhere than the one you've just completed.

ADAMS AND MOUNT GREYLOCK

Adams, first East Township, then East Hoosuck, was finally named for Revolutionary War hero Samuel Adams in 1778. Its remarkable ethnic heritage began with English Quakers, whose vitality carved an industrial center from the wilderness, and continued through successive waves of immigrants who came to labor in those industries: Irish, Scots, Germans, French Canadians and Poles. Although the textile mills have ceased and although its northern end was lopped off to form No. Adams, Adams remains a bustling town of 10,000, with all the accommodations and services a walker could want. Most stores and restaurants are along Rte. 8, which goes by different names such as Columbia and Park streets. The statue of William McKinley in front of the library honors a friend of a foremost Adams family, the Plunketts. McKinley's high tariff policies benefited the local cloth manufacturers.

Although the summit of Mt. Greylock lies in the town of Adams, the Mt. Greylock State Reservation encompasses 12,000 acres of hilly land in the towns of Adams, Cheshire, Lanesborough, New Ashford, No. Adams, and Williamstown. But you only have to look upwards in Adams to understand why the town feels a special regard for the mountain that looms over it. Mt. Greylock is a close, intimate friend.

Greylock is the tallest peak in southern New England at 3,491 feet. It is surrounded by half a dozen lower eminences, most of which are still higher than anything else in Massachusetts, Connecticut and Rhode Island: Saddleball (3,238), Mt. Fitch (3,110), Mt. Williams (2,951), Mt. Prospect (2,690), Stony Ledge (2,580), and Ragged Mtn. (2,451).

So it is not as high as some of the Adirondacks or the White Mtns. or the Green Mtns. even — which you can see from Greylock. At one time the Appalachians, of which Greylock is a part, stood Himalayan high, six times their present altitude, but time and weather have eroded them. Even in the early 19th century, before the more spectacular, western scenery in this country was accessible, Greylock created a lot of excitement.

All the great American writers and naturalists, like Thoreau, Hawthorne, and Melville, made their pilgrimages to Greylock. The first person to publish an account of his visit, in 1800, was the former president of Yale, Timothy Dwight, who said "the view was immense and of amazing grandeur. . .". It inspired prose, poetry, fiction and energetic enjoyment of the out-of-doors.

A popular destination as it has been and still is, not surprisingly, paved roads from No. Adams (Notch Rd.) and from Lanesborough (Rockwell Rd.) meet a mile from the summit, to which they travel together as Summit Rd. A gravel-surfaced road, known as New Ashford or Greylock, climbs from the west to Rockwell Rd. not far below a gravel spur known as Sperry Rd. This provides a way to the public campgrounds (which have no recreational vehicle hookups, showers or flush toilets). Tent sites are distributed discreetly in a spruce grove. Stony Ledge, at the end of Sperry Rd., provides a spectacular view of the Hopper, a V-shaped wedge worn by erosion on the western side.

The summit has limited development, such as broadcast towers and communications dishes. A 100-ft.-high War Memorial Tower, designed originally to be a lighthouse in the Charles River estuary, 130 miles away, was erected on Greylock in the 1930s to pick up the spirits of local residents during hard times. The state-owned Bascom Lodge, built by the CCC during the New Deal and run by the AMC, provides modest accommodations and good, hearty food, in season (reservations required). The hikers' breakfasts and Tuesday evening barbecues are not to be missed. Enthusiastic interpreters lead walks and conduct programs to explain the natural and human history of the mountain.

A 7.8-mi. segment of the 2,050-mi.-long AT transects the reservation from S. to N., a ribbon that hangs over most of the peaks. Remember: the AT is blazed white. Of the 5 three-sided shelters on the reservation, two are associated with the AT. Ten side trails to the AT, blazed blue, together with 11 other trails and the AT, total 43 mi. of hiking in the Greylock range — routes shorter or longer, steeper or more gentle, fit just about every walker's time and ambition.

The War Memorial Tower, open during posted hours, extends the view from the summit to 70 or 100 miles in clear conditions. Innumerable more local views reveal Adams from the east of the summit, the farms of Williamstown from the trail intersection on Mt. Prospect, the peak itself from Ragged, the lakes and rounded hills of mid-Berkshire from Jones' Nose or Rounds' Rock.

Views on the mountains include tumbling streams. March Cataract flows best when the snows melt. You can see it from Rte. 7 in front of Mt. Greylock Regional High School. A trail from the campground lead to it. The Deer Hill Trail from the campground passes a falls on Roaring Brook. Money Brook Falls, also tucked into the Hopper, can be reached by a side trail to the Money Brook Trail.

Most of the vegetation on Greylock is northern hardwood: beech, birch, maple and few evergreens. In the southern portions of the reservation, recent second growth fills formerly farmed fields. Here and there on the mountains' steep slopes stand aged trees, in areas not cut for railroads or other development over the years. Especially the 1,600 acres of the Hopper, on the west side contain red spruce stands nearly 200 years old. The state has designated the Hopper a Natural Area. The federal government, together with the Society of American Foresters, has recognized these spruces as a National Natural Landmark. To protect the Hopper, it is a low-impact area, excluding vehicles, camp fires, and camping but available for study and hiking.

Its upper reaches are covered by a boreal type of balsam and yellow birch forest, probably the only example of such woods in Massachusetts. The bogs and stunted fir growth near the summits of Greylock and Saddleball are similar to the vegetation on the Canadian Shield — the fir forest of the far north. Your experience as a hiker arriving in them is exhilarating.

The variety of wildlife matches the diverse vegetation. Forty state-listed rare or endangered species have been seen on the reservation, as well as birds as unusual as Swainson's thrush and the blackpole warbler. Viewers come to watch a variety of hawks performing their aerobatics by taking advantage of updrafts on the steepest part of the east face. Common wildlife include the whitetail deer, bobcat, snow shoe hare, cottontail rabbit, ruffed grouse, woodcock, raccoon, red squirrel, chipmunk, fox, skunk, woodchuck and the porcupine that hang around the shelters to chew your hiking boots if you leave them unattended. Bear, the eastern coyote, wild turkey, fisher, and raven have recently returned to the reservation, as surrounding farm fields grow over.

Berkshire County is blessed by 150,000 acres of land protected from development, approximately one-quarter its total area. The Greylock Reservation stands as the flagship of the state's park system and as the jewel of the county's public and private holdings.

This book describes walks and hikes in the summit area, and in the campground area. The walks are the Overlook Trail, Stony Ledge, March Cataract and Deer Hill. It describes 5 hikes: one from Notch Rd. in to the ridge of Prospect Mtn.; Cheshire Harbor Trail, from the southwest; Bellows Pipe Trail from the north; Hopper Trail from the west; and Stony Ledge/Roaring Brook from the southeast. Dogs are only allowed on leash at the campground.

WALKS

OVERLOOK TRAIL

2.5 miles (1 hour)

Try the Overlook Trail from the summit, fairly rigorous going that passes by fine overlooks into the Hopper. Depart from the television tower, except turn right instead of following the Hopper Trail. Descent is constant through mixed woods to Notch Rd. Cross it into the woods again at about 10 min., continuously losing altitude until the stream crossing just above March Cataract Falls (40 min.). The overlooks, down short trails, are in this vicinity. Shortly you come out on the Hopper Trail, at which you turn left to climb back up to the TV tower.

CAMPGROUND TRAILS

Stony Ledge, 2 miles; March Cataract, approximately 2 miles; Deer Hill, 2.25 miles

Several trails depart from the campground, including a self-guided nature and cultural walk. Consult the supervisor at the contact station for detailed information on their present state. The most spectacular is simply to continue up gravel Sperry Rd. 1.0 mi. from the contact station to Stony Ledge, with its breathtaking view over the sheer depths of the Hopper to Greylock and Fitch. The road rises but this is an easy walk on an open road, suitable even for sneakers. It is also possible to drive, although there is a slight fee for driving to picnic at Stony Ledge. The afternoon is the best time to make the trip, because the sun strikes on the far ledges. An intriguing alternative from the same perch, however, is watching the sun rise over the highest peak in Massachusetts.

Other walks include a good bit of up-and-down, and so require stout shoes. A short but rugged trail departs across from the contact station, up a former road and then right, up and along a sidehill, then steeply down, less than a mi. in total, to the foot of March Cataract. Although a good flow of water tumbles down at all seasons, the walk is especially recommended in high water, when you will be well wetted before you stand on the midstream rocks — if you can — gazing up the gleaming wet stone face. It is dangerous to make this trip in the winter, because the trail cuts uncertainly along the sidehill, but it is a thrill to hear the water plunging beneath the ice. Note: this trail is less worn than most in the reservation and therefore harder to follow.

Departing Sperry Rd. on the same side as the contact station but a few hundred feet farther in, the Deer Hill Trail follows Roaring Brook, sharing the Roaring Brook Trail at first but turning left after 200 yds., passing Deer Hill Falls (1 mi.), and starting fairly steeply up, past a recently reconstructed lean-to, and coming out on the carriage road. Turn left to arrive at Sperry Rd. and left again to return to

the contact station (2.25 mi.) If you don't turn on Sperry
Rd., you will come out on the Hopper trail above the
campground.

MOUNT PROSPECT FROM NOTCH ROAD

1 mile (30 minutes)

Climbing from the valley to the peak of Prospect is the
steepest hike around (it begins part-way along the Money
Brook Trail, which in turn begins at the same point as the
Hopper Trail). It is possible to get the same view, however,
by driving up Notch Rd. 3 mi. from the gate to the AT crossing at the stand of tall spruce trees. There is an obvious
parking area on the right and a big sign. Follow the white
blazes down and then up. Where the AT meets the Prospect
Trail, on the ridge (.5 mi.), an opening gives a fine view of
Williamstown and especially the Galusha Farm, with cleared
fields below you.

HIKES

CHESHIRE HARBOR TRAIL

6.6 miles (2 .5 hours)

Road approaches

At the statue of former President McKinley in front of the library in Adams turn W. off Rte. 8 onto Maple St. At .4 mi. turn left on West Rd.; .5 mi. later, right on W. Mountain Rd. at sign for Mt. Greylock Greenhouses. The road ends at a turn around, the site of a former farmhouse, after 1.6 mi.

Camping

Peck's Brook shelter, a three-sided, Adirondack lean-to, is attained by a separate, 1-mi. trail that departs from the junction of Rockwell, Notch and Summit roads. Bascom Lodge, at the summit, has limited accommodations (reservations required) as well as food. It is run by the AMC. All summit buildings are closed from late October until Memorial Day, but some protection can be found at the Thunderbolt Ski Shelter, an open-sided shelter with a fireplace on the AT just below the summit parking lot, to the north of the War Memorial Tower.

CHESHIRE HARBOR TRAIL

Mt. Greylock is very close to its east side approaches, although the summit is more of a haul than it looks as you stand on the old field at the end of the open section of W. Mountain Rd. Cheshire Harbor Trail is the shortest and easiest of the hiking routes to the summit, not only because of its directness but because it begins at a good elevation. It rises from 1,800 ft. to 3,491 ft. It is also heaviest traveled. Every Columbus Day, hundreds climb this route during the Greylock Ramble, sponsored by the Adams Chamber of Commerce. The trail has been badly eroded, mostly due to off-road vehicles, which have now been banned here (except for snowmobiles). Cheshire Harbor is the community in the town of Cheshire where the trail actually starts, about a mi. SE of where you start.

The unblazed trail leaves as a woods road, heading from the SW corner of the field. Old walls and trash mark the site. Almost immediately the portion of the trail rising from Cheshire Harbor enters left. Riveted drainage pipes and barbed wire harken to the time when this road served active farms.

At 11 min. you come to the first switchback and, in 3 more min., to the second, where a trail enters left (ignore it). Soon, depending on the condition of the foliage, you see the summit, with its tower, rising over Peck's Brook ravine. At 17 min. you round the third switchback and, 4 min. later, the junction with Old Adams Rd. makes the fourth. Old Adams Rd. follows more or less at this contour to the base of Jones' Nose, crossing the AT, which rises from the south. It was a stage route joining Adams and New Ashford; a farmhouse (no longer standing) at Jones' Nose served as a stop. Apparently the place was named for the profile of the farmer.

You bear right, staying on the Cheshire Harbor Trail, however, continuing up the moderate grade that characterizes this entire trail. The trail has been blazed blue or orange from time to time, although blazes are not needed. As you rise, the trail erosion diminishes. The northern hardwoods through which you pass are severely stressed, the effect of atmospheric pollution. Scientists have designated plots in the area to study the decline of high altitude forests in New England. The results to date are disturbing. You see many dead birch, beech, and maple. The ledges (left) rise to the ridge that connects Greylock with the next peak south, Saddleball.

At 54 min. you cross Peck's Brook. Soon a snowmobile trail, known as the Super Highway, drops right to the Gould Farm. Continue on to Rockwell Rd., an hour from the car. At this point you join the AT, following its white blazes to the summit. The next stretch parallels the road but is in the woods — which are, suddenly, the boreal, high elevation forest of balsam firs and bogs, which the trail crosses on bog bridges. The unnamed pond on the left was dug out of a wet spot by the CCC to serve as a water supply for Bascom Lodge.

At the 3-way road junction (1:08), follow straight ahead, back into the woods. The trail to Peck's Brook Shelter departs across the road, right. You follow the AT, with the old water pipe from the pumphouse on the pond; now the lodge has a drilled well. The next sound you hear may well be the wind in the guy wires of the television and radio broadcast tower, which you pass at 1:14. In 3 more min. you pass through the break in the stone walls and come to the War Memorial itself. For those who do not suffer from vertigo, the 92-ft. climb up stairs to the lookout is worthwhile, extending your view. It is also worthwhile to tour the summit on ground level, especially looking over the eastern side, directly down to the town of Adams — and, considerably nearer, Greylock Glen.

Remember to start down by the broadcast tower. The road crossings can be confusing, too. Cross the first, staying on the AT. After the second crossing, the AT continues straight (S.) while the Cheshire Harbor Trail bears left. The trip down takes just about the same time as up.

Since the summit is the focus of 43 miles of trails in the Greylock Reservation, numerous variations on this basic, east side climb are possible. If you can get someone to serve as chauffeur, an east to west hike across the ridge could begin on the Cheshire Harbor Trail and end on the Hopper Trail. Or, with the aid of a Berkshire Regional Transportation Authority bus from No. Adams to Cheshire, an east to north climb would link the Cheshire Harbor Trail with the Bellows Pipe Trail. (Hopper and Bellows Pipe trails are described farther on.) A loop, eschewing the summit, begins on Cheshire Harbor Trail, follows S. on the AT over Saddleball and past the Bassett Brook Campsite to Old Adams Rd. Follow left (N.) 1.5 mi. on Old Adams Rd. until it joins the Cheshire Harbor Trail again (about 15 mi.). Cheshire Harbor Trail and Old Adams Rd. are skiable with deep snow cover.

BELLOWS PIPE TRAIL

4.0 miles (1.5 hours) one way

Road approaches

Turn S. on Notch Rd., off Rte. 2 between Harriman-West Airport and the turn that leads to downtown No. Adams. The road climbs through a residential area and woods, turning sharply left at Mt. Williams Reservoir. After 2.4 mi. from Rte. 2, park along Notch Rd. before it turns right to enter the Mt. Greylock State Reservation; the road by Notch Reservoir comes in from the left. Do not park in such a way as to interfere with the private home at the corner. Bellows Pipe Trail is the gravel road straight ahead. (You can reach the same point via Reservoir Rd., also from No. Adams, or by Pattison Rd., the continuation of Luce Rd. in Williamstown.)

Camping

You pass a lean-to, a ski shelter and Bascom Lodge on this hike. The lean-to is a bit more than halfway in time, where the Bellow's Pipe Ski Trail meets the Bellows Pipe (hiking) Trail. It faces south. The ski shelter is next to the parking lot at the summit, and therefore inclined to be trashy regardless of how rigorously it is cleaned. With a large fireplace in the middle and open sides, it is meant for day use but is available at night for emergencies in the winter. Bascom Lodge stands firmly on the summit, a warm and cheery destination in summer and early fall.

BELLOW'S PIPE TRAIL

Although this trail is too steep for a comfortable descent (see end of description for alternatives), it is hard to think of a better place to be under certain conditions than climbing the Bellows Pipe. One set of conditions is a sunny day on light, powdery snow — on skis. Another is a warm morning, as the fog burns off in the valley, perhaps in late May, when the ephemeral flowers are blossoming and all the brooks are running high. The sun bursts yellow through the trees, suddenly creating shadows where there had been none and picking out the dew on the shrubbery.

You are starting at 1,304 ft. in elevation and climbing to 3,491. In places, particularly on the Bellows Pipe Ski Trail, the going is quite steep. As you cross the chain on the road, it's clear you're on No. Adams watershed property, which protects Notch Reservoir, an impoundment of the brook that cut the valley you climb. There are no blazes on city land, which extends to the Notch. The large sugar maples beside the gravel road have been there many generations; the pines were planted as a way of having trees beside a reservoir that would not fill the water with leaves. You pass several cellar holes and old walls you probably won't notice if the foliage is out. But you may notice the road was uncommonly well made: edged with stone, built with a crown, ditched on the sides. In places it appears to have been cobbled.

For this and many other man-made features of the route, credit Jeremiah Wilber and his descendants, who cut a spacious and productive farm out of the wilderness of this mountain about 1800, built the first road to the summit, grew hay, boiled off enormous quantities of maple syrup, grazed his cattle, killed marauding wolves and bears, built three mills and raised a dozen children by two wives.

Yours is the route Henry David Thoreau took in 1844, when he heeded Hawthorne's and Emerson's advice to visit Greylock. (Emerson called it "a serious mountain.") At one of these homes, now a cellar hole, Thoreau stopped to converse with a lady who was combing her long tresses. You can read about it in *A Week on the Concord and Merrimack Rivers*. He spent the night on a wooden tower on the summit. When he awoke, the clouds had closed in below him, and he found himself, "in a country such as we might see in dreams, with all the delights of paradise."

In 10 min. you come to a yarding area used for timber cutting, but continue straight on the unblazed trail. The

going gets a bit steeper. Soon, through breaks in the foliage, you can see the ridge of Ragged Mtn. (which rises
2,451 ft.), to the east, over Notch Brook valley. The next
landmark, at 31 min., is a bridge. Just why this area is
called Bellow's Pipe remains a mystery. Thoreau said
"bellows" because of the force of the wind rushing through
the notch, like a fireplace bellows. Why "pipe" then? Maybe
as in a musical instrument played by the wind?

Having crossed a dozen or more tributaries, you finally
cross the main stem of Notch Brook at 40 min. and after a
short, very steep eroded section, are in the notch (2,197 ft. in
elevation) clear not long ago as an orchard. At the site of informal camping under spruces at the left, an unmarked trail
follows the wall up to the cliffs on Ragged. Thoreau may
have climbed up there to check his bearings before his final
bushwack to the summit. Now that you are on state land,
look for orange and blue blazes that lead to the summit.

Follow a level section, looking down into Adams. At 50
min. turn right on the blazed trail (the original road continues down to become Gould Rd. in Adams; see under alternate ways home). The shelter is on your right, almost
immediately. You are now on the Bellows Pipe Ski Trail, cut
by the CCCs in the 1930s, as you will recognize from the
series of steep sharp switchbacks. At 1:02 do not take the
unmarked trail straight ahead, which leads to the Thunderbolt. Instead, follow right, on a section that is a real workout
if you are on skis. As a matter of fact, it's a workout on foot.

The trees are becoming lower and more scraggly on the
steep eastern face — more beech and birch, somewhat
stunted. After 5 switchbacks and testing ascents, you come
out at 1:17 on the white-blazed AT, heading S. to the summit. Trees are often ice-covered on this stretch in the winter;
if you catch them when the sun hits, the effect is of walking
through a lighted chandelier. If a breeze is blowing, the
branches clink together like cut glass, as well. Within a minute the AT joins the Thunderbolt Trail for the final assault.
If you plan to descend this way, be sure to turn around at
this point to check the lay of the land, which can be con-

fusing on the way back. As the Indians said, "every trail is two trails, one going and one coming." Soon a blue blazed trail heads right, crossing nearby Notch Rd. to Robinson's Point. You continue on the steep Thunderbolt to cross Summit Rd. (1:26). The ski shelter the CCC built at the head of the Thunderbolt is right. You skirt the parking lot and arrive at the memorial tower at 1:30.

Remember, if you decide to return by this route, that you start on the AT N., by the parking lot. The AT S. takes off by the TV tower only part-way around the compass. But the Bellows Pipe Ski Trail is too steep to be a pleasant descent, so choose a different way home. In the winter, ski down Notch Rd. to your car. Leave on Summit Rd. and turn right at the first intersection. You don't want to walk down a road with traffic in the summer, however, so you need to arrange a 2-car hike, with someone meeting you at the summit or at the base of another one of the trails described here. Cheshire Harbor, Hopper, and Roaring Brook are good trails down as well as up. A long alternative would be to make a loop by descending the Thunderbolt, again very steep, or the Gould Trail (a snowmobile trail across private property) to West Rd. to Notch Rd. in Adams (different than the 2 other Notch roads you've been on), which soon degenerates to a 4-wheel vehicle road and meets Reservoir Rd. at Notch Reservoir. That would add 16 mi. to your trip, for a total of 20. in effect, you would make a loop around Ragged; a shorter version would leave out the summit by following straight to Gould Rd. at the Notch.

THE HOPPER TRAIL

8 miles (3.5 hours)

Road approaches

Beginning at Field Park in Williamstown, follow Rte. 2 E. to Water St., which becomes Green River Rd. (.5 mi.). Turn right. Hopper Rd. turns left at Mt. Hope Park (2.5 mi.). Follow Hopper Rd. along the brook, past Bresset Rd., until it swings left (straight ahead is Potter Rd.) beyond some open fields. It turns to gravel, ending at a gate between barn and farmhouse (2.75 mi.). Park in the designated area.

Camping

As well as Bascom Lodge at the summit, on this route you hike through Sperry Rd. Campground, with 34 tent and 5 group sites, including 2 three-sided shelters. No showers, no flush toilets, no hookups. The state collects a small fee in season for overnight parking, picnicking, or camping. The Deer Hill shelter, reconstructed by an Eagle Scout and his father, is within .5 mi. of the campground. Please note that the Hopper itself is classified as a low impact area: No fires, camping, or vehicles permitted, except for tent camping at the Haley field, at the beginning of the Money Brook Trail. The Sperry Rd. Campground is also convenient for the Stony Ledge and Roaring Brook Trails.

THE HOPPER TRAIL

This is the classic Greylock hike, from 1,096 ft. to the summit, 3,492 ft., on a historic trail, through the deeply eroded "grain hopper" that marks the western side of the Greylock massif. Hopper Rd. didn't originally end at the gate; instead, it passed between the stone walls you walk between and then forded Money Brook, continuing up the far side into the inner Hopper. The route you are following was originally laid out by Almond Harrison, who pioneered a farm at the campground site about 1800. President Edward Dorr Griffin dismissed his Williams College students from class on a May day in 1830 to improve this road and extend it to the summit, where they built the first tower. At the time, the summit was tree-covered, so the tower was the only alternative to shinnying up the stunted fir trees for a view. Later the CCC built its camp where Harrison's farm had been; still later the state developed its campgrounds in the same spot, as the spruces grew into the once-open fields.

Be sure to close the gate at the trailhead. No dogs allowed. Stroll down the road between the hayfields, on which cows were recently pastured. Leave the old road, which continues as Money Brook Trail, at the sign (8 min.) for Hopper Trail, bearing right following the blue blazes to the edge of the upper field. There the trail plunges into the woods. At 13 min. you pass through a stile. For the next quarter mi. or so the trail has been carefully engineered to make it as dry as possible.

This steady, no nonsense rise, cut into the sidehill, was the first leg of the Berkshires-to-the-Cape Bridle Trail, which wandered across the Commonwealth in the later 19th century. The large birch trees seem to have reached the ends of their lives, as beech and maple crowd them out. At 34 min., the Money Brook cut-off drops into the valley. You can probably hear the song of Money Brook, floating from the floor. Just shy of an hour you reach Sperry Rd. and the campground. Turn left and, in 2 min., left again, across from the contact station, as the Hopper Trail, still blazed blue, leaves the road.

This climb (from here on identical to that described in the Stony Ledge hike) is fairly steep and worn, along the upper reach of Roaring Brook. You pass a lovely brook the CCCs developed as a water source when they had their camp at Sperry Rd. Turn left on the Deer Hill Trail, which was once a carriage road (1:15). This is relatively level and stone-covered, as erosion has removed the thin soil. Where the Overlook Trail exits (1:27), your trail turns steeper. Large trees are less frequent at the higher elevation, giving way to more shrubbery. Nick a corner of Rockwell Rd., at a spring, but stick to the woods, which soon turn to spruce. You emerge on the road again, but duck in across from a sign indicating the Cheshire Harbor and Appalachian trails. From here to the summit, follow the white blazes. You cross swampy areas on foot bridges. At 1:35 you pass the pond, no longer used, dug to serve as a water supply for Bascom Lodge. Follow the AT across the road intersection a min. later. Study these road crossings so that you will know what to do on the return trip.

Climb steeply, through fir and spruce, crossing the old water line, for 8 min. until you reach the broadcast tower and 2 more min. to the Memorial Tower (1:46).

For the return, the broadcast tower is the landmark for the proper direction to depart the summit on the AT. At 10 min. you cross the intersection, still on the AT, even though the "Adams" sign may momentarily confuse you. You pass the pond. Six more min. take you to the next road crossing where, instead of following the AT, you turn right, down the road and back into the woods at the "Hopper" sign. Continue on the Deer Hill Trail until the Hopper Trail exits, right, at a brook (35 min.). After you turn right on Sperry Rd., look for the Hopper Trail angling off to the right. The return trip takes 1:30, for a total travel time of 3:17.

You needn't return the way you came, of course. The most obvious circuit — up the Hopper trail and down Money Brook — is lengthy if you include the summit: 11 mi., via the AT over Mt. Williams to Tall Spruces. After you cross Notch Rd., take a left towards the shelter on the Money Brook Trail. You can save more than a mi. by cutting off the AT prior to Mt. Williams and hiking down the road .5 mi. to the cutoff for the Money Brook Trail. Shorter still would be to omit the summit of Greylock — all right to do after you've hit the summit a few times. Take the Hopper Trail to the Overlook Trail. Follow the Overlook

Trail until it meets Notch Rd. Take Notch Rd. 100 yds. N. to the cutoff to the AT on top of the ridge, and continue as described above. This route runs about 8 mi. A more attractive, although steep, shorter (6.5 mi.) hike links Money Brook and Prospect Trails.

STONY LEDGE AND ROARING BROOK TRAILS

9.0 miles (3.75 hours)

Road approaches

Beginning at Field Park in Williamstown, drive S. on Rte. 7, 5.5 mi. to Roaring Brook Rd., left just before the Massachusetts Department of Public Works garage; alternately, coming from the S., after entering Williamstown, turn right immediately beyond the garage. Drive 1 mi. up the gravel road until you see the sign indicating the private Mt. Greylock Ski Club. Use the parking area large enough for 3 or 4 cars just downstream from the sign; in the unlikely event that area is filled, you will have pull over nearer Rte. 7.

Camping

See description under Hopper Trail.

STONY LEDGE TRAIL

You can call this loop Stony Ledge for the first eminence, with its spectacular view of the Hopper, but you actually hike on several other trails: Hopper, Appalachian, and Roaring Brook, for instance. You rise from a deep valley, through the plateau that hosts a campground, to the summit, and back down through a hemlock forest. Both ascent and descent have steep sections. This hike is the most logical one if your goal is to sit on the edge of the abyss at Stony Ledge.

The trailhead is streamside, across from the ski club sign. You begin on a well-established old woods road, blazed blue for the most part although some of previous white blazes persist. In 3 min. you ford Roaring Brook just as wagons and horses did years ago. You climb, passing a trail that rises into the fields, left. After 10 min. you drop down to the brook again and cross it on a log bridge. The old trail, exiting right, rises to the ski club. At 13 min. you cross a plank bridge. Just beyond, bear left on Stony Ledge rather than straight on Roaring Brook, on which you will return.

The sign indicates the wide, grassy trail to be an "intermediate ski trail," which refers to downhill skiing. Nordic skiing here is "advanced." Although you can see how the CCCs laid it out wide enough to enable some maneuvering, it hasn't been maintained for skiing.

Soon the trail picks up an old road, which it follows most of the rest of the way. From time to time you will see the telltale charcoal bits indicating charcoal burning sites. The product was used to smelt iron ore until the late 19th century when the Bessemer process came in. At 30 min. the trail begins to bear left and climb sharply, which it continues to do, with a branch of Roaring Brook left, to the ridge you soon will see to the right.

You arrive at Sperry Rd. at 53 min. Walk straight ahead to the gravel turn around. Sit and absorb the summit and ridge across the chasm. The morning is not as good a time as evening because of shadows, but on the wall opposite you can see dark stands of red spruce, some nearly 200 years old, probably the oldest stands in the Commonwealth. You can also see March Cataract, to the southeast. It won't be prominent when late summer reduces the water flow, however.

Walk down the road about a mi., between azaleas and berry bushes into the camping area. You can easily see why Sperry Rd. is regarded as the best laid out campground around. Autos stay by the road; campers walk in 50 or 75 ft. to the sites, which are separated from one another for privacy. At 1:10 the Hopper Trail enters the road from the left. You see the Roaring Brook Trail entrance, right. At 1:13 the Hopper Trail exits, with you, to the left, across from the contact station.

Climb fairly steeply on a well-worn path, still blazed blue, which joins Deer Hill Trail (actually a carriage road), on which you turn left at 1:25. The path is relatively level until the Overlook Trail exits, left (1:37). You are surrounded by the big leaves of the hobble bush, known as the woodsman's toilet paper. You come out on a corner of Rockwell Rd. but stay to the woods, which soon turn to spruce. You emerge on the road, ducking back into the woods across from the sign indicating the Cheshire Harbor Trail and the AT. You cross bridges over swamp. At 1:45 you pass the pond the CCC dug, no longer used. Follow the AT across the road intersection a min. later. Study the layout of these road crossings for the way back.

Eight min. later you climb steeply to the broadcast tower and 2 min. later (1:56), the War Memorial Tower. Cross to the E. side, drop over the edge a bit, and look down on the cleared fields and ponds of Greylock Glen. Look close, don't they?

The broadcast tower is your landmark for the proper direction to depart the summit on the AT. At 10 min. you cross the intersection, on the AT, even though the "Adams" sign may momentarily confuse you. You pass the pond. At 10:16, the next road crossing, instead of following the AT, bear right. Turn off the Deer Hill Trail, right, at 35 min., following the brook, more or less, to the campground.

In 42 min. from the summit (2:38), turn right on Sperry Rd. and shortly left, where the sign says "Roaring Brook Trail," blazed blue (occasionally white), across a bridge, and right along the brook. The Circular Trail leaves left in 5 min., but you cross the bridge; just beyond the bridge the Deer Hill Trail leaves left. Stay with Roaring Brook. You pass through hobble bush, black raspberries, beech, and maple. You descend steadily through hemlock, aware of a brook on each side. The descent becomes steep.

Gradually the two brook branches come closer, as you descend, until you must cross the smaller (3:16). You are at the junction with Stony Ledge Trail. After crossing the bridge and attaining some height, look down into the scenic, rocky gorge, where you can see the remains of a mill run. Farther downstream, in the day lilies, is the cellar hole for the mill. At 1:35 from the summit or 3:31 round trip you will be back at your starting point.

Skiers should do the loop by climbing Roaring Brook to Sperry Rd. and returning via Stony Ledge. Hikers go the opposite direction purely for the aesthetic satisfaction of coming out at the end of the climb on Stony Ledge. They might prefer the 3-mi. shorter version, however, omitting the summit. In season, the hike could be spiced up with a visit to March Cataract or Deer Hill falls. You can link all other Greylock trails to these 2, for 2-car variations on this hike.

ADAMS: MT. GREYLOCK

ADAMS: MT. GREYLOCK

WILLIAMSTOWN

Soldiers at Fort Massachusetts, once located where the Price Chopper supermarket now resides on Rte. 2 in No. Adams, built the first homes in the township west of the fort and held their first Proprietors' Meeting there in 1753. Then a flare-up of the French and Indian War drove them out; of the original residents only Benjamin Simonds returned, with a wife, after having been in prison in Quebec. Their daughter, Rachael, was the first child of European stock born in the area. Simonds' River Bend Tavern still stands, run now as a bed and breakfast, on Simonds' Rd. (Rte. 7 north of town).

Still an active farming town, Williamstown is more famous for the college that has grown up with it. Ephraim Williams Jr. was a commander at the fort; on his way to battle at Lake George in 1755, he rewrote his will to establish a secondary school for the children of his command. Town and school were named for his generosity. The trustees converted his school into Williams College, which opened in 1793.

The college has attracted to the community the Clark Art Institute, with its ravishing collections of French Impressionists and 19th-century American artists and sculptors, and the Williamstown Theatre Festival, busy all summer with myriad main stage and experimental productions, readings and cabarets. Both have been singled out by tough critics as the best of their kinds in the United States.

So, should the weather turn sour, despair not. The Clark (open daily except Monday) provides an eyeful that can last all day. Other undercover destinations: the Williams College Museum of Art, the Hopkins Forest Farm Museum, the Chapin Rare Books Library, and the planetarium show at the Old Hopkins Observatory (reservations required). As well as shopping on Spring and Water streets, visitors may take tours of the Williams College campus, which originate at the admissions office, Main St.

WALK

STONE HILL

1.5 miles (1 hour)

For Williamstown's favorite walk, drive S. on South St., beginning at Field Park, across from the Williams Inn. At a half mi., turn right into the Clark Art Institute. Drive under the bridge and turn left for the far side of the parking lot, behind the main building.

This leisurely stroll will take you from the Clark parking lot, 750-ft. in elevation, on a meandering path through old-growth, northern hardwood forest, to a stone seat at 1,000-ft.; then down through open fields, with a striking view of downtown Williamstown and the surrounding hills, and back to the parking lot.

To find the trailhead, look for 2 small gravestones that mark the eternal resting place of dogs that belonged to a previous owner of the property, Dr. Vanderpool Adriance. Sterling and Francine Clark purchased his land and built the white marble building for their art collection. It was opened to the public in 1955. The darker building to the right was built as an addition to the institute in 1973. The trail and footbridge were built in 1985 to help celebrate the Clark Institute's 30th anniversary. The orange-flagged trail passes through a variety of birch, beech, and maple stands, as well as some hemlock and pine, so that the stroller can compare and enjoy, working gradually uphill.

At about 15 min., note a signed trail that turns right to the open fields you will pass through later. You continue straight to the remains of the colonial Stone Hill Rd., which preceded Rte. 7 as the main north-south route in the county. The road has been improved as access to the town's water tank, buried under a field. Follow up the hill to the stone seat erected as a memorial to George Moritz Wahl, a professor of German at Williams College who was incorrectly suspected by some of being a German spy during World War I. He was accustomed to climbing to this spot in the evening to watch the sunset — in those days the fields were open. This monument was the town's apology and tribute.

This is the far point of the hike, but you might like to continue S. on the old road, to see how the hill got its name. If you look through the trees to your left, you will see the schist outcroppings. After returning, walk through the gate across from the seat, carefully closing it behind you because cows may be pasturing in the fields. (Cows are curious enough to look you over but are harmless.) Head down, following the open land as it swings right. Although the trail remains clear, it passes through a short stretch of forest, emerging at the head of a long, sloping field. Set your sights to the right of a clump of trees on the ridge ahead, dipping down and then rising to a view that includes the Clark, Main St. and college, the Dome in southern Vermont, East Mtn. (encompassing Pine Cobble and Eph's Lookout), the Hoosac Valley heading into No. Adams, the Hoosac Range beyond the city, and the Grey-lock Range. The ridge is the ideal picnic site on this trip. You can keep the view in sight as you wander down the field, looking for the stone gateposts at the lower left corner.

Follow across the next field, heading down the hill to the wooden gate. Note: you are now part of the view for museum-goers. Perhaps you are being compared to the pastoral subject of an old master. Act accordingly. You are passing through what was called a "haha" in the 18th century. This device enclosed stock by a ditch with a fence at the bottom — invisible from the level of the manor house.

Picnic tables rest under the trees around the parking lot. In the summer months an outdoor cafe serves light lunches on a terrace off the end of the newer building, if that fits your strolling plans. Longer walks are possible, although they cross private land not necessarily open to the public. The Taconic Golf Course, across South St., is open for cross-

WILLIAMSTOWN: STONE HILL

country skiing.

Many other strolls in town are yours for the walking. The description of the Triple-R Brooks Trail tells you how to get to a collection of them in Hopkins Forest. Walking guides to the town, available at the Williams Inn or at the Information Booth nearby, show numerous strolls that also reveal something of the history of Williamstown.

HIKES

BERLIN MOUNTAIN

5.25 miles (3 hours)

Road approaches

From Field Park at the Williams Inn in Williamstown, drive S. on Rtes. 7 and 2 for 2.5 mi. until they diverge. Follow Rte. 2 W. (right). A half mi. up the hill, turn left on Torrey Woods Rd. (a sign directs you towards the Carmelite Fathers). Follow straight at the bottom of the hill onto a gravel road, sometimes called Bee Hill and sometimes Berlin. From the point at which a closed road enters to the right, it is part of a 1799 post road between Boston and Albany. Bear left at the fork, passing a few houses to a small (3 car) parking area on the left. Blue trail blazes are visible heading into the woods 100 ft. nearer town.

Alternatively, you can continue .5 mi. to the old Williams College ski area and leave your car there. The route you will be taking comes out at the ski area.

No drinking water is available. Hemlock Brook is not as clean as it looks. At the junction of Rtes. 7 and 2, Margaret Lindley Park, a town-owned swimming area, provides a pond with water diverted from Hemlock Brook, changing rooms with plumbing, snack machines and lifeguards. The town charges a modest day-use fee for parking.

BERLIN MOUNTAIN

From the parking area to the summit is a demanding hike, ascending from 1,400 ft. (probably 100 ft. lower in the ravines), across 2 branches of Hemlock Brooks and directly up the side of the ridge to an altitude of 2,798 ft. in 2.5 mi. Members of the Williams Outing Club originally laid out the trail in 1933 — clearly they were a no-nonsense group. The remainder of your trip, down into the pass and down the post road, is fairly easy going. The reward is an unusual

360-degree view, in clear weather everything from Mt. Greylock to the Adirondacks. You see some land-use history, as well as sampling old-growth hemlock woods and hardwood forests of more recent vintage. Blueberrying is good here in July and August.

Wear layered clothing, because the wind on the summit is apt to be cool, particularly if you decide to take in the sunset. There are wet as well as steep spots in the hike, and brook crossings, so hiking boots work better than tennis shoes.

The wet spots begin as you follow easterly on an old woods road for 5 min. until turning right to cross the first branch of Hemlock Brook. Be particularly vigilant for the blue blazes at both brook crossings. Scramble up the far side, jogging right and left as the trail jumps from one logging road to another. This part, a 1980 re-routing to avoid private property, is a bit hard to follow, as it doesn't seem to be tending in any direction. Soon, however, you start up a steep logging road and turn left over the ridge and down to the outing club's former cabin site, at about half an hr. The only building remaining is the outhouse. Misuse of the old trail and cabin led the landowner to request the cabin be razed and the trail re-routed: the moral is obvious.

After a sharp right turn, the trail drops down to cross the second branch of Hemlock Brook. Scrambling up the other side you turn right on a broad woods road, following the brook W. Back on this older portion, the trail is easier to follow. Soon it leaves the road and begins a steep ascent up the side of the ridge, leveling out and joined by a day-glow orange blazed trail at about an hr. This trail rises from the Carmelite Fathers' property and accompanies the 1933 trail to the summit. Look back from time to time during the climb for views of Greylock.

At 1:25 a hemlock grove provides a lovely lookout at the Dome and East Mtn. with its Pine Cobble. Then the trail rises steeply once again until it joins the upper end of the college's downhill ski trail. Turn uphill (left) for the brief distance to the windswept summit (1:30), just over the

New York state line. The four concrete piers anchored a fire tower. Blueberries and raspberries surround you; this is an excellent picnic site. To the east the Greylock massif broods over Williamstown. The ski runs to the south are cut on the sides of Jiminy Peak. If the weather is clear enough, you may be able to pick out the Catskills to the southwest and the Adirondacks to the northwest. To the northeast rise the Green Mtns. of Vermont. You are standing in the township of Berlin in New York State, looking directly down into the valley of the Little Hoosic, which threads through Berlin and Petersburg, New York. If it is noon, you may hear one bark of the fire siren in Berlin.

The Taconic Crest Trail (TCT) goes off to the S. and N. It is marked by diamond-shaped metal blazes, painted white. You will hardly need them, however, as you follow N. the deeply rutted jeep trail, once the access road to the fire tower. (Detours around large puddles might be momentarily confusing; near Berlin Pass a different trail heads W.) After 20 min. you approach the pass. The former post road, a surfaced section you were driving on, rises from Berlin, to the west. You can see the TCT continuing up the slopes of the open ridge to Petersburg Mtn., straight ahead. To the east the badly eroded post road descends to the start of the hike. You may want to linger in this area to enjoy the view of Williamstown, to pick the blueberries that abound, or to picnic. The trail bikes and jeeps that come through the intersection can be annoying; however, the state of New York has acquired much of the land along the Taconic Crest in this area and may soon impose controls on off-road vehicles.

Turn right down the post road for a mi. You soon cross near the origin of one branch of Hemlock Brook, high in a mountain spring. Immediately to the right of the trail is a foundation for Alexander Walker's early-19th-century tollgate farmhouse. At about 15 min., look left to see the old stone marker at the state line, also left over from post road days. From the college ski area, it is .5 mi. down the road to where you began your hike, 3 hrs. of hiking altogether.

An alternative route, shorter but harder on the legs, would be to descend the ski run from the summit to the parking area. If 2 cars are available, you might consider leaving one at Petersburg Pass, on Rte. 2. The distance from Berlin Pass to Petersburg Pass, 1.5 mi., is the same as from Berlin Pass to the parking area. A less strenuous outing, although still a hike rather than a walk, would begin at the heights of Petersburg Pass, climb most of Petersburg Mtn. (Mt. Raimer), and end down at the college ski area.

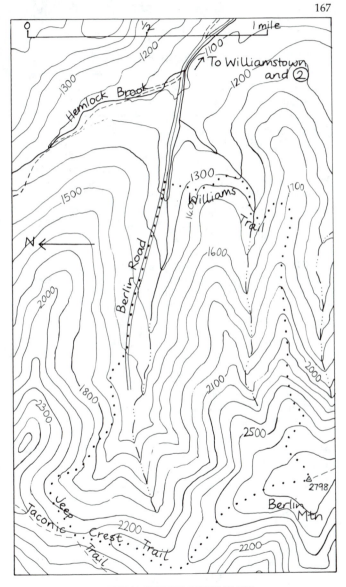

WILLIAMSTOWN: BERLIN MTN.

PINE COBBLE AND BROAD BROOK TRAILS

Williamstown and Pownal, Vermont, 10 miles (5 hours), plus 3 miles to complete the loop

Road approaches

From Field Park in Williamstown, drive N. on Rte. 7, over the Hoosic River at the bottom of the hill, and right at the first turn, N. Hoosac Rd. Follow that until Cole Ave. enters right. Park at a lot on the access road to the Williams College housing development. The hike starts on the private road with a Long Trail sign at the bottom. With the addition of 3 mi. to the total trip, you can make this hike a loop; otherwise, you will want to leave a second car at the Broad Brook trailhead. To get there: back-track on N. Hoosac until Bridges Rd. bears right. Follow that to White Oaks Rd. Turn right again. Follow White Oaks to the Vermont line, where the road surface becomes gravel. Park in the area just to your right over the line.

Camping

The Seth Warner shelter, a three-sided Adirondack-style lean-to, is your destination. The local chapter of the Green Mtn. Club keeps it well maintained, with firewood and a clean privy. A tent camping area is nearby. Broad Brook is presumed safe drinking water, as it serves the city of No. Adams. Sand Springs Pool (slightly farther W. on Bridges Rd. than White Oaks Rd.) is a private swimming spa open to the public for a fee.

PINE COBBLE AND BROAD BROOK TRAILS

Pine Cobble is one of the most popular climbs in Williamstown, but few hikers venture N. along the ridge to Eph's Lookout; little traffic, other than AT through-hikers, continues N. to Seth Warner. Although the lower end of Broad Brook Trail sees many hikers, the upper end is only slightly used, in part because it is tough going. This hike covers East Mtn., the hunk that, located mostly in Vermont together with the Dome, makes up the north skyline from Williamstown. The route contrasts hiking a highland plateau (1,880 to 2,000-ft. in elevation) with following the rocky, mountain stream as it knifes down 1,000 ft. Views out are excellent towards the beginning of the trip. Views in, later, include several glacial erratics, towering hemlock, and mossy brook chasms. From the Vermont line the AT and the Long Trail are one.

Go E. on North Hoosac Rd. to the east end of Pine Cobble Rd. Look for signs and blue blazes as you work your way around a Williams College housing development. As you climb moderately, you can look back to see the Hoosic River and the town. The trail shows some gravel and sand, evidence of the hill being shore to a glacial lake 10,000 years ago.

After 20 min. you should start climbing steeply for another 10 min. to the top of a plateau on scree (loose accumulation of stone). The second growth birch and oak, in poor soil conditions, are thin and small. At about 34 min., bear left where a former trail enters right. The trail gradually increases in angle until (44 min.) you pass a large boulder on the left. Then it climbs steeply to the ridge. Turn right and follow any one of the paths for 3 min. to the quartzite rock pile for which, together with the prevailing tree species, Pine Cobble was named (1,894 ft.).

You are looking at Mt. Williams reservoir and mountain — one of the Greylock peaks. You overlook Williamstown and, to the east, No. Adams, in the valley. The Hoosacs rise farther east and the Taconics to the west. You are standing on the southern extremity of the Green Mtns. Behind you, in that dark valley of Sherman Brook, rises the AT, which you will meet later on, unless you decide to descend as you came up, for a 3.2 mi. jaunt and view. The route from here on is both more remarkable and challenging than the standard day hike.

Backtrack to the trail junction. If you decide to continue, instead of descending, follow the blue blazes N., winding through scrawny growth, past the anchors of an old tower (1:02). The vegetation opens up at a burn area, now covered with blueberries. Blazes are painted on stone; look for some cairns as well. The highest pile of loose stone (1:10) is Eph's Lookout (2,254 ft.), named for the college's benefactor, soldier of the king, Ephraim Williams, who probably never stood where you do. The Hoosac Valley links the communities of Williamstown and Pownal below you. The dwarfed pitch pine behind the rocks are at their northern extent. The AT enters right almost immediately, with several handsome signs: Williamstown 2.1 mi.; Rte. 2, 2.7 mi. S.; Vt. line, 1.3 mi. N. Follow the white blazes N., into the woods.

The vegetation is beginning to pick up an evergreen flavor: some spruce and white pine. Ignore the private trail that enters left (1:29). Occasional lumbering roads cross from now on. At 1:45 you hit the Vermont border and the beginning of the Long Trail, duly signed. Only 263 miles to Canada! Add your name to the register. You may want to sign with your trail name, as AT through-hikers do.

Although you are on a plateau, it is cut by ravines and sprinkled with boulders (erratics) left by the glaciers. One is nearly a balancing rock. You venture in Green Mtn. National Forest, yet much of the land you are passing through belongs to the city of No. Adams as watershed. Parallel logs form the pathway through bogs. At 2:29 a woods road crosses. Scrambling up the far, steep side, you arrive on a ledge with a deep ravine right. After another section that may remind you of spruce bogs much farther north, you arrive at the gravel West Rd. from Clarksburg (2:49). Ignore, temporarily, blue blazes heading N. along the road.

Instead, follow straight on the AT/Long Trail for .2 mi. until another blue-blazed side trail heads left to the Seth Warner Shelter (3.0), elevation 2,000 ft. Warner was a patriot and Green Mountain Boy in the American Revolution. This form of immortality is perpetuated by those folks, GMC members and hikers, who take good care of the shelter. A good spot for a picnic or the night.

Backtrack to West Rd. and follow the blue blazes. The

blue-blazed Broad Brook Trail departs the road just before the culvert through which the brook passes (3:14) and follows the brook, losing elevation at a steady rate. At 3:22 you arrive at the first of numerous brook crossings, followed by a very steep ascent on the far side, into a hemlock forest. Just as rapidly you drop down over a promontory between 2 brook branches (3:31), making your second and third brook crossings. Follow the side for a ways, leaving the stream on your left before yet another steep ascent. If your legs are logy from the exertion so far, you may begrudge these ascents; but there just isn't room for the trail by the brook.

You are starting to find the innumerable logging roads in this area, but follow the blazes over the fourth branch brook crossing (3:50) and then up! again. In 5 min. you come out on what was clearly once a road and soon, as further evidence of the lumbering activity, the stone remains of a mill and tail race, the route made for the water to flow from the wheel back to the brook (4:02). You cross that waterway for the fifth crossing. You see the remains of an old wagon, said to have served the lumbermen as a chuckwagon. Directly across the brook is the end of Henderson Rd. (here just a woods road). You make your sixth stream crossing but instead of taking the road, continue downstream, south side, and up the steep sidehill. At 4:13, make your seventh crossing, followed in 10 min. by the eighth and last. The Agawon Trail leaves from the far side to rise to the Dome Trail.

At 4:50 you cross on a bridge over the public water supply through the fence kindly left open for hikers by the city of No. Adams and in 4 min. you arrive at the parking area where, if you didn't leave a vehicle, you probably wish you had. After all, you just completed nearly 5 hrs. of hiking, with a great deal of up and down.

If you are afoot, turn left on White Oaks Rd., follow down to the intersection with Bridges Rd., turn left, following Bridges — which becomes N. Hoosac — back to your point of departure.

As well as choosing to return back down Pine Cobble,

you could have made a loop with the AT, ending up on Rte. 2 in Blackinton, a village in the city of No. Adams. Or you could have continued past the Seth Warner cutoff, ending up .5 mi. later on County Rd., (barely) drivable in the summer and a place to leave a car if you wished to do half the trip only. To get to County Rd., take Rte. 7 N. in Pownal to Barber's Pond Rd. Follow right, past the pond. The road turns sharp right and then sharp left. Turn right immediately on a gravel road. Bear left at the fork.

If you left your car at the base of Pine Cobble and are walking the complete route, taking Henderson Rd. from the chuckwagon would save you a mi. of road hiking.

WILLIAMSTOWN: PINE COBBLE/BROAD BROOK/THE DOME

RRR BROOKS TRAIL

7.75 miles (3 hours), plus 2 miles to complete loop

Road approaches

From Field Park in Williamstown drive S. on Rtes. 2 and 7, going .25 mi. to Bee Hill Rd., bearing right. Drive this gravel road up and then down, across a bridge, where there is parking on the shoulder for one or two cars. This is the end of your hike. If you have 2 cars, drive 1 or hike 2 mi.: back to Rtes. 2 and 7, N. 100 yds., left on Thornliebank Dr., left on W. Main, right on Northwest Hill Rd. past the end of Bulkley St.; left into a parking lot on the Hopkins Forest drive. Since parking is tight on Bee Hill, you may prefer to leave your car along Thornliebank or W. Main or Hopkins Forest.

Camping

The Williams Outing Club cabin in Hopkins Forest is available through the club to people associated with Williams College. It has a wood stove, running water, and a sleeping loft. No other shelters or camping are available on this route. Buxton Gardens, the re-creation of a 19th-century flower garden; the Barn Museum of farming; and the exhibits in the Rosenburg Center, all at the beginning of this hike, are worth a visit. Hopkins Forest, a 2,500-acre tract bordering New York and Vermont, is an ecology laboratory for Williams College. Please do not wander off the trails because you might inadvertently disturb experiments. Signs explain some of the work in progress, much of which currently has to do with monitoring the effects of acid rain on trees. As alternatives to this route, many strolls, other hikes, and ski tours beckon in Hopkins Forest. Pocket maps are available at the large map near the barn.

RRR BROOKS TRAIL

Although this hike is called the Triple-R Brooks Trail, actually it travels 5 trails. A vigorous outing, you climb from 800 ft. to 2,200 ft. As well as evidence of past land use, you view two spectacular brook valleys and, standing 300 ft. above the highway, an eagle's eye look at the old Petersburg Pass ski area, Berlin Mtn., the Hopper on Greylock, and the Williamstown valley. Remember that cold comes with altitude and that the Taconic Ridge can be extremely windy. On the other hand, standing on the top of this piece of the world in snow and ice crystals is unforgettable. Azaleas and blueberries are found here in season. Equally exciting, the three states, Williams College, and Williamstown are cooperating to create a public recreation area for 3,500 acres in this area.

Beginning at the Hopkins Forest lot, walk up the private drive to the barn. Turn right, past the WOC cabin and the maple sugar house. Continue on this woods road, well made by the CCC when the U.S. Forestry Service ran an experimental forest here. Pass without entering a weather station (4 min.) that gathers important information for experiments in the forest. Looking down to your right, you will soon see Ford Glen, in the chasm it has cut for itself.

You are on what is known as the Loop Trail. Bear right at the first intersection (18 min.) and straight at the second (23 min.). You gradually gain elevation through second-growth birch and maple — all this land was open fields two generations ago. Bear left where a private trail enters right (33 min.). Just before the brook crossing, turn right on the Birch Brook Trail (36 min.).

After the broad and carefully constructed Loop Trail, Birch Brook Trail appears indistinguishable in places from a stream bed; nevertheless, follow at a moderate rise for 4 min. Then turn right, up the side of a shoulder. This trail soon follows the remains of a stone wall, swings left on top of the rise, and soon another wall and forest boundary appear right. The large maples here were never cut because they were (and are) line trees, marking a property boundary.

At 50 min. the trail crosses a spring, beginning a steep, steady ascent to the ridge on the left. The forest is older, although the birches and maples are not healthy. You think you've been climbing pretty hard, yet if you look sharp, on your left, you see a cellar hole within spitting distance of the trail. It wasn't just that people farmed these ridges, they lived on them. If you lived up here, you'd think twice about going back to town because you forgot to pick up a spool of thread at the store.

Climbing over phyllite outcrops, after watching your elevation approach the ridge's for some time, at last (1:18) you attain the Taconic Crest Trail (TCT), blazed white. Make a hard left at the yellow sign. Motorized vehicles are not allowed, although you see the evidence of how they have sliced up the trail. You are in New York, .5 mi. south of the Vermont border, which juts .5 mi. west of Massachusetts. A *New Yorker* cartoon (1989) showed a real estate broker greeting hikers here.

Although the vegetation along the crest is thin, due to wind and soil conditions, there are no views from this section of trail. To remedy the situation, climb to the open expanse of Smith Hill, spotted with quartz outcrops, by taking a largely unmarked trail (1:26) off to the left. With a little luck you'll be able to follow the route in a loop back to the TCT. (Side trip not included in elapsed time.)

Continue S. on the TCT. Yellow signs and blue blazes warn of the Shepherd's Well Trail, left at 1:41. Take it. Farmer Shepherd dug a well, still extant, nearby — another sign of high altitude farming. You will soon confirm you're on the trail by seeing Hopkins Forest postings to your left. Work up the sidehill. Where the trail may appear to go straight through a clearing (1:46), it actually angles left along a ridge. Soon (1:53), you break out into steep-sloping blueberry bushes, high over the highway (Rte. 2), facing the old Petersburg Pass ski area now owned by the New York State Department of Environmental Conservation. As you work your way around a shoulder, you see Berlin Mtn., with the telltale streak of the old Williams College ski trail, and the fields rising to the Hopper on Mt. Greylock. Winter wind and ice can be a problem here, obscuring the trail, which soon returns into the woods.

You work down at first gradually and then steeply, coming out on an old cut, where trees have been removed to let telephone wires through (2:01). The wires are gone, now. Turn left, down hill, with views of the Congregational church spire and college chapel tower lined up. Turn right (2:06) on a wide and grassy logging road, which soon (2:08) joins the Triple-R Trail. Dean of the college, RRR Brooks, built a log home you will see across the pond at the foot of this trail and laid out the trail, largely on existing old roads. For example, the trail here appears to have been on Petersburg Rd. before the lower Taconic Trail State Highway was built in the 1930s. Brooks dug the lowest part of the trail out of the sidehill, by hand.

For a way you follow a wall, left. There are azaleas along this stretch. At 2:23 jog left, swing right, and cross old Petersburg Rd. (gravel) to come out on an old farm field the state mows occasionally, part of Taconic Trail State Forest. The run across this field on skis can be exciting; at other times of the year follow the beaten path through the brush for the corner farthest down. The clump of trees to the left marks a cellar hole.

Back in the woods (2:32), follow a shoulder between two rivulets, across a bridge at a boggy area (2:36). Flora Glen, which you keep on the left for the rest of this hike, is named not for a person but for plants. Dropping moderately, in 10 min. you cross a second bridge, soon entering a lovely hemlock forest. The trees find it difficult to cling to the steep valley walls, as storms hurl them, roots and all, into the valley. Western Massachusetts' foremost early poet, William Cullen Bryant, was inspired by the wild romanticism of Flora Glen. Eventually the trail drops right into the streambed (2:50), where the going can be wet and difficult. Then it climbs somewhat up the valley walls, on a narrow ledge. In 12 more min. you arrive at a dam, beside Bee Hill Rd.: the end, unless you must continue walking to your car.

It is possible to ski this route on cross-country skis, in the same direction. It can be tough climbing Birch Brook, and the Flora Glen section requires good control. A pleasant stroll would take you on the Loop Trail in Hopkins Forest to the second intersection. Turn right to return by Northwest Hill Rd. Completing the Loop Trail is more of a hike. It is possible to park your car at Petersburg Pass to hike either the TCT or RRR Brooks, allowing the automobile to gain most of the altitude for you.

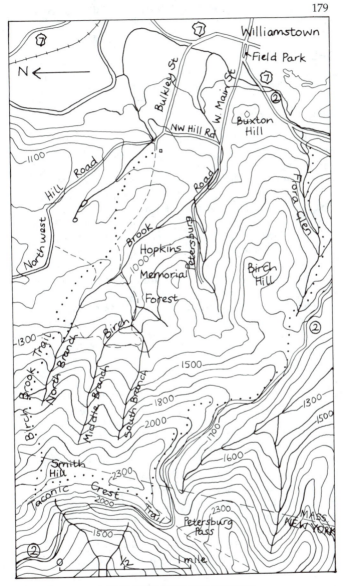

WILLIAMSTOWN: RRR BROOKS

THE DOME

Pownal, Vermont, 6.4 miles (3 hours)

Road approaches

Although located in Vermont, the Dome is accessible by road only from Williamstown. See map for Pine Cobble and Broad Brook Trails. From Field Park, drive N. on Rte. 7 across the Hoosic River. Take the first right onto N. Hoosac Rd. and the second left onto White Oaks Rd. Follow White Oaks until you have gone about 4 mi. from Field Park. At the Vermont line the road turns to gravel; immediately on your right is a parking lot that also serves the Broad Brook Trail. You can park here or drive another quarter mi. to the trailhead, on the right.

Sand Springs Pool (left at the junction of Sands Springs and White Oaks roads) is a private spa open to the public for a fee. No shelters on this trail. The trail is unusual in that water is available almost the entire route. Since it is the protected water supply for No. Adams, it should be safe to drink.

THE DOME

The Dome, at 2,748 ft., is a favorite hike of the few who know it, especially in cool weather when its rocky crest reflects the sun and in the winter when its highest vegetation is spectacularly snow- or ice-covered. Although the mountain lies in Vermont, it is distinctly a part of the northern Berkshire skyline, like the East Mtn. that borders the north of Williamstown. As the trail dead ends, you must come back down the way you went up. From the parking lot at about 1,000 ft., it is a steady climb; nowhere overwhelming but demanding. The bald stone summit is unusual, although the view is gradually being obscured by the spruce fringe growing up around it. But the Dome joins only Greylock in this collection of hikes in that you climb out of a second-growth, mixed hardwood forest into a distinctly different environment: a Laurentian plateau of spruce and fir bogs of the kind found in northern Canada.

The times in this description assume that you leave your car at the Broad Brook trailhead. Continue up White Oaks Rd., gravel now. Pass the small reservoir; the woods road up the Dome leaves to the right after 5 min., beside a branch of Broad Brook — an excellent source for a drink. If you miss the trailhead you will soon come to a division of White Oaks Rd.: a woods road continuing straight, eventually meeting the County Rd. that crosses southern Vermont. This very old road passes through wild country; the traveled branch swings westerly to serve a few homes.

Back on the trail — vehicles drive into former fields, growing over, that have served as a logging yard and more recently as a party site. Perhaps when you visit, the area will not be as trashed as it has been. The Williams Outing Club once blazed the trail white; more recently, orange. The trail is broad and blazes clear. One stone of a small family cemetery stands on a knoll to the right: "Polly 1830," it reads. Continue on the old lumber road, bearing right, out of the second field into the woods, at 8 min.

The road begins a moderate climb along the shoulder of the Broad Brook valley, passing through a gap in a stone wall at 13 min. and continuing up at a steady rate until the first terrace, about 5 min. later. The lumber road goes straight but you should follow the trail left for 15 min. of strenuous hiking, with occasional detours around the most seriously eroded sections. Erosion, particularly from motorized vehicles, is severe in this section.

The Agawon Trail drops off to the right, down to join the Broad Brook Trail. Just beyond is Meeting House Rock, a large boulder halfway to the summit. And just beyond that, the trail emerges on the second terrace, an open area where azaleas bloom with their haunting fragrance in late spring. The trail rises more gently, swinging westerly. The quartzite ledges are covered in some places with gravel and even white sand, left over from the time when the sides of the Dome, like all northern Berkshire ridges were shore to a glacial lake that covered the valley to a depth 1,300 ft. or more. The deposits left by the glaciers formed the shoulders and plateaus so evident on the Dome, creating a situation typical of Berkshire climbs: the steepest part is at the beginning (you've done it), followed by a leveling or series of plateaus, and ending with a steep but short scramble to the summit.

Surprise: at about an hr., an old Chevy truck stares balefully at you. Presumably someone drove it up the logging road that enters from the left, where it died. Turn right on this road, past intimidating signs that aim to control hunting, not hiking on the trail. Bear left where the logging road continues straight, up a short steep section to the third terrace. Few motorized vehicles get beyond this point.

Now begins a pattern of emerging on successively wetter terraces and bearing right up the slope after attaining each one. Short ascent to fourth terrace. Angle right; short ascent to fifth terrace. The trail begins to follow a brook. Turn right for ascent to sixth terrace. Right again to seventh. Cross the brook where usually there's sufficient depth to drink. Then back across it, right, to the eighth and last terrace. Have you kept count? Turn right through spruce and fir forest to the rocky ridge.

Follow the ridge to the false summit (1:15): no view because of vegetation. Still following the blazes, push through the evergreen down into a bog, similar in ecology to what you might find hundreds of miles north. Scramble up the quartzite outcroppings to the ridge that leads to the real summit. The blazes are now painted on the rocks, augmented by a few cairns. You will know the summit because there isn't any more *up* (1:30). Furthermore, you get the first real views: west to the Taconics and southeast to the Hairpin Turn and the Hoosacs. The view of Greylock is pretty well obscured by spruce now, although an ice storm may improve visibility one of these winters.

When descending, while still on the summit ridge, note the blazes and bear left where it appears the trail continues straight. As well, on the way down remember to turn left at the Chevy. The trip back to the parking lot will take about 1:20 for a 3-hr. round trip.

An alternative route would be, either going or coming, to use the Agawon Trail between the Dome and Broad Brook trails. It is steep and requires a stream crossing troublesome at high water. Pretty near the entire trail is skiable, except for the two summits.

NORTH ADAMS

North Adams was formed from Adams' rib in 1878, as an immediate result of the railroad coming through the Hoosac Tunnel into the north part of town — which then outstripped the south part. The incision was already there, though, created by a military line for recruiting soldiers for the Revolutionary War, and based on topography. The Hoosic River floodplains of the southern part lent themselves more to agriculture; the swift falling streams of the north part more to industry.

The slack in employment when the textile mills moved to the southern United States was taken up by the electronics industry, especially during World War II. But after the war, electronics, too, gradually faded. More recently, in the 1980s, the state has tried to help. It created Western Gateway Heritage State Park, an effort to revitalize the downtown by building a memorial to the railroad past and a home for shops and restaurants. The state purchased Natural Bridge, a marble span carved by a stream, from private interests. And the state is working with Williams College and other private groups to develop the largest museum of contemporary art in the world, Massachusetts MOCA, in the former textile/Sprague Electric Co. mills.

Turn S. off Main St. on the Curran Highway for the Heritage State Park, which features various interactive displays about tunnel building and railroading. North off Main St. on Marshall St. leads to the site of the proposed MOCA. No. Adams' Windsor Lake, on the east side of town beyond No. Adams State College, is available for public swimming at a nominal fee, as is the pond at Clarksburg State Park, north of the city, beyond Natural Bridge, on Rte. 8.

WALK

THE CASCADES

1 mile (30 min.)

No. Adams' slightly known treasure is the Cascades. Drive W. of town on Rte. 2; turn left on Marion Ave., a residential street. If you miss it, turn up Notch Rd. and take either the first or second left and then right on Marion. Park where the road ends (there's not much room). The trail follows along Notch Brook, switching from side to side, for .5 mi. Major blow-downs have not been cleaned out as this is written, making the going slow, but at least they keep out the dirt bikes.

The water tumbles down about 50 ft. with a satisfying roar, although the amount of water varies, generally it is a heavy flow. The folds in the rock that create the falls are worth seeing in themselves. The large hemlocks in the overstory keep the temperature down; the area, virtually in the middle of town, is surprisingly wild and undeveloped. The trail continues on the west side of the brook above the Cascades, really an old woods road, eventually coming out on Reservoir Rd. Parts are grown over, however. The Cascades present a fine picnic and cooling off spot.

NORTH ADAMS: THE CASCADES

FLORIDA AND SAVOY

In 1753 Capt. Elisha Hawley, commander at Fort Massachusetts, then the westernmost wilderness outpost of the Bay Colony and now No. Adams, began to build the first road east over the mountains to Charlemont to provision his fort, largely following an Indian route. It climbed to the Western Summit (as it's called now) about as does present Rte. 2 but then followed the line of what is now Central Shaft Rd. to the Cold River, west of the present highway. Samuel Rice, a few years later, built a route closer to the present one, up from Charlemont; for some reason he generally gets all the credit. But then, the Trail is in the Mahican Indian hunting grounds, yet the auto road is called the Mohawk Trail. The first Savoy settlers, in 1777, called the wet, rocky town, located at nearly 2,000 ft. in elevation, New Seconk, but at its incorporation it was named after the mountainous Savoy section of Europe. Florida was incorporated in 1805, at a time when the whole country was excited about a proposed land purchase from Spain. New State Rd., by the way, was not named for a construction project by the Commonwealth, but a religious community active in the area in the 19th century.

In those days Savoy and Florida were busy farming and manufacturing towns. You come across many cellar holes, mill sites, and cemeteries, as well as old roads, as you walk through them. The lack of good farm land and the appeal to go west, especially after the opening of the Erie Canal in 1825, drained this hilly land of its population. On February 9, 1875, the first three flatcar-loads of dignitaries passed beneath Florida, signaling the opening of the Hoosac Tunnel, then the longest in the world (4.75 mi.); more convenient than Hawley's provisioning route. The state purchased a few acres around Borden Mtn. in order to erect a fire tower there in 1917, adding 10,000 acres in 1920 to fill out Savoy Mtn. State Forest. Construction of the Mohawk Trail led the state to purchase 3,000 acres for the Mohawk Trail State Forest in 1921, the first state campgrounds. Over the years, the state has added more land in Florida and Savoy to its holdings, so that it now owns fully half of Savoy.

Several CCC units made camp in Savoy in the 1930s. They built many of the dams and the roads, together with stone culverts and bridges. They also planted vast areas of spruce in order to provide for a forestry industry. They built the cabins at South Pond and the picnic facilities at North Pond. Forest HQ is located in former CCC buildings. There was a camp at the parking lot at Burnett and New State roads. and one at Tannery Falls. The CCC "boys" must have cursed the blackflies in the summer and the snow, which accumulates deeper here than anywhere else in the county, in the winter. In fact, one vicious winter storm nearly flattened one of their bunkrooms.

Road approaches

From Dunkin' Donuts on Rte. 2 in No. Adams, follow E. on Rte. 2, up around the Hairpin Turn and farther up into Florida. After you pass the Wigwam Gift Shop, bear right at the second turning (5 mi.), where a chocolate and white sign directs you to Savoy Mtn. State Forest. Bear right at the next 2 intersections. Both are signed. On your left is the ventilation shaft, originally a construction shaft, for the Hoosac railroad tunnel, 583 ft. below. Hence the name of the road: Central Shaft. Pass forest HQ on the right. Next on the right is the trailhead for the Spruce Hill hike where Old Florida Rd. enters. Next comes the North Pond parking lot and South Pond camping area. The road, which is in poor shape, changes to gravel. Turn left on Burnett Rd. On your left, soon, is an unpaved parking area, the starting point for the stroll to Tannery Falls. Drive right, cross the bridge and continue S. on New State Rd. Bear left where Adams Rd. enters right and then straight where Center Rd. drops right. You are still on Adams Rd., a gravel road now and possibly rough, climbing until a paved road exits right. That is 51 Rd., leading up Borden Mtn. In Savoy you drive the gravel roads and hike the paved roads. To reach 51 Rd. from the south, east or west, take Rte. 116 or Rte. 8A to Savoy Village, then follow Center Rd. N. to Savoy Center, turn right and follow Adams Rd. to 51 Rd. on right.

Camping

The Savoy Mtn. State Forest camping area is located on South Pond, a mile south of forest HQ on Central Shaft Rd. As well as tent and trailer sites (no hookups but toilets and showers), 3 very popular cabins, used year around, look out over the pond. No reservations are accepted for any state campsites, but the cabins must be reserved in advance (413-663-8469). The state maintains a campground a few miles east on Rte. 2, at Mohawk Trail State Forest. Chilson's Pond Campground, north of Rte. 2 at Whitcomb's Summit, is privately owned. Swimming is available at South Pond, without lifeguards, and North Pond, with lifeguards, for a modest parking fee. Maps of the many hiking and skiing trails are available at the contact station at South Pond.

WALKS

BORDEN MOUNTAIN AND TANNERY FALLS, SAVOY

Various distances

Insects of a biting nature favor this wet, boggy area, so take precautions. They are attracted to perfume and shampoo. Because these 2 strolls are on gravel roads, sneakers are adequate. Both of these routes are skiable. The strolls can be connected together to make a hiking loop and the roads to make a biking loop.

Park at the end of 51 Rd. to walk up Borden Mtn. Fifty-one refers to the number of the fire tower the road was built to serve. The climb takes 20 min. The trail that bears off to the right part-way up makes a loop with Bannis Rd. that swings you around Borden Mtn. and back to Adams Rd.; instead follow straight up the hill to the Walker Lookout Tower — which will likely be locked, because forest fire spotting is apt to be by airplane these days. You can climb the stairs as far as you dare to get above the trees and take in a marvelous view of Greylock, Spruce Hill and the various undulations of the peneplain (cut off mountain) that makes up the Hoosacs. Without climbing the tower you won't get much of a view. Your elevation at the top of the tower (2,586 ft.) slightly surpasses that of Spruce Hill (2,566). It would be nice to think people wouldn't drop bottles from towers, but apparently the temptation is too much.

You can drive directly to Tannery Falls, either up Black Brook Rd. from Rte. 2 at the eastern foot of the trail, or via the gravel Adams or Tannery roads. On the principle that the value of an experience improves if it is earned, however, park in the dirt lot near the Gulf Brook bridge. Walk across the bridge and turn left on Tannery Rd. (The old road signs in Savoy are rusted and nearly illegible.) Simply stay on the road, mostly downhill, for 1.5 mi., about 40 min. You will find a family cemetery tucked in to the stands of spruce, on the right.

You probably won't see a sign for Tannery Falls, but you will see a parking lot on the left. You have gone past it when Tannery Pond appears on your right. Follow the blue blazes from the lot as you work your way down Ross Brook, under wonderful hemlocks. The first falls and chasms in the folded rock are prologue. Follow where wire protects you from the edge, at the top of the long, delicate falls over a slab of rock. Then, as you work your way to its foot, you discover another brook and falls entering right, Parker Brook — the one the CCCs dammed to make Tannery Pond. After their union they are Tannery Brook, joining Cold River. Be sure to allow plenty of time to observe the rock, the water, and the trees; read a book or have a picnic here, at least.

Many of the trails in the area are designed for snowmobiling, kept up either by the state or a club, Adams Sno-Drifters. They are not all blazed. Two of these trails connect Adams Rd. and Tannery Rd., a distance of 1.25 mi. The Ross Brook Trail begins on Balance Rock Rd., which leaves Tannery Rd. at its sharp turn north and comes out on Adams Rd., east of 51 Rd. It has some orange blazes. The other, called Lewis Hill Rd., runs parallel to it but farther west. Thus it would be possible to park your car at one end or the other and connect both of the destinations with a 5 mi. hike. A pleasant uplands bicycle loop would connect New State, Adams, Black Brook and Tannery roads: about 8 mi.

FLORIDA & SAVOY: BORDEN MTN. & TANNERY FALLS

HIKE

SPRUCE HILL

Florida and North Adams, 4 miles (1.5 hours)

Road approach

Follow directions (p. 187) given under Florida and Savoy, up to the trailhead for Spruce Hill Hike.

SPRUCE HILL

A relatively short walk over a wide, well-marked although wet trail, this one-trail hike could easily be matched with a picnic at Tannery Falls or a swim at North Pond — or both. The patina derives from lovely, dense, spruce plantations and interesting foundations and stone walls. The last few hundred feet require clambering over some rock. The cliff lookout is not for those who suffer from vertigo. The view, especially west and north, is fine, however.

Walk in Old Florida Rd. for a few feet before turning right on the Busby Trail, blazed with blue triangles (in state iconography these limit the trail to non-motorized uses). In 2 more min., pass beneath the first of 2 sets of power lines; the second is 11 min. into the hike. Stay left where an old road enters right. The first part of the trip the trail rises gently on a wide although somewhat puddly woods road.

The first evergreens you pass between are hemlock, but soon you come to spruce plantations, planted by the CCC, which had three camps at various locations in Florida and Savoy. You notice Staples Brook on your right. Soon you see where the stream side was walled for a millrun. In fact, Chester Tower owned a mill there in 1855. At 22 min. you ford a joining brook; the next section of trail is at times indistinguishable from a brook.

At 27 min. you pass foundations, left, presumably for some sort of a barn, and larger foundations, right, which

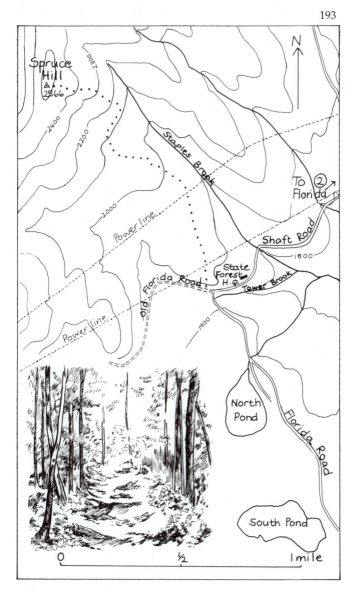

FLORIDA & SAVOY: SPRUCE HILL

supported the considerable dwelling. The cellar stones were cut; where the house faced downhill are elaborate terraces, now overgrown, connected by steps. This site appears to have been a farm that by 1904 started taking in summer boarders. It was donated to the Florida-Savoy Land Trust in 1916 and thence to the state. George Busby, however, was granted the right to cross the property to the town road (Central Shaft Rd.) via the county road (Adams-Florida).

From here on, the trail rises more steeply. After 5 min. it crosses through a wall, apparently with a former road on the up side. Soon you reach the first of 2 steep but brief ascents over rocks. You come out on the outcroppings, looking east, after 45 min. You parked your car at 1,900 ft. in elevation; this summit rises to 2,566, the highest on the Hoosac plateau (except the tower on Borden Mtn.). The view down into the Hoosac Valley and up to the Greylock massif rewards your final burst of effort. The view south, over the Hoosac plateau, is no slouch, either. A bit of exploration on the summit will take you to other cliffs, where the view of the Green Mtns. improves. These cliffs are an excellent vantage point to watch kettles of hawks cavort in the warm air rising from the valley during the fall migration.

What with taking it easy on the steep sections and examining the artifacts, it will take you about as long to get down as to climb. If you take the ski option, presumably you park them to climb the last few feet of rocks.

FLORIDA AND MONROE: TUNNEL AND TURBINE

Driving to the trailhead for Spruce Mtn. you pass 2 man-made points of particular interest. The first, in Florida, Massachusetts, is the eastern end of the Hoosac Tunnel. Look left as you cross the railroad tracks. On February 9, 1875, a steam engine first chugged from the Deerfield River Valley to the Hoosic River Valley, in No. Adams, through a 4.75-mi.-long tunnel, the longest in the world at the time, bored at a cost of 24 years, $15 million, and 195 lives. Discarding an idea dating back to 1825 to surmount the Hoosac Range by canal, those who wanted to join Boston and Albany by this northern route used the best available technology, drilling by hand and blasting with black powder through the rock. Two huge power drills, intended to do the work, both proved incapable; however, an air drill was successfully introduced in 1865. At the same time, George A. Mowbray tried a new explosive called nitroglycerin, a great improvement in blasting but dangerously unstable. A crazy, drunk assistant learned the lucky way that it could be frozen and carried safely. Freight trains still use the line, even though passenger service has long since faded from the northern Berkshire scene.

Florida was a boom town when the tunnel was under construction, especially the village known as Hoosac Tunnel, at the eastern end. Now you hardly know you are passing through a town. That anything more still exists than a few farms is probably because of the New England Power Company's Bear Swamp pumped storage hydroelectric project in the next town upriver and across the Franklin County line, Monroe. Although several hydroelectric units had existed in the valley previously, the Bear Swamp project was built in the 1970s. The Bear Swamp Visitors' Center, on River Rd. north of the tunnel, shows an interesting slide-tape on the history of the valley and a working exhibit of pumped storage. The local Massachusetts Electric Co. office can arrange a tour of the power plant. You drive across the dam and walk down a tunnel into the side of Rowe Mtn. for 690 ft. until you are in the powerhouse. Then you descend

5 stories, viewing control equipment and getting a look at the huge, twin pump-turbines that generate electricity during peak load periods as water is let out of the Upper Reservoir. The process is reversed, pumping from the Lower Reservoir 770 ft. up to the Upper Reservoir, during off-peak times. The penstock that carries the water is 17.5 ft. in diameter. Construction of the powerhouse involved removing 97,800 cubic yards of stone.

Road approaches

Going E. from Florida, above and east of No. Adams on what is known locally as the Trail (the Mohawk Trail, Rte. 2), take the next left after Whitcomb Summit; then the next right. You head down on a steep road to a T at River Rd. The river is the Deerfield. Go left at the T, continuing through the village of Hoosac Tunnel. Soon you pass the Bear Swamp Visitors' Center, right, where you might wish to stop. The parking area you want to find for the hike is on the left, .75 mi. beyond the visitors' center, 4.5 mi. from the Trail.

Camping

You will pass 3 lean-tos (three-sided) shelters, all of which are well maintained (by the state and power company), and numerous fireplaces and informal camping areas. A word of caution, though: all the shelters are within a couple miles of a road and show evidence of being sites for parties. Ideally, as well, shelters should be located a bit off the trail. Using these is like sleeping in the hall. Few services or accommodations are available in Hoosac Tunnel or the next town up, Monroe Bridge, so plan accordingly.

Do not confuse the Spruce Hill hike in Florida with this one on Spruce Mtn. in Monroe. Several other spruce hills and mountains exist in the area, for the obvious botanical reason.

HIKE

SPRUCE MOUNTAIN

9 miles (4 hours)

Spruce Mtn. in Monroe State Forest, Franklin County, is a pleasant hike, not too steep on the south side. There are fine vistas from wire cuts — that is, swaths opened for powerlines — and three cliffs along the way. The mountain does not have a cleared summit. A short sidetrip, part-way up, leads to Raycroft Lookout, for a view of the Deerfield Valley. Other links of this loop, all blazed blue, climb up the Dunbar Brook Valley and pass over former and present woods roads. The best is last: the truly scenic walk down Dunbar Brook Trail, beside the tumbling waters of the clear, mountain stream, through glades of enormous hemlock, which look as though the underbrush were swept out every day. The Commonwealth has declared the Dunbar Valley, like Alander Mtn. and the Hopper on Mt. Greylock, special Backcountry Areas.

(Due to technical difficulties — the author having forgotten his watch — the times on this hike are estimated; add about 20 min. overall for the actual elapsed time.)

The Dunbar Picnic area, maintained by New England Power Co., is on the east side of River Rd. Your trailhead, a smaller parking lot, is directly across from it. Start up to the powerline, at the SW corner of the lot. Above the dam, the trail detaches itself from the jeep road and drops towards the brook, which it follows under spreading hemlock. Look for the blue blazes. Solomon's seal, trilliums and other spring ephemerals flower in profusion, so that in late May it is impossible to avoid stepping on their beautiful blossoms. After 6 min. the trail turns left at a bench and fireplace, following close to the river for 4 min. You turn up the hill at the trail junction just before the bridge — which you will cross on your return.

For the next 15 min. you zigzag up the Dunbar Brook

Valley wall. A stone cairn is the sign you are almost at the first shelter; 5 more min. takes you to Raycroft Extension, a dirt road with large puddles. This is prime mosquito and blackfly land; wear your favorite bug repellent. Turn right, following the blue dots. In 3 min. you turn left on a former woods road, somewhat grown in. At 48 min. from departure you pass the second shelter of the outing, almost immediately turning sharp right. Straight ahead is deceptively like a path, but actually an intermittent brook bed.

In 50 min. you pass under a powerline you will cross 3 more times. If the trail has not been bushed recently, it may be hard to spot the opening directly across the cleared area. You could follow the line, left, as a short cut, but aren't you in this to hike? The route is steep and rocky, as well. Ignore extraneous woods roads. Follow the blazes. An hr. from the parking lot, turn left on South Rd. As a check, almost immediately you should see a cement boundary marker, right. In 5 min. you will cross under those familiar wires, which alert you that you will soon turn. In 3 more min., at an intersection of gravel roads, follow the trail, still blazed blue, right.

Shortly you pass under those wires, again: This time the cut gives you a nice view of the church spire in Florida. You climb moderately to a plateau, through spruce, oak and maple, over quartzite outcroppings. In 20 min. you come to a view, left, over a cliff, of the Hoosac peneplain, the truncated remains of a mountain range. You are in a beech forest. You may think you've reached the summit when the trail begins to descend; but like the boat *Mary Ellen Carter*, it rises again, for about 20 more min., to the summit (2,751 ft. in elevation; you began at about 1,100 ft.). Cliffs to the left show you a view south similar to one you've seen before.

Beginning its descent, the trail bends right. At 1:58 you arrive at a trail junction in a bog; stay right, still following the blue. The trail begins to descend sharply, pausing for one more outlook, this time over the hydroelectric project. You pass some beautiful ash specimens before reclaiming the hemlock. At 2:20, turn left on that same

FLORIDA & MONROE: SPRUCE MOUNTAIN

South Rd. you trod before. Look left for some enormous boulders in the woods.

At 2:23 you cross Dunbar Brook on a wooden, automobile bridge. To orient yourself, you may want to follow straight a few hundred feet to the junction with a paved road that leads, as a section called Tilda Rd., from the top of the Mohawk Trail and under other names to Monroe Bridge — an alternate driving route. Your trail picks up downstream, just an the north side of the bridge, past some old mill foundations. The brook beckons for swimming or sunning; less public places lie down below.

Thus begins the longest as well as the loveliest leg of the trip, down Dunbar to the car. The trail you are on swings away from the water to join a woods road (2:26), which soon tapers down to a trail through a magnificent hemlock grove. One thousand needles cushion your every tread. As you descend to the brook, bear right before the large boulder; then zig and zag down. You cross several brooks joining from the side . . . and then, yes, once more the wire cut (2:55).

And just 5 min. later, the third shelter, where a large brook joins Dunbar, stands right in the trail. Of several choices, you want to bend left. You pass, under continual hemlocks, several informal fireplaces. Five more min. bring you to the bridge you saw but did not cross 3 hrs. ago. Cross it now. It hangs across Dunbar Brook on 2 telephone poles. At 3:10, on the south side of the brook now, you come to that turn at the bench; 10 min. more returns you to your car.

Because the dam on Dunbar Brook has a fence across it, don't bother to walk down the trail to it. A shorter, attractive hike would simply leave Spruce Mtn. out, turning N. on South Rd. after the second shelter, if you follow those directions.

WALKS FOR THE BLIND
AND DISABLED
by Robert J. Redington

Robert J. Redington lost his sight in 1982. Previously an ardent Berkshire hiker, he had an important role in establishing the southern end of the Taconic Skyline Trail (see Long Hikes*). Since then he has been working to help blind people enjoy the out-of-doors. Redington describes the following trails for the use of sighted people in assisting the blind to walk in the woods. He suggests that generally the sighted person walk beside the visually handicapped person, explaining any obstacles and also describing the wildlife and views. Where the trail is narrower, the sighted person should walk in front, holding one end of a stick or rope that the blind person also holds with a hand on the same side. A walking stick for the blind person can also be fun and useful. Redington chose relatively smooth trails. The Commonwealth of Massachusetts wishes to cooperate by designating appropriate trails for the blind. In addition, the state has created a wheelchair accessible path, known as Tranquility Trail, at Pittsfield State Forest (for directions see Pittsfield, this section). Bob Redington graciously allowed us to edit his descriptions for this book.*

SOUTH COUNTY

GREAT BARRINGTON AND MONTEREY

WALKS

BEARTOWN STATE FOREST, BENEDICT POND

l.5 miles or more

Road approach

Coming down Rte. 7 from Stockbridge, turn left just beyond the high school onto Monument Valley Rd. Follow it to Stony Brook Rd. where you turn left. Stony Brook becomes Blue Hill Rd. Continue to Beartown State Forest entrance, left. The pond is uphill into the woods. Parking is provided. From Gt. Barrington, go east on Rte. 23 to Blue Hill Rd. in Monterey, turn left, continue past state forest headquarters to the entrance road to the pond.

BENEDICT POND

Beautiful Benedict Pond lies in Beartown State Forest. It is surrounded by woods where mountain laurel bloom in late June and early July. Canada geese are on the pond in the summer. Alternative hiking routes around the pond can be taken. One, which is nearer the shore with more views of the pond, is the Pond Loop Trail, marked by triangular blue painted blazes and 1.5 mi. long. The other route, which is longer and easier walking, follows a road, a wood road (a route with a natural surface and wide enough for a four-wheel vehicle), and a cross-country ski trail. A combination of the 2 routes can also be followed.

Benedict Pond is the recreation center of Beartown State Forest, with hiking, picnicking, camping, swimming, and, if you bring your own boat — or rent a boat from the concessionaire — canoeing, rowing and fishing (no motors). A day-use fee is charged per car during the Memorial Day weekend to Labor Day season, but not if the occupants are only going hiking or include a handicapped person suitably identified.

POND LOOP TRAIL

This trail is rough in places, with rocks and roots under foot and a few steep steps. There are also log bridges and walkways along the trail. These sections call for close guidance by the sighted guide. Hiking is mostly single file along the trail, so the blind hiker and guide should use a guiding stick or rope tether.

The trail starts from the parking area at the Pond Loop Trail sign and blue blaze. Follow it E. along the south side of the pond, passing viewpoints at the edge of the pond a few paces to the left of the trail.

The Loop Trail turns left onto the white blazed Appalachian Trail (AT), which it follows at the eastern end of the pond. At a point here you can go left a short distance to a fine vantage point at the edge of the pond.

The trail turns left again on a wood road, and in a few yds. the AT goes right while the Loop Trail continues ahead on the wood road, now on the east side of the pond. Next, the trail turns left from the wood road at the sign and follows the northeast and north sides of the pond. Finally, the trail turns down the west side of the pond, passing through the campground and ending at a trail sign at the shore of the pond a few yds. before the dam at the pond's outlet. There are picnic tables here and a swimming beach nearby.

To complete the circuit back to the parking area, cross on the dam, and go through the picnic area on the wooded knoll to the parking area.

THE LONGER CIRCUIT ROUTE

This route is a mile or so longer than the Loop Trail. It provides smoother walking and is mostly wide enough to permit the blind hiker to walk beside the guide. From the same parking area, take the paved road, which is blocked by a metal gate and has a sign saying, "To the Appalachian Trail," and follow it eastward parallel to the Loop Trail on the south side of the pond. After the AT crosses the road, the pavement ends at a triangular Y junction, where you take the left fork onto the previously mentioned wood road. Soon the combined AT-Pond Loop Trail enters the wood road from the left. Follow the wood road northward on the eastern side of the pond, passing the point where the Loop Trail turns away from it. In another half mi., a few yds. before the wood road reaches the paved Beartown Rd., turn left onto the cross-country ski trail marked by triangular red blazes. Follow this ski trail SW to the camping area where it crosses the Loop Trail. Turn right on the Loop Trail for the short distance to its end near the dam.

CENTRAL COUNTY

BECKET

NATURE TRAILS

OCTOBER MOUNTAIN STATE FOREST, FINERTY POND

4 miles

Road approaches

From Lee go left (N.) off Rte. 20 on Becket Rd., which soon becomes Tyne Rd. as it enters Becket from Lee. A half-mile from the junction with Rte. 20, turn left into a wood road and park immediately on the right.

FINERTY POND

Hike north for about a mi. on the wood road gravel, which is easy walking with a gradual ascent, and reach a junction with a left and right fork. Take the right fork, an old CCC road made with a cobblestone base. There are 2 rough rocky sections along it, but the route continues to be relatively level. After less than a mi. on this wood road the AT, with white painted blazes, crosses it. Turn left on the AT, which descends towards nearby Finerty Pond. Soon reach a junction where the AT turns left and an unmarked trail goes right. Continue straight ahead on a faint trail a short distance to the edge of the pond and go a few yds. to the right to a large log at the edge of the pond, which is good for several people to sit on. Sighted persons have a good view of the attractive pond from here.

Return to the starting point, retracing your steps over the same route. If you wish to walk farther, when you reach the AT from the edge of the pond, turn left on the unmarked trail and follow it along the southeast side of the pond to the dam at the pond's outlet. There are views over the pond along here. Then retrace your steps. The dam can also be reached by continuing a short way along the wood road beyond the AT crossing, and descending left to the aforementioned unmarked trail to follow it right to the dam.

207

OCTOBER MTN. STATE FOREST: FINERTY POND

PITTSFIELD

NATURE TRAILS

PITTSFIELD STATE FOREST

There are two self-guiding interpretive nature trails in the main recreational area of Pittsfield State Forest, an area also containing hiking, ski and snowmobile trails, picnic areas, campsites, a swimming pond, and a ski jump. A notable feature of the state forest is the Berry Pond area on the crest of the Taconic Range, reached by a one-way, paved circuit road. Here there are splendid views, the largest stand of wild (Pinkster) azaleas in Massachusetts, the highest natural pond in the state (Berry Pond at 2,060 ft.), and another self-guiding nature trail especially rewarding for blind persons.

Road approaches

See directions under "Pittsfield, Berry Pond."

TRANQUILITY TRAIL AND WOODS RAMBLE

At the entrance there is a contact station where an attendant collects day-use fees from cars during the late May to early September season. There is no charge if the occupants of a car are to go hiking or include a handicapped person. Just beyond the contact station you can either turn left and drive to the parking area by the ski lodge, which is the access to the 2 nature trails of the area, or you can drive straight ahead to reach the HQ building and to drive up to the Berry Pond area.

The two self-guiding nature trails, called the Tranquility Trail and the Woods Ramble, start from the same place near the ski lodge. Each one is about a half-mi. long, has numbered signposts along it and makes a loop, which you follow in a counterclockwise direction, keeping to the right where the loop starts. Each trail is wide enough for the blind person to walk beside the guide. The Tranquility Trail is paved, so it may be used by persons in wheelchairs and by those who walk with difficulty. The Woods Ramble Trail is rougher and climbs a way. There are blue painted blazes on part of the trail and on the Hawthorne Trail, which branches off it, so care should be taken to remain on the route with the numbered signposts, shown on the map contained in the Woods Ramble Trail leaflet.

The self-guiding leaflet for each trail, entitled "Nature's Secrets" in the case of the Tranquility Trail, has numbered paragraphs giving information regarding the plant life and other natural features near the corresponding numbered posts. Each leaflet contains information not provided in the other, and the Wood Ramble leaflet gives additional information of interest concerning the natural history and ecology of Pittsfield State Forest. The two leaflets, as well as the one for the nature trail near Berry Pond, may be obtained from the contact station. The sighted persons can help the blind feel plant life and other natural objects along the trail. If blind persons walking the Tranquility Trail prefer to listen to a recording of the information on the leaflet, they may obtain, at the HQ building, the necessary cassette player and tape.

An additional walk of a mi. or so to state forest recreational sites may be taken. Start off by walking along the paved road past the ski lodge for some distance. Then turn right on the gravel crossroad, and near its end turn left onto a trail that leads to the ski jump and the swimming pond, formed by a dam in Lulu Brook. You can then either retrace your steps or return via the paved road which passes the HQ building. The walk will also take you past picnic grounds and campsites. You can consult a state forest leaflet and map obtained from the contact station or the HQ building.

BERRY POND AREA

BERKSHIRE HILLS RAMBLE

During the non-snow season, usually mid-April through October, you can drive up the Berry Pond Circuit Rd., a one-way route which climbs 1,000 ft. to the crest of the range and descends again to the main recreational area. As you reach the crest, look for a broad trail going left from the road where there should be a sign, and where on the right there is a space for 2 or 3 cars to park. This is the beginning of the Berkshire Hills Ramble, an interesting, self-guiding nature trail with numbered signposts corresponding to numbered paragraphs on the trail's leaflet. The trail descends somewhat and makes a loop (followed in the clockwise direction), which passes the edge of Berry Pond, the distance ending back at the starting point about .75 mi. Blind persons can enjoy the fragrance of the ferns, balsam firs, and the azalea bushes when in blossom, and they can listen to the frogs in the pond.

Drive another .25 mi. or so along the road on the crest of the range, past the azalea stands, and park on the right where there is a fine panoramic view over New York State to the west. Then walk up the broad trail to the right of the parking area for a short climb to the top of Berry Hill 2,200 ft. in elevation. Here there is a bushy growth and further views. Continue down the other side of the hill, following occasional white trail markers, to the paved road. Turn right to walk back along the road to the parking area. Alternatively, if you did not visit the nature trail on the drive up, you can go a few yds. along the road to reach that trail on the left. When you have finished the trail, you walk left on the road for the .25 mi. back to the parking area. The walk over Berry Hill and along the paved road, as well as on the nature trail, is the best way to view the azalea bushes when they are in bloom, usually during the first week in June.

If you continue walking along the road past the parking area, you will descend a short distance to Berry Pond on the left. Here an open grassy area gives access to the shore of the pond. You can then follow a broad trail marked with an occasional white painted blaze, which goes between the road and the pond and passes several campsites by the pond. Each one has a picnic table and fireplace. You can then walk back to the parking area and continue driving along the one-way road back down to the main recreational area of the state forest, where the road passes the ski lodge and the access to the 2 nature trails.

WASHINGTON

WALK

WARNER HILL / APPALACHIAN TRAIL

2 miles

Road approaches

Drive E. on Williams St. in Pittsfield, fork left on Kirchner, and make the long climb up the highland to where the AT crosses the road 3.1 mi. from the junction below. The trail crossing here is in Washington, where Kirchner becomes Blotz, although there is no sign indicating the name change. From the east one can reach the trailhead from Rte. 8 in Hinsdale, from where it is 1.4 mi. along the Blotz/Kirchner side road westward to the trailhead.

Park in the space, if empty, on the north side of Blotz Rd. where the white blazed AT crosses the road.

WARNER HILL / APPALACHIAN TRAIL

Hike N. on the AT, the blind person using a guiding stick or rope tether with the sighted guides. Near the start of the hike pass several fragrant balsam fir trees and cross 2 muddy spots on stones, if possible. Gradually ascend Warner Hill, passing an extensive stand of red spruce trees and fragrant fern beds. After almost a mi., reach the summit of Warner Hill, at 2,050 ft. A short, narrow side trail loops right from the AT to go over the high point of Warner Hill. From this rocky summit there is a view of Pittsfield to the northwest, of the Taconic Range beyond, and of Mt. Greylock to the north. Trees have been cut down to open up this view.

Continue N. on the AT a short way down from the summit to an extensive stand of fragrant ferns. Before retracing your route to the trailhead, you may wish to hike farther N. on the trail, as it gradually descends Warner Hill.

From the trail crossing of Blotz, you may wish to hike another half-mile or so S. on the AT. This is pleasant, level walking, past some conifer trees, and you can turn back where the trail starts to climb. There are log walkways over wet places along this trail section.

NORTH COUNTY

ADAMS

MOUNT GREYLOCK STATE RESERVATION, MOUNT PROSPECT

Road approaches

See directions (and information about facilities) under "Adams and Mt. Greylock."

MOUNT PROSPECT

This excursion is recommended to last from morning into the afternoon, including lunch. It should be between Memorial Day weekend and mid-October. Generally, the walking is more difficult than on other recommended paths for the handicapped. There are 2 short, self-guiding nature trails in the Mt. Greylock State Reservation. One starts from the east end of the parking lot of the Visitors' Center on Rockwell Rd. as you begin your drive up the mountain, and the other is located on the mountain range above on the north side of Sperry in the public campground. If you wish to visit either trail, or both, ask at the Visitors' Center for the self-guiding leaflet for the trail. At the numbered stops along the trail, the sighted guide can read to the blind person the information in the leaflet concerning the plant life and other natural features at these locations.

After visiting the Greylock summit, drive back down to the fork and turn right on Notch Rd., which is a continuation N., along the range, of Rockwell Rd. You pass on the left open viewpoints westward to the Taconic Range. In 3.5 mi. from the fork, park on the right and walk another

100 yds. ahead to the AT crossing. Take this trail (white blazes) to the left, passing an open area called Tall Spruces over a rough section of trail. After .5 mi. of hiking, reach the Money Brook Trail going left from the AT. Before turning onto this trail, you may wish to continue on the AT another .5 mi. or so, ascending to an open section of the crest of Mt. Prospect where there is a fine view, northwest, of the Taconic Range and Williamstown. Retrace your steps down the AT and take the Money Brook Trail, now on your right, southwest, through a stand of red spruce trees. The trail is marked with triangular blue state forest markers. After about .3 mi. from the junction with the AT, turn right on a red blazed side trail which takes you about 100 yds. to the Tall Spruces or Wilbur's Clearing. Back at the Money Brook Trail, you have a choice of routes, as described below.

You can turn left on this trail and retrace your route, turning right at the AT to reach Notch Rd. and your car. The other choice is to take a longer loop, involving some climbing, by going right farther along the Money Brook Trail. In about a third of a mi., turn left on a side trail with triangular blue painted blazes. As indicated by a sign, this goes to Notch Rd. on the east. There is a considerable climb up this trail to the road, where you turn left and walk down northward for a half-mile to your car.

APPENDICES

HIKES & WALKS BY DEGREE OF DIFFICULTY

Hikes and walks are ranked here by a simple system. Walks are rated "A," "B" and "C" — "A" being the easiest and "C" the most difficult. Hikes are rated "1," "2" and "3," with "1" being the easiest, "2" somewhat more challenging and "3" the most difficult. Where specific distances and/or times are available, these, too, are cited for convenience.

Walk / Hike   **Difficulty / Distance / Time**

SOUTH COUNTY

Mount Washington
  Hikes: Alander Mountain/
             Bash Bish Falls 2   7 mi./3 hrs.
             Mount Everett....................2   5.5 mi./2.75 hrs.

Sheffield
  Walks: Salisbury Road ....A   7 mi./2.5 hrs.
             Bartholomew's Cobble/
             Ashley House ....B   approx. 2 hrs.

Egremont
  Walk: Baldwin Hill Road
             North & South.................A   6 mi./2.5 hrs.

New Marlborough
  Walks: Harmon Road ....A   7 mi./2.5 hrs.
             Campbell Falls ....A   4.5 mi./2 hrs.
             York Pond ....A   1 mi./30 min.

Great Barrington
  Walks: Seekonk ....A   3 or 6 mi./1 or 2 hrs.
             Benedict Pond ....A   5 mi./2 hrs.
  Hike: Monument Mountain 2   3 mi./1.5 hrs.

Tyringham
     Walk: Tyringham Cobble .... B   2 mi./ 1 hr.

Stockbridge
     Walks: Ice Glen C   3.5 mi./1.5 hrs.
                 Bowker's Woods .... A   5 mi./15 min.
                 Prospect Hill .... B   3 mi./1 hr.
                 Glendale .... B   various options
                 Gould Meadows and
                 Bullard Woods .... A   various options

CENTRAL COUNTY

Lenox
     Walks: Kennedy Park .... A   3-4 mi./1.5 hrs.
                 Reservoirs .... B   8 mi. or less
                                                              3 hrs. or less
                 Golden Hill .... B   2.5 mi./ 1hr.
     Hike: Pleasant Valley/
                 Lenox Mountain 1   various options

Richmond
     Walk: East Road .... A   4.6 mi./ 2 hrs.

Peru
     Walk: Rice Sanctuary .... B   various trails

Pittsfield
     Walks: Downtown .... A   8 blocks/30 min.
                 Canoe Meadows .... A   various trails
     Hike: Berry Pond 1   5 mi./ 2 hrs.

Hancock
     Hike: Shaker Mountain 2   6.5 mi./3 hrs.

Dalton
     Walk: Wahconah Falls .... A   few hundred ft.

Windsor
     Walk: Windsor Jambs .... B   3 mi./1.5 hrs.
     Hike: Notchview/Judge's Hill 1   5.5 mi./2.25 hrs.

NORTH COUNTY

Cheshire
 Walk: Hoosic River Railroad ....A 4.5 mi./2 hrs.

Adams and Mount Greylock
 Walks: Overlook Trail ....C 2.5 mi./1 hr.
    Campground Trails:
     Stony Ledge ....A 2 mi./50 min.
     March Cataract ....C under 2 mi./45 min.
     Deer Hill ....C 2.25 mi./1 hr.
    Mount Prospect
    from Notch Road ....2 1 mi./30 min.
 Hikes: Cheshire Harbor Trail ......2 6.6 mi./2.5 hrs.
    Bellows Pipe Trail ....3 4 mi./1.5 hrs.
    The Hopper ....2 8 mi./3.5 hrs.
    Stony Ledge and
    Roaring Brook Trail ....2 9 mi./3.75 hrs.

Williamstown
 Walk: Stone Hill ....B 1.5 mi./1 hr.
 Hikes: Berlin Mountain ....3 5.25 mi./3 hrs.
    Pine Cobble and
    Broad Brook Trails ....3 10 mi./5 hrs.
    RRR Brooks ....3 7.75 mi./3 hrs.
    The Dome ....2 6.4 mi./3 hrs.

North Adams
 Walk: The Cascades ....A 1 mi./30 min.

Florida and Savoy
 Walks: Borden Mountain and
    Tannery Falls ....B various distances
 Hike: Spruce Hill ....1 4 mi./1.5 hrs.

Florida and Monroe: Tunnel and Turbine
 Hike: Spruce Mountain ....3 9 mi./4 hrs.

LONG HIKES AND
TRAIL SYSTEMS

Hikes and Walks in the Berkshire Hills is designed for day trippers, only tangentially describing the long distance trails in the county. They are well covered in guides specific to them, noted here and in the bibliography. Nor does this book cover more than a fraction of the trails in the county. In particular, many more hikes in northern Berkshire are described in the Williams College Outing Club's guide.

The Appalachian Trail

In the 1920s, Benton McKaye and others used available state-owned land located between convenient small town inns and lodges to plan the Berkshire section of the 2,050-mi. footpath from Springer Mtn. in Georgia to Mt. Katahdin in Maine. It is intended to be a passive, recreational trail. No vehicles are allowed. The 262-mile Long Trail, the length of Vermont to the Canadian border, begins on the AT at the Vermont line, north of Pine Cobble.

The more than 86 miles of the AT in Berkshire enter in South County at Sage's Ravine and wander through Mt. Everett State Reservation, East Mtn. State Forest, Beartown State Forest, October Mtn. State Forest, Mt. Greylock State Reservation, and Clarksburg State Forest, in the north, from whence they exit the county. In recent years, the National Park Service has been attempting to move sections in between state forests onto protected lands and away from the original conception of connecting towns. The AT is blazed with white rectangles, with side trails blazed blue.

Shelters will eventually be placed within a day's hike of each other over the entire length of the trail. Bascom Lodge, on Mt. Greylock, is a storied rendezvous for through-hikers, who can get a reduced rate for a night in a real bed, cooked food, and showers by helping in the kitchen. See: *Appalachian Trail Guide — Massachusetts-Connecticut.*

The Taconic Crest Trail

The Taconic Hiking Club, founded in 1932 in Troy, New York, sponsors various kinds of outings. In 1948 its members began to develop the Crest Trail, 29 miles from Berry Pond in Pittsfield State Forest to No. Pownal, Vermont. The trail runs generally north and south along a ridge through 3 states. The club also maintains 7 miles of the Taconic Skyline Trail from Berry Pond south to Rte. 20 in Pittsfield. The trail is marked by white diamond-shaped markers or paint; side trails are marked by blue diamonds. As well as Pittsfield State Forest, the TCT runs through newly acquired New York Department of Environmental Conservation property at Petersburg Pass, Williams College's Hopkins Forest, and other private land. Once every other year, the club sponsors a 1-day, end-to-end hike, beginning with breakfast before dawn at Berry Pond and continuing past dusk. See: *Guide to the Taconic Crest Trail.*

The Taconic Trail System

The entire Taconic system includes the Taconic Crest Trail, the Taconic Skyline Trail, and the South Taconic Trail. The 23-mile-long Skyline Trail runs from Richmond to Williamstown, including the 7-mile section south of Berry Pond maintained by the Taconic Hiking Club. It follows along the Brodie Mtn. extension to the Taconics. About half is in Pittsfield State Forest and half on private land. The blazes are painted white, round or square in shape. The trail is not consistently maintained.

The South Taconic Trail extends 15.7 miles, mostly in New York State's Taconic State Park and Mt. Washington State Forest in Massachusetts. It runs parallel to the AT, to the west, and is maintained by volunteers from the New York chapter of the AMC, the Mid-Hudson chapter of the Adirondack Mountain Club, the New York/New Jersey Appalachian Trail Conference, and the Sierra Club. The crest it follows provides almost continuous, open, extensive views east and west, including Alander and Bash Bish (see the description of that hike). Numerous side trails and camping areas provide circuit routes. See: *Guide to the Taconic Trail System*.

Williams Outing Club Trails

Founded by Albert Hopkins as the Alpine Club in 1863, the Williams Outing Club is the oldest mountain-climbing organization in the United States, preceding both the White Mtn. and Appalachian Mtn. clubs. Volunteer college students maintain some 75 miles of trails in northern Berkshire, southern Vermont, and the corner of eastern New York. Its trail guide (see Williams Outing Club's *Trail Map and Guide*) details trips on 35 trails in the Williamstown area.

Berkshire Hiking Holidays

A tour business brings individuals, families and groups of hikers (twelve maximum) to the Berkshires for 2-, 3- and 5-night hiking excursions. Many of the hikes cover trails described in this book. The program, *Berkshire Hiking Holidays*, arranges for accommodations at country inns, prepares all meals, transports luggage while you're on the trail, and provides a guide who is knowledgeable about the Berkshires. For information, call 413-499-9648.

BOOTS, BOOKS, MAPS, PACKS

Stores throughout the county sell items useful to hikers, for example, ice cream cones. Nevertheless certain kinds of stores are of particular value.

Arcadian Shop, Pittsfield-Lenox Rd., Lenox
Berkshire Outfitters, Rte. 8, Adams
Besse-Clarke, 273 North St., Pittsfield
Cosby Gerry & Co., Undermountain Rd., Sheffield
Dick Moon Sporting Goods, 114 Fenn St., Pittsfield
The Mountain Goat, Water St., Williamstown
Pittsfield Sporting Goods Co., 70 North St., Pittsfield

Albion Bookstore, Water St., Williamstown
The Book Maze, Lenox House Country Shops, Rte. 7, Lenox
The Bookloft, Barrington Plaza, Rte. 7, Gt. Barrington
The Bookstore, 9 Housatonic St., Lenox
The Village Book Store, Inc., Spring St., Williamstown
Either/Or Bookstore, 122 North St., Pittsfield
Lauriat's Books, Berkshire Mall, Rte. 8, Lanesborough
October Mtn. Books, Allendale Shopping Ctr.,
    Rtes. 8 & 9, Pittsfield
Railroad St. Books, 44 Railroad St., Gt. Barrington
Village Bookstore, Park St., Adams
Waldenbooks, Berkshire Mall, Rte. 8, Lanesborough
Water Street Books, 26 Water St., Williamstown

BIBLIOGRAPHY

Appalachian Trail Guide to Massachusetts-Connecticut (1988), P.O. 807, Harpers Ferry, WV, 25425-0807.

Binzen, William. *The Berkshires* (a book of photographs) (1986), Globe Pequot Press, Chester CT.

Brady and White. *Fifty Hikes in Massachusetts* (1983), Backcountry Publications, P.O. 175, Woodstock, VT 05091.

Burns and Stevens. *Most Excellent Majesty: A History of Mount Greylock* (1988), Berkshire Natural Resources Council, 20 Bank Row, Pittsfield, MA 01201.

Cuyler, Lewis. *Bike Rides in the Berkshire Hills* (1990), Berkshire House, P.O. Box 915, Gt. Barrington, MA 01230.

Drew, Bernard. *A History of Notchview* (1986), Attic Revivals Press, Gt. Barrington, MA 01230.

Federal Writers Project. *The Berkshire Hills* (1939), reprinted by Northeastern Univ. Press (1987).

Griswold, Whit. *Berkshire Trails for Walking and Ski Touring* (1986), The East Woods Press (out-of-print).

Ryan, Christopher J. *Guide to the Taconic Trail System* (1989), New England Cartographics, P.O. Box 369, Amherst, MA 01004.

Sternfield, Jonathan. *The Berkshire Book: A Complete Guide* (1990), Berkshire House, P.O. Box 915, Gt. Barrington, MA 01230.

Taconic Hiking Club. *Guide to the Taconic Crest Trail* (1988), 810 Church St., Troy, NY 12180.

Thoreau, Henry David. *A Week on the Concord and Merrimack Rivers* (1893), Houghton Mifflin Co., Boston, MA.

Williams Outing Club. *Trail Guide and Map* (1989), Williams College, Williamstown, MA 01267.

A Note on the Author

Lauren R. Stevens, author with Deborah Burns of *Most Excellent Majesty: A History of Mount Greylock*, and of *Skiing in the Berkshire Hills*, has lived and walked in Berkshire County for 30 years. Founder in 1981 of *The Advocate*, more recently as a freelancer, he has written on outdoor recreation and the environment for most Berkshire regional publications. He has also published a novel, *The Double Axe* (Scribners). As an environmental consultant, he was a principal author of *2003: A Study of Williamstown Over the Next 20 Years*; *The Hoosic River Action Plan*; and the GOALS study: *The Mount Greylock State Reservation*. The father of three, Lauren Stevens lives in Williamstown, where he has taught and served as Dean of Freshmen at Williams College.

have seen them from so many angles that the picture they finally make seems at once comprehensively complete and incomprehensibly complex. . . . The associations that *Apeirogon* suggests are inescapable, of course, not random at all, but as wide as they ripple and as heady as they sometimes seem, they always come back to the book's human heart."
—Minneapolis *Star Tribune*

"A quite extraordinary novel . . . Colum McCann has found the form and voice to tell the most complex of stories, with an unexpected friendship between two men at its powerfully beating heart."
—KAMILA SHAMSIE, author of *Home Fire*

"Astounding . . . [McCann] paints another masterpiece. . . . [*Apeirogon* is] his most important novel to date."
—*The Free Lance-Star*

"[McCann is] a beautiful writer: his sense of rhythm, alliteration, and assonance all emerge wonderfully in this book's prose. . . . He is also deft with metaphor and understands how to use juxtaposition to upend conventional perception. . . . What is most evident in this novel, hanging above it like a nimbus, is how deeply McCann cares."
—*Los Angeles Review of Books*

"*Apeirogon* has the fractured, associative quality of poetry, as much meditation as narrative. . . . It's suffused with hope."
—*The Christian Science Monitor*

"This beautiful, deeply felt book is first and foremost an extraordinary act of listening."
—NATHAN ENGLANDER, author of *Dinner at the Center of the Earth*

"A mind-bending and momentous new novel . . . groundbreaking."

—*San Francisco Examiner*

"A powerful and heart-wrenching story."　　　　—*Business Insider*

"Every significant novel is an act of reckless originality. Colum McCann's *Apeirogon* is nothing like any book you've ever read. Think of reading David Mitchell's *Cloud Atlas*, Anne Carson's *Autobiography of Red*, or George Saunders's *Lincoln in the Bardo* for the first time. Think of discovering an entirely unprecedented, and profoundly true, narrative form. Think about feeling that the very idea of the novel, of what it can be and what it's capable of containing, has been expanded, forever."　　　　—Michael Cunningham, author of *The Snow Queen*

"What's remarkable . . . is the wildly imaginative way McCann tells this tale: through hundreds of short segments, some with only a quote, that create a moving whole."　　　　—AARP

"Ambitious . . . McCann mixes history and fiction, shifting narrators, place and time into a seamless though sprawling whole. . . . McCann's protagonists believe that if a country's commitment to peace leads the way, the most complex politics will sort themselves out. *Apeirogon* makes space for this belief, a placeholder for a future where irreparable loss transforms violence, where grief leads to reconciliation."

—*Bookpage* (starred review)

"*Apeirogon* is a brilliant dramatization of the tensions behind a universal problem, the contentious ownership of land and the location and nature of its borders. This novel arrives at a crucial time for us in the history of the world."　　　　—Barry Lopez, author of *Outside*

By Colum McCann

FICTION

Apeirogon

Thirteen Ways of Looking

TransAtlantic

Let the Great World Spin

Zoli

Dancer

Everything in This Country Must

This Side of Brightness

Songdogs

Fishing the Sloe-Black River

NONFICTION

Letters to a Young Writer

The Book of Men (EDITOR)

APEIROGON

APEIROGON

A NOVEL

COLUM McCANN

RANDOM HOUSE

NEW YORK

2021 Random House Trade Paperback Edition

Published in the United States by Random House, an imprint and
division of Penguin Random House LLC, New York.

RANDOM HOUSE and the HOUSE colophon are registered trademarks
of Penguin Random House LLC.
RANDOM HOUSE BOOK CLUB and colophon are trademarks of Penguin
Random House LLC.

Originally published in hardcover in the United States by Random House, an
imprint and division of Penguin Random House LLC, in 2020.

Grateful acknowledgment is made to WC Music Corp. and Universal Music
MGB Ltd./Universal Music–Careers (BMI) for permission to reprint an excerpt
from "Once In a Lifetime," words and music by Tina Weymouth, Chris Frantz,
David Byrne, Brian Eno, and Jerry Harrison, © 1980 Index Music, Inc. (ASCAP),
and WC Music Corp. (ASCAP), published by Universal Music MGB Ltd./
Universal Music–Careers (BMI). All rights on behalf of itself and Index Music,
Inc., administered by WC Music Corp. Reprinted by permission.

Illustration credits are located on page 465.

LIBRARY OF CONGRESS CATALOGING-IN-PUBLICATION DATA
Names: McCann, Colum, author.
Title: Apeirogon : a novel / Colum McCann.
Description: New York : Random House, 2020.
Identifiers: LCCN 2019022848 (print) | LCCN 2019022849 (ebook) | ISBN
9780812981933 (trade paperback) | ISBN 9780679604600 (ebook)
Subjects: LCSH: Jewish-Arab relations—Fiction. | Palestinian Arabs—Fiction. |
Israelis—Fiction. | Political fiction. lcgft
Classification: LCC PR6063.C335 A65 2020 (print) | LCC PR6063.C335 (ebook) |
DDC 823/.914—dc23
LC record available at https://lccn.loc.gov/2019022848
LC ebook record available at https://lccn.loc.gov/2019022849

International edition ISBN 9780593131451

Printed in the United States of America on acid-free paper

randomhousebooks.com
randomhousebookclub.com

468975

Book design by Simon M. Sullivan

For Sally

AUTHOR'S NOTE

Readers familiar with the political situation in Israel and Palestine will notice that the driving forces in the heart of this book, Bassam Aramin and Rami Elhanan, are real. By "real" I mean that their stories—and those of their daughters, Abir Aramin and Smadar Elhanan—have been well documented in film and print.

The transcripts of both men in the center section of the book are pulled together from a series of interviews in Jerusalem, New York, Jericho and Beit Jala, but elsewhere in this book Bassam and Rami have allowed me to shape and reshape their words and worlds.

Despite these liberties, I hope to remain true to the actual realities of their shared experiences. We live our lives, suggested Rilke, in widening circles that reach out across the entire expanse.

2016

1

The hills of Jerusalem are a bath of fog. Rami moves by memory through a straight stretch, and calculates the camber of an upcoming turn.

Sixty-seven years old, he bends low on the motorbike, his jacket padded, his helmet clipped tight. It is a Japanese bike, 750 cc. An agile machine for a man his age.

Rami pushes the bike hard, even in bad weather.

He takes a sharp right at the gardens where the fog lifts to reveal dark. Corpus separatum. He downshifts and whips past a military tower. The sodium lights appear fuzzy in the morning. A small flock of birds momentarily darkens the orange.

At the bottom of the hill the road dips into another curve, obscured in fog. He taps down to second, lets out the clutch, catches the corner smoothly and moves back up to third. Road Number One stands above the ruins of Qalunya: all history piled here.

He throttles at the end of the ramp, takes the inner lane, passing signs for *The Old City*, for *Giv'at Ram*. The highway is a scattershot of morning headlights.

He leans left and salmons his way out into the faster lane, toward the tunnels, the Separation Barrier, the town of Beit Jala. Two answers for one swerve: Gilo on one side, Bethlehem on the other.

Geography here is everything.

2

THIS ROAD LEADS TO AREA "A"
UNDER THE PALESTINIAN AUTHORITY
THE ENTRANCE FOR ISRAELI
CITIZENS IS FORBIDDEN
DANGEROUS TO YOUR LIVES
AND IS AGAINST THE ISRAELI LAW

3

Five hundred million birds arc the sky over the hills of Beit Jala every year. They move by ancient ancestry: hoopoes, thrushes, flycatchers, warblers, cuckoos, starlings, shrikes, ruffs, northern wheatears, plovers, sunbirds, swifts, sparrows, nightjars, owls, gulls, hawks, eagles, kites, cranes, buzzards, sandpipers, pelicans, flamingos, storks, pied bushchats, griffon vultures, European rollers, Arabian babblers, bee-eaters, turtle-doves, whitethroats, yellow wagtails, blackcaps, red-throated pipits, little bitterns.

It is the world's second busiest migratory superhighway: at least four hundred different species of birds torrent through, riding different levels in the sky. Long vees of honking intent. Sole travelers skimming low over the grass.

Every year a new landscape appears underneath: Israeli settlements, Palestinian apartment blocks, rooftop gardens, barracks, barriers, by-pass roads.

Some of the birds migrate at night to avoid predators, flying in their sidereal patterns, elliptic with speed, devouring their own muscles and intestines in flight. Others travel during the day to take advantage of the thermals rising from below, the warm wind lifting their wings so they can coast.

At times whole flocks block out the sun and daub shadows across Beit Jala: the fields, the steep terraces, the olive groves on the outskirts of town.

Lie down in the vineyard in the Cremisan monastery at any time of day and you can see the birds overhead, traveling in their talkative lanes.

They land on trees, telegraph poles, electricity cables, water towers, even the rim of the Wall, where they are a sometime target for the young stone throwers.

4

The ancient sling was made of a cradle of cowskin, the size of an eye-patch, pierced with small holes and held together with leather thongs.

The slings were designed by shepherds to help scare away predatory animals from their roving flocks.

The pouch was held in the shepherd's left hand, the cords in his right. Considerable practice was needed to operate it with accuracy. After placing a stone in the pad, the slingman pulled the thongs taut. He swung it wide above his head several times until the moment of natural release. The pouch opened and the stone flew. Some shepherds could hit a target the size of a jackal's eye from two hundred paces.

The sling soon made its way into the art of warfare: its capacity to fire up a steep slope and battlement walls made it critical in assaults on fortified cities. Legions of long-range slingmen were employed. They wore full body armor and rode chariots piled with stone. When the territory became impassible—moats, trenches, dry desert gulches, steep embankments, boulders strewn across the roads—they descended and went on foot, ornamental bags slung over their shoulders. The deepest held up to two hundred small stones.

In preparation for battle it was common to paint at least one of the stones. The talisman was placed at the bottom of the bag when the slingman went to war, in the hope he would never reach his final stone.

5

At the edges of battle, children—eight, nine, ten years old—were enlisted to shoot birds from the sky. They waited by wadis, hid in desert bushes, fired stones from fortified walls. They shot turtledoves, quail, songbirds.

Some of the birds were captured still living. They were gathered up and put into wooden cages with their eyes gouged out so that they would be fooled into thinking that it was a permanent nighttime: then they would gorge themselves on grain for days on end.

Fattened to twice their flying size, they were baked in clay ovens, served with bread, olives and spices.

6

Eight days before he died, after a spectacular orgy of food, François Mitterrand, the French president, ordered a final course of ortolan, a tiny yellow-throated songbird no bigger than his thumb. The delicacy represented to him the soul of France.

Mitterrand's staff supervised the capture of the wild birds in a village in the south. The local police were paid off, the hunting was arranged, and the birds were captured, at sunrise, in special finely threaded nets along the edge of the forest. The ortolans were crated and driven in a darkened van to Mitterrand's country house in Latche where he had spent his childhood summers. The sous-chef emerged and carried the cages indoors. The birds were fed for two weeks until they were plump enough to burst, then held by their feet over a vat of pure Armagnac, dipped headfirst and drowned alive.

The head chef then plucked them, salted them, peppered them, and cooked them for seven minutes in their own fat before placing them in a freshly heated white cassole.

When the dish was served, the wood-paneled room—with Mitterrand's family, his wife, his children, his mistress, his friends— fell silent. He sat up in his chair, pushed aside the blankets from his knees, took a sip from a bottle of vintage Château Haut-Marbuzet.

—The only interesting thing is to live, said Mitterrand.

He shrouded his head with a white napkin to inhale the aroma of the birds and, as tradition dictated, to hide the act from the eyes of God. He picked up the songbirds and ate them whole: the succulent flesh, the fat, the bitter entrails, the wings, the tendons, the liver, the kidney, the warm heart, the feet, the tiny headbones crunching in his teeth.

It took him several minutes to finish, his face hidden all the time under the white serviette. His family could hear the sounds of the bones snapping.

Mitterrand dabbed the napkin at his mouth, pushed aside the earthenware cassole, lifted his head, smiled, bid good night and rose to go to bed.

He fasted for the next eight and a half days until he died.

7

In Israel, the birds are tracked by sophisticated radar set up along the migratory routes all over the country—Eilat, Jerusalem, Latrun—with links to military installations and to the air traffic control offices at Ben Gurion airport.

The Ben Gurion offices are high-tech, dark-windowed. Banks of computers, radios, phones. A team of experts, trained in aviation and mathematics, tracks the patterns of flight: the size of the flocks, their pathways, their shape, their velocity, their height, their projected behavior in weather patterns, their possible response to crosswinds, siroccos, storms. Operators create algorithms and send out emergency warnings to the controllers and to the commercial airlines.

Another hotline is dedicated to the Air Force. *Starlings at 1,000 feet north of Gaza Harbor, 31.52583°N, 34.43056°E. Forty-two thousand sandhill cranes roughly 750 feet over southern edge of Red Sea, 20.2802°N, 38.5126°E. Unusual flock movement east of Akko, Coast Guard caution, storm pending. Projected flock, Canada geese, east of Ben Gurion at 0200 hours, exact coordinates TBD. Pair of pharaoh eagle-owls reported in trees near helicopter landing pad B, south Hebron, 31.3200°N, 35.0542°E.*

The ornithologists are busiest in autumn and spring when the large migrations are in full flow: at times their screens look like Rorschach tests. They liaise with bird-watchers on the ground, although a good tracker can intuit the type of bird just by the shape of the flock on the radar and the height at which it is coming in.

In military school, fighter pilots are trained in the intricate patterns of bird migration so they can avoid tailspins in what they call the plague zones. Everything matters: a large puddle near the runway might attract a flock of starlings; an oil patch might slicken the wings of a bird of prey, disorienting it; a forest fire might throw a flock of geese far off course.

In migratory seasons the pilots try not to travel for extended periods at lower than three thousand feet.

8

A swan can be as fatal to the pilot as a rocket-propelled grenade.

9

In the fall of the First Intifada, a pair of birds migrating from Europe to northern Africa were found in the mist nets on the western slopes of Beit Jala. They were tangled together side by side, their feet caught in a single strand, their wings frantic against the filaments, so they appeared at first to be just one oddly shaped bird.

They were found by a fourteen-year-old boy, Tarek Khalil, who thought at first they were too tiny to be migrants: perhaps they were blackcaps. He leaned closer. Their agonized chirping astounded him. He untangled the birds, put them in two cloth pouches and brought them up the hillside to the bird-ringing station to be identified and tagged: the wing length, the tail size, the weight, the sex, the percentage of body fat.

It was the first time Tarek had seen such creatures: green-headed, beautiful, mysterious. He leafed through guidebooks and searched the records. Songbirds, most likely from Spain, or Gibraltar, or the south of France. He wasn't sure how to deal with them. It was his job to put a tiny metal ring around their legs, using pliers and a numbered band, so their migration could be documented before he let them go.

Tarek prepared the rings. The birds were so thin that they weighed no more than a spoonful of spice. The metal bands might, he thought, unbalance them in flight.

He dithered a moment, put the birds back in their cloth bags and brought them to his family home in Beit Sahour. He walked up the steep stone streets, cradling the birds in their bags. Cages were hung in the kitchen. For two days the ortolans were fed and watered by Tarek's two sisters. On the third day, Tarek took the songbirds back out to the hillside to let them go, unbanded, amid the apricot trees.

One of the birds remained in the palm of his hand for a moment before flying away. He rolled it around in his fingers. The talons pinched a callus on his hand. The tiny neck turned against the soft of his palm. It rose, unsure, then flitted away.

Both birds would, he knew, go undocumented. For a keepsake the teenager hung the original aluminum rings—with their sequential numbers—on a thin silver necklace.

Tarek felt the rings bouncing at his throat two months later when he went down to Virgin Mary Street alongside his older brothers to sling stones.

10

The bird-ringing station at the Talitha Kumi school is one of two of its kind in the West Bank: it is part of an environmental center with a natural history museum, a recycling program, a water treatment project, an educational unit, and a botanical garden filled with jasmine, hollyhocks, thistles, Roman nettles and rows of yellow-flowered African rue.

The center looks down on the Wall coiling its way across the landscape. In the distance the ordered terra-cotta roofs of the settlements step across the hilltops, surrounded by electrified fences.

In the valley there are so many new roads and bridges and tunnels and apartments that the birds gravitate toward the small section of hillside where they can rest and feed among the fruit trees and long grasses.

Walking through the ten-acre environmental center, amid the tamarisks and olive trees and sabra cactus and the flowering shrubbery of the terraces, is like walking the rim of a tightening lung.

11

A white blimp can often be seen rising over Jerusalem and floating above the city, disappearing, then rising again, disappearing. Watching from the hills of Beit Jala—a few kilometers away—the unmarked blimp looks like a small cloud, a soft white welt, a botfly.

At times birds perch upon it, hitching a lift, drifting lazily for a mile or two before swooping off again: a nightingale celebrating off the back of an eagle.

The airship, nicknamed Fat Boy Two by its Israeli crew and the radar technicians, usually hovers at about a thousand feet in the air. It is made of kevlar and aluminum. A glass cabin is attached to the bottom of the blimp. The thirteen-man room is equipped with a range of computers and infrared cameras powerful enough to pick out and identify the numbers and colors of every single license plate on the highway, even those passing swiftly along.

12

Rami's license plate is yellow.

13

He glances at the clock on the bike, then at his watch. A moment of confusion. A one-hour difference. Daylight savings time. Easy enough to fix the watch but it will, he knows, penetrate the day in other ways. Every year it is the same: for a few days at least, Israel and Palestine are mismatched an hour.

Nothing to be done about it now. No point in turning home. He could kill some time staying on the highway a little longer. Or scoot around some of the back roads in the valleys. Find himself a little stretch where he can push the bike, instill a little torque in the day.

He clicks back into fourth, watches the red line of the revometer. He shoots past a long truck, then eases into fifth.

14

A rubber bullet, when shot from a metal tube on the end of an M-16, leaves the barrel of the gun at more than one hundred miles per hour.

The bullets are large enough to be seen but too fast to be avoided.

They were tested first in Northern Ireland, where the British called them *knee-knockers:* they were designed to be fired at the ground, then bounce up and hit the legs of rioters.

15

The bullet that killed Abir traveled fifteen meters through the air before it smashed into the back of her head, crushing the bones in her skull like those of a tiny ortolan.

She had gone to the grocery store to buy candy.

16

For two shekels Abir could have bought a bracelet with *He Loves Me, He Loves Me Not* imprinted along its rim. Instead she bought two *iswarit mlabase:* hard pills of pink, orange, yellow, and light blue candy braceleted together on a string.

She slipped the money across the counter into the palm of the shop owner, who fished the bracelets out of a deep glass jar.

As they made their way out towards the school gates, Abir gave the second bracelet to her sister Areen.

17

Every day since Abir was killed, Bassam has walked to the mosque in the hour before sunrise to join the optional pre-dawn prayers.

Forty-eight years old, he moves through the dark with a slight limp, a cigarette cupped in the well of his hand. He is thin, slim, fit. His limp imprints him into the world: otherwise he might slip through almost unnoticed. Still, an agility lurks underneath, a wiry surprise, as if he might burst away from the limp at any moment and leave it abandoned behind him.

He drops his cigarette on the path outside the mosque, scrunches it with his sneaker. In his isolation he smooths his white shirt with his palm, walks up the steps, removes his shoes, enters first with his right foot, kneels at the rear of the hall and bows himself before his limitless God.

He prays for his wife, his five children, the memory of Abir. *Allah, save us from enormities whether open or hidden.* One by one, the prayer beads drop slowly from his fingers to the other side of his hand.

As sunrise claws along the windows, a little splinter of shadow purls along the stone steps. Bassam sweeps the floor with a twig broom and rolls out the mats that stand cylindrical against the east wall.

The smell of charcoal and hemp drifts in from outside. The thrum of awakening traffic, the comfort of the muezzin, the barking of stray dogs.

Bassam works methodically down the length of the hall, covering the entire floor with mats, followed by skullcaps and rosaries for the first of the day's prayers.

18

A town of neither here nor there, Anata appears like an odd urban archipelago—a Palestinian town, in the West Bank, under Israeli occupation, within the Jerusalem governate. It is surrounded almost totally by the Separation Wall.

A few fine homes stand perched on the upper hillsides—white stone, marble columns, tall arches, high windows—but they soon give way to a chaos below.

The descent is steep and sharp. Satellite dishes mushroom the roofs. Pigeons squawk from cages. Laundry flaps on washing lines strung between apartments. Bare-chested boys swerve their bikes between potholes. Downhill they go, among the overflowing dumpsters and the piles of rubbish.

The streets are all traffic without traffic lights. Everywhere is neon. Tire shops, bakeries, cellphone repair kiosks. Men feign nonchalance in the shadows. Clouds of cigarette smoke hover over them. Women hurry underneath their hijabs. Carcasses of lamb hang forlorn on steel hooks outside the butcher shops. Pop music slides out from the loud-speakers. Bits of rubble lie everywhere.

The town shoulders up against the Shu'fat refugee camp. Shu'fat builds itself upwards, apartment block upon apartment block. Nowhere else to go but the sky.

It is easy to get into the camp—just slide through the metal revolving gate at the checkpoint and walk down the road—but it is tougher to get out. To travel to Jerusalem an ID card or a permit is needed. To get to the rest of the West Bank—which, like Bassam, you must do if you own a green license plate—only a single potholed road allows escape.

19

The rim of a tightening lung.

20

Think of it like this: you are in Anata, in the rear of a taxi, cradling a young girl in your arms. She has just been rubber-bulleted in the back of the head. You are on your way to the hospital.

The taxi is stuck in traffic. The road through the checkpoint to Jerusalem is closed. At best you will be detained if you try to pass through illegally. At worst both you and the driver will be shot while carrying the shot child.

You glance down. The child is still breathing. The driver puts his hand to the car horn. The car behind blares its horn. The car in front joins in. The noise doubles and redoubles. You look out the window. Your car nudges past a mound of trash. Plastic bags whip in the wind. You go nowhere. The heat bears down. A bead of sweat drops from your chin onto the plastic seat.

The driver blares his horn again. The sky is blue with torn ribbons of cloud. When the car moves, its front wheel sinks into yet another pothole. The clouds, you think, are the fastest thing around. Then there is movement: two helicopters blading the blue.

A part of you wants to get out and carry the smashed-up child in your arms, but you have to keep her head cradled and try not to move while nothing else on the ground moves either.

21

The Biblical Jeremiah—known also as the Weeping Prophet, chosen by God to warn of impending disaster—is said to have been born in ancient Anata. His image can be found on the ceiling of the Sistine Chapel in Rome, painted by Michelangelo in the early sixteenth century.

In the painting, which appears to the side of the high altar, near the front of the chapel, Jeremiah sits, bearded and brooding, in long salmon-colored robes, his finger extended across his mouth, his eyes cast downward.

22

To this day, Bassam is haunted by his daughter's candy bracelet. In the hospital he was met by the taxi driver and the shopkeeper who had traveled in the back with Abir. Abir's shoe had been slipped back on her foot, but the candy bracelet had disappeared: it was not in her hand, not on her wrist, not in her pockets.

In the operating room, Bassam kissed her forehead. Abir was still breathing. The equipment beeped weakly. It was the sort of hospital that needed its own hospital. The doctors were doing everything they could but they had little working equipment.

It was decided to transfer her to Hadassah in Jerusalem. A twenty-minute journey, beyond the Wall.

Two hours later—still stalled in an ambulance near the checkpoint—Bassam reached into her schoolbag and found the candy beneath her math book.

23

The shot came from the back of a moving jeep. Out a metal flap in the back door, four inches by four.

24

The Commander of the Border Police wrote in his report that rocks were being pelted from a nearby graveyard. His men were, he said, in mortal danger.

25

Abir was ten years old.

26

She was coming out of the tin-roofed grocery store with Areen and two friends. It was just after nine in the morning. The winter sun shone slant. School was in recess for an hour. They were just about to return for a math test, multiplication tables.

Twelve times eight, ninety-six. Twelve times nine, one hundred and eight.

The street was cut open with sunlight. The girls passed the concrete bollards set up across the roadway, made their way past the bus stop. Their shadows stretched across the roadblock.

Twelve times twelve, one hundred and forty-four.

27

28

When the armored jeep turned the corner, the girls began to run.

29

The bullet was metal at the core, but tipped with a special vulcanized rubber. When it hit Abir's skull, the rubber deformed slightly, but then bounced back to its original shape without any evident damage to the bullet itself.

30

The soldiers called the bullets Lazarus pills: when possible, they could be picked up and used again.

31

In the year after the millennium, a rogue artist in Beit Jala hung hollowed-out rubber bullets as tiny improvised bird-feeders in the trees: the bullets were perforated with small incisions, filled with seed and hung with wire from the branches.

Dangling in midair, the bullets attracted a number of small birds: yellow wagtails, sparrows, red-throated pipits.

32

The border guard who fired the shot was eighteen years old.

33

In the 1980s, during operations in Lebanon, Israeli soldiers were sometimes asked to pose for official photographs with their platoon members before they went out on their missions.

As they lined up the soldiers were told to stand far enough apart that there would be ample space between them in the photo.

The photographers made no other demand. The soldiers could smile, they could frown, they could turn directly into the camera, or they could turn their gaze away. No matter—the only thing they had to do was to give each other room, a handsbreadth of space so their shoulders wouldn't touch, that was all.

Some of them thought it was a ritual, others figured it was a military directive, others considered it to be a matter of decorum and humility.

The soldiers gathered in groups by tanks, in tents, along rows of bunk beds, in armories, bandstands, canteens, by sheets of aluminum siding, against the green hills of Lebanon. They adjusted an array of berets: olive-drab, pitch-black, pigeon-grey.

The photos were a theater of expression: fear, bravado, anxiety, unease, bluster. Confusion, too, at the request to stand a little farther apart. After the photos were taken, the soldiers went out on their missions.

In some cases it was days later, in others weeks, in others months, before the reason became apparent: the space between the soldiers was needed in case the photograph had to be printed in the newspapers, or shown on TV, with the dead identified by a crisp red ring drawn around their faces.

34

Ringing a bird involves a simple twist of the metal with a banding pliers around the leg.

35

The newspaper editors and TV producers were eager to avoid the optics of intersecting lines. Sometimes there were five or six rings in one single photograph.

36

To free a bird from a hanging mist net, the first thing an ornithologist must do is unknot the thin strip of nylon from between the bird's toes and then—depending on the degree of struggle and the length of time it has spent suspended in the net—to calmly untangle the feet, the knees, the belly, the armpit and finally the bird's head, all the time holding the wings against its hammering heart, making sure that it doesn't try to tear open your fingers with its beak or talons.

It is akin to unlooping a tight knot in a silver necklace that, as you open it, wants to spread itself and thrash alive in your hands.

Often the ornithologist will slip a pen or pencil beneath the talons to give the bird a grip for its feet. For larger birds they use branches or shorn-off broom handles.

Some birds, after tagging, have been known to fly off with pieces of broom still held in their talons.

37

The prototypes for rubber bullets were discovered in the 1880s when small pieces of splintered broom handle were fired by the Singapore police at rioters in the streets.

38

Some Israeli soldiers in Lebanon were killed by French-made Milan anti-tank missiles, many thousands of which had been sold by François Mitterrand's government first to Syria, then on the black market to Hizbollah fighters.

Several others were killed by fire from Soviet T-55 tanks, machines that had been considered cumbersome and unwieldy until it was suggested by one general that the tanks should be buried in the ground and used like pillboxes. Only the barrel of the tank's gun stuck out. They were known to the fighters as coffin tanks. Camouflaged, they were difficult to locate from the air, but when discovered these buried targets were easily blown to smithereens.

Six soldiers were killed by fighters who—in an operation known as the Night of the Gliders—floated across the Lebanese border on homemade hang gliders powered by lawn-mower engines and attacked an Israeli camp. They were armed with Russian-made AK-47s as well as hand grenades manufactured in the Czech Republic, not far from Theresienstadt, the German-run concentration camp.

39

Folklore has it that, to this day, migratory birds avoid flying over the fields of Theresienstadt.

40

On the Night of the Gliders, in 1987, one of the Israeli guards, Irina Cantor, glanced up at the movement of a faint light in the dark sky. Cantor, who had emigrated from Australia two years before, had just begun her military service.

She was sure that the hang glider was something distant or spectral, a trick of vision against the scraggly cloud.

Afterwards, at the military tribunal, Cantor testified that when the shooting began the sight of the glider confused her so much that she thought that a large bird—something huge and prehistoric—had flapped out of the darkness.

41

Imagine the swan sudden-sucked into the engine of the fighter plane. *Mayday, mayday, mayday.* The brisk crunch of bone and long wing. A whirl of machinery. *Mayday mayday mayday.* The stutter of metal, the crush of feather, the rip of ligament, the chew of bones. Fragments of beak being spat out from the engine. *Mayday mayday mayday.*

42

Imagine, then, the pilot ejecting from the plane, still strapped to his seat, dreideling through the air with a force not unlike that of a rubber bullet.

43

The term *mayday*—coined in England in 1923, but derived from the French, *venez m'aider,* come to my aid—is always repeated three times, *mayday, mayday, mayday.* The repetition is vital: if said only once it could possibly be misinterpreted, but said three times in a row, it cannot be mistaken.

44

The M-16 used to shoot Abir was manufactured near the town of Samaria, North Carolina. Samaria being the name of so many villages and towns around the world: eight in Colombia, two in Mexico, one each in Panama, Nicaragua, Greece, Papua New Guinea, Solomon Islands, Venezuela, Australia and Angola.

Samaria also being home of the ancient capital of the Kingdom of Israel.

45

A metal tube is locked onto the muzzle brake of an M-16 service rifle in order to shoot rubber bullets. The tube can contain up to eight bullets. They are powered by blank rounds fired from the gun's magazine. Inside the attachment are a number of grooves which help the bullets maintain proper trajectory. The grooves are curved like the stripes on a candy cane so that the bullet emerges in a perfect spiral.

46

Seelonce mayday, or mayday silence, is maintained on the radio channel until the distress signal is over. To end the alert the caller says, at least one time, *Seelonce feenee,* an English-accented corruption of *silence fini.*

47

François Mitterrand was buried in Jarnac on the banks of the river he played in as a child, a swiftly moving bolt of brackish green criss-crossed with shadows cast by the hanging trees.

Shortly before he passed away, his eyes flickered and he said to his doctor: I am eaten up inside.

48

Abir wore her school uniform—a white blouse, a navy cardigan, a blue skirt with ankle-length pants underneath, white socks, dark blue patent shoes, slightly scuffed. Apart from the candy bracelet, her brown leather schoolbag contained two exercise books and three children's books, all Arabic, although Bassam had contemplated teaching her some words of Hebrew, which he had learned as a teenager, many years before, in prison in Hebron, locked away for seven years.

49

His fellow prisoners liked his quiet manner. There was something mysterious about the seventeen-year-old with a limp, his dark skin, his wiry strength, his silence. He was always the first to step up in the canteen when the prison guards came. The limp gave him an edge. The first one or two baton strikes seemed almost reluctant. Often he was the last prisoner standing: the most brutal beatings were yet to come.

Bassam spent weeks upon weeks in the infirmary. The doctors and nurses were worse than the prison guards. They reeked of frustration. They punched him, jabbed him, shaved his beard, denied him medicine, put his water out of reach.

The Druze orderlies were fiercest of all: they understood the Arab consciousness of the naked body, how aware they were, how close it could come to shame. They took away Bassam's clothes, his sheets, tied his arms back so he couldn't cover himself.

He lay there. The ceiling tiles were perforated. He made mental patterns from the tiny holes. Playing cards, diamonds, spades. A form of solitaire. The nurses were unsettled by his quiet manner. They expected shouts, complaints, curses, allegations. The longer his silence, the worse the extra beatings. He could see the weaker nurses begin to twitch with worry. In the end, he thought, he would occupy their brains.

When Bassam finally spoke, his voice rattled the medics: there was something calm about it. He learned the art of the mysterious smile, but he could drop it in an instant, turn it into a stare.

He listened to the doctors talking in the corridor: more and more he understood what they were saying in Hebrew. He decided, even then, that he would one day become fluent.

Word went around that he had become commander of the prison Fatah unit. He grew his beard out. The beatings became more regular.

He turned nineteen years old with two missing teeth, several fractured bones and an empty drip bag in each arm. There were cameras above his prison hospital bed: he angled himself towards the wall so that he could not be seen while he wept himself to sleep.

The days hardened like loaves: he ate them without appetite.

50

After a year in lockup Bassam established a schedule for classes. English. Hebrew. Arab History. Israeli Law. The Fall of the Ottoman Empire. The History of the Zionist Movement. Pre-Islamic Poetry. The Geography of the Middle East. Life in Palestine under the British Mandate.

Know your enemy, know yourself.

51

In Beersheba prison the married prisoners used cardboard blowguns to send love notes to their wives and children waiting outside the prison gates.

As many as twenty toilet-roll cylinders were taped and glued together to make blowguns that could measure up to five feet. Prisoners wrote messages on small scraps of paper, folded them, then extended the cardboard guns as far as possible out the cell windows.

The men filled their lungs and blew the notes out the window.

The prisoners learned to make curves in the cardboard, soft angles for reaching around corners to catch favorable winds. Sometimes it took two or three men to handle a blowgun so the paper pipe would not sag or bend.

Most of the time the messages ended up scattered in the prison yard or caught underneath the barbed wire, but every now and then one would catch a strong current and make it all the way to the parking lot where the wives waited. *Tell Raja to be strong. That day we met was the best of my life. Give the Mecca jigsaw to Ahmed. I cannot wait to leave this place, it rots my heart.*

Bassam watched the women from his cell window. When the notes cleared the prison wall, they hurried over, unfolded the paper and shared them with one another. Once in a while he would see the women dance.

52

In the library—under the Open University system—Bassam found a Hebrew version of the *Mu'allaqat,* the series of sixth-century Arabian poems, translated in a kibbutz by an Israeli literary group just after the Yom Kippur War. It came as a surprise to him. He knew the words by heart in Arabic and so he could compare the languages, learn the Hebrew. He lay on his bare bed and read the poems aloud, then copied them. He brought the poems to one of the prison guards, Hertzl Shaul, a part-time guard and a student of mathematics.

They were still slightly reluctant with one another, the prisoner and the guard, but in recent months had come to think of themselves as acquaintances: Hertzl had saved Bassam from a canteen beating one afternoon.

Bassam had written the words of the poems on the labels from water bottles. Hertzl stuffed the labels inside his shirt, took the poems home. He touched the mezuzah on his door: hidden prayers.

Later in the evening, when his wife Sarah had gone to bed, Hertzl took out the label and began reading.

53

In the hospital where Abir lay dying, Hertzl—who had quickly removed his kippah as he walked down the corridor—remembered a line from those prison days: *Is there any hope that this desolation can bring us solace?* He stood by Abir's bed, his head bowed, noticing the pattern of her labored breathing. A mist lay on the inside of her oxygen mask. Her head was swathed in bandages.

Bassam came and stood beside him, their shoulders not quite touching. Neither man said anything. Many years had gone between them since Bassam's release from prison.

Bassam had co-founded Combatants for Peace two years previously. Hertzl had come to one of the meetings. He was amazed when Bassam began speaking of the peace he had learned in prison, the heft of it, *salaam, shalom,* its confounding nature, its presence even in its apparent absence.

Now Bassam's daughter was dying in front of their eyes. The red lights shone and the hospital equipment beeped.

Hertzl reached across and held his friend's shoulder, nodded to the dozens of others who had gathered around the bedside, including Rami, his wife Nurit, and their oldest son, Elik.

Hertzl slipped the kippah back on his head as he left the hospital. He made his way to the Hebrew University to teach his class in freshman mathematics.

54

Later Hertzl wrote: If you divide death by life, you will find a circle.

55

When a bird has been ringed, the serial number is entered into a global database. The birds, then, are identified with the country where they were tagged: Norway, Poland, Iceland, Egypt, Germany, Jordan, Chad, Yemen, Slovakia. As if they have been ascribed a homeland.

Ornithologists in Israel and Palestine sometimes find themselves in competition if a rare bird, a diederik cuckoo, say, or a windblown stone curlew, is spotted in the seam-zoned sky between both.

Sometimes whistles are used to coax the bird down into a mist net so it can be taken and tagged.

For the ornithologist, it is always a matter of disappointment if the bird has already been ringed elsewhere.

56

When out cataloguing birds in the field, Tarek could feel the ortolan tags moving on the necklace at his throat.

57

Songbirds produce an elaborate call: a meld of territorial protection and courtship.

58

The original meetings of Combatants for Peace took place amid the pine trees of the Everest Hotel in Beit Jala, in Area B, just across the hill from the bird-ringing station.

The two sides met in the hilltop restaurant. Nervously they shook hands and greeted one another in English.

The room had two large sofas, a long table and eight red chairs. Nobody took the sofas at first. They sat at opposite ends of the table. The language that they might use for each other was already fraught: Muslim, Arab, Christian, Jew, soldier, terrorist, fighter, martyr, occupier, occupied.

Eleven of them altogether: four Palestinians, seven Israelis. The Israelis took the batteries out of their phones, placed them on the table. It was safer that way. You never know who's listening, they said. The Palestinians glanced at each other and did the same.

The initial talk was about the weather. Then the journey past the checkpoints. The roads they had taken, the turns, the roundabouts, the red signs. They had different names for the areas they had traveled through, varying pronunciations of streets. The Israelis said they were surprised how easy it had been to get there: they had driven only four miles. The Palestinians replied that they were not to worry, it would be just as simple to get back. An uneasy laughter went around the table.

The talk returned to the weather once more: the humidity, the heat, the strangely clear sky.

The Palestinians drank coffee, the Israelis carbonated water. All the Palestinians smoked. Only two of the Israelis did. Plates of olives arrived. Cheese. Stuffed grape leaves. The specialty of the restaurant was pigeon: nobody ordered it.

An hour slid by. The Israelis leaned into the table. One of them had, he said, been a pilot. Another, a paratrooper. One had spent much of his service as a commander at the Qalandia checkpoint. They had been in the forces, yes, but they had begun to speak out: against the Occupation, humiliation, murder, torture. Bassam sat stunned. He had never heard an Israeli mention such words before. He was certain they were on an operation. Intelligence, surveillance, an undercover ploy. What confused him was that one of them, Yehuda, looked like a settler. Stout and spectacled, with a long beard. Even his hair wore the mark of a kippah. Yehuda had been an officer in Hebron. He had, he said, begun to rethink it all, the conscription, the operations, all the talk of a moral army. Bassam leaned back in his chair and scowled. Why would they send such a glaring ruse? What kind of mockery was this? Perhaps, he thought, it was a form of double-think, triple-think: the Israelis were known for it, their mesmerizing chess, their theater, intricate and ruthless.

The sun went down over the steep hills. One of the Israelis tried to pay, but Bassam put his hand on the man's elbow, and took the bill.

—Palestinian hospitality, he said.

—No, no, please, let me.

—This is *my* home.

The Israeli nodded, bowed his head, blanched. The two groups shook hands, bid each other goodbye. Bassam was sure they would never see each other again.

That evening he put their names in a search engine. Wishnitzer.

Alon. Shaul. They had used some of the same words in blogs he found online: *inhumane, torture, regret, Occupation*. He closed out the files, reloaded his search engine, just in case: perhaps his computer had been interfered with somehow. He would put nothing past them. He searched again. The words were still there. He put a message through to Wishnitzer that he was ready to meet with them again.

A few weeks later they ate dinner at the Everest Hotel. Two of the Israelis ordered pigeon. A toast was made. Bassam raised his water glass.

It slowly dawned on Bassam that the only thing they had in common was that both sides had once wanted to kill people they did not know.

When he said this, a ripple of assent went around the table: a slow nodding of heads, a further loosening. A shiver went amongst them. My wife Salwa, my daughter Abir, my son Muhammad. Then, from across the table: My daughter Rachel, my grandfather Chaim, my uncle Josef.

It was an idea so simple that Bassam wondered how he had ignored it for so long: they too had families, histories, shadows.

After two hours they extended hands to shake and promised they would try to meet a third time. The light slanted through the tall trees. Some of the Israelis were still worried about getting home: what if they strayed by mistake into Area A, what would happen?

—Don't worry, said Bassam, drive behind me awhile, I'll show you, just follow me.

The Israelis laughed nervously.

—I'm serious. If there's any trouble I'll take care of it. I'll tap my brakes three times. I go right, you go left.

They sat for another half hour over coffee and discussed what names they might use if they really were to create an organization together. It was a difficult thing to find a good name. Something catchy, provocative, yet neutral too. Something with meaning but not offensive. Combatants for Peace. That might work. It held contradiction.

To be in combat. To struggle to know.

59

On the wall of the restaurant were photographs of frigatebirds scissoring over the sea.

60

Area A: administered by the Palestinian Authority, open to Palestinians, forbidden, under Israeli law, to Israeli citizens. Area B: administered by the Palestinian Authority, with shared security control with Israel, open to Israelis and Palestinians. Area C: an area comprising Israeli settlers and mostly rural Palestinians, administered by Israel and containing all the West Bank settlements.

61

Among the Israeli contingent in the Everest Hotel was Rami's twenty-seven-year-old son, Elik Elhanan, who had served in an elite reconnaissance unit in the army.

At the second meeting Elik talked about his late sister Smadar, killed in a suicide bombing in Jerusalem, but the story did not register fully for Bassam until many months later.

Bassam himself was just a few years out of prison. Abir was still alive. Bassam had not met Rami. Rami was a member of the Parents Circle, but Bassam was not yet.

All of that confusion was still to happen.

62

(Area A being comprised of the main Palestinian cities and villages, hemmed in, patchworked, and secured by dozens of Israeli checkpoints, patrolled by Palestinian security forces but open, at any time, to the Israeli army.)

(Area B, under Palestinian civil administration, under Israeli security control with cooperation from the Palestinian Authority police, so that the Palestinian security forces operate only with Israeli permission.)

(Area C, the largest of the areas, containing most of the West Bank's natural resources, controlled by Israel, with the Palestinian Authority responsible for providing education and medical services to Palestinians only, with Israel providing exclusively for the security and administration of the settler population in over one hundred illegal settlements, with ninety-nine percent of the area being heavily restricted or off-limits for construction or development to Palestinian residents, it being almost impossible to secure a permit for any building or water project.)

(Also, Area H1 and H2 in the West Bank city of Hebron, eighty percent of the city administered by the Palestinian Authority and twenty percent controlled by Israel, including areas open only to Israelis and those with international passports, known as sterile streets.)

(Also, Zone E1, twelve square kilometers of disputed/occupied undeveloped land outside annexed East Jerusalem, home to Bedouin tribes and bounded by Israeli settlements, falling within Area C.)

(Also, the Seam Zone, the land between the Green Line and the Separation Barrier, in the West Bank, also known as the closed zone, also known as No-man's-land, lying entirely in Area C, populated mostly by Israelis living in settlements, accessible to Palestinians by permit only.)

63

Beyond their immediate calls of distress, it is not known exactly how, or even if, different species of birds communicate with one another.

64

Rami likes the feeling of entering the tunnel while it is still dark outside. A bit of comfort. It's different than entering during daytime when he feels subsumed by the darkness. This early in the morning it is almost the opposite: he enters the light, fluorescent as it is.

The motorbike purrs along in the fast lane. He shifts up into fifth gear, leans into the machine a little, his knees touching the petrol tank. In his helmet, the sound of the stereo. The Hollies. The Beach Boys. The Yardbirds. The Kinks.

It is a cold morning with a late October chill. He reaches down and zips the vent in his riding pants, tightens his fingers in his gloves. Nothing in his side-view mirrors, he slides across into the slower lane, keeping the revometer steady.

A kilometer long, the tunnel was blasted out from the mountain under the supervision of French engineers. A number of New York–based sandhogs were brought across to supervise the work.

The tunnel runs under the town of Beit Jala, dovetailing in parts with the Way of the Patriarchs, the ancient Biblical route.

Rami emerges beneath the concrete blast walls into the still-dark, and after a few moments passes the large red sign—in Hebrew, Arabic, English—without even thinking about it.

THE ENTRANCE FOR ISRAELI CITIZENS IS FORBIDDEN

The engine scoffs slightly as he turns the handle on the throttle. He will circle around and take the back road this morning, past the yellow gates and beyond. No nerves, no fear. He is well used to it: he makes the trip to Beit Jala at least twice a week.

All morning he has driven fast, but he likes the moments when things slow down to a near-halt and he can feel the space around him, everything held in suspension like in a photograph where he is the only moving thing.

It never ceases to astound him what a difference a border can make: the arbitrary line, drawn here, drawn there, redrawn further along.

No soldiers in sight, no border guards, nothing.

The road rises in a steep ascent. He knows the area well, the barbed-wire fence, the rusting cars, the dusty windshields, the low houses, the hanging flowerpots of fuchsias, the gardens, the wind chimes made out of tear gas canisters, the black water tanks on the roofs of apartment blocks.

Once, long ago, these roads were so much easier to travel. Even in the bad times. No bypasses, no permits, no walls, no unapproved paths, no sudden barricades. You came and you went. Or you didn't. Now it is a tangle of asphalt, concrete, light pole. Walls. Roadblocks. Barricades. Gates. Strobe lights. Motion activation. Electronic locks.

He is not surprised by the three dark-haired Palestinian boys who seem to appear straight out of the ground. The first hops a section of broken concrete and puts one foot on a roadside tire as if to trampoline off it. The boy is lean and jaunty. The others are older, slower, wary, keeping to the side of the road. Fifty yards, forty yards, twenty, ten, until Rami is almost level with the lead boy. He lets off the throttle and edges the bike closer, beeps the horn in tandem with the slap of sandals.

Dark feet, white soles. A long scar on the back of his calf. A blue-and-white striped shirt. Smadar's age. Younger even.

The boy's legs piston. His chest strains against the small swoosh on his T-shirt. The muscles in his neck tighten. The boy grins, an expanse of white teeth. The road rises further. Just beneath a grey light pole— the yellow bulb still shining in the morning—the boy lets out a high yell and then stops abruptly, throws his arms in the air, turns, vaults over a concrete barricade.

In the rearview mirrors, the other two boys meld into the roadside ruin.

Rami can't quite tell if it was the exertion of the run, the yellow license plate, or the sight of the bumper sticker on the front left of the bike—זה לא ייגמר עד שנדבר—that makes the boy stop so quickly.

65

זה לא ייגמר עד שנדבר

It will not be over until we talk.

66

He clicks back to third to accommodate the rising road.

Further up the hill is the bird-ringing station at Talitha Kumi, the steep streets, the stone walls, the center of town, the Christian churches, the careful iconography, the tin roofs, the high limestone houses looking out over the lush valley, the hospital, the monastery, the small countries of light and dark rushing across the vineyard, all the atoms of the approaching day stretching out in front of him.

Today, like most days, just another day: a meeting with an international group—seven or eight of them, he has heard—in the Cremisan monastery.

He turns the corner at the top of Manger Street.

67

In the distance, over Jerusalem, the blimp rises.

68

He followed the blimp one Sunday, a year ago, for a couple of hours, surveilling it, surveilling him, wondering if he could find a pattern to its movement.

He went corner to corner, street sign to street sign, out into the countryside, then parked his bike at the overlook at Mount Scopus, sat on the low stone wall, shaded his eyes and stared upwards, watching the blimp drift in the blue. He had heard from a friend that it was a weather machine, gauging moisture levels and checking air quality. There was always a backup for the truth. And, in truth, how many sensors? How many cameras? How many eyes in the sky looking down?

Rami often felt that there were nine or ten Israelis inside him, fighting. The conflicted one. The shamed one. The enamored one. The bereaved one. The one who marveled at the blimp's invention. The one who knew the blimp was watching. The one watching back. The one who wanted to be watched. The anarchist. The protester. The one sick and tired of all the seeing.

It made him dizzy to carry such complications, to be so many people all at once. What to say to his boys when they went off to military service? What to say to Nurit when she showed him the textbooks? What to say to Bassam when he got stopped at the checkpoints? What to feel every time he opened a newspaper? What to think when the sirens sounded on Memorial Day? What to wonder when he passed a man in a kaffiyeh? What to feel when his sons had to board a bus? What to think when a taxi driver had an accent? What to worry about when the news clicked on? What fresh atrocity lay on the horizon? What sort of retribution was coming down the line? What to say to Smadari? What is it like being dead, Princess? Can you tell me? Would I like it?

Below him, on the slope, young boys lazed on the hillside on the backs of thin Arabian horses. The boys wore immaculate white jeans. Their horses muscled beneath them. Rami wished he could somehow reach out to them, approach them, say a word. But they knew already who he was from his license plate, *what* he was, just from the way he carried himself. They would know from his accent too, even if he spoke to them in Arabic. An older man on a motorbike. His pale white skin. His open face. The hidden fear. I should go and tell them. I should stride across and look them directly in the eye. Her name was Smadar. Grape of the vine. A swimmer. A dancer too. She was this tall. She had just cut her hair. Her teeth were slightly crooked. It was the start of the school year. She was out shopping for books. I was driving to the airport when I got the news. She was missing. We knew. My wife and I. We knew. We went from hospital to police station, back again. You cannot imagine what that is like. One door after another. Then the morgue. The smell of antiseptic. It was unspeakable. They slid her out on a metal tray. A cold metal tray. She lay there. Your age. No more. No less. Let's be honest here, guys. You would have been delighted by the news. You would have celebrated. Cheered. And I would once have cheered for yours too. And your father's. And your father's father.

Listen to me. I admit it. No denial. Once, long ago. What do you think of that? What sort of world are we living in? Look up. It's watching us, all of us. Look. Look. Up there.

After a while the blimp began to press down further upon him, like a light hand upon his chest, the pressure growing firmer, until all Rami wanted to do was find a place where he could not be seen. It was so often like this. The desire to vanish. To have all of it gone in a single smooth motion. To wipe it all clean. Tabula rasa. Not my war. Not my Israel.

Show me, then. Convince me. Roll back the rock. Return Smadar. All of her. Gift her back to me, all sewn up and pretty and dark-eyed again. That's all I ask. Is that too much? No more whining from me, no more weeping, no more complaints. A heavenly stitch, that's all I ask. And bring back Abir too, for Bassam, for me, for Salwa, for Areen, for Hiba, for Nurit, for all of us. And while you're at it bring back Sivan and Ahuva and Dalia and Yamina and Lilly and Yael and Shulamit and Khalila and Sabah and Zahava and Rivka and Yasmine and Sarah and Inaam and Ayala and Sharon and Talia and Rashida and Rachel and Nina and Mariam and Tamara and Zuhal and Riva and every other one under this hot murdering sun. Is that too much to ask for? Is it?

He felt the bike galloping underneath him as he drove back to his house and sat in his office, closed the curtains, rearranged the photographs on his desk.

69

Smadar. From the Song of Solomon. The grapevine. The opening of the flower.

70

Abir. From the ancient Arabic. The perfume. The fragrance of the flower.

71

He has only ever been stopped once on his motorbike. He had heard that the back road from the West Bank was closed, but it was the easiest and quickest way home. The rain hammered down in slanting sheets. He took the chance. What was the worst that could happen: to be stopped, to be questioned, to be turned away?

He had, he knew—even at his age—an impish grin, a chubby face, a soft pale gaze. He sat low and throttled the engine. The bike sprayed up droplets behind him.

A sudden spotlight funneled a shot of fear down his spine. He throttled back, sat up on the bike. His visor was blurry with raindrops. The spotlight enveloped him. He braked in the pool of brightness. The back wheel skidded slightly in the oily rain.

A shout insinuated itself into the night. The guard was trembling as he ran through the downpour. The light was scattershot with silver spears of rain. The guard pointed his gun at Rami's helmet. Rami raised his hands slowly, opened the visor, greeted him in Hebrew, *Shalom aleichem, shalom,* in his thickest accent, showed him his Israeli identity card, said he lived in Jerusalem, he had to get home.

—The road's closed, sir.

—What do you want me to do, go back *there*?

A raindrop fell from the barrel of the soldier's rifle: Go back, yes, sir, go back, right now, this road is off-limits.

A tiredness had crawled into Rami's bones. He wanted to be home with Nurit, in his comfortable chair, a blanket over his knees, the simple life, the ordinary mundanities, the private pain, not this forsaken rain, this roadblock, this cold, this shaking gun.

He lifted the visor further: I was lost, I got lost, and you want me to go back there, are you mad? Look at my I.D. I'm Jewish. I got lost. Lost, man. Why in the world would you want me to go back?

The boy's gun swung back and forth wildly.

—Go back, sir.

—Are you fucking crazy? You think I have a death wish? I got lost, I took the wrong road, that's all.

—Sir. I'm telling you it's closed.

—Tell me this—

—What?

—What Jew in their right mind would go to the West Bank in the first place?

The boy's face puzzled. Rami tightened the throttle, gave the engine some throat.

—Go ahead, habibi, shoot me if you have to, but I'm going home.

He watched a fault line develop further on the boy's brow, a little earthquake of confusion as Rami closed the visor, turned on his hazards and drove on, his whole body conspired into the bike, all the time thinking of the gun aimed at him, a bullet slamming into the small of his back.

72

When, the next day, in the office of the Parents Circle, he began to tell Bassam the checkpoint story, he stopped short and remembered the shiny blue shoe sailing through the air and the bullet ripping into the back of Abir's skull. He had no desire to tell last night's story anymore.

73

The shopkeeper was named Niesha the Ancient, even though she was just thirty-four years old. She heard the pops. One, two, three, four. A screech of tires. For a moment there was silence. Her hands remained on the long wooden counter. Then the shouting began: the high pitch of schoolchildren, girls mostly, an unusual sign: the girls were usually quiet. Niesha reached for her keys from the cash register.

Outside, a commotion. A child on the pavement. A blue skirt. A white cotton collar blouse. A discarded shoe. Niesha dropped to her knees. She knew the child's name. She leaned down to check the pulse.

—Wake up, Abir, wake up.

Screams rang out. A crowd huddled over the child. She was unconscious. Men and women keyed their telephones for a signal.

Word went around that traffic had been blocked by the soldiers at the far end of the road. Nothing was being allowed through: no ambulances, no police, no paramedics.

—Wake up, wake up.

Minutes passed. A young teacher crossed the roundabout, wailing. A battered taxi pulled up. The young driver waved his arms. Kids streamed from the school gates.

Niesha helped pick Abir from the ground and bundle her into the back seat of the taxi. She wedged herself into the well between the front and back seats to keep the child from rolling off. The driver glanced over his shoulder and the taxi lurched. Someone had thrown the lost shoe into the back of the car. Niesha slipped it on Abir's foot. She felt the warmth of the toes. She knew instantly that she would never forget the surprising warmth of the flesh.

The taxi raced through the heart of the marketplace. Word had already jumped around Anata and Shu'fat. Calls went out from the mosques, the balconies, the side streets. Kids ran from the alleyways, streamed down towards the school. The driver braked only for the speed bumps. He hit traffic on the far side of the market. He laid his hand on the car horn. The cars around them joined in the hellish symphony.

Niesha lay on the floor beneath Abir, reaching up, keeping the child's head still. Abir's eyes fluttered. She made no sounds. Her pulse was slow and irregular. Niesha touched the child's toes once more. They had grown colder.

The windows of the taxi were down. Loudspeakers outside. Flags unfurling. The prospect of riot. The car jolted forward. The driver invoked the name of Allah. The tumult rang in Niesha's ears.

The hospital building was low-slung and dingy. A team waited on the steps. Niesha took her hand from Abir's head and opened the rear door before the taxi had even stopped. Shouts went up for a gurney. The front steps of the hospital were mayhem.

Niesha watched the gurney disappear in a swamp of white coats. These were the days of small shrouds: she had seen so many of them carried along the streets.

She suddenly recalled that she had forgotten to lock the door of her shop. She put her forearm to her eyes and wept.

74

The cameras in the blimp remotely swiveled and the lenses flared. Already helicopters were circling over Anata.

75

Down below, the shebab threw stones. They landed on rooftops, bounced against light poles, clattered against water tanks.

76

On the day Smadar was killed, the television cameras were there even before the ZAKA paramedics.

Rami saw part of the footage years later in a documentary: the outdoor restaurant, the afternoon light, the milling bodies, the overturned chairs, the table legs, the shattered chandeliers, the splattered tablecloths, the severed torso of one of the bombers like a Greek statue-piece in the middle of the street.

Even listening with his eyes closed was unbearable: the rush of footsteps, the sirens.

After the screening, he realized that he had clasped his hands so tightly together that his fingernails had drawn blood.

What he wanted the filmmakers to do was to somehow crawl inside time and rewind it, to upend chronology, reverse it and channel it in an entirely different direction—like a Borges story—so that the light was brighter, and the chairs were righted, and the street was ordered, the café was intact, and Smadar was suddenly walking along again, her hair short, her nose pierced, arm in arm with her schoolgirl friends, sauntering past the café, sharing her Walkman, the smell of coffee sharp in her nostrils, caught in the banality of not caring what happens next.

77

The sky was a radiant blue. The cobblestone street was crowded with September shoppers. Music was being piped from a raffia-fronted loudspeaker. The blasts ruptured the sound system. The silence afterwards was uncanny, a stunned interval, until the street erupted in screams.

78

In Aramaic, *Talitha Kumi* means: Rise up, little girl, rise up.

79

The bombers were dressed as women, their explosive belts strapped around their stomachs. They had shaved closely and wore headscarves to hide their faces.

They had all come originally from the village of Assira al-Shamaliya in the West Bank. It was, for two of them, the first time they had ever been in Jerusalem.

80

Jorge Luis Borges, when walking with guides through Jerusalem in the early 1970s, said he had never seen a city of such clean searing light. He tapped his wooden cane on the cobbles and the sides of the buildings to figure out how old the stones might be.

The stones, he said, were pink as flesh.

He liked walking in the Palestinian neighborhoods, around the souks where as a blind storyteller he was treated with particular reverence. There had always been a tradition of the blind among Arabs. The imam in the marketplace. Abdullah ibn Umm Maktum. Al-Ma'arri. Those who were *basir*, sighted in the heart and mind. Their ways of seeing, their ways of telling.

Crowds of young men followed Borges, hands clasped behind their backs, waiting for a chance to talk to the famous Argentinian writer, the *rawi*. He wore a grey suit jacket, shirt and tie, even in the warm weather. He had been given a red fez as a welcome present. He wore the hat unabashedly.

When he stopped, the crowd stopped with him. He enjoyed the sound of the alleyways, the flitter of laundry, the swoop of pigeons, the remnants of ghosts. In particular he liked the trinket shops in the Old City where he could pick small charms from the trays, attempt histories from the feel of them alone.

Borges sat drinking coffee in the small shops, amid the smoke and the bubbling water pipes, listening to ancient stories of larks and elephants, of streets that turned endlessly, of pillars that contained every sound in the universe, of flying steeds, of mythical marketplaces where the only things for sale were handwritten poems that scrolled out infinitely.

81

To be or not to be with you is the measure of my time.

~ BORGES ~

82

Sivan Zarka, fourteen years old, was blown into the air alongside Smadar. Her parents were French: she had lived once in Algeria. They had recently moved to Jerusalem where Sivan was studying, with

Smadar, at the Gymnasia high school in Rehavia. Yael Botvin was also fourteen. She had just begun ninth grade at the Israel Arts and Science Academy. She had made aliyah from Los Angeles with her parents eight years before. Rami Kozashvili was twenty years old. He worked as a clerk in the Yehuda Bazaar, selling sports clothes. He had emigrated from Georgia in the Soviet Union. Eliahu Markowitz, an office clerk, a book lover, a pacifist, was forty-two. His family had come originally from the Black Sea coast of Romania.

83

To make aliyah: to ascend.

84

Markowitz was having lunch in an outdoor café with his eleven-year-old son. The boy was thrown backwards through the air but his fall was softened by a potted palm situated in front of the window.

85

So often, thought Rami, the ordinary can save us.

86

When Rami came back from the Yom Kippur War—long-haired, blue-eyed, exhausted—he began work as a graphic designer, drawing posters for the right wing, the left wing, the center too. He was a maverick. He didn't care. If they wanted fear, he would give them fear. If they wanted glamour, he would give them glamour. Controversy, nationalism, pessimism—anything at all. Schmaltz too: no problem, he could easily deliver a bouquet of bullshit. A raised fist for the new

Israel. An expansive border, the Nile to the Euphrates. A wide-eyed child. A sinister stare. A wounded dove. A long elegant leg. Anything at all. Make it smart, make it crude, make it rude, he didn't care, he had no politics. No party allegiance. No safe alignment. To have a house, a family, to be undisturbed: an *Israeli* life, that's what he wanted. A good job, a mortgage, a safe street, leafy, no knock on the door, no midnight phone calls. What he wanted was the spectacularly banal. The worst of it would be a long line at the falafel joint, a shortchange at the cheese store, a mistake by the mailman. Rami did what he did best: drawing, sloganeering, provoking with paintbrush and pencil. He started his own firm. Advertising and graphic design. He delighted in ruffling feathers. Most everyone liked him—if they didn't, he laughed it off, always the clown, the joker, the man at the edge. He met Nurit: she was a beauty. Fiery. Red-haired. Liberal. She didn't care what others thought. Smart as a whip. From a good family. A general's daughter, a pioneer, an original, she went generations back. She took the oxygen from the air. He was rougher-edged, raw, more working class, but she liked his charm, his wit, his ability to turn on a word. He was reckless. He made her laugh. He wasn't going to let her go. She had the brains, he had the instinct. He courted her, wrote her letters, drew pictures for her. She was a peacenik. He sent her red roses. She returned them for white. He was smitten. He had served as a tank mechanic in the army. He fixed her father's car. The General approved. They were married in Nurit's house. A rabbi held the service. Together they broke the glass. *Mazal tov* rang around the house. They had their eighteen minutes of yichud, it was tradition, why not? The years tumbled on. They had kids: one two three four. Beauties. Whippersnappers. A little wild, all of them. Especially Smadar. A ball of energy, a magnifying glass: she was all focus and burn. The boys too—Elik, Guy, Yigal—all of them had their mother's eyes. *Tiger eyes*, he called them, something to do with an English poem he couldn't quite remember. They were extraordinary years. Rami was sharp. Witty. A little sardonic when he needed to be. He knew politicians, artists, journalists. He got invited to parties. Jerusalem. Tel Aviv. Haifa. He played the jester. He developed a taste for motorbikes. Bought himself a leather jacket. Came home bearing colorful dresses and scarves as presents for Nurit. She laughed at his poor taste, kissed him. She let her hair fall. At parties he could hear her talking to her professor friends. *Occupation* this, *Occupation* that. Ah, my wife, the liberal, the beauty. She wrote articles. She didn't hold back. She said what she wanted. It thrilled him. She brought him to the edge. His lungs were bursting. There were more wars, yes, but there were always wars, weren't there, this was Israel after all, there always would be another war, this was the price the people had to pay. Somehow he was able to slide through it all, one eye open, both closed. Vigilance. That was the word. Vigilance. He knew the routines even if he didn't like them. Watch for the dark face on the buses. Always know where the exit is. If the Arab bus is beside you in traffic pray for the light to be green. Measure the roll of the accent. Look out for cheap shirts and tracksuits. Flick a quick look for dust on the shoes. He wasn't prejudiced, he said, he was just like everyone else, he was logical, he was practical, he simply wanted to be tranquil, to be undisturbed. He read the papers, he said, in order to ignore the news. It was the only way to get by. He didn't want to be pinned down. He wanted to maintain his freedom. He could argue anyone, at any time, in any corner. He was Israeli, after all: he would argue against himself if need be. It was all about appetite. He developed a double chin, filled out his shirtfronts. He didn't fly flags, but like everyone else he stood stock still every Memorial Day. His work sustained him. He was doing well. His fees were large. He doubled them, tripled them. The more he charged, the more work he got. He was surprised when he won awards. Silver decanters. Cut-glass bowls. Trophies. They lined the shelves of the house. Half the billboards around Jerusalem were designed by him. The phone didn't stop ringing. The kids grew. The boys were full of pep. Smadar was a pistol, a firecracker. She loved to run around the house. She danced on the table. Cartwheeled in the garden. Skinned her knees. Knocked a tooth out. Girl stuff. Time sauntered on. High school degrees. Theater. And then came military service—Nurit didn't like it, but Elik, the oldest, went anyway. Shined his shoes and twirled his beret on his finger. It was the done thing. To refuse to serve was to isolate. To isolate was to lose. To lose was un-Israeli. It was duty, pure and simple. Rami recognized it: he had done it and his sons would do it, and eventually his daughter too. Rami took photos of Smadar in her grandfather's army fatigues and her brother's red beret on her head and they laughed as she marched, keystone-style, around the room.

He would describe it years later as his life in a bubble, his years in an open-neck shirt, his role in a Talking Heads song.

87

The sound of the rollers on the cold metal tray. The slide of the plastic shoe covers on the shiny tile floor. The soft hiss of the refrigerator door sealing behind them. The morgue, then, silent as Rami walked through.

88

And you may ask yourself, What is that beautiful house?
And you may ask yourself, Where does that highway go to?
And you may ask yourself, Am I right, am I wrong?
And you may say to yourself, my God, what have I done?

89

For the first few years after the bombing it worried Rami that he was repeating himself. He sometimes had to tell Smadar's story two or three times a day. Once in the morning at a school. Once in the afternoon at the Parents Circle offices. Then again at night in a synagogue or a community hall or a mosque. To pastors. A'immah. Rabbis. Reporters. Cameramen. Schoolkids. Senators. Visitors from Sweden, Mexico, Azerbaijan. The bereaved from Venezuela, Mali, China, Indonesia, Rwanda, who had come to visit the holy places.

On occasion—early on, before he allowed himself to be comfortable in the repetition—he found himself pausing in mid-sentence, wondering if he had just said the same thing twice in the span of minutes, not just a general repetition, but the exact same words in a row, with the same intonation, the same facial expressions, as if somehow he had reduced the story to the mechanical, the rhythm of the everyday. It bothered him to think that the listeners might look at him as a broken-down reel, trapped by the sameness of his grief.

Afterwards he would realize he had left out whole chunks of what he truly wanted to say.

It flushed him with fear that he might appear fraudulent, theatrical, rehearsed. As if his story was a brand, a commercial, bound to repetition. He could feel the heat rise in his face. His palms grew sweaty. On the second or third telling in a day, he found himself pinching the skin on his forearms to jolt himself awake, to make sure he wasn't retreading old territory. *My name is Rami Elhanan. I am the father of Smadar. I am a seventh-generation Jerusalemite.*

He wondered how actors did it. To say the same thing meaningfully, performance after performance. What sort of discipline did it take? Once a day. Twice on matinee days. How could they, in that endless repetition, continue to make it real? How could they keep it alive?

But the more he went on—the more the story took on a singular shape—the more he began to realize that it did not matter. There was, he knew, always an end to the run of an actor, but he had no such end. No final curtain call. No ovation. No grand finale for him. No walk out the stage door, overcoat on, collar turned up. No streetlit alleyway. No rain falling on the grey cobbled street. No morning review. No fawning adulation.

He began to understand that it wasn't a performance. His was a beginning without an end. There was nothing theatrical about it at all. He could make of it whatever heaven or hell he wanted. He settled into the repetition: it was his blessing and his curse.

He spoke to academics, to artists, to schoolkids, to Israelis, to Palestinians, to Germans, to the Chinese, whoever would listen. Christian groups. Swedish scientists. South African police delegations. The country was, he told them, written on a tiny canvas. Israel could fit inside New Jersey. The West Bank was smaller than Delaware. Four Gazas could be shoehorned inside London. One hundred Israels could be placed inside Argentina and you'd still have some room for the pampas. Israel and Palestine together were one-fifth the size of Illinois. It was infinitesimal, yes, but something pulsed at its core, something spare, original, nuclear: he liked that word, *nuclear*. The atoms of his story pressed against one another. The force of what he wanted to say. There were times he felt he was standing outside himself, hovering, watching himself, but it didn't matter: he connected with the words now, they were his, he owned them, they were spoken for a purpose. He wanted to waken the sleep in his listeners. To see a jolt in them. Just for a split second. To see an eye open. Or a lifted eyebrow. That was enough. A crack in the wall, he said. A crease of doubt. Anything.

When he spoke he saw Smadar again. Her oval face. Her brown eyes. Her turn-to-the-shoulder laughter. In a garden. In Jerusalem. With a white band in her hair.

90

Soon they were meeting virtually every single day. More than their jobs, this became their jobs: to tell the story of what had happened to their girls. Rami handed over the reins to his partner in his graphic design company. Bassam cut back on his working hours in the Sports Ministry and the Palestinian Archives. The two began working officially with the Parents Circle. They were paid a living wage. They traveled whenever they could. Met with philanthropists. Lectured at foundations. Had dinner with diplomats. Spoke at military schools. They carried their stories with them.

It didn't matter that they were repeating the same words over and over again. They knew that the people they spoke to were hearing it for the first time: at the beginning of their own alphabets.

91

It sometimes surprised Rami that he could reach so far inside he could discover new ways of saying the same thing. He was, he knew, making Smadar continually present. It slid something sharp and burning into his rib cage, pried him even further open.

Once or twice, at the lectures, he looked across to see the surprise on Bassam's face, as if the new phrase had just sliced him open too.

92

The force of the blast on Ben Yehuda Street knocked her high in the air.

93

There are times I think she might have been hitching a lift to heaven.

94

I can still hear the slide of the rollers on that cold metal tray.

95

Physics stole her soar.

96

Bassam kept different pieces afloat in his mind, tried them out for size, rearranged them, jumped around, juggled them, shattered their linearity.

He liked to put the groups at ease. I spent seven years in prison, and then I got married. You want to know about occupation? Try six kids in two bedrooms. Hey, who in their right mind gives the job of lookout to the guy with the limp?

The groups weren't sure how to take his quips at first. They fidgeted, glanced away. But there was something magnetic about him and slowly he drew them back again. I'm the only man who ever went to England, he said, and liked the weather.

His accent was thick. He rolled the words around in his mouth. But he spoke softly, musically. He could quote poetry: Rumi, Yeats, Darwish. It didn't matter if he fractured the story here and there: it was more like a song than story to him, he wanted to get to the deep rhythm of it.

97

A bony structure at the bottom of the trachea—the syrinx—is integral to the voice box of birds. With its surrounding air sac, the syrinx resonates to sound waves created by membranes along which the bird forces air. The pitch of the song is created when the bird shifts the tension on the membranes. The volume is controlled by the force of exhalation.

The bird can control two sides of the trachea independently so that some species can produce two distinct notes at once.

98

At night Rami read Smadar a children's version of *One Thousand and One Nights* in Hebrew.

Her eyes fluttered as she listened. Sinbad the Sailor. Julnar the Sea-Born. Ali Baba and the Forty Thieves. Aladdin and His Wonderful Lamp.

Smadar always seemed to wake about three-quarters of the way through each story.

99

Certain birds are said to sleep in mid-flight. They do so in short ten-second bursts, usually after nightfall. The bird is able to switch off one side of its brain in order to rest, while the other side continues its rhythmic vigilance to avoid crashing into a fellow flier and to watch out for predators.

100

A frigatebird can stay aloft for two whole months without touching down on either land or water.

101

One afternoon, in a souk on Al-Zahra Street, Borges said to his listeners that *One Thousand and One Nights* could be compared to the creation of a cathedral or a beautiful mosque, and perhaps it was even more splendid than that since, unlike a cathedral or a mosque, none of its authors, or creators—the actual builders—were aware that they were contributing to the construction of a book. Their stories had been gathered at different times, in myriad places, Baghdad, Damascus, Egypt, the Balkans, India, Tibet, and from different sources too, the *Jataka Tales* and the *Katha Sarit Sagara,* and then were repeated, refined, translated, first in French, then in English, changed once again and passed on, entering yet another lore.

The stories existed on their own at first, said Borges, and were then joined together, strengthening one another, an endless cathedral, a widening mosque, a random everywhere.

It was what Borges called a creative infidelity. Time appeared inside time, inside yet another time.

The book was, he said, so vast and inexhaustible that it was not even necessary to have read it since it was already an intricate part of humankind's unconscious memory.

102

They were so close that, after a while, Rami felt that they could finish each other's stories.

My name is Bassam Aramin. My name is Rami Elhanan. I am the father of Abir. I am the father of Smadar. I am a seventh-generation Jerusalemite. I was born in a cave near Hebron.

Word for word, pause for pause, breath for breath.

103

Arrangements for Smadar's funeral were made immediately. Phone calls. Emails. Telegrams.

Jewish law requires that a body be buried as soon as possible, complete with all its limbs and organs: the soul is considered to be in turmoil until it is in the ground.

104

Muslim law too, though at first the police didn't return the bodies of the three bombers to their families.

For years afterwards they were stored in blue plastic bags in a locked refrigerator vault in the morgue in Jerusalem.

105

Certain small patches of the Sistine Chapel's ceiling have been purposely left untouched so that future generations can understand the layers of restoration.

As early as the mid-1500s, deposits of saltpeter began coming through cracks in the ceiling. The growths gathered and began to creep across the paintings: crystalline deposits that appeared like small rock formations.

The Italian artist Simone Lagi—hoping to prevent the disintegration of the murals—spent much of his life mopping the accretions away with soft linen cloths and pieces of wet bread.

The untouched areas of the ceiling show what might have happened if the chapel had been left alone.

106

The thirteenth-century Syrian chemist Hasan al-Rammah described the process of making gunpowder: the saltpeter was boiled down and mixed with wood ashes to make potassium nitrate, which was then dried and mixed into an explosive. The gunpowder was known in Arabic as Chinese Snow.

107

In the ninth century, the Chinese accidentally created the explosive mixture—75 parts saltpeter, 15 parts charcoal, 10 parts sulfur—when they were looking for the elixir of life.

108

Seven others were killed on Ben Yehuda Street. Scores of people lay injured. Sirens flashed red and blue against the white stone buildings. The night was raw with raised voices.

The ZAKA paramedics received their calls—*mayday mayday mayday*—and arrived within minutes of the bombings, on scooters and in cars. Their long beards. Their kippahs. Their hanging tzitzit. They set to work in their orange vests and latex gloves alongside the police and the Magen David Adom.

The night pressed down against them. They aided the living first. They were bulky men, but they moved lightly, absorbed in silhouette.

They leaned over the victims, whispered consolation to the still living, careful not to step in the slick blood.

After all the injured or dying were taken to hospital, the ZAKA set to their real work: to collect the body parts for burial. They paused a moment. Theirs was a concentration born from repetition. A form of prayer. They nodded at one another, reversed their vests to forensic yellow, put on new sets of latex gloves, slipped new bags over their shoes.

Silently they went about it. In small groups. Quick and terse through the scattered human jigsaw. A finger. An earlobe. A foot, still in its shoe, leaning, almost brazenly, against a garbage can.

They removed gutter grills, combed the surfaces of manhole covers, pushed open jammed doors. They sifted the glass and debris, looking for any sign of life or flesh. They reached into shattered glass with long tweezers to pick up a severed thumb. They picked bloody shrapnel from the windshields of cars, shone flashlights on the underside of tables, climbed trees to scrape the skin of the victims from the branches, dabbed cartilage from the street signs, coiled intestines back into half-torsos, vacuumed up any available liquid from the pavement into portable machines.

The shadows of the ZAKA moved under intense floodlight. One man passing along the street, becoming the next, becoming the next again. A hushed, abbreviated form of communication.

They assembled the corpses together on sheets of white plastic, bagged them and handed them over to the Israeli police. They were meticulous. Rigorous. Precise. Special care was taken not to mix the blood of victims and the bombers.

Within a couple of hours their work was done.

When they walked back towards their scooters they let their arms hang slightly away from their bodies, as if their hands had been exposed to a contaminant. One man washed a trace of blood that had soaked into a stray tzitzit. Another leaned down to remove the plastic booties from his shoes. Carefully he folded them into another plastic bag. They arranged their clothes into the metal boxes on the back of their scooters, put on their helmets, and then they dissolved, once again, into the city, bearing their sorrows.

They didn't wait around, didn't exhibit themselves with prayer. No ritual. No closure. It was their duty. Simple as that.

For this the scripture had been written.

109

Seelonce feenee.

110

Two of the ZAKA came back on their scooters the next morning to pick up a single eyeball that had been missed.

The eyeball was noticed by an elderly man, Moti Richler, who, at dawn, looked down from his upstairs apartment on Ben Yehuda Street and saw the piece of severed flesh lying on top of the tall blue awning of the Atara café.

A long string of optic nerve was still attached to the pupil.

111

The workings of the human eye are still considered by scientists to be as profoundly mysterious as the intricacies of migratory flight.

112

With age-related macular degeneration, a patient develops a central blind spot and can generally only see objects on the periphery. Everything at the center of vision appears dark. The patient sees edges: everything else becomes a fuzzy circle. If looking at a dartboard, all that might be seen is its rim.

To combat this, the surgeon removes the natural lens and implants a tiny metal telescope in one eye. The surgery does not repair the macula, but magnifies the patient's vision. The blind spot might be reduced from the size of a person's face to the size of his or her mouth, or maybe even to an area as small as a coin.

The operation—which was pioneered in New York and perfected in Tel Aviv—only takes a couple of hours, but afterwards requires a new way of seeing. The patient has to learn to gaze through the tiny implanted telescope and at the same time scan the periphery with the other eye. One eye looks directly forward, magnifying things up to three times their usual size, while the other searches sideways. In the brain the two sets of visual information are combined into a complete picture.

Sometimes it takes the patient months, or even years, to properly retrain the vision.

At the time of the bombing, Moti Richler was in his second month of recovery. He turned from the window and told his wife, Alona, that he wasn't sure, but he had been looking down on the scene of yesterday's bombing and thought he saw—through his implanted telescope—something odd lying on the awning below.

113

It looked to Moti like a tiny old-fashioned motorcycle lamp with wires dangling.

114

One of the earliest texts on the eye—its structure, its diseases, its treatments—*Ten Treatises on Ophthalmology*, was written in the ninth century by the Arab physician Hunayn ibn Ishaq.

The individual components of the eye, he wrote, all have their own nature and they are arranged so that they are in cosmological harmony, reflecting, in turn, the mind of God.

115

The doctors came to Bassam in the corridor of the hospital. They wore ties underneath their crisp white coats. They asked him to sit down. He felt a rush of cold to his arms. He said he preferred to remain standing.

One doctor was Jewish, the other a Palestinian, from Nazareth. He addressed Bassam in Arabic: softly, his voice measured. If Abir were to die, he suggested. If things take the wrong turn. If the worst was to happen. If we are unable to revive her.

The other doctor touched him on the shoulder: Mister Aramin, he said, do you understand what we're telling you here?

Bassam looked beyond the doctor's shoulder. Further down the corridor Salwa sat, surrounded by her family.

Bassam replied, in Hebrew, that yes he understood.

The first doctor talked, then, about harvesting organs. Of creating life from life. Her liver, the kidneys, her heart. The second doctor followed.

—We have a renowned eye transplant unit, you know.

—We would take very good care of her.

—There's a severe need.

—Some people are reluctant.

—We understand that.

—Mister Aramin?

For a moment Abir's eyes seemed to hover in the room: large, brown, copper-flecked at the core.

—Please take a minute. Talk with your wife.

—I will.

—We'll be back.

Dreidels spinning on a kindergarten floor. The Aleph. The Torah. A bat mitzvah dress. Military service directives. The checkpoint from behind the glass. Permits and stamps. The blue and white fluttering above her. Yellow-plated cars. Israeli television, Israeli books, Israeli recipes. She might go home for Shabbat and bake the challah and light the candles and make her mitzvahs and wake to her husband and kiss his eyes and raise her children and bring them to the synagogue and teach them the Hatikvah and their kids might have kids and their own ways of seeing, and, yes, there were other ways of seeing beyond Muslim law, he knew—Druze, Christian, Bedouin too—but it was not just that, no, it was so far beyond that, he wanted to explain it to the doctors, there was something deeper here for him, something fundamental, something he needed to say, he wasn't sure how to explain it, he had always wanted Abir to see the sea, it was the thing he had promised her for so many years, his pledge to his daughter, that he would bring her the short drive to the coast at Akka, along with her sister and brothers, allow them to wade in the blue of the Mediterranean, run along the wooden piers, to give them access to what was denied, and he wondered what it was that the doctors saw when he lowered his gaze and he said, in perfect Hebrew: No, I am sorry, we cannot do that, my wife and I, sorry, we cannot allow that, no.

116

Shortly after Abir's funeral—she was carried, flag-draped, through the rutted streets of Anata—Bassam called Rami on the telephone and said he needed to join the Parents Circle.

He was, he insisted, ready to get involved. He would start as soon as possible, the next day if needed.

Bassam put the phone down and went walking through the broken, dusty streets. The smashed sidewalks. The piles of rubble. The pyramids of tires.

He had seen photographs of Anata in the national archives, how beautiful it once was. The marketplaces. The villas. The mosaic faces. The men in fezes. The women in their long dresses. The cafés.

Gone now. Walled in. Garbaged up.

He passed the school gates and slipped around the back of the shop. He held his breath as he walked by the graveyard.

117

My name is Bassam Aramin. I am the father of Abir.

118

In the '48 war Moti Richler guarded a primitive cart that ran on a metal cable strung across the Hinnom Valley in Jerusalem. The cable was two hundred and forty meters long. It ran from a room in the eye hospital to a schoolhouse on the side of Mount Zion. The wire was pulled taut by winches and propped up by makeshift cavallettis.

The cart, made of wood and reinforced steel plates, ran only at nighttime. It brought injured soldiers and medical equipment from one side of the valley to the other: the soldiers who were still conscious could feel the cart swing and sway as they traveled through the air.

Every evening Moti drove a motorbike through the valley underneath the cable to make sure the wire was still intact and not booby-trapped. He wore dark clothing and blackened his face, neck and hands with shoe polish so as not to attract Jordanian sniper fire.

The Italian-made bike was painted dark, even its handlebars and spoked wheels. Mufflers were put on the engine. The rear lights were disabled and Moti took out the front light completely so that the glass didn't catch the moonlight.

The disabled headlamp sat by Moti's bedside all through the war, the wires dangling.

119

The morning after the bombing Moti looked out from his apartment window to the awning below.

—Alona, come quick, he called to his wife over his shoulder. Down there. Look at that. Is that what I think it is?

120

Years later the French high-wire artist Philippe Petit strung a three-quarter-inch steel wire on almost the exact same trajectory as Moti's cable, and walked, on an incline, across the valley.

121

In David's fight with Goliath in the Valley of Elah, David used a slingshot to hit the giant in the forehead with one of five stones taken from a nearby brook. The stones from the valley are made up primarily of barium sulfate, twice as dense as most ordinary stones. They are rumored among throwers to fly quicker, farther and more accurately than other stones.

122

The rubber bullet knocked Abir face-forward to the ground.

123

Goliath is said to have fallen forward, where he was decapitated by David on the spot, but every sling thrower will tell you that what happens when you hit the enemy with a stone is that he falls backwards, unless you hit him in the lower legs.

124

What the British would call a knee-knocker.

125

So that Goliath, if conscious, would have been looking straight up into David's eyes. As John the Baptist might have been looking in the eyes of his killers, at the behest of Salome, in the town of Sebastia, not far from the village of Assira-al-Shamaliya, where the Ben Yehuda Street bombers were raised amid the yellow wheatfields and winding roads and olive groves with rickety wooden ladders leaning up against the trees.

126

When a suicide bomber activates his or her belt, his head is nearly always separated from the top of the torso: it is known to the police as the mushroom effect.

127

There are two to three seconds of consciousness after decapitation when the brain is still functioning: the mouth can make a sound and there can be ocular movement, a twitching of the eyeball or the opening—or closing—of an eyelid.

It is said that decapitated men often look surprised as their bodies separate from their heads: as if their final thoughts are in flight, visions of loved ones in Stockholm, in Savannah, in Sierra Leone, in so many small and scattered Samarias.

128

The Beit Jala teenagers spent hours on end painting their stones with flags, insignias, the jerseys of their football teams, Shabab al-Khader and Wadi al-Neiss.

Tarek's brothers used to paint their stones in the colors of Beit Jala Orthodoxi, and sometimes even in the blue and white of the Dheisheh team from the nearby refugee camp.

Some of the stones also took on the insignia of foreign teams, mostly Barcelona and Real Madrid, though a few used the colors of Al Ahly in Egypt, or Olympique Lyonnais in France, or Glasgow Celtic in Scotland.

On occasion a pissed-off Israeli soldier, under orders not to shoot, launched the stones back at the rioters by arm. These stones were picked up again and again, launched back and forth between soldiers and boys, almost comradely in flight.

129

130

The frigatebird is dark and stealthy, with a hooked beak and a deeply forked tail. It belongs to the family of seabirds found in tropical and subtropical oceans. Their wings can span up to eight feet. They cannot dive beneath water or even rest on its surface since their feathers will absorb moisture and they will drown.

They are known to swoop beneath cumulus clouds where the rising currents of warm air pull them into the heart of the vapor. In the currents they simply open their wings as if in the tube of a sky vacuum, a thunderous swirl of air. As they ascend they sometimes sleep. They are hauled upwards, thousands of feet, like hollow-boned gods through the narrowing gyre.

High in the air they finally break from the current and flap out of the envelope of cloud. For a moment the buffer shakes them, but then the turbulence ends. In the still air they can glide horizontally downwards for up to forty miles without even flapping, finishing often with an annihilating drop.

While still in flight, they stay alive by robbing other seabirds for food, or skimming the ocean surface for fish and squid, snatching their prey from the water with their long razor-sharp bills.

131

To ancient mariners they were called Men-of-War.

132

While camped on Mount Scopus in 1099 the Christian Crusaders perfected a giant slingshot that could fire large balls of flaming pitch great distances through the air.

133

In art class, at school in Anata, Abir sketched out a picture of the blue Mediterranean that she had only ever seen from the tops of tower blocks. It was drawn in her childish hand, with a globe of yellow sun, a swath of squiggled cloud, two dark gulls in the upper corner flying over a boxy ship with four small circles penciled in at the hull.

134

When designing the forerunner of the Predator drone, Israeli aerospace engineers studied the form and stream patterns of the frigatebird.

A pair of scientists was sent to the Galápagos Islands in the late 1990s where they filmed flocks in flight. They captured some of the birds and strapped tiny sensors to the undersides of their bodies, tracked the path and the arc of their fall.

Later the Israeli team journeyed to Seattle where they created a series of computer models and began working to see if they could adapt any of the movements of the birds to the development of their drones and the missiles they would let fall into the twenty-first century.

135

The computer graphics were designed to echo popular video games with an intricate mathematical map laid over the cartoon visuals, so the drone lazed in at first, high in the sky, waiting, circling, until the missile zoomed down at the stroke of a key or the tap of a joystick. The models replicated the grace of the frigatebird's drop.

The visual landscape was drawn from a number of places, but in particular they used a computerized map of Gaza: the streets, the alleys, the markets, the fishing huts, the patches of farm, the border ditches, the rubble, the refugee camps.

136

During Operation Cast Lead in late 2008—also known, at the time, as the Gaza War, also known as the Battle of al-Furqan, also known as the Gaza Massacre—the drones were used to fire Spike missiles into the city, arriving from the clouds into the mayhem below.

The Spike missiles were of a type known as *fire-and-forget*.

137

Even as a child, Abir showed an amazing gift for memorization. She knew ancient songs, poems, an array of lengthy verses from the Qur'an which she could quote at will.

Salwa sat by her bed and told her stories that had come down through her own family, not just the traditional Kalila and Dimna or Clever Hassan or Omar the Just, but other tales that had been filtered through the generations too. Linen cloths with special healing powers. Ancient olive trees that went off walking on night journeys. Silver tea kettles capable of entrancing even the most jaded. Jackals able to turn into tiny hummingbirds.

The young girl would wake in the morning and ask for a part of the story she might have missed: often she could recite her mother's exact words from the night before.

Abir also showed a penchant for mathematics, so that, on the morning just before her death, Bassam had no doubt that she would pass her exam: the multiplication tables tripped off her tongue. She wandered around the apartment creating rhymes from the numbers.

When she jaunted out the door towards school, Bassam handed her two shekels and told her to make sure that she continued reciting the tables so that her older sister Areen—who had already gone on ahead—could pass the exam too.

138

She slid the shekels over the counter to Niesha the Ancient.

139

Trauma to the back of the skull. Contusions on the front of her head. A weak pulse, a fluttering of the eyelids, no lucidity.

The doctors huddled. They had seen this sort of injury before, but seldom in a child so young. Most likely an epidural hematoma, the blood slowly collecting in the space between the skull and the outer lining of the brain.

What was needed was a skull decompression, but that would require a CT scanner. Their only scanner had been inoperative the past month. But perhaps they should drill anyway. They had done it before in emergencies. Make an incision into the skull. Relieve the tension. Drain the blood.

The shouts ricocheted along the corridor. We need permission. Where are the parents? Do you hear me? We should wait. Monitor her pulse. Have we called the parents? Check her heart rate. We need permission from the parents. Watch for bradycardia and respiratory collapse.

140

Bassam was ushered into the operating room. Salwa didn't want to go. She couldn't bear the thought of it. The air was so dense he felt as if he was fighting through water. He pushed it aside but it collapsed over him, wave upon wave. Abir was laid out, tubes in her arms, a breathing apparatus at her mouth, her head bandaged, a small wave of dark hair at the nape of her neck. He walked across and kissed her eyelids. He had told her that morning that she could not stay over at a friend's house. He had been sharp with her. Wake now, he thought. Just wake and you can go wherever you want. Open your eyelids and I will never say another stern word, I promise, all you have to do is open your eyes.

Bassam turned to the doctor behind him: We have to get her to Hadassah. They have all the proper equipment there.

—You can't, said the doctor. Everything is closed off.

—I have friends in Jerusalem. I can call them. They can help. They can get an ambulance here.

—It's all locked down.

Bassam was already moving out into the corridor to look for Salwa. She was by the benches, surrounded by other women, but entirely alone. The dark of her eyes glistened. The left side of her lip twitched slightly. The women surrounding her bowed their heads, let him through. He took her elbow, guided her to the operating room. The door swung. He held it open with his good foot.

Salwa stood there frozen until her hand went to her mouth. She could see the rise and fall of Abir's chest.

—We're going to switch her to Hadassah, he said.

141

The Israeli hospital. At Ein Kerem. An ancient Palestinian village, once.

142

Where Smadar was born.

143

At first it seemed as if it would be just a small delay. Protocol. Security. The army needed to accompany the vehicle to the hospital. The route had to be prepared. There was trouble outside. A calm was called for. The ambulance could move soon. An hour passed. The situation was under control, they said. Remain alert. They would be moving again soon. They were in touch with the authorities. Repeat. It was for the safety of everyone. A route was being established. Stay calm. Instructions would be on their way. Repeat. They would be moving soon. Helicopters had been deployed. There was still rioting near the checkpoint. Repeat. Moving soon.

Bassam sat in the back of the ambulance with Abir. She was laid out on the gurney in her hospital gown, hooked up to the drip bags. The monitor machines beeped softly. Two paramedics sat in the front of the ambulance, another one behind with Bassam. They whispered softly, glancing at each other as the instructions came over the radio. A route has been established. We will be going soon.

Bassam's mobile phone died after an hour and fifteen minutes. He could see no rioting out the back window. There were, he knew, other routes the ambulance could take. In the front seat the paramedics were shouting into the radio: they wanted to loop around. The answer came back. Negative. Stay where you are.

A small plastic bag lay at the foot of the gurney. Abir's school socks, her shoes, her school tunic. Beside it, her leather schoolbag. He reached down and opened the clasp. In it, her schoolbooks. Mathematics. Religious Studies. A copybook. Her lunchbox, untouched.

In the bottom of the schoolbag, he found the bracelet of candy. For a moment he thought about slipping it on her wrist. He tucked it back in the bag, kissed her forehead.

He reached for a clean linen sheet in the rear of the ambulance, opened the doors and stepped outside. A jeep sat idling not five meters away. A voice came over the loudspeaker telling Bassam to step back into the ambulance, that everything was under lockdown.

—Step back, sir. Step back now.

He didn't turn. He carried the bedsheet over to a concrete bollard at the side of the road. He glanced up at the sun, established due east, unfolded the sheet into a rectangle on the ground, knelt down. He was surprised that nobody tried to stop him. He could hear, in the distance, the sound of helicopters.

A soldier came towards him, a gun strapped across his shoulder. His eyes were brown and tender. He said nothing until Bassam finished praying.

—You have to get back in the ambulance now.

Bassam felt a surge of hatred for the apology in the soldier's voice.

The soldier's hand touched his elbow. Bassam swung his arm away and walked across to the ambulance. The door closed behind him. He bent over Abir. He could still see the soft fog of her breath on the oxygen mask.

The ambulance lurched in increments. One hundred yards, two hundred, fifty, ten, one hundred again. It reversed, stopped once more, turned around. Static on the radio. Another half hour passed.

A call came to return to the first hospital. Strike that. Remain in position. You will be moving again soon. Repeat. You will be moving soon.

When he opened the doors once more, Bassam realized that they were still near the checkpoint. Some soldiers were arguing behind an orange barrel. There were three empty deck chairs set up alongside the barrel. Far away, a dog barked. All else was quiet.

After two hours and eighteen minutes the ambulance was given the okay to drive to West Jerusalem.

144

In the hospital Abir was kept alive for another two and a half days.

145

The waiting room was filled with activists. Bassam had come to know them well over the previous fifteen years. From the courthouses. From mosques. From synagogues. From churches. From prison. From peace conferences, meetings, rallies.

Theirs was a small world: cliques, factions, splinter factions. Nothing of that mattered now. They crowded together, waiting, drinking coffee, waiting, holding hands, waiting, slipping outside to smoke, waiting, whispering into phones, waiting.

A silence fell over the crowd when Bassam walked in. He knew every face: Suleiman, Dina, Rami, Alon, Muhammad, Robi, Chen, Elik, Yitzak, Zohar, Yehuda, Avichay.

He stood quietly with his head bowed. He did not want to address any single person. The ceiling pulsed down upon him. Only the ticking of the wall clock could be heard.

—*Ma feesh khabar baed*, he said in Arabic, then repeated it in Hebrew, and then in English: No news yet.

146

The newspaper reports said that a ten-year-old child had died in the hospital after an incident in the West Bank. It was said in some reports that her father was a prominent member of Combatants for Peace. It was said in others that he had spent seven years in jail for terrorist activities in Hebron. Some reports mentioned both. *Haaretz. Al Quds. The Jerusalem Post. Felestin. Yedioth Ahronoth. Israel-Nachrichten. Al-Hayat al-Jadida. The Palestine Telegraph.* The Army released an official statement denying any involvement. A TV segment said that rumors of an incursion were spurious. Later there were reports of rioting in protest against the Separation Barrier being built through the school playground. Another report said the girl had been seen at the school gates holding a stone. She was killed by a rock to the back of her head from nearby rioters. She was shot by Palestinian Authority forces. She was epileptic, she smashed her head when she fell. She implicated herself by running away from the jeep. She was found to have stones in her pocket. She picked up a shock grenade which had exploded in her hands. She was buying candy. She threw her arms in the air in surrender. She was walking defiantly away. She had been mistreated in a Palestinian hospital. They had dropped her from a gurney and she had hit her head. She was air-lifted immediately to the Hadassah where she had been given priority care. The Muslim parents had refused to get help from a Jewish doctor. She had no I.D. Reports of an illegal incursion were categorically untrue. The girls had been throwing stones, it was caught on closed-circuit television from the school gates. Her father was an active ranking member of Fatah. The teacher in her school was a known Hamas activist. No such Border Police operations were logged that morning. The delay in the ambulance absolutely did not hasten her death and was directly linked to riots on the ground.

147

In civil court, four years later, the judge questioned the assertion that Abir's head injury was the result of Palestinian boys slinging rocks from a nearby graveyard. She pointed out that the nearest graveyard was located behind a four-story building, a hundred meters away from where the jeep would have been located. The rioters would have had to be able to sling their stones up over the building to clear the water towers and arc precisely downwards to land anywhere near the tin-roofed grocery store.

It was an entirely impossible feat, the judge added, even in the most vivid imagination.

Not to mention, the judge said, the autopsy commissioned by the Aramin family, or the discovery of the rubber bullet yards from where Abir fell, or the evidence from eyewitnesses that at least two rounds of rubber bullets had been fired.

148

The newspaper reports said that a fourteen-year-old girl had been murdered in a suicide bombing in West Jerusalem. Some said that four people had died in the attack. Others said five. There were two bombers in some reports, three in others. Fifty-eight were injured, seventy-seven, one hundred and twenty. The bombers had been dressed as Orthodox men. It was a Hamas splinter group. They had come from East Jerusalem. They had escaped from prison in the West Bank. They were on a Wanted list that was ignored by the Palestinian Authority. They had passed through Qalandia checkpoint. They had been living undercover as merchants in the Old City for many months. They had hidden in West Bank caves. They had targeted a group of teenage girls for maximum shock. They had originally planned to attack the Mahane Yehuda market. A secondary plan was to take out a music school. It was a direct reference to the bombings which had taken place on the same street in 1948, led by British deserters who had joined the Jewish underground. It was a bombing funded by the Islamic Republic of Iran, masterminded by Yasser Arafat. It was a brand-new splinter group belonging to a radical underground network. The bombers were heard to yell *Allahu akbar* seconds before they pulled the tabs on their belts. It was a direct attack on the family of Matti Peled, Smadar's grandfather, a former Israeli general. It was a sophisticated operation planned out amongst the most senior members of Hamas. Another nearby car bomb failed to go off. The shrapnel was laced with rat poison which was rumored to maximize bleed-out. It was a new type of explosive stolen from the Israeli Defense Forces. The bombers had spread themselves out evenly on the street for full impact. The girls were shopping for schoolbooks. They were going to sign up for jazz dancing classes. They were last seen walking along, passing a small silver Walkman between them, two of the girls leaning together to share a single pair of earphones.

149

The smashed Walkman was found and entered into evidence. Later, Uri Esterhuzy, a forensic scientist from Tel Aviv, examined the machine and determined from the scorched cassette that they had been listening to the Sinéad O'Connor album *I Do Not Want What I Haven't Got.*

The plastic tape rollers were melted and jammed on the song *Nothing Compares 2 U.*

150

Smadar danced to the song in her baggy shorts and her red sleeveless T-shirt, her late grandfather's watch on her wrist.

In the living room, she was always bumping into the oak coffee table so that there was a little ring of bruises on her knee. The bruises became apparent when she stood on the table to dance, a darkening tattoo.

She listened to the album with her white headphones on, so that Rami was forever wondering what part of the song she was inhabiting as she mimed along to the music.

151

The bombs were so loud that they shattered windows at a distance of thirty yards.

152

When she was a baby, Smadar became the poster child for the peace movement. The poster appeared in union halls and student centers and kibbutzim all over the country. It could be found posted in left-wing offices and school hallways and bakeries and bars and falafel stores.

Rami had taken the job, but it was just that: a job.

He snapped the photo and designed the poster himself: its size, the font, the weight of the paper. Smadar's hair was fair and bobby-pinned. Her eyes were large. Her face was cherubic. Her little finger was hooked up near her top lip.

Already, at one year of age, there was something intense and concerned about her. Like she might have known something in advance.

153

154

The poster asked: What will life in Israel be like when Smadar reaches fifteen?

155

She was two weeks away from fourteen.

156

The three suicide bombers had an accumulated age of sixty-eight. They went up in a pink mist.

157

The weight of each bomber's vest was forty to fifty pounds. The Semtex was packed with ball bearings, screws, nails, glass and shards of sharp porcelain. Forensic tests concluded that, despite reports, the shrapnel had not, in fact, been laced with rat poison to make the victims bleed out quicker.

158

Semtex was invented by two Czech chemists who named it after an abbreviation of its parent company, Explosia, and Semtín, a suburb of the city of Pardubice. The explosive was mass-produced first in the 1960s in response to a request from the North Vietnamese government of Ho Chi Minh.

It was malleable and putty-like, so it could fit just about anywhere. A tiny handful could bring a plane down.

For years, representatives of the Czech government gave out Semtex in neatly ribboned gift boxes to visiting heads of state, most notably to Colonel Muammar Gaddafi, who eventually bought seven hundred metric tons of it and distributed it to the PLO, Black September, the IRA and the Red Brigades.

The original compound was almost impossible to detect by airport scanner until a taggant was added in 1991 so that it would emit a distinctive vapor.

The removal of the taggant from the Semtex emulsion was not an easy task for even the most experienced chemists, and the process usually rendered the explosive useless.

159

In manufacturing a rubber bullet, the rubber is coated around a rounded steel core. Wax from the carnauba palm is used as a lubricant, and molybdenum disulfide, known also as moly, helps the rubber stick to the metal on contact.

160

Bassam and Rami gradually came to understand that they would use the force of their grief as a weapon.

161

Seven hundred and fifty years ago al-Rammah, the Syrian chemist, postulated the idea of rocket-propelled torpedoes in his book *Military Horsemanship and Ingenious War Devices*.

His handwritten treatise was lost for many years until it was discovered in a battered leather traveling trunk in a small Ottoman village market.

The manuscript changed hands several times until it found its way into the Topkapi Palace library in Istanbul, known to scholars—with its domed ceilings and decorated Iznik tiles—as one of the most beautiful libraries in the world.

162

Perdix drones are named after the mythological partridge. The flying machines are small enough to sit in the palm of your hand. They are released from pods mounted on the wings of fighter jets, a cloud of them all at once—like a flock of starlings seeding themselves into the sky.

They are sturdy enough to be released at Mach 0.6, almost five hundred miles per hour.

After the initial orders are programmed in remotely by human operators, the drones are designed to act autonomously.

They are sprayed out in a flock of twenty or more, sending signals to one another, creating their own intelligence as they go along. Theirs is the ultimate in digital communication, a perfect specimen of math and computational intuition, able to tell itself what to do and when to do it. Turn left, turn right, realign coordinates, hit moving car, engage now, rifle! rifle! rifle! weapon away, reconnoiter, abandon mission, retreat, retreat, retreat.

They can make a decision to carry an explosive right through the window of your home.

163

Flying so fast that it would be a miracle of precision if a slingman could hit one with a stone.

164

When Rami found out that a drone could be built remotely on a 3-D printer, the plastic casing created from the bottom up, slice by slice, embedding the microchips, cooling until fully formed—so that anyone, anywhere, in possession of the right chips, could feasibly create a flock of drones—he stood up from his desk in his home office and went into the living room to mention it to Nurit.

She was at the kitchen table, writing. The light caught her hair. Something about her seemed ethereal. Out the window a single swallow went by.

Nurit looked up from her computer, gestured with two open hands, and said: And we think the myths are startling.

165

Rami had heard the story once that, during World War Two, a series of bombs filled with live bats were designed to make Japan burn. Each of the bombs, developed first by the U.S military, had thousands of compartments, a vast metallic honeycomb.

A Mexican free-tailed bat was placed in each compartment with a tiny incendiary firebomb attached to its body. The controlled detonations took place, at first, in laboratories and large airplane hangars.

The bombs were to be released by a series of high-flying bombers at dawn: they would be let go at five thousand feet. It was anticipated that the casings would open somewhere above Osaka, and the bats would seed out into the air, a flotilla of doom. They would wake from hibernation and drift down into a vast urban area where, at dawn, they would hide in the dark eaves of houses, or sneak under wooden beams, or make their way into hanging paper lanterns, or even enter open windows to nestle in curtains until their timers went off.

Then the bombs—and the bats themselves—would explode.

Japanese houses were largely built of wood, paper and bamboo, and so it was thought that the burning bats would set off a spectacular firestorm.

A mock village was built in Utah with information gleaned from several Japanese Americans who had been incarcerated in internment camps. The Issei, the Nisei, the Sansei. They advised on village houses and shrines and model tatami rooms. Their height, their shape, their position. The shape of the eaves. The curl of the tiles. The height of the walls.

The village sat in the middle of the desert as if dropped from afar, not unlike something from a movie set. The soldiers called it Nip-Town. Every day different parts of the village burned.

The originators of the project were quite sure it would work, but by late 1943—after spending tens of millions of dollars—the research was running far behind, and instead of bat bombs the focus shifted to a more promising secret operation, the Manhattan Project in Los Alamos.

166

What nobody admitted during the testing of the bat bombs was that most of the time when the Mexican free-tails were released in midair, they were still in a state of hibernation. The bats dropped from the bomb casings without waking up.

By the end of the experiment the scientists knew that they might just as well have released a cascade of stones.

167

Nurit and Rami were convinced that Smadar would become a doctor: she was always running around the house after her younger brother, Yigal, soothing him, applying poultices to his knee, holding his head back when he had a nosebleed, putting ice on his arm after a bee sting.

168

On August 9, three days after the atomic bomb was dropped on Hiroshima, a second bomb was slated to be dropped on the city of Kokura on the island of Kyushu. The main target was the Nippon Steel factory, a fulcrum of the Japanese war effort. Kokura had a large military presence, but there was a huge civilian population too. The factory was located by the sea at the head of the Onga River, hemmed in by mountains.

The plane, the *Bockscar*, took off from Tinian in the Northern Mariana Islands and flew towards Kyushu, accompanied by another B-29, *The Great Artiste*. On the nose of the Fat Man bomb the crew had stenciled the word JANCFU: *Joint Army-Navy-Civilian FuckUp*.

The planes took off into clear weather, but by the time they reached Kyushu the sky had clouded. Thin sheets of grey smoke rose from the factory below.

The commander of the operation, Major Charles Sweeney, had been told that—despite the sophisticated radar at his disposal—he had to be able to see the target with his naked eyes before the bomb could be unleashed.

Sweeney looked out on the landscape of white and grey. He figured they had enough fuel to circle the city a dozen times or more. The plane rose and dropped again, looking for a clear vantage point, circling as it went. The cloud subsided and Sweeney could see the outline of the steel mills, the coast, the seashore, but there was still the problem of smoke billowing from below.

The factory spires appeared again, barely visible. A forest. A pier. More factory smoke. A line of trucks. A tanker out on the water. Another thin sheet of cloud. Wisps of white out the window. The fuel indicator dropped.

Sweeney ordered his planes to continue circling. He was amazed by the sight of a baseball diamond through his binoculars, immediately obscured by a cloud. A line of fishing shacks appeared along the shore and then were swallowed by smoke.

The major scribbled the calculations out on a sheet of lined yellow notepaper: the longer he held on to the bomb the more fuel he would use. The *Bockscar* had already circled ten times in ever-widening arcs.

He had three choices: firstly, drop the bomb on Kokura without clear visuals; secondly, switch the mission to a different city; thirdly, dump the Fat Man out at sea.

Sweeney called for another update from his superiors and circled for the eleventh time. The cloud was, he felt, dissipating. He was sure he would have visuals shortly. The fuel line dropped further. He looked out the window into an unexpected wall of cloud.

The call went through on the radio and the coordinates were switched.

There were, Sweeney was told, no clouds over Nagasaki.

169

The plutonium core of the Nagasaki bomb was the size of a throwable rock.

170

And we think the myths are startling.

171

Often Rami thinks of this: but for an accident of cloud vapor—a small defect in the weave of atmospheric weather—seventy-five thousand lives were lost in one place and preserved, then, in another.

172

But for a turn toward the book store. But for an early bus. But for a random movement on Ben Yehuda Street. But for a trip to Ben Gurion airport to collect her grandmother. But for a late sleep-in. But for a break in the babysitting routine. But for the homework to do later that night. But for a crush of pedestrians on the corner of Hillel Street. But for a hobbling man that she had to loop around.

173

Geography is everything.

174

But for an early recess in the Anata school. But for multiplication tables. But for a long wait at the shop counter. But for two shekels in her pocket. But for a pause in the candy store. But for the open school gate. But for a turn of the jeep's steering wheel. But for the sound of a siren. But for a concrete barrier that forced her to veer out into the street. But for some boys rumored to be rioting near the graveyard.

175

From the age of eight, Abir wanted to be an engineer. Her older brother Araab had a plastic see-through ruler and a silver bow compass. She liked to draw circles on the back of her copybooks and then intersect the circles with straight lines.

For her tenth birthday she asked for a book on Galileo.

176

Occasionally the motorbike allows Rami a state of flow, present in the moment, his senses keyed in, keen, fully aware. He finds a stretch free of potholes, no litter, no barriers, no slick road paint, no pebbles, no twigs, no ridges, no tar lines, no cracks, just a straightaway with a properly banked curve at the end. Nothing behind him, nothing in front, nothing to slow him down. He passes through a delicate ridge of fear, presses his palm against the handlebar to bring the machine left, recorrects, adjusts, curls his fingers around the throttle, revs it up. A hum in his ears, a small vault in his lungs. The bike disappears, the heft of it gone, no rubber, no steel, no gravity, no force. The frame of the landscape dissolves and everything is momentarily gone until the road interrupts him once more.

177

The white apartment blocks of Beit Jala. The black water tanks. The satellite dishes mushrooming the roofs. The flap of laundry from the balconies. The houses fronted with pale Bethlehem stone. The occasional bullet holes. The dusty windows. The young boys, outside, playing marbles on the manhole covers.

Further up the road, he passes the majestic Palestinian villas overlooking the valley, many of them empty now, scantily clad, the families long gone, emigrated, the doors locked, the windows plyboarded up.

The houses like portraits. A different time. More loneliness than rage.

178

It is a town that never ceases to amaze him: on the walls outside the restaurants he has often seen thin pink plastic bags of bread left out in accordance with the local custom that no food should be wasted or thrown away.

The bread should go first to the needy, or the poor, so the plastic bags are tied in a knot and placed carefully on the top of any available wall.

Most often the bags are not taken. The food must then be offered to animals, and so it is the tradition of the older men of Beit Jala— Christian and Muslim both—to go around in the early morning, up and down the steep hills, carefully unknotting bag after bag after bag, like small pink purses.

It is not unusual to see a bird swoop down to grab the bread, and on occasion a whole pink plastic bag rising up in the air over Beit Jala.

179

When he was young, Rami was the schoolyard jester, the clown. A smirk accompanied his shyness. He ran around at recess, quick, exuberant, his breath coming so fast that he didn't know quite how he could handle it. He put a can of muddy water on top of the classroom door so when the teacher came in, the can fell from the frame and the water splattered.

At the school gate—on the day he was expelled—Rami clicked his heels together in the air in a Charlie Chaplin move as he walked away.

Inside he was terrified, thirteen years old, no idea what he would do now.

180

In the industrial school the only thing that really interested him was graphic design: he found himself taken by ideas of color, of shapes.

181

Apeirogon: a shape with a countably infinite number of sides.

182

Countably infinite being the simplest form of infinity. Beginning from zero, one can use natural numbers to count on and on, and even though the counting will take forever one can still get to any point in the universe in a finite amount of time.

183

There always seems, to Rami, to be more dust in the West Bank than anywhere else. Dust on the cars. Dust on the windowsills. Dust on the handlebars. Dust in his helmet. Dust on his eyelashes.

Turning the corner, he brakes gently and comes up against a small jam of cars. A boy with a metal tea-cart is backing out into the street, hitching the cart to the back of a van. The traffic behind waits, the drivers with their elbows out the window, drumming their fingers on their doors, cigarette smoke drifting out their windows.

Normally, in Jerusalem, he would beep his horn and skirt around the cart, but now he waits carefully, the engine idling, the revometer at rest, the engine fan kicking in, the day dull, a little cool, a huge flock of swifts rising over the rooftops.

184

Bassam showed him photographs from the archives once: the ancient Palestinian villas on the rim of the valley. They were among the most beautiful houses Rami had ever seen. The Ottoman life. The Mandate life. The Jordanian life.

In one of them a small boy, maybe eight or nine years old, was walking along the edge of an intricate ironwork fence. He was dressed in a crisp white shirt and dark pants, his hair very neatly combed, carrying in his hand a small leather school valise. In his other hand he held a thin switch and he was running the piece of wood along the middle of the metal bars.

In another photo a very beautiful woman, with large black sunglasses, sat on a veranda in the shade of an apricot tree, in a long white dress, her slender shoulders bare, a large glass of iced water held against her cheek, a few sprigs of mint floating. She smiled at the camera as if all the coolness of the world were to be found in the glass.

In his favorite, there was an Arab man in wide white trousers and a billowy shirt, standing on the tiled roof of one of the houses with, for whatever reason, a badminton racket in his hands. The man looked as if he had just returned a shuttlecock to a party below, maybe even, thought Rami, to the woman cradling the ice, or to the boy with the valise running music along the fence.

185

On the clearest of days, from the highest vantage points of Beit Jala, you can see all the way to the Mediterranean in one direction and to the Dead Sea in the other.

The eye cannot rest. Down below, in the valley, an orchard, a watchtower, a terraced field, the roof of a synagogue, a minaret, a military gate, a series of mist nets among the remaining trees.

Stay here long enough, looking down into the valley, and you will notice the settlements emerging in a pattern around Jerusalem: red tile, red tile, red tile.

Coming together, a perfect ring: the rim of a tightening lung.

186

For the first two years, whenever he was giving a lecture, Bassam slipped his hand into his jacket pocket and pulled out Abir's candy bracelet.

He didn't want to slip the bracelet over his wrist for fear that the string might break, so he gripped it in his fingers, held it in the air, showed it to the audience: the blues, the pinks, the oranges, the yellows.

—This, he said, is the world's most expensive candy.

187

Driving home alone from the lecture, Bassam was ordered to get out at a flying checkpoint. A hot day. Ramadan. The sun was still up. He stepped forward, his shadow slanting in the light.

—Show me your hands, show me your hands!

The soldier was older, a streak of grey down the center of her hair. She had, he thought, a slight Russian accent. Her rifle swung at her hip and then suddenly she pointed it at him.

—What is that, what the fuck is that?

Bassam turned his lofted hand around, stared at it for a second. It looked like something that didn't belong to him. His palm was coated in pink. He had no idea why. He brought it to his nose. It smelled sweet.

—On your knees, on your fucking knees!

Bassam knelt in the dust at the side of the road. He made sure to face east just in case they kept him there a long time: facing east at least he could pray.

Three other soldiers ran towards him. Bassam stared at his hand again. He thought for a split second about licking the pink coating off, then remembered he was fasting.

—Lift your shirt! Lift your shirt I said!

For an instant he felt unashamed, even in front of a woman. A surge of anger. A defiance. He hiked his shirt up around his chest. The soldiers stepped forward again.

The butt end of a rifle jabbed the small of his back. He was shoved forward. Dust rose in his face. Black boots. The woman cuffed his hands with zip ties. He was yanked up by his hair, thrown into the back of the jeep.

188

In the station later that evening, after five hours of interrogation, she softened and said to Bassam that she was sorry, yes, but that Semtex, too, was known to stain the hands a pinkish-orange color.

189

After that, Bassam never again displayed the candy bracelet in his lectures.

190

During Ramadan there were always more flying checkpoints than at any other time: random patrols stopping wherever they wanted, jeeps strewn across the road, soldiers crouched down, orange cones laid out, rifles pointed at the oncoming cars.

At dusk, with fasting about to finish, the checkpoints appeared more frequently than ever: at that stage the Muslims were irritable, tired, hungry, ready for a cigarette. The interruptions got under their skin. It seemed to Bassam that the soldiers reveled in the moment. They wanted confrontation. It justified them, he thought.

Bassam never knew where or when he would come across a truck or a barricade or even a large rock rolled into the middle of the road. He rounded the corner and his whole day would go on pause.

He knew not to say much when he rolled down the window. No confrontation, no rancor, but he didn't want to be obsequious either. He nodded, waited for them to speak. Most of them used English. A few of them had Arabic. He seldom showed recognition of any Hebrew, nothing fluent anyway: it could be a sign he had been in prison. He spoke to them slowly and with precision.

Always he kept his hands in view. He knew never to make a sudden move. He drove away carefully, checking the rearview mirror.

191

He had learned that the cure for fate was patience.

192

The avian migratory paths go all the way from northern Europe over and along the Rift Valley, from Syria to central Mozambique, over the shifting tectonic plates of the world, to the tip of Africa.

A single bird can travel from a nesting site in Denmark to Tanzania, or Russia to Ethiopia, or Poland to Uganda, or Scotland to Jordan in a matter of weeks, even days.

Whole flocks of them, up to three hundred thousand strong, sometimes blot the sky over the bottleneck of land.

Six out of every ten don't make it because of high-voltage lines, pylons, factory chimneys, spotlights, skyscrapers, drilling rigs, oil pits, poison, pesticides, diseases, droughts, failed crops, repeating guns, baited traps, poachers, birds of prey, sudden sandstorms, cold spells, floods, heat waves, thunderstorms, construction sites, windows, helicopter blades, fighter jets, oil spills, rogue waves, bursts of sewage, islands of debris, blocked drainpipes, empty feeders, fetid water, rusty nails, shards of glass, hunters, gatherers, bird-dogs, boys with slingshots, the plastic rings from six-packs.

193

The route over Palestine and Israel has long been known as one of the bloodiest migratory paths in the world.

194

In parts of southern Africa bird bones are used for musical instruments, the theory being that the ancestral memory is regained when you blow air along the hollow bone.

195

In prison, Bassam's cellmates made musical instruments out of anything they could find: strips of wood and metal shower rings for riqs, tightened canvas and shaped metal strips for dafs, even the ligaments from chicken carcasses rolled together, stretched and then varnished to approximate the strings of a primitive lyre.

Any time a prisoner got his hands on fishing wire or dental floss, they were immediately put to use. Any nylon string was considered to be a treasure.

If nothing else could be found, music was played on canteen trays or tapped out rhythmically on the side of empty soup cans.

196

There was a reek to the prison. In the canteen, the shower stalls, the phone booths, even in the tiny prison mosque. Mice fell dead in the corners. Cockroaches. Lizards. The place was ripe with decay.

The days stretched out on a rack. The prisoners pondered the anatomy of boredom. Time was endless and hollow. They rolled messages to each other along the floor, played games of shatranj by knocking out codes on pipes. Rolled tobacco skittered along the ground. They shaped horses, camels, rooks, pawns from chickpeas to make chess pieces.

They were not allowed any traditional dress. They improvised keffiyehs from whatever they could find, kitchen rags, dishtowels, elastic from their underwear. They spent weeks stitching them together, had them confiscated straightaway.

At night, along the corridor, verses from the Qur'an rang out. *Nor will they enter the garden until the camel can pass through the eye of the needle. Have you no faith in Him who created you from dust?* Classes were organized in poetry and song, shouted along from cell to cell. Antar, Abu Zayd al-Hilali, Sayf ibn Dhi Yazan, Marx and Lenin too.

The poems of Mahmoud Darwish were chanted with the regularity of prayers: *A prison cell with a cold window. A sea for us, a sea against us. I work with comrades in a stone quarry. Perfume me with basil water.*

Bassam was able to handle the beatings. Mostly in the canteen. The guards came in full riot gear. They lined the prisoners up. They were told to take their clothes off. They stood there naked. Bassam used a plastic food tray as a shield. It split perfectly in the middle, right above his head.

He limped into the shower fully dressed so he could wash the blood from his clothing, then hung the clothes from the bars of his window. He got down on his knees and prayed into the damp of his shirt.

Much of his time was spent in solitary confinement. Ritual called on him to pray on a clean prayer mat. He used a blue cloth upon which he drew a mihrab. The prison guard, Hertzl, risked giving the cloth to him. Bassam rolled it up meticulously and put it away without drawing attention.

They had fought at first, he and Hertzl. Hertzl was tall and thin and sharp-faced with a prominent Adam's apple. He was raised an Orthodox Jew and had studied mathematics as a student in Tel Aviv. He was taken by the fact that Bassam's prison number was 220-284. Something to do with what he called amicable numbers.

Bassam tried to remember a school lesson about al-Khwarizmi and the House of Wisdom. He couldn't recall it entirely, but told Hertzl that all good math had come from the Arabs, everyone knew that. The two started talking. Quietly and insistently, at the door of his cell.

—Hey, Hertzl, we've been doing your math for a thousand years, who's the settler here now, tell me that?

He learned Hebrew because he wanted to know the enemy. *Ivrit hee sfat ha'oyev.* Keep him close. Learn how to bury him. Read the Torah. Know his foul idolatry. Break his jail down. Imprison him with his imprisonment.

Just about everything that surrounded Bassam was enemy. The food he ate. The plexiglas windows he scratched. The air he breathed. The way it shaped his lungs. Even someone like Hertzl was an enemy.

It was only in the fourth year of his seven-year sentence—after watching a documentary in his cell—that Bassam's balance got all knocked to hell.

197

> —Why did you leave the horse alone?
> —To keep the house company, my son.
>
> ~ MAHMOUD DARWISH ~

198

The prison guard arrived with two bottles of Coca-Cola in a grocery bag, hid them in a water tank in the warden's office to keep them cool. He brought them to Bassam in the dead of night, tucked under his shirt. He made a special presentation of a glass cup.

The next day Bassam distributed one swallow of Coke to every prisoner in the unit. He cut the empty bottles apart, crushed them into tiny pieces, flushed them down the toilet.

The glass cup smelled syrupy for days: the prisoners came to his cell simply to inhale the scent.

199

None of the leaders in the prison block ever mentioned that one of Darwish's lovers was a Jewish dancer, Tamar Ben Ami. He had written the poem *Rita and the Rifle* about her. Later Bassam would think of the great dark-eyed Palestinian poet pulling the covers back from her long white body, the strap-mark of a gun, an M-16 or an M-4 perhaps, still across her shoulder.

She accompanied Darwish when he reported to prison once, kissed him at the gates, went off to rejoin the Israeli forces: she was part of the Navy's performing troupe.

She wrote Darwish letters from the decks of frigates and gunboats and carrier ships—in one photo she is perched in front of the railing of a submarine chaser.

Without you, she wrote in Hebrew, *I am without any depth, I am on the surface here, waiting.*

200

Bassam was six years old when a helicopter bladed the sky in the hills outside Hebron. He had never seen a machine quite like it before. The soldiers, when they leaped out, looked to him like green insects, crouching and running up the hillside, fabulous with fear.

His mother ran down from their home in the hillside caves, grabbed his sleeve, shooed him home along the rocky path. He knew every pebble underfoot.

She ripped across the curtain of the cave, blew on the candle that swung in the glass lantern from the rock ceiling.

The light clung a moment to the handmade rugs on the wall, then all went dark.

201

The caves outside Hebron were some of the most coveted places for farmers to live—cool in summer, warm in winter, fragrant with olives kept in ornate pots on rows of carefully built wooden shelves.

Bassam was one of fifteen children. In summer he slept outside on a straw mat under a tarp alongside his father, a privileged position, coveted by his brothers.

It was, Bassam knew, because of his father's guilt: of all the children, Bassam was the only one who had missed the polio vaccine.

202

In a shallow cave, Bassam found the stashed grenades he and his friends used for the assault. When they explored further inside the cave they found the rifle.

The grenades were the size of large stones. The rifle, when his friends cocked it, flaked dust.

203

The army jeep crashed through the cactus, the shrubs, past the fence. Engine-roar. Shouting. A bird he couldn't name swung low past his ear. His right foot dragged. He felt a blow on the side of his head. He crumpled while still running.

The ground was dry and hard. The dust came up to his nostrils. A sand-colored lizard darted in front of his eyes.

He tried to rise. A foot landed on his neck. The soldiers wore black boots, square-toed. The boots made them seem as if they had something wrong with their feet: as if they would limp badly if they were to walk long distances in them.

His arms were pulled behind his back. A blow to the back of his neck knocked him out.

204

He was tied to a chair, hooded and beaten. The hood was coarse, brown, dirty, with a smell of burnt straw, not sleek and black like the ones that were used later in Beersheva. He whispered his prayers into the hood. *I invoke the perfect words of Allah from which neither a good person nor a bad one can escape.*

They lifted him up from the chair with a rope tied around his neck. They looped the rope over a steampipe and stretched him in the air while he stood on the chair. They rocked the chair back and forth. He took a blow to his kidneys, his stomach, his groin.

He invoked the name of God again. He was thumped several times in the side of the head until he collapsed.

When he woke he was in a cell, six feet by three. His testicles were so swollen that he could hardly move his legs to swing himself out of bed.

205

He was seventeen years old.

206

When he was thirteen he hoisted a flag in the school playground: green, red, black, white. Just to piss the soldiers off. So he could throw stones at them when they came to tear it down. To see the cords in their necks tighten. To have them blaze around the corner, jolting to a halt.

What he liked most of all was the sound of the jeep tires when they plowed past the school gates. Not the soldiers anymore, not the vehicle, not the guns, just the noise of the spinning tires: there was something hungry about them.

The sounds of his boyhood.

207

The silence, then, afterwards, while out walking in the dusty hills.

208

Another cave in southern Hebron had a small shaft open to the sky. When he was young, Bassam lay there under the moving stars, watching the pinpoints turn above him.

Occasional flocks of night birds darted across the face of the opening, disorienting him a moment.

In prison he tried to replicate the memory. Poems and stories slid from cell to cell among his fellow prisoners: the tale of a mechanical vulture, a herder of giant ostriches, the flight of a centaur, a weeping lion, the sacrifice of virgins along the banks of the Nile.

209

Memories hit Rami, too, all the time. A closing door. A beeping sound from the motorbike. The bristle of a razor against a chin. The call for a stretcher. The sound of the metal rollers in the morgue.

210

During the first of his three wars Rami drove an army truck for a technical medical team. He brought in the ammunition and carried the Israeli dead out from the Sinai desert.

One night in an abandoned warehouse in El-Arish, on the north coast of Egypt, the Commander of Rami's unit sat down in the middle of a pile of grain. They had already lost eight of eleven tanks. The Commander counted out the pieces of grain, dropping them from his fingers one by one. Three, four, five. He dropped the ninth grain by mistake. It seemed to Rami like a brutal piece of theater.

He walked outside into the dark. Streaks of bomblight went across the sky, an aurora borealis.

He thought of the war afterwards as a sort of awful artwork: the stretchers went in white and came out red. The beds were hosed down and put back in the truck and he drove into the desert again to pick up men whose faces would soon be ringed in the newspapers.

211

When he returned from the war he said to Nurit that he wasn't sure that all of him had come home.

212

From great distances come the starlings
Beating to these death-ponds: always they come.

~ ELISHA PORAT ~

213

In the late nineteenth century, rare falcons could be found for sale in the markets of Bethlehem.

The falcons were captured in the desert by Bedouin boys who dug deep pits at night, covered them with brush and interlaced twigs, and concealed themselves underground. They tied pigeons on long straps as lures, and made the terrified birds fly about in the air at the end of the leather, making slingshot circles in the air.

The boys waited, peeking out from beneath their camouflage. They knew it was best to capture the birds at sunrise when the winds were calmer and, because of the angle of the light, the traps were less likely to be seen.

The boys held the long straps in their hands. They wore long camel-hide hand coverings that reached to their elbows. Every now and then they jerked on the straps to distress the pigeons, causing them to flap about.

The birds of prey, noticing the anguish below, circled on the thermals, then began swooping lower and lower, in careful circles.

As the falcons descended, the boys pulled the screaming pigeons closer and closer to the hole.

When the falcons were near enough to the pit—about to swoop upon the tethered pigeon—the boys exploded upward from the hole and grabbed the falcons by both legs, hauled them into the pit, quickly folded back their wings, tied their beaks, hooded them, subdued them.

The neck of the pigeon was immediately broken and it was fed to the captured falcon in order to calm it down.

The boys caged the falcons and strapped them to the sides of camels, then moved in caravan through the scrubby hills, wary of ambush. They hurried the camels along, slapping their brindled hides, feeding them grain from their hands.

The birds commanded considerable money, especially among British aristocrats who put bells on their legs and trained them for game-hawking around Jerusalem.

214

Sir Richard Francis Burton, the nineteenth-century explorer, was a keen falconer. Born in Torquay, he learned his craft at Oxford in the 1840s, where he studied Arabic, one of his twenty-nine languages. Tall and thin, he had famously dark eyes, not unlike those of his adored birds. In the army in India he was known as the White Nigger. It was rumored that he was of mostly Romany, or Gypsy, blood. Burton could pass himself off as a trader, diplomat, dervish or holy wanderer.

He had a penchant for fighting and was known to his fellow soldiers as Ruffian Dick. Sometimes, in the middle of a fight, he would stop and twirl the ends of his thick dark moustache, then continue the scrap undaunted. He took to calling himself the Amateur Barbarian.

Burton traveled the world in pursuit of *gnosis:* he wanted to discover the very source of meaning and existence. He made a hajj pilgrimage to Mecca in 1853. He knew full well that non-Muslims were not allowed in the city, under pain of death. He developed what he said was an Arab gait: what he liked to think of as a surrounded walk where he appeared at ease, long-limbed, dismissively nonchalant, while acutely aware of everything that was going on around him. He considered himself a follower of the *tariqa,* or the mystic path, which was to lead to heaven. He studied Islamic law and learned to play the rubab. He worked on his accent, grew out his hair, darkened his skin with boiled grass, applied kóhl to his eyelids, wore flowing muslin shirts, practiced squatting on the ground for hours on end. He apprenticed himself to a blacksmith to learn how to shoe: he thought he might eventually find a trade in Arabian horses.

Burton made a point of praying five times a day. At night, in the caravan of two hundred worshippers, he led the prayer ceremonies. He rode the camel at the front of the procession, using a giant yellow umbrella for shelter from the brutal sun.

On the way to Mecca, he managed to help stave off several attacks from roving bands.

He was well known among his fellow travelers for his ability to spot those places where water might be found in the desert: it wasn't simply his sensitivity to the flight of the desert birds, but an ability also to intuit smaller clues in the landscape, the slant of the dunes, the dart of a lizard, the coarseness of the sand.

215

One of the few all-Arab units in the Israel Defense Forces is comprised almost entirely of Bedouin trackers: they are known among themselves as the Khamsin Unit. A volunteer unit, they are reputed to be able to follow or track even in the middle of pelting sandstorms.

216

The Khamsin winds are named after the Arabic word for fifty. They blow from the south to the northwest—hot and sand-filled—for fifty days.

217

Imagine the terror of the captive pigeon as the falcon descends. A cloud of dust as it is pulled toward the hole. The tightening of the strap

around its leg. The collapse of the camouflaged twigs. The sudden swell
of air. The disappearance underground. The darkness. The silence of
the boys. A hand reaching up. The shriek of the falcon, its wings folded
back. An underground burst of feathers.

218

In the desert the best time to track is the early morning or the late
afternoon when the sun's oblique rays create shadows, darkening a
footprint or a tire track.

When the sun is high in the sky the Bedouin use portable paper
shades of varying weight and thickness to shadow the ground and to
detect nuances in the dirt.

The trackers also pride themselves on what they can learn from the
smell and the feel of the wind.

219

After the Ben Yehuda Street bombings, a Bedouin unit was sent out
to the West Bank to flush out the cave where the suicide bombers had
lived for almost a year. The task was called Operation Icarus. One of
the hideouts was traced to Wadi al-Hamam, the Valley of the Dove.

220

Amicable numbers are two different numbers related in the sense that
when you add all their proper divisors together—not including the
original number itself—the sums of their divisors equal each other.

The numbers—esteemed by mathematicians—are considered
amicable because the proper divisors of 220 are 1, 2, 4, 5, 10, 11, 20, 22,
44, 55 and 110 which, when added together, reach 284. And the proper
divisors of 284 are 1, 2, 4, 71 and 142, of which the sum is 220.

They are the only amicable numbers under 1,000.

221

As if those different things of which they are comprised can somehow recognize one another.

222

On the day he left prison, Bassam cut out his number from the chest of his prison uniform. Later he sent the cloth badge to the prison guard Hertzl.

Hertzl framed the badge—220-284—and hung it on the wall in his office in the Department of Mathematics in Hebrew University where he had begun to work on ideas of harmonic integration.

223

Sir Richard Francis Burton translated *Arabian Nights*, also known as *The Book of a Thousand Nights and a Night*, also known as *One Thousand and One Nights*.

224

One of Smadar's favorites was the Tale of the Hunchback, the story of an amusing hunchback who was assumed dead over and over again, resulting in a string of confessions from all the supposed murderers, only for it to turn out in the end, as revealed by a barber, that the Hunchback was never dead at all.

225

A few weeks after the bombing, Rami went into Smadar's room. Everything had been kept exactly as it had been the day she left: her copybook open on the table, the earrings spread out on the windowsill, the photo of Sinéad O'Connor in the corner of the mirror.

He removed *One Thousand and One Nights* from the shelf and began to read the hunchback story.

You see, cried the barber, he's not dead at all.

226

Burton was wary of being seen as a spy or a sorcerer: on his pilgrimage to Mecca he did not want to be seen taking notes of any kind, even in Arabic. He carried what appeared to be a small Qur'an slung on a leather cord over his shoulder. The book had three compartments—one for his watch and compass, another for his money and the third for pencils and numbered slips of paper that he could hide in the palm of his hand. He kept a small pistol in a pocket and carried a packet of opium which he smoked when alone.

If Burton had been exposed as a nonbeliever, he would have been beaten with sticks, stoned, disemboweled and left alive in a shallow grave in the unbearable heat, subject to attacks by jackals and vultures, until nothing recognizable was left.

227

Once, during Salman Rushdie's fatwa, the Indian novelist received a single pebble in the mail, alone in a white envelope with no note included. The pebble sat on his desk for years until a New York house-cleaner mistakenly swept it up and threw it away.

228

Burton—who also translated the *Kama Sutra*—was a notorious liar.

It was said that he killed a young Bedouin boy after the boy saw him lifting his robe to urinate rather than squatting in the traditional manner. The story was that Burton knifed the boy to save himself from being exposed as a non-Muslim.

Burton claimed it was just pure fantasy, a piece of prejudiced apocrypha, but years later, drunk in a brothel in Rio de Janeiro, he suggested to friends that he had once killed a child and he would carry the weight of the guilt with him into the grave.

229

You see, cried the barber, he's not dead at all.

230

What Bassam hated most about the prison beatings was that the guards would take away the prisoners' clothes and leave them standing there in the great humiliation of their nakedness.

The guards locked them in the canteen. He soon discovered that it wasn't the first thump of the baton that was the worst: it was the second or third, when he realized it wasn't going to stop. By the time the seventh or eighth blow landed it almost felt routine. He balled up, with his hands over his head, unsure where the next blow might land.

He woke up in the prison hospital covered in a thin bedsheet.

Only Hertzl would not take part in the beatings. Once he threw himself over Bassam to prevent the baton coming down. Another guard pinned Hertzl up against the wall, headbutted him, asked him if he had a penchant for camels. Hertzl replied that, yes, he was quite interested in the camel's ability to spit, without fear, in an owner's face.

231

During the twelfth-century Crusades, Christian warriors tied naked prisoners—Jewish, Muslim, Turk—to mountaintop rocks and then released trained eagles with sharpened talons upon them.

The eagles worked around the liver, the kidneys and the heart until they pecked the prisoners to death.

Artists were employed to depict the Promethean scene in charcoals, bronzes, watercolors.

232

Godfrey of Bouillon, who became Defender of the Holy Sepulchre, decorated his eagles with a pure-silver cross tied around their necks. They left the perch of his armored hand and flew—sinewy and majestic—toward the prisoner.

233

Imagine, then, the swing of the cross as the eagle approached.

234

235

The way of the patriarchs.

In the early 1990s, eight New York sandhogs were brought to Israel to work on portions of Highway 60, also known as the Tunnels Road. Hard men, fierce, unflappable, some of the best tunnel workers around. Two were American-born, two were Irish, one was Polish, one was Italian, one was Canadian and the other was Croatian.

They packed up their work on the upstate water tunnels in Poughkeepsie and moved to Jerusalem where they lived together in a seedy hotel in the east of the city.

For eight months it was a steady stream of hangovers for all the sandhogs except the Croatian, Marko Kovačević, who was a teetotaler. He was a tall, brooding man, broad-shouldered, intent. He stayed quiet, living on a separate floor from the others.

Every morning Kovačević drove them all to work in their white van. They worked the dynamite, crimping the fuses, blasting out the rocks, supervising the removal of the rubble from under the mountain.

Kovačević's specialty was using small precise amounts of explosives in tight situations: the men nicknamed him the Mole.

In the evening Kovačević drove the sandhogs home in a cloud of cigarette smoke and then disappeared to walk the holy city by himself. Kovačević was never around on a Friday or Saturday. He grew his hair out and began a beard. He looped his hair in ringlets. Toward the end of the job he disappeared altogether. The sandhogs reported his disappearance to the Israeli police, but Kovačević was nowhere to be found. Foul play wasn't suspected: suicide seemed the only possibility. The sandhogs contacted his wife at home in the Bronx but she had heard nothing from him either, nor had any money appeared from him in her bank account for three months running.

A missing persons report went out for Kovačević, but the Croatian was not found.

When the tunnel was finished the sandhogs gathered for a ritual they had performed many times before, in New York, Pennsylvania, Florida. The electricity was cut, candles were lit, and together they paraded through the darkness in traditional fashion, their shadows flickering, carrying the memory of their disappeared colleague, along the Way of the Patriarchs, under Beit Jala, from one end of the tunnel to the other.

237

King Hezekiah, in the year 700 B.C., ordered his men to build a tunnel in Jerusalem to bring water from the Gihon Spring to the Pool of Siloam. The tunnel was a meter wide, half a kilometer long.

The men began on opposite sides of the mountain using chisels and hammers and axes. The two tunnels were due to meet in the middle, but the stonecutters had no way of knowing how or where they might collide. At certain times of the day one team would drop their tools and put their ears and hands to the rock to see if they might hear the other.

When they eventually heard the faint vibration of hammers and chisels through the limestone, the tunnelers swerved toward each other. They kept chiseling, the sounds growing clearer and clearer the closer they came. It took one last final S-swerve to bring them together.

When they broke through, water flowed down the gradient between the pool and the spring.

238

Halfway through the Gilo tunnel, the sandhogs tucked a plaster of paris statue of Saint Barbara—patron saint of tunnel diggers—into a crevice near the ceiling.

They were not surprised to learn that the Palestinian workers had their own rituals too: arrows carved in the ceiling every hundred feet, pointing toward Mecca, and a tiny piece of thread tucked under the paving stones to ensure safety.

239

In the winter of 2010, two Palestinian ornithologists went on a field trip into the scrublands halfway between Gilo and Beit Jala. They were out studying the patterns of the shrike, a small bird known for catching insects and impaling them on barbed wire. The ornithologists—Tarek Khalil and Said Hourani—were careful not to wear anything resembling traditional clothing, and were easily visible in their neon vests.

In the late morning, several shots were fired over their heads. The men had been subject to warning shots before, both from the settlers and from houses on their own side in Beit Jala.

The men lay on the dusty ground and raised Tarek's white T-shirt on a length of stick. Their cellphones had no signal. The men began to crawl back through the shrub among the hard rocks and stunted olive trees. The area—much of which had become a no-man's-land—was heavily decorated with barbed wire where the shrikes had left their insects. When the men were fairly sure they had crawled back to safety, near a small clay ridge, they again raised a white shirt in the air. Six more shots were fired.

The two men lay together on the ground. At nightfall they were rescued by a joint force of Israelis and Palestinians.

Where the shots had come from became a subject of debate until six months later a tall, thin settler, Mark Kovack, was arrested after a tip-off. A search of his house revealed several sniper rifles. A further search revealed that he had built a series of tunnels out from the settlement into No-man's-land, where he could shoot at intruders from any angle.

Kovack, who was known by other settlers as a quiet recluse, claimed to have been born in Jerusalem, but his accent was Eastern European. A quick background check revealed one of his previous jobs: he had worked as a sandhog in the Bronx.

240

The impaling of insects along the wire by shrikes is known to be part of their courtship behavior.

241

Kovack is said to have bought a house in Ariel, a Jewish settlement in the West Bank. He is the owner of a swimming pool company. For years a billboard could be seen over Highway 1, a photo of a sparkling pool beside a red-roofed villa, a phone number, and a single phrase: *Your Oasis Awaits.*

242

During the 2004 operation on Nablus, Israeli soldiers advanced into the city.

Instead of moving through the narrow streets and the densely packed alleyways, soldiers moved through walls and ceilings, cutting holes and blasting their way aboveground, house to house, shop to shop, stealthily worming their way through, painting fluorescent arrows on the walls to show other soldiers behind them which way to go.

When they stopped, they used thermal-imaging goggles in order to see what lay on the other side of each wall. Men and women tucked together in embrace. Sleeping children. Young men with keffiyehs over their mouths.

The burrowing was known to the soldiers as walking through walls.

243

The phone call came in the middle of the evening. Fourteen years after the bombing. Rami was taken aback. A documentary filmmaker. She had been in contact with the families in Assira al-Shamaliya. The mothers and fathers of two of the three bombers were willing to meet with him. In the heart of the West Bank, she said. It was unprecedented. They would allow themselves to be filmed by a Western crew. In their village. In their houses. In their living rooms.

She would arrange transportation, security too. He had nothing to worry about. She could guarantee it. He would have to be smuggled into the West Bank, but he knew already that that part would be easy.

They would be waiting for him, the parents of the men who had murdered his daughter.

244

Rami could see himself in a high-arched house, sitting on a sofa with patterned cushions, a tray of cardamom coffee and sweets laid out in front of him, flowers, pottery, a miniature Dome of the Rock in white mother-of-pearl alongside a careful arrangement of photographs on the high wooden shelf.

245

In the summer of 1932, as part of an exchange of letters between several noted intellectuals, Albert Einstein wrote to Sigmund Freud.

Einstein praised the Austrian's devotion to the internal and external liberation of man from the evils of war. This liberation was the profound hope of all moral and spiritual leaders from Christ to Goethe and Kant, universally recognized as leaders who existed beyond their own times and countries. And yet, Einstein asked, was it not significant that these very persons had been essentially ineffective in their desires to change the course of human affairs? That they had, for years, been unable to stem the savagery? That the patterns of violence could not be mitigated, even in the face of the most meaningful pleas?

The essential question that he wanted to ask Freud was if he thought it might be possible to guide the psychological development of humankind so that it became resistant to the psychoses of hate and destruction, thereby delivering civilization from the hovering menace of war?

246

Even as he said yes, Rami knew that it would likely never happen.

247

He drove that night to Bassam's apartment in Anata. On the motorbike. He peeled off the bumper sticker before he went through the checkpoint. *It will not be over until we talk.*

They huddled together for hours in the living room. The offer stunned Bassam, but it might, he said, cause more grief than anything it might ever solve. The villagers were simple people. They farmed olives. They cut wheat sheaves. They had no idea how to deal with cameras or microphones. They might be out of their depth. Something could go wrong. Perhaps they wouldn't understand him, his straight talk, his honesty. He was an Israeli after all, face it, he was loud, he was forceful, he might go too far, his anger could overflow. It might end up a sound bite. Tensions were high. The villagers, too, could get in trouble. They might not follow the proper political lines. Ramifications. Repercussions. Word could spread. They could be called collaborators, accused of normalization. One could never know. It was a minefield. Someone might get hurt.

They walked out of the apartment, down the stairs, into the night. On the horizon a fire was burning in the nearby Shu'fat camp. Another protest. Beyond that, over the Wall, faint stars hung dull over the scrublands. The two men stood on the sloping pavement, silent awhile.

—Don't do it, my friend, said Bassam.

248

When the British beat a hasty retreat from Mandate Palestine in 1948, among the things that army corporal Paul Hartingtone left behind were his prize falcons.

Hartingtone, who had been decorated several times in North Africa during the Second World War, had bought and trained two cherished peregrines during his time in Palestine. Sympathetic to the Jewish cause, Hartingtone left a note for a local leader of the underground resistance asking him to take care of the birds, which were kept on the balcony of a large white limestone house in Jerusalem. The prizewinning peregrines had been left in silver cages with enough food to last them a few days. He left veterinary certificates and grooming instructions and even a little money to make sure the birds were looked after.

A couple of days later a fierce gunfight erupted in the vicinity of the limestone house. Arab forces beat back the Jewish fighters and the birds fell into the hands of a local man, Jafer Hassan, who groomed them and looked after them until he, too, a few days later, was forced to retreat, carrying only the birds and the keys to his locked house.

Hassan and his family—and their falcons—eventually ended up in the mud streets of Nablus. Their home was shoddily constructed. Thin industrial carpet laid over bare cement. Walls of styrofoam. Electricity pirated from dangling wires. A broken sewage pipe gurgled just down the road. Hassan made applications for permission to return to the limestone house in Jerusalem, but the requests were turned down. He fashioned locks to fit the keys rather than the other way around. The locks were put on the falcon cages. Months slid into months, years into years.

Hassan kept the birds on the roof of his house. The only way to build in the refugee camp was upwards. His house began to extend higher and higher as his family grew, adding extension after extension. For a while Hassan liked this: the falcons were constantly rising, as if there were some sort of generational thermals underneath. Beneath them, children were born to children.

The home grew, rickety, sheeted, scaffolded, the cages perched precariously above.

Throughout the 1960s and '70s, Hassan made a living breeding the birds, but had to pay a series of fines for owning the rooftop cages. He had no permits. When he applied for them, he was refused. The fines continued until he had to sell the birds at auction. The last of the offspring were finally sold in the 1980s when Hassan was an old man and knew he would never be able to return to his house in Jerusalem. The locks and the keys, he kept.

He used the money to buy a large stone house in the village of Assira al-Shamaliya, near the camel stables, but he died shortly after moving his family in.

The birds ended up being exported to Abu Dhabi where their offspring commanded huge fees, sometimes hundreds of thousands of dollars, not only for their beauty, but for the value of their story too. They were carefully bred with other prizewinners. Falcon hoods were made for them out of pressed gold and jewels.

249

The Abu Dhabi sheikh who owns the most famous of the peregrine's offspring refers to them as his Birds of Sorrow. They were photographed in 2012 for the cover of the catalogue of the state-of-the-art Abu Dhabi Falcon Hospital on the Sweihan Road.

250

One of the most intricate operations at the Falcon Hospital is the repair of broken feathers. Whole drawers of falcon feathers in every shape and hue are to be found in the climate-controlled room next to the first-floor operating theater.

The feathers are carefully sewn and glued to the bodies of injured birds.

Afterwards, their new flight patterns are captured on camera and transferred to a computer program. Further adjustments are then made to the new feathers in order to streamline the birds for perfect flight.

251

One of the most sought-after makers of falcon hoods in the world is Mona Akilah Saqqaf who works from a dusty warehouse on the outskirts of eastern Los Angeles. She uses grass-fed bison leather, with stitches, no glue. Her designs are originally Persian, but she also incorporates Native American styles into the hoods, not least in the knots and in the color schemes, mostly Comanche designs. With the hoods come leashes, jesses, anklets and perches too.

Often the falcons are brought directly to her on private planes from the Middle East. Depending on the jewels involved, and the gold leafing or silver embroidery, Saqqaf can take up to two weeks to make a single hood.

In her home in Santa Monica—where she lives with her Chilean husband and their son Kamil—Mona has built a huge outdoor swimming pool in the shape of an Arabian hood: the bright blue pool is often photographed from above in architectural magazines.

For a while in 2004 her business dropped off when she was photographed for a style magazine standing poolside in a bikini. Several prominent sheikhs canceled their orders until Saqqaf's agent assured them that the hoods were made by traditional methods.

A photograph was circulated of Saqqaf applying the finishing lacquer while at her workbench in modest Middle Eastern attire.

252

The reason a falcon is hooded is exactly the reason a falconer is not: the birds can see so well that they would most likely be distracted by other prey much further away.

The falconer hoods the bird and waits. He wants the falcon to only see what he sees.

253

Saqqaf's Los Angeles swimming pool holds 32,000 gallons of water.

254

In September 1932, Einstein received a reply from Sigmund Freud, and the psychoanalyst apologized for the delay.

The proper reply to the thorny problem of preventing war would be coming sometime soon, but Freud suggested that he was nervous at the thought of his own incompetence. His answer would probably not be very encouraging. He had grown old, he said, and all his life he had been telling people truths that were difficult to absorb.

A week later Einstein wrote a second note to Freud saying that he eagerly awaited the contents of the forthcoming letter.

In his eventual reply—which came several weeks after the initial request—Freud said that he was flattered to be asked, but that in his opinion there was not much likelihood of anyone being able to suppress humanity's most aggressive tendencies. There are not many people in the world whose lives go gently by, he said. It is easy to infect mankind with war fever, and humanity has an active instinct for hatred and destruction. Still, Freud said, the hope that war will end is not chimerical. What was needed was to establish, by common consent, a central authority that would have the last word in every conflict of interest.

Beyond that, anything which creates emotional ties between human beings inevitably counteracts war. What had to be sought was *a community of feeling*, and *a mythology of the instincts*.

255

By the time the exchange between Einstein and Freud was published in 1933, Adolf Hitler was already in power. The original German- and

English-language editions of the letters, titled *Why War?*, were limited to just two thousand copies.

Both men left their homelands to live in exile, Freud in England and Einstein in America, to avoid the full fate that neither they nor anyone else could possibly yet imagine.

256

My name is Rami Elhanan. I am the father of Smadar. I am a seventh-generation Jerusalemite. Also what you might call a graduate of the Holocaust.

257

Immediately on release from the concentration camp in Auschwitz, Yitzak Elhanan Gold was given a ticket to travel on a ship to Tel Aviv along with a dozen other Hungarians, several Romanians and two Swedes. The men had no official papers.

On arrival, Yitzak was met by underground Jewish forces. He was disguised as a British soldier and put on a bus to Jerusalem. A job was arranged for him as a police officer in the Old City. He was nick-named Chet Chet Gimmel for the numbers on his chest: British Mandate Police Officer Number 883.

Yitzak was injured in the war of '48 and adopted, at the hospital, by a family who had lived in the city for six generations. He soon learned the language and began to fit in, but he never spoke to his children about his experiences during the Holocaust until decades later, when he was asked by Smadar for a school genealogy project.

258

At the age of fourteen, Yitzak was assigned to work as a runner for the rabbi in Gyor, smuggling gold down to the market. The money was used by the rabbi for food and medicine.

Yitzak was quick and lithe. He wore no stars on his jacket. No garrison cap with a military brim. He knew the alleyways and rooftops. He was able to make his way across the town without being spotted, sometimes jumping from chimney to chimney or shimmying down to street level on a drainpipe.

He dashed through the red-light district to get to the market, near the square. The women were all lipstick and dare. In winter they wore short coats. He ran past them and into the market. In the evening he hung around the cinema and began to scalp tickets, selling them at a little over face value.

One evening, with a single ticket left, he decided he would go in and treat himself to a Zarah Leander film.

He had just settled in his seat—the curtains had pulled across on *The Great Love*—when an officer from the Gestapo slid into the seat beside him and blocked his exit.

259

One of the most popular German songs of the time, *Davon geht die Welt nicht unter*—The World Will Not End Because of This—was written expressly for the film.

260

On June 23, 1944, the Nazis allowed representatives of the International Committee of the Red Cross to visit Theresienstadt in order to counter rumors of death camps. There were, the Germans said, no such thing.

Among the visitors to the Czech camp were the head physician of the Danish Ministry of Health and the top representative from the Foreign Ministry. They were guided around by SS first lieutenant Karl Rahm and his deputies.

For weeks prior to the visit, the Germans forced the Czech and Jewish prisoners to clean the streets. They brought in flowers, fixed broken roofs, installed park benches. The lower floors of the dormitories were renovated. They painted fake shop fronts. Gave the streets civilian names. Signs appeared, pointing to a nonexistent post office, a swimming pool, a café. They opened up the central square, put down a new lawn and planted rosebushes. They carved signs for cafés and bakeries and a luxury spa. They printed decorative posters and hung them from the boughs of the trees. Handed out belt buckles, clothes brushes, combs. Distributed fresh yellow armbands. Rehearsed a performance of a children's opera written by Hans Krása, a camp resident. Put together a series of shows under the guidance of the camp's official music critic, Viktor Ullmann.

Then, when the town was spruced up, they deported thousands of Jewish prisoners—mostly the sick and the elderly—to Auschwitz so the streets wouldn't seem too crowded.

On the day of the visit, the Germans instructed all remaining camp residents to ignore any questions the Danish guests might ask if they passed through. Compulsory salutes were abolished, and the residents could only speak if addressed by the fake mayor and his underlings, or a uniformed officer. The artists, actors, poets, professors, psychologists, children and a number of elderly all complied with the order.

The Red Cross delegation walked around the town following a pre-ordained red line drawn on a map.

Afterwards, when the delegation had left, deeming it to be a functioning internment camp operating within international law, the Nazis decided to make a propaganda film for the site. It was directed by Kurt Gerron, a Jewish prisoner, who had been a cabaret and film actor in Germany: he was known as the voice behind *Mack the Knife*, and had also played a minor role in a film with Marlene Dietrich.

Under instruction, Gerron made the film in eleven days. His crew was over a dozen strong. He used a 16mm Leica camera. The German officers told him what exactly they wanted. Film a performance of *Brundibár*. Capture for us the musicians tuning their violins. Show us the children playing hopscotch just beyond the swing. Film a teacher in the schoolhouse with chalk on the board behind her. Capture an old man at ease over his chessboard. Portray the sun rising up between buildings.

When he was finished, Gerron and his wife were put on a train, along with the film crew, and brought to Auschwitz where they were put in a chamber and gassed.

261

The Germans called it Operation Embellishment.

262

Most of the 23-minute film was later destroyed.

263

The title was to have been *Der Führer schenkt den Juden eine Stadt:* The Fuhrer Gives the Jews a City.

264

A special bureau known as the Hygienic Institute was responsible for delivering Zyklon B pellets to the SS soldiers in Auschwitz. They rushed the canisters by ambulance to the gas chambers.

The pellets—which had a shelf life of three months—were dropped through vents in the ceiling.

265

The rim of a tightening lung.

266

What fascinated Smadar most about her grandfather's story was that a well-dressed man had slipped Yitzak a piece of seedcake at the train station in Gyor. The cake was wrapped in a piece of newspaper.

On the train, he unfurled the newspaper and found, in the bottom corner, an advertisement for the film *The Great Love*.

Yitzak ate the cake in one sitting—he always regretted this, he told Smadar. He wished he had made it last longer, but he kept the piece of newspaper folded in his pocket all the way through his days in the camp.

267

Bassam had a small black-and-white television set in his prison cell. It received Channel One in Hebrew with occasional Arabic programs, nothing else. He placed it on a wooden table at the head of his bed and it played in the background as he slept.

He had to hold his hand on the aerial to get better reception. It felt odd to him to think that the news of the day was flowing through him in Hebrew. Mostly what interested him was the weather: he could imagine what it was like back in Sa'ir.

On the night before Holocaust Memorial Day he switched it on to a documentary. It came as no surprise. Bassam was tuned in to their propaganda. He would watch anyway.

He wanted to see Jews die. One after the other. To watch them fall. Starve. Collapse in ditches. To see the gas spurt through the ceiling. Retribution. To experience them being annihilated.

Twenty years old, lying there on the bed, Bassam was waiting for the moment he could applaud.

268

In the final stages of hypothermia, a person suffering from extreme cold will experience a sudden surge of blood to the extremities when the peripheral blood vessels become exhausted.

The victims may even take off their clothes because of what they think is an unbearable heat.

269

At lunchtime the next day Bassam walked along the metal floors to the canteen. He could hardly see down through the latticework of iron: his balance was all knocked to hell.

270

The hard bed folded down from the wall. He lay back against it. Arms behind his head. Shouts rang along the corridors. Music from the cells. The pluck of a single wire. A distant radio. There was, he thought, some other layer to the emptiness that lay beneath him. He rested his head on the stinking pillow and grasped the thin metal aerial. He had wanted at first to cheer the falling corpses. Watch them being pitched forward again and again in their hideous contortions. Know your enemy, keep them close. Under your feet preferably. In the ground. He turned to the wall, pulled up the thin blanket. *To lighten the sorrow of the sorrowful.* He repeated his prayers. A small roach crawled from the gap in the plasterwork. Its antennae pulsed. He crushed it with his shoe. He rewrapped the blanket, reached for the aerial once more. He wondered why they did not fight back. One after the other. Their bodies pitched forward again and again. In their nakedness. On the other side of the cell, the toilet, the metal sink. A faint tapping came through the pipes. Each sound was amplified. He felt as if something had taken over the sprockets of his mind, driving the mechanical gears forward like the constant pitch of the bodies.

271

The most excellent jihad is that for the conquest of self.

272

Over the loudspeakers came the order for a camp census. It was November: the morning so cold outside that the branches of the trees snapped.

Thousands of prisoners filed into the open. Some were hustled from their beds in their nightshirts. Others wore thin jackets, camp trousers, dresses, whatever gloves and hats they had fashioned in their barracks. They lined up in neat rows. Men, women, children. They were ordered to drop their blankets to the snow. Immediately the blood backed away from their fingers, their toes, their legs, their arms. Every ounce of warmth went into the way they shivered.

Anton Burger, the camp commandant, walked along the long lines in his high black boots and his fur-collared coat, his hands clasped behind his back. From his waistband looped a beautiful silver time-piece. He flicked it open, closed it again. The count went five minutes, eight, ten.

Some collapsed fully clothed and were dragged away, but soon—as Burger had predicted—a hat came off. A coat was thrown away moments later. Another. And then another. Any prisoner who stooped for a discarded item, or to help another prisoner, was shot. A woman began fingering at her buttons. An elderly man stripped to his undershirt. Two more minutes went by. Three. Four. Burger checked his watch. The prisoners began to fall in pairs. Clothes littered the ground. Twenty-seven minutes altogether. Burger waved his hand: he would try the experiment again, in even harsher weather next time. The prisoners were ordered to return to barracks.

Scores of bodies lay on the ground. Burger ordered the discarded clothes to be immediately collected and burned.

State your name. Bassam Aramin. From? Hebron. Age? Forty-two. Who are you traveling with? My wife and children. Destination? England. Where in England? Bradford. Never heard of it. It's a university. What's your purpose? To go to university. Are you trying to be smart with me? No. Where did you get this permit? I explained that to the other officers. Do I look like the other officers? From the office in Jerusalem. What's your purpose in going to university? To study. Are you a professor? No. How old are you? Forty-two, I told you. And you're *studying*? Yes. Where did you go to school? The village in Sa'ir. Where's that? Near Hebron. Did you finish school? My studies were interrupted. What does that mean, *interrupted*? I didn't finish school, no. Why are you smiling? I always smile, it's part of what I do, I like to smile. Do you want to miss another plane, Bassam? No. Then wipe that grin off your face and tell me where did you learn Hebrew? After school. *After school,* is that so? Yes. I have your file here, I know who you are. Then why did you ask? Don't be a smart-ass, answer the question. After school, I learned it after school, then I worked for the Authority, first in Sports, then in Archives, then I was accepted into the program at Bradford, I have a special permit, I have the right to go there. Answer my question, why are you going to university *now*? I was offered a place. You do like that smile of yours don't you? Not especially. State your name again. Why? I said state your name again, do you hear me, are you listening? Bassam Aramin. Twenty-five years without studying and all of a sudden, Bass-sam Ara-min, you're an intellectual? I never said that, I'm going as a student. You're going for how long? A year. The permit is for two years. Yes. And you're going to study what? The Shoah. Pardon me? The Holocaust. I heard you, you're studying the Shoah, you're an Arab, you're a Muslim, you're a terrorist, seven years in prison, you attack us, you throw grenades, you terrorize us, and now you're studying the Shoah, you say you're an intellectual, is this some sort of joke, Bass-sam, what do you think I am, stupid? I don't think you're stupid at all. Is that what you're telling me, you're going to England so you can tell us how the Shoah didn't happen? No. What do you mean, *No*? One of the things I have learned is that nobody wants to be expelled from history. What the fuck are you talking about? I am not interested in denying the truth. Is that so? I don't believe in violence of any sort. Since when? Since a long time ago. Really? Yes. How many terrorists are you going to be meeting in Bradford, Bass-sam? I don't know, what's a *terrorist*, can you define it for me? You're asking *me*? My wife is waiting, my children are waiting, we're going to miss another plane and I have to say that I'm a little terrified right now, yes. Oh you're a real smart-ass, Bass-sam, aren't you? I don't think so. Don't smile. I'm not smiling, I'm not laughing, I'm not doing anything, I'm just sitting here, answering your questions, waiting for my plane. State your name. I gave it a dozen times already. Name! Bassam Aramin. Is that your child crying? I can't see through walls. Why is she crying, Bassam? I don't know, probably because she's tired, we've been waiting a long time. Can't your wife shut her up? My wife is tired too, we have been here for eight hours, I don't know how many flights we've missed. How many children do you have, Bassam? Five, I used to have six.

274

One of the first photos he saw in the library was of the camp in Theresienstadt. It showed a young man in a tuxedo and a white bow tie in front of a music stand, busy putting rosin on a violin bow, staring straight at the camera, about to play.

275

Later he would meet Englishmen who rolled their eyes when he mentioned Bradford and he could almost see their disdain, nothing like Oxford, nothing like Cambridge, nothing like Edinburgh, nothing like Manchester, but he and Salwa loved it, the openness of the town, the space, the green park, the clean path along the river, the rows of low redbrick houses, the chimneys, the bright tinny shops, the music in the elevators, Manor Row, Mirror Pool, North Parade, Tumbling Hill,

Rawson, the stretches of neon, the cafés, the shops, the waft of vinegar, the falafel stall, the red double-decker buses, the men in bowler hats, the women in burqas, the fire engines, the rubbish trucks, the ringing of church bells, the call of the muezzin, the postman, the Indian cop on Cheapside with the dreadlocks, the slack-wire walker outside the Peace Museum, the walk home along Pemberton Drive, the quiet street, the grass verge, the lopsided gate, the yellow climbing rose along the wall, the blue door, the white bell, the silver letter slot, the hatstand, the creaking stairs, five bedrooms, their own bedroom looking out to a small patch of garden, the ticking of radiators, the kids allowed out in the afternoon to the park without worry, watching them run along the water, ripping bread to feed the ducks—the surprise of it all, even under the bowl of grey English sky—walking through the rain, and, yes, even the rain itself, the slanting sheets, the sun showers, the night drizzle, the hammering storms, and the endless jokes about umbrellas, some of which Salwa, brand-new to the language, found quite funny.

276

What goes up, Salwa, when the rain comes down?

277

In the library he read Primo Levi. Adorno. Susan Sontag. Edward Said. He watched *Schindler's List*, searched out other films, documentaries, combed through reams of news footage. Dug out pictures of the camps. Found everything he could about Theresienstadt. He read, too, about the effects of trauma and its intersection with memory; Adler, Janet, Freud. The acquisition of fear. The disintegration of memory over time. The task of language.

At times it seemed to him that his brain had caught fire. He would come home to Salwa late at night, exhausted, thrilled: he would fall asleep on the sofa, books open on his chest, feet propped up on the coffee table.

He began work on his master's thesis: *The Holocaust: The Use and Abuse of History and Memory*. He wrote it in longhand. He thought in Arabic, but wrote in English. He was aware that these were not new ideas, just new to him. Still, it felt as if he were in the territory of the explorer. He had cast himself out to sea. Most of the time he ended up crashing back on the shore, but every now and then he chanced upon a small rumor of land. Still, when he tried to find purchase, the land disappeared before his eyes. This was the true terror, he thought. His was a responsibility not to diminish. He wanted to talk about the use of the past in the justification of the present. About the helix of history, one moment bound to the next. About where the past intersects with the future.

He was the oldest in his class. Peace Studies. He sat in the second-to-last row of seats, to the side of the room, kept as quiet as possible. Hardly ever spoke above a whisper. He seldom volunteered, but if he did it was slow-spoken, soft, considered. He left class with his head bowed. Smoked alone, away from the buildings. Kept his prayer mat out of view.

Still, the word leaked out: he was a Palestinian, an activist, he had lost his ten-year-old daughter, he was studying the Holocaust.

He knew the names of the janitors, the groundsmen, the canteen ladies. He nodded to them as he went along. They were open and jovial. They wanted to know what football team he supported. He wasn't interested in the game, but he began to wear a claret-and-amber Bradford scarf. They loved the way he pronounced the town, his thick Arabic English. *Brr-ad-a-fort*. They nicknamed him Kayser Söze for his limp. They told him he looked a bit like Kevin Spacey, an Arab version. He had no idea what they were talking about so he rented the film and watched it with Salwa. They laughed at the idea of him being one of the Usual Suspects. The life of a Palestinian. The small ironies.

He was invited out to parties, to dinners, to symposiums. He accepted the invitations, one in Glasgow, one in Copenhagen, one in Belfast. It was his curse: he hated to disappoint people, he could never say no.

He had one simple answer to the questions that inevitably came his way. There was no symmetry between the jailer and the jailed. Destroy the jail. The Occupation was based on the fallacy of security. It had to end. Nothing else would be possible until that happened.

A sort of haze drifted over his listeners. He knew that his answer disappointed them. They wanted something else—one state, two states, three states, eight. They wanted him to dissect Oslo, to talk about the right of return, to debate the end of Zionism, the new settlements, colonialism, imperialism, hudna, the United Nations. They wanted to know how he felt about armed resistance. About the settlers themselves. They had heard so much, they said, and yet they knew so little. What about the strip malls, the stolen land, the fanatics? He demurred. For him everything still came back around to the Occupation. It was a common enemy. It was destroying both sides. He didn't hate Jews, he said, he didn't hate Israel. What he hated was being occupied, the humiliation of it, the strangulation, the daily degradation, the abasement. Nothing would be secure until it ended. Try a checkpoint just for one day. Try a wall down the middle of your schoolyard. Try your olive trees ripped up by a bulldozer. Try your food rotting in a truck at a checkpoint. Try the occupation of your imagination. Go ahead. Try it.

The listeners nodded, but he wasn't quite sure if they fully understood. The thing about the Occupation was that it never let you decide. It took away your ability for choice. Banish it and choice would appear.

Still, his listeners pressed him. Where was his moral line on violence? Were his politics not obsolete? What sort of concessions would he make to the right of return? What sort of territorial swaps? What would happen to the town of Ariel? What about the Bedouin? The unrecognized villages? Why would he not study the Nakba instead of the Holocaust?

The questions exhausted him. He changed, then, the tone of his voice. He leaned in. He whispered. Their questions were valid, and he would answer them, he said, but give me time, give me time, the only way I can work towards it is to leverage the power of my grief, do you understand? He no longer wanted to fight. The greatest jihad, he said, was the ability to talk. This is what he did now. Language was the sharpest weapon. It was a mighty thing. He wanted to wield it. He needed to be careful. *My name is Bassam Aramin. I am the father of Abir.* Everything else rose out of that.

He felt himself so often back in prison: that moment when he saw the documentary, the naked bodies above the ditches, the wrist numbers, the freezing cold snapping the branches in midair. How he left prison, not so much a man of peace—even the word *peace* itself was awkward at times—but a man who wanted to pit himself against the ignorance of violence, including his own. The irony, then, of the years that followed: his marriage, his children, the apartment in Anata, the peace work. And then that rubber bullet flying through the air, on an ordinary January day, out of the blue, the smash of his daughter's forehead against the pavement.

Sometimes he left the symposiums early. He wanted to be home. To be quiet. To be undisturbed. He was amazed to open the back door of the house and see Salwa out weeding the garden, her headscarf down among the rhododendrons.

278

A community of feeling. A mythology of the instincts.

279

Late at night he walked around the streets of Bradford, reading. There were cul-de-sacs, alleyways, roundabouts. He began to carry a notebook. He stood under globes of uneven lamplight and scribbled, walked on and on, a flat English hat on his head. He avoided the center of town: it was loud with alcohol. Sometimes he circled the park endlessly. When he got home, the hieroglyphics of his notebook were difficult to decipher. Sometimes the pages were damp with mist. He unpeeled them and began to transcribe. Memory. Trauma. The rhyme of history and oppression. The generational shifts. The lives poisoned with narrowness. What it might mean to understand the history of another.

It struck him early on that people were afraid of the enemy because they were terrified that their lives might get diluted, that they might lose themselves in the tangle of knowing each other.

There was a sort of burn to the ideas, he thought, a scorching. After a while he wanted to stop writing altogether and just read. At every turn of a page there was something new to discover. He liked the notion, now, of being thrown off balance.

He immersed himself in the library. He was often the last one to leave. He sat in stillness. The lights flickered off. He gathered the books and scattered papers. His backpack was full to bursting. He bent toward home. His body felt lighter somehow, his limp less pronounced. He could see a change come over Salwa too. She was looser, happier. She hired a tutor, a young French girl, to teach her English. He could hear them together in the kitchen, giggling over the pronunciation of words. *Um-ber-ella.* He went walking with the children in the park.

Bassam knew that it would not last, it was temporary, he would have to go back, the scholarship moment would run out. He found himself one night out walking the streets in his long white sleeping thobe and sandals. This was not Anata, this was not East Jerusalem, this was not the West Bank: this was England. It was not his. He knew that in his happiness he had grown ready for return.

Above his desk he tacked a line he remembered from the Persian poet, Rumi: *Yesterday I was clever, so I wanted to change the world. Today I am wise, so I have begun to change myself.*

280

One of the things that Steven Spielberg knew—even as a young filmmaker in Hollywood—is that history is in constant acceleration, but sooner or later a force, any force, must hit a curve: that curve, then, is a story that must be told.

281

If you divide death by life you will find a circle.

282

Rami was in his car when he heard the news. On his way to Tel Aviv to pick up his mother-in-law at Ben Gurion. The traffic was light. Early afternoon. He was listening to the radio. The Beatles. The music stopped abruptly. A man's voice. Breaking news. Within the past half hour. Ben Yehuda Street. A café. Unknown number of casualties. Police on the scene.

It was always the same: a dip in the stomach, an awareness of his throat, a travel of dark behind his eyes. He performed the quick mathematics of where everyone was—Nurit at the university, Smadar at home babysitting with Yigal, Elik on duty, Guy at swim practice. All accounted for, good, yes. Breathe.

Some drivers in front of him touched their brakes, like they had just heard the news too, a flash of red. Already there were sirens on the other side of the highway: police and ambulances on their way.

He calculated again. Thursday. Nurit in university, yes. Smadar babysitting, yes. The older boys safe, yes.

Take it easy. Breathe. Just breathe.

Up ahead, he saw a clutter of cars moving toward the exit. He hit the blinker, pulled back into the lane again, touched the blinker a second time. The car drifted. It felt like it was operating apart from him. There was something here, he couldn't quite locate it, a tingle of doubt, that faint gnarl in the gut. There was always somebody who would know somebody. Nobody in Israel lived unbombed.

He hadn't charged his phone. He should find a phone booth, he thought, give Nurit a quick call. He hit the blinker again and nudged halfway into the lane, halfway out.

An eruption of car horns sounded behind him.

Rami reached for the dial, flicked through the stations. Bomb in Jerusalem. Bomb in Jerusalem. Bomb in Jerusalem.

Breathe. Keep calm.

He left it on 95.0 FM. A woman's voice this time. They were waiting for a live update. It was believed now to be two bombs. Police activity. The city was on alert for other incidents. Traffic chaos. Stay tuned for more updates. Dozens injured. Possible fatalities.

A horn blared. He was surprised to see so much space in front of his car. He lifted his foot from the clutch and the car lurched forward, off the ramp. What exit was this anyway? He couldn't remember. So many of them looked the same. He scanned the horizon for a gas station or a fast food joint. Anywhere with a telephone. Just for reassurance. To tell them that he was okay, no worries, no need to panic, he was on the road, three-quarters of the way to the airport. The routine check-in. Hi honey, everything's fine.

Two bombs for certain, said the radio again. Possibly three. A number of casualties. The street was thronged with shoppers. Back-to-school time. The area was in full lockdown. Unconfirmed reports now of a death, possibly several.

283

Back-to-school time.

284

285

He saw a row of three telephones at the side of a Paz station. He pulled to the curb, locked the door, dug deep in his jeans for his wallet, his Telecart. Two of the phones were taken. The third was free. A row of business cards was stuck haphazardly along the edge of the phone: a strip club in Tel Aviv, computer repair, lawn mower service, dog walker. He lifted the receiver. No dial tone. A second time, a third time. *Come to Where the Baby Dolls Play. Ariel Landscaping. Mobile Repair ₪ 50. We Have You On Our Leash. Pussycat, Pussycat, Where Have You Been?*

He slammed the receiver. The phone slipped off the cradle, dangled down. He stepped back off the curb.

At the middle phone stood a young girl, not much older than Smadar. She tossed her hair and laughed. Rami paced behind her. Just get off the phone please, he wanted to say, I have to call my wife, I just want to check in, can't you hurry?

The caller at the other phone was young too. Mid-twenties, dark-skinned, a tracksuit top, sunglasses on his head. He was leaning close to the phone, his hand cupped over the receiver, whispering. Rami paused a moment. Was he talking in Arabic? Rami stepped along the curb, leaned forward, listened. No, it was Hebrew, he had no accent at all.

Rami felt a faint flush of shame in his stomach.

Two other cars had pulled up quickly. A man in one, a woman in the other. The woman—tall, thin, curly-haired—was first to the bank of phones. She picked up the dangling cord.

—It's not working, said Rami.

Her eyes were an alarming shade of blue. She replaced the receiver, stepped off the curb, began pacing back and forth.

—Did you hear?

—Yes.

There was something of the stalked about the woman: the pupils of her eyes seemed to have fully disappeared. Already the other man—short, wiry, electric—was at the phone.

—It's broken, said the woman.

The short man slid his Telecart into the slot.

—It's kaput, said Rami.

The man shrugged, pressed his finger on the hook switch anyway, tapped it up and down.

One of the business cards fluttered to the ground. *Ariel Landscaping: Let Us Mow You Down.* The short man kicked the card away, went back to the phone, put his ear to the receiver once more.

—We already tried it, said the woman, we're waiting, we're in line.

The short man stepped past the tracksuit man, then stared at the girl still flicking her hair and laughing.

Rami leaned forward and tapped the girl on the flesh of her shoulder, said: We're waiting, honey, can't you see that we're waiting?

286

Bomb in Jerusalem. Bomb in Jerusalem. Bomb in Jerusalem.

287

Rami's first call was to Nurit's office. It rang through to her answering machine. He paused a moment, waiting to see if she would pick up. Hey, buttercup, it's me, are you there? He heard the machine beep. Hi buttercup, he said again. No response. He closed the line, fished in his shirt pocket for the Telecart again. The second call was home to Smadar. It was picked up instantly. Hello? He was thrown by the voice a moment. I've been trying to call you, Nurit said. My phone's dead. Where are you? On the way to the airport. I called your office. I came home. Why? I let Smadar go downtown, I let her go with her friends, she wanted to buy some books, she said something about a jazz class. Where? Downtown. Have you heard from her? Not yet. Okay, okay, what about her friends? Nothing. Who is she with? I don't know, Sivan, Daniella, a few others, she went by bus. Did something happen on the bus? Nothing, no, no, I don't know, I just haven't heard from her, normally she calls. She doesn't have a phone with her, does she? She can use a pay phone. Maybe the lines are jammed. I can just about hear you. Everyone here's trying to use the phone. I can hardly hear you, speak up. Rami. She'll be fine, love, she'll be fine, where are the boys? They called, they're okay. Where did you say she went again? Shopping. Should I come back? Maybe, yes, maybe. The radio said the traffic is chaos. I'll leave a message with my mom, she can get a taxi from the airport, the buses will be hell, I'm going downtown, have you got your phone? I told you, my phone's dead. How long will it take you to get here? I don't know, half an hour, forty-five minutes? Okay. You should get a babysitter for Yigal, just in case. Rami. Yes? Hurry.

288

Seventy kilometers per hour, eighty, eighty-five. Every single hole in the traffic seemed to open up for him. Even in the breakdown lane. He felt as if he was not in a car at all, but on his motorbike, a series of sliding gates in front of him, a gap here, a space there, nobody tailgating, nobody honking, nobody flipping him off, not even when the traffic backed up outside the city and he got in behind a police car that moved like a myth in front of him, parting the waves. He would puzzle over it later. The journey defied all expectations. The cop even pulled off to the side of the road and waved him on for no reason he could fathom. The exit ramp was clear. Every traffic light he hit was yellow.

289

We will mow you down.

290

Traffic in front. Traffic behind. There was nothing he could do. He knew the streets of Anata so well. There were no shortcuts. He couldn't swing left, he couldn't swing right. There was no pavement to mount. No room to move. Bassam reached across and touched Salwa's hand. She keyed her phone alive. No more news, she said. Moments later she keyed her phone again. They're waiting for us, she said, she's going to be okay. He resisted the urge to blow the horn. He opened his window. Helicopters spun overhead. Something was happening somewhere. He scanned the skyline for smoke. I just hope, he said, she doesn't need stitches.

291

The men stirred outside the shops. There were teenagers running now between the cars. Some already had their scarves over their faces. Bassam stepped out into the street. He put his hand up. They ran past him. Someone's been shot. Where? At the school. They streamed past. He put his hands up again to slow them down, but they slalomed around him. Stop, he pleaded. Stop. He thrust his hand into the chest of a tall young boy. The urgency froze him. Which school? The girls' school. Are you sure? I think so, yes.

292

They abandoned their vehicle half a kilometer from the hospital. He left the keys in the ignition. They ran together. She wore a long green dress and headscarf. He was in a dark shirt and pants. His limp was more pronounced when he hurried, but even in his haste there was a quietness to Bassam.

At the clinic there was a hush when they entered. The crowd in the corridor parted for them. They knew. They hurried toward the operating rooms. Bassam was taken aside by a doctor. They recognized each other from the mosque and from Bassam's peace work.

A hand against his chest: It's critical, Bassam. Prepare yourself.

—I'm prepared.

It had always been, Bassam thought, his duty to keep others calm: ever since prison he had been called upon to deliver news.

He returned to Salwa. She was standing under a flickering fluorescent. He squeezed her hand. She turned quickly and sobbed into his shoulder.

—We have to prepare ourselves, he said.

293

When he stepped outside, his car was there, parked in the hospital lot, with a note in Arabic to say that they were praying for Abir and that the keys had been left at the front desk. Underneath the note, a single tulip with a Post-it note: *Get Well Soon.*

294

Just exactly how, Bassam wondered later, would Spielberg have filmed the rubber bullet flying through the air? Where would he have placed the camera? How would he have framed the sharp turn of the jeep on the street? How would he capture the crunch of the wheels? How would he portray the slide of the small metal grate in the rear door? The burst of light onto the border guard's face? The inside of the jeep, the mess of newspapers, the uniforms, the trays of ammunition? The emergence of the M-16 through the rear door? The curl of the finger against the trigger? The shell emerging from the candy cane of grooves? The rifle's kick into the border guard's shoulder? The bullet's spiral through the sharp blue air? The shot sounding out against the school bells? The crash of the bullet into the back of Abir's head? The vault through the air of her leather schoolbag? The shape of her shoe as it flew off her foot? The twirl of it? The tiny bones being crushed at the back of her brain? The delay of the ambulance? The gathering at the hospital? The flat line of the machine?

295

The deaths occurred ten years apart: Smadar in 1997, Abir in 2007. At a lecture in Stockholm Bassam stood up to say that sometimes he felt as if the rubber bullet had been traveling a whole decade.

296

So much of what Spielberg did in *Schindler's List* was achieved in the opening frames when the flame of the Shabbat candle was lit. It was one of only five instances of color in the film: a tiny flicker of yellow light.

297

Every year in the Church of the Holy Sepulchre in Jerusalem—where Christ was crucified, entombed and then believed by Christians to have risen from the dead—a holy fire is said to erupt spontaneously, lighting candles which eventually spread a flame that is carried around the world.

On Holy Saturday before Easter, the Greek Orthodox patriarch of Jerusalem enters the darkness of Jesus's tomb, where all the lights have been extinguished. The doors have been sealed with wax and the tomb searched for any item that might contribute to fire: flame, flint, lighter, magnifying glass.

Inside and outside the church huge crowds wait for news of the fire: loud, fierce, electric, raw, packed together.

At the door of the tomb, the patriarch takes off his robe and is thoroughly searched for anything that might ignite. He is then ceremoniously allowed into the sealed room. He kneels at the foot of the stone where a blue light is said to rise slowly.

The light is, at first, cool to the touch. It forms a column from which the patriarch lights his two candles.

Once the candles are lit they are passed through openings on either side of the tomb. The Orthodox patriarch gives the flame first to the Armenian and then to the Coptic patriarch. The flame is raced by priests up to the Patriarch's Throne.

The church comes alive in a blaze of light and a clatter of bells. Shouts ring out. Ancient drums boom. Arguments erupt. Laughter. The flame is passed backward through the crowd, candle to candle.

The fire is then carried through the narrow streets of the Old City, into Christian homes and in some cases those of Muslims and Jews too. It spreads, then, to all the Orthodox churches in the Holy Land.

In centuries gone by the flame was carried by mule out of the city, or by camels across the desert, or taken in glass containers on steamer ships around the world. By the middle of the twentieth century, the flame was being driven out of the city by police car to Ben Gurion airport where—like an Olympic torch—it was put in specially designed vacuum tubes and placed on flights to Greece, Russia, Argentina, Mexico and beyond.

298

In 2015 a representative of the Greek Orthodox church entered into negotiations with representatives of Elon Musk to bring the flame into outer space through Musk's rocket manufacturing company, SpaceX. The talks went unresolved.

299

On the back of Sir Richard Francis Burton's silver compass he engraved an inscription from the Qur'an: *Travel through the earth and see what was the end of those who rejected Truth.*

300

During Operation Embellishment the prisoners were told to remain silent as the Red Cross contingent moved through the town: any word out of place would result in certain death.

301

Imagine, then, the Danish ministers moving politely through the spruced-up streets, listening, nodding, their hands entwined behind their backs as if in some form of inquisitive prayer.

302

There are many theories about how the Church of the Holy Sepulchre flame might be made to spontaneously appear: the candles may have been dusted in white phosphorus so that they self-ignite, or a piece of flint has been secreted in the floor, or a jar of naphtha is hidden in the tomb, or the patriarch manages to sneak a lighter inside, hidden in his beard or in a tangle of his hair.

These possibilities are scoffed at by the legions of faithful who say that the fire is simply ignited by the Holy Spirit.

303

When Sinéad O'Connor sang the ancient Irish ballad *I Am Stretched on Your Grave*—on the album which Smadar loved to dance to—her performance was, she said, influenced by her readings in the Kabbalah, the mystical interpretation of the Bible.

304

The Kabbalists, in their attempt to examine the nature of the divine, are known to envision two aspects of God. The first, known as *Ein Sof*, finds God to be transcendent, unknowable, impersonal, endless and infinite. The second aspect is accessible to human perception, revealing the divine in the material world, available in our finite lives.

Far from contradicting each other, the two aspects of the divine—one locatable, one infinite—are said to be perfectly complementary to one another, a form of deep truth to be found in apparent opposites.

305

Borges, too, was fascinated by the Kabbalah. He suggested that the world might merely be a system of symbols and that the universe, including the stars, was a manifestation of God's secret handwriting.

306

Borges wrote that it only takes two facing mirrors to form a labyrinth.

307

When Bassam was a child he found a picture of Muhammad Ali in a magazine article about Vietnam: he brought it home, cut out the picture, tacked it on the wall of the cave right near the hanging kerosene lantern.

In the photo Ali was standing over Sonny Liston, arm cocked, eyes ablaze, triumphant, angry. Liston was supine on the floor beneath him, his arms behind his head in dazed surrender.

In the rear of the cave, Bassam stood in a mirror of Ali's stance, the grin, the clenched fist, the body of a soldier at his feet.

308

Muhammad Ali was known in the Muslim world as a *da'ee:* one who strives to convey the message of Allah to the world. One of his prized possessions was a silver Timex watch, with a qibla compass hand always pointed in the direction of Mecca.

309

The ceiling of the cave formed a dome. Ventilation holes had been bored out with a thin handmade auger. Chambers were dug out of soft rock. Ledges were used as natural shelves: they were used also as steps into the upper reaches of the cave. Alcoves were cut deep in the walls.

Bassam's brothers called it Sesame after the cave in *Kitab Alf Layla wa Layla.*

Flat paving stones lay at the front entrance. Deeper in, rugs covered the floor. The kitchen and living room walls were plastered smooth and brightly painted. Kitchenware and earthen jars of olives were ranged on high wooden shelves, above the taboon oven.

A row of books and photographs decorated the southern wall. The northern wall was bare except for a hanging carpet that was said to have been in Bassam's uncle's family since the days of the Ottoman empire.

The water came from a well half a kilometer away. The other families in neighboring caves pirated electricity from the grid, but Bassam's father preferred their own cave without electricity.

There was a light shaft in the ceiling near the front of the cave: as a child Bassam could tell the time of the day to within minutes.

310

He led the donkey up and down the rocky slope, carrying carpets, shelving, mattresses, chairs and cookware. The journey to the village took forty-five minutes, the donkey straining under the weight and the piling heat.

Each time Bassam returned to the cave, he bathed the donkey's feet with a poultice, then set off again. The donkey placed each hoof precisely, buckling a moment before catching itself, braying, and moving on.

All along the hillside, in the shade, stood armed Israeli soldiers. Most of them, he noticed, didn't even turn to watch him as he moved the contents down the hillside.

The soldiers—his Sonny Listons—had somehow perfected the art of sleeping while standing.

311

The caves were demolished the evening after the eviction, blown asunder with sticks of dynamite.

Bassam, playing in the rubble a month afterwards, found the stone which had arrowed out the direction of Mecca.

312

Years later, in Boston, Bassam recalled the story of the eviction from the cave while he sat in a swivel chair in the office of Senator John Kerry.

Earlier in the conversation he had seized the Senator's attention by leaning forward in his chair and saying: I am sorry to tell you this, Senator, but you murdered my daughter.

313

He had such a distinctive way of talking, quietly but forcefully, always laying emphasis on the final syllable—*you muh-der-red my dawt-ter*—so that everything emerged in a kind of singsong.

314

At the end of the meeting—which had lasted an hour and a half beyond its allotted time—Senator Kerry bowed his head and led everyone in his office in prayer. He would, he vowed, never forget the story of Abir.

315

The tear gas used by the Israel Defense Forces was once made in Saltsburg, Pennsylvania, but in 1988—after federal investigations ruled the gas had been misused—the sales were suspended. Lobbyists were called. Congressional meetings took place. Local meetings were held. Editorials were posted to say that the people of Pennsylvania had a kinship with Israel. Jobs were at stake. The tear gas, they said, would be made elsewhere anyway. It was time to make a stand.

After eighteen months, production started up again, and then, in 1995, manufacture was switched to a company in Jamestown, Pennsylvania, one hundred miles away.

316

In order to throw back a tear gas canister, a protester—already shrouded in clouds of gas—must be nimble. The canister must be picked up with a gloved hand. The direction of the wind needs to be immediately judged. The can is placed in the sling in such a way that, for just a moment, the gas is blocked from escaping.

If the rioter does not have a gas mask, he wears swimming goggles or welder's glasses, and covers his mouth with a scarf moistened with diluted baking soda. The can is swung above his head and released as quickly as possible, especially if the canister is of the triple chaser variety, a special container designed by Israeli scientists to split into three parts on impact.

The fling-back is known, tongue-in-cheek, among rioters as *the right of return*.

317

At the Western Wall in Jerusalem's Old City, flocks of swifts migrating from South Africa arrive back in January or February of each year. They nest in the cracks in the ancient limestone blocks.

Some swifts can be seen entering the tiny cracks in head-on flight, a marvel of speed and agility. Others go into their nesting holes by taking sharp 90-degree turns in the air, one wing tip pointing down, the other slanted skyward.

They share the brickwork with pigeons, jackdaws and sparrows. Feral pigeons sometimes block the entrance to the holes and so the swifts have to wheel about, waiting for a chance to get back into their nests, thirty feet above the ground.

The evening journeys are known as vesper flights. At dusk the birds carve the space above the heads of the faithful, many of whom cram prayers scribbled on tiny slips of paper into the wall while they put their heads against the stone to pray.

Sometimes, in a strong wind, the prayer slips loosen and the notes are caught by the swifts in midair.

Make me a vessel, Lord. Forgive me my sins. Make Dana love me back. Cure my strep. G-d protect me. Beitar Jerusalem for the Champions League! Give Jeremiah hope. Grant true rest upon the wings of the Shechinah.

The swifts fly so low and fast that the men and women below are forced to duck. If seen from the blimp above, it looks like a wave of hats and headscarves, a dip and a rise, a dip and a rise, a dip and a rise again.

318

Twice a year sanitation workers remove the tiny slips of paper crammed into the holes of the Western Wall.

The slips are collected in plastic bags and then buried in the cemetery on the Mount of Olives. A large backhoe digs the hole and the prayers are placed inside and covered with soil.

The local gravedigger tends the site which he ritually replants each season with new grass.

319

A giant steel key sits on top of a keyhole-shaped archway in the Aida refugee camp in Bethlehem, a reminder of the houses left behind by Palestinians in 1948. The key is nine meters high and weighs almost a ton. It has been inscribed in several different languages. It is known locally as the Key of Return. A *Not For Sale* sign is imprinted along its shaft, alongside several bullet marks and scratches from the impact of tear gas canisters.

320

In the Cremisan monastery in Beit Jala the vespers sound out when the sun disappears behind the surrounding hills.

In decades gone by, a hundred monks or more would gather in the light-streamed chapel to recite their prayers, the chants slipping around the building, along the stone floors and out the high windows.

After the prayers, the monks would walk out the arched doorway, down the gravel path, toward the vineyard in the gathering dark. They carried dented silver buckets and watering cans. They spread out around the vineyard, pouring small circles of water around the bases of the plants. The best time to water the vines was at night: it decreased the evaporation rate.

Many of the monks were Palestinian. Others were Italian and French and Portuguese. To make wine so close to Bethlehem and Jerusalem was a sacred pursuit.

They sent bottles back to their hometown churches in Tuscany, Sicily, Jura, Languedoc, Umbria, Aix-en-Provence, Porto, Faro.

It was marked in shipping vats as holy wine, the Blood of Christ, to be handled with care.

321

Mitterrand said that his last supper—the ortolans—would combine the taste of God and the suffering of Jesus and man's eternal bloodshed all together in one single meal.

322

At harvest time, the nuns from the sister convent, a quarter mile down the road, came to help the monks out.

The women shuffled under the starlight in their long habits, kneeling to pick the ripe fruit. On the darkest nights they carried candles as they moved through the fields, their white robes spectral among the vines.

At sunrise it was not unusual for local children, on their way to the convent school, to see a line of nuns walking back along the road with their dresses stained, small dots of purple at the knees.

323

324

After a decade alone at a monastery in Aleppo, the fifth-century ascetic Saint Simeon proclaimed that God wanted him to prove his faith by becoming immobile: to move as little as possible, to be static, to embrace the mind rather than the body.

He climbed to the top of an abandoned pillar in the Syrian town of Taladah, built himself a small platform, and tried not to move in any excessive way. He lashed his body to a pole with palm fronds to keep himself upright even while sleeping. He remained standing even in the fiercest heat and sandstorms.

He collected drinking water in jars. A rope-and-pulley system was devised to deliver food. Small boys from nearby villages sometimes climbed the pillar to give him bread and goat's milk.

Besieged by other ascetics and admirers from all over the world, Simeon decided to move the platform higher—his first pillar was said to have been just nine feet tall, but the final one was over fifty feet from the ground. He could not, even in this, find solitude: admirers still flocked to see him.

Simeon's monastic elders began to wonder whether his desire for isolation was an act of genuine faith. They ordered him down from the pillar under the assumption that if he descended willingly his was a truly holy act, but if he stayed it would be a sin of pride.

Simeon announced that he would come down of his own accord, and they allowed him, then, to stay.

He died after spending thirty-seven years on the pillars.

325

The wine-making in the monastery—grape crushing, bottling, labeling—was fully automated in the 1970s, taken away from the monks, and bought by local Palestinian businessmen.

The number of monks living in the monastery began to drop. Those who came to live there were mostly retired. They had the air of exhausted saints. They could be seen wandering the grounds, through the garden and down through the vineyard, their hands clasped behind their backs.

Rami had heard that there once used to be as many as a hundred monks, but now there were no more than five or six.

326

Every Saturday, in Bradford, Bassam pulled on a white string under-shirt and old tracksuit bottoms. The push mower was kept in a coal shed at the side of the house. He slipped open the stiff metal bolt on the door and wrestled the rusty machine out.

The mower fascinated him. At first it just tore the grass, but he sharpened the blades by running a metal file along the edges. He oiled and tightened the bolts on the side wheels. He rolled the mower back and forth a few times to make sure it was working properly and then set to work: he liked the churning sound the blades made.

The garden was small, so he took to mowing the verge on the ser-vice road outside. It took him hours with the primitive mower, back and forth, back and forth.

During Eid al-Adha that year Salwa bought him a pair of gardening gloves. He immediately slipped them on and went out to weed the garden.

327

Bombing operations in Gaza and raids into the West Bank are often referred to by Israeli officials as *mowing the lawn*.

328

As a teenager, Bassam learned to carry an onion in his pocket to combat the scorch of tear gas in his lungs.

329

When Bassam returned from England to the West Bank—to the apartment on the slopes of Anata—the first person to come see him was Rami. He arrived by taxi to avoid any hassle at the checkpoint.

Rami knocked on the door and they embraced, two kisses on each cheek. The table was laid out: a casserole of maqluba with chicken and savory yogurt.

Later they walked down the hill together to the schoolyard where a memorial playground had been built for Abir: monkey bars, a slide, a sandpit, a spinning wheel.

Together the two men tended a tiny patch of grass at the entrance. There were no clippers, so they borrowed a plastic-handled scissors from a schoolteacher who sat by the window and watched them as they chatted.

330

The motorcycle thrums as he moves through Beit Jala.

331

332

It will not be over until we talk.

333

He knows the way through the old section of the town, a steep climb and then a smooth corner up into Area B again: good sightlines, he can take it fast.

He turns the bike at the end of Manger Street, halfway toward Bethlehem.

He adjusts the music on his phone, taps the side of his helmet to seat the earbuds in place, pulls back on the throttle and drives up, alongside the Wall, toward the Everest Hotel.

A cup of coffee, perhaps. Or a bite to eat. Somewhere to sit and rest awhile.

334

The bar-headed goose can fly at almost thirty thousand feet, allowing it to migrate over the Himalayas before sweeping south. Pairs of them have been spotted over Mount Makalu, the fifth-highest mountain on earth.

In certain villages the birds are caught and the names of the dead are written in dark ink on the underside of the birds' bellies.

The geese are said to bring news of the dead to the heavens.

335

The hotel, he knows, is now Russian-owned. It was, before the Wall went up, a far busier place—weddings, christenings, ameens, parties, fine meals—but it has in recent years become a little shabby and run-down.

At the top of the hill he passes through the ornate gates, swings right, parks the motorbike away from two large buses. He clicks off his phone, removes his helmet.

A moment of relief. Like emerging from a caisson. He flips open

the top box at the back of the bike and places the helmet inside, makes
his way toward the hotel entrance.

Never a good idea to walk in anywhere in the West Bank wearing a
helmet, even at sixty-seven years of age.

336

He is always surprised by the sight of pigeon on the menu.

337

They seemed the most unlikely of friends, even beyond the obvious,
one being Israeli, the other Palestinian.

They had met first in the Everest Hotel. On a Thursday. It was that
time of the evening when Beit Jala willed itself to cool down: the land
breathed, the sun dipped, the birds rose, the hills took on a sudden
burst of dark green.

They were sitting outside at the hotel picnic tables, a dozen of them,
eight Israelis, three Palestinians, one Swedish reporter. Rami had been
invited by his son Elik. Rami was curious about Combatants for Peace.
The organization had begun to gain traction. He was proud of what
his son could stir.

The group had launched into discussion about who was a
combatant and who was not: the question mattered to determine who
was eligible for membership. What exactly was a *combatant* anyway?
Was it simply someone who had just fought in a war? Was it anyone
who had served in the military? What about someone who had served
outside the Territories? Wasn't someone who sat in an army office a
combatant too? Why did it matter? Surely a combatant could be
in combat for anything at all? Perhaps everyone was a combatant?
What about women and children? If Israeli women were combatants
because of military service, surely Palestinian women were combatants
too? And what if they were Jordanian or American or Lebanese or

Egyptian? Who could be a founding member? Who could be a sustaining member? Would the organization be compromised if it cast too large a net? What would happen if the definition was too small? Was it something they should put in the bylaws?

Rami and Bassam were seated next to each other. Rami nursed a lemonade. Bassam drank coffee and chain-smoked. The talk went in circles. Rami could see the shadows of the trees lengthening.

After a moment, he found himself speaking. He wasn't sure how it had happened. He had come to observe, to hang out, to watch his son in action. He hadn't intended to speak, but the talk had drifted to his own organization, the Parents Circle, and how they dealt with membership and language. In order to be a member of the Circle one had to have lost a child, to be one of the bereaved, what an Israeli would call the *mispachat hashkhol*, what a Palestinian might call *thaklaan* or *mathkool*. There were a few hundred members already: it was one of the rare organizations that wished they were smaller in number. The bereaved were not just parents, they were brothers and sisters, aunts, uncles, cousins too. But, then again, like a combatant, maybe everyone was bereaved, and perhaps there were issues with the word *parent* too—what if a child were adopted, or what if the parents themselves were dead? What about family members? One could spin through language endlessly, looking for a word or a term, perhaps they should simply all just gather the organizations together under a giant umbrella.

After a while—he didn't know how long—Rami looked down and was amazed to see that he was smoking. There was an ashtray beside him and he was flicking the ash with a practiced ease. It had been years since he had smoked. He hadn't even realized that he had lit one. He certainly could not remember having asked for one. Somehow he had just reached for the Palestinian's box and he had helped himself. Smoking with a stranger, and not just that, but they had reached into the same pack, and not just that, but Bassam was silent, and not just that, but his eyes were closed and he was listening. There was something elemental about it. As quickly as the feeling arrived it seemed to vanish. Rami stopped speaking, the words disappeared from him and the cigarette tasted awful. The conversation went back once again to the question of naming, but he was still sitting there, alongside Bassam, in the Everest Hotel, in this unexpected guild.

Only his son Elik had seemed to notice. He was nodding quietly: he was a smoker too.

338

The only other time he smoked with Bassam was two years later, outside the hospital, shortly before Abir's heart monitor flatlined: they sat quietly, on the benches under the dark trees, sharing one back and forth, the red ash pulsing between them.

339

Bassam, when he prayed, touched his head lightly against the ground, but never quite firmly enough to develop a prayer bruise.

340

Save us from enormities whether open or hidden.

341

Upon arrival in the Ritz hotel in Washington, D.C.—where, in the fall of 1993, his entourage was staying on the entire top floor—Yasser Arafat was given a welcome basket.

In the wicker basket—along with a schedule, a flashlight pen, two bottles of sparkling water, a bag of honey-flavored pecans and a White House thermos—was a carefully wrapped cookie in the shape of a dove. The icing was white and the eyes were two tiny dots of blue.

In the elevator down to the lobby, Arafat—wearing an ill-fitting suit and his customary keffiyeh—turned to his bodyguards, stroked his scraggly beard, and with a straight face said: What am I going to do, eat it?

342

In May of 1987 the French artist Philippe Petit decided that a white dove should be part of a planned high-wire performance across the Hinnom Valley.

Petit thought of his walk as an olive branch: he would release the dove midway across the wire, cast it free in the air, watch it fly away.

The day before the walk, Petit scoured the streets of the Old City— market to market, alleyway to alleyway, among the stalls of sweets, herbs, fruit, vegetables, clothes, souvenirs, crosses, mezuzahs, trinkets. He talked to vendors, hotel concierges, butchers, and even searched in upscale delicatessens for anyone who might know where he could buy a small dove to release on the walk. He found parrots, partridges, large pigeons, but no doves.

A part of Petit relished the acute irony: *No doves in Jerusalem,* but still he continued his search in obscure corners, market to market, spreading the word on the street.

On the morning of the walk, in the streets of the Old City, he was waved down by an elderly man with a scraggly beard and a dark robe. The stranger spoke in broken English. He took Petit by the arm and led him down a warren of cobbles and corners.

On the counter of a tailor shop, amid bolts of colorful cloth, sat a row of birds in ancient bell-shaped cages. The elderly man began to take the birds out, one by one. Petit recognized immediately that they were useless: too big, too dark, too unwieldy.

—It's a pigeon, said Petit. I need a dove. Something white. Small. This size. Not this.

Petit turned to leave the shop but the seller held his elbow, grinned, and took out the smallest, lightest-colored pigeon from the cage: it appeared slightly grey but off-white in the light.

The elderly man bowed. As Petit gestured to leave, he felt the bird placed in his hand.

—Take it, said the man. Free.

Petit stroked the belly of the bird. It was still too big, too grey, but at a distance it might actually work.

—Free, the man said again. For you.

Petit shook the shop owner's hand, paid him fifty shekels, walked the caged bird back through the Old City. Nothing, he knew, was ever free.

In his room at the Mount Zion hotel on the Hebron Road Petit practiced releasing the large bird from a specially designed pocket sewn into the thigh of his billowy trousers.

It flapped awkwardly around the room and landed on Petit's bed.

343

As he grew older, the Spanish artist José Ruiz Blasco lost some of the dexterity in his fingers. The blood backed away. He found it hard to grip his paintbrushes. He could no longer properly paint the feet of the rock doves he had become famous for depicting.

In Málaga he had earned the name El Palomero, the Pigeon Fancier, and he kept numerous birds around his house, some in cages, some flying freely in the downstairs rooms.

Saddened by the loss of agility, José asked his young son Pablo to help him complete the delicate work of the feet. The boy had already shown a talent: he could often be found in the Plaza de la Merced, sketching birds in the dirt with a sycamore stick, making outlines in the dust with his bare toe.

When José Ruiz saw the work his son could do—the intricate beauty of the dove's feet—he gave the boy his favorite palette and brushes.

—Now, go paint, he said.

344

At the World Peace Congress in 1949, Pablo Picasso unveiled a drawing of a dove carrying an olive branch in its mouth. The sketch—inspired by the Biblical story of Noah and the ark, the dove returning with a leafy branch signifying that the floodwaters had receded—immediately became a universal symbol of opposition to war.

345

In 1974, Mahmoud Darwish wrote Yasser Arafat's speech to the General Assembly of the United Nations: *Today I have come bearing an olive branch in one hand and a freedom fighter's gun in the other. Do not let the olive branch fall from my hand.*

346

I repeat: do not let the olive branch fall from my hand.

347

348

On her bedroom wall, just below a picture of Sinéad O'Connor, Smadar hung a Picasso dove. It was positioned on the wall so it angled upwards rather than moving in brisk sideways flight. The beak was exaggerated to hold the olive branch.

Beneath it, a second ghostly dove had bled through the page. On the ghost image the beak was slightly sharper.

The sketch remained on her wall for years after her death until Rami's grandchildren took it down and put it, along with many of her other possessions, in a see-through plastic box kept at the end of her bed.

349

The Hinnom Valley is also known as Gehenna, where, in Biblical times, ritual sacrifice took place in the warren of caves and altars to honor the fire god Moloch. Babies were placed in pyres of olive wood, strapped to stakes, or attached to cantilevered platforms which slowly turned towards the fire, roasting the children alive bit by bit. Loud drums were played by priests to drown out the cries of the children as they burned. The smell from their smoldering bodies reached through the valley.

It was also where Judas bought his Field of Blood after betraying Jesus for thirty pieces of silver. Judas later hanged himself from a tree and then fell headlong in the field where his body burst open and his intestines spilled out.

It was said that the gates of hell could be found in the valley, and they were often depicted in monumental works of art.

In the Qur'an, too, the valley was a place of torment for sinners and those who did not believe.

350

Petit said that he could hear the sounds of the centuries turning beneath him as he crossed the valley.

351

He wore the loose white outfit of a court jester. The right leg was decorated with pale Israeli blue, the left leg with the intertwined colors of the Palestinian flag.

He stepped out from the roof of the Spanish Colony building, just yards from the Mount Zion hotel.

The wire was strung three hundred meters across the valley. He had called the performance *Walking the Harp: A Reach for Peace*. The profile of the walk appeared to him like a harp: the bowl-shaped depth of the valley, the level edge of the tightrope, the eleven cavallettis strung in place to keep the wire taut.

The walk was three hundred meters long at an incline of twenty meters. The wire was three-quarters of an inch thick. Crowds gathered to watch from all parts of the city, some perched along the walls of Jerusalem, others by the Cinematheque, others gazing up at him from the ground below.

It struck Petit that, because of the incline, he would be ascending into the sky.

Below him was the valley with its pockets of green and its burial chambers and its ancient caves and its stories of hellish sorrow.

A strong summer wind had whipped up. The valley appeared beautiful in the early evening light. Antennae glistened on the distant rooftops. The blimp hovered. Petit stepped off the roof of the Spanish Colony building to huge roars and applause.

His outfit billowed. He held the captive white pigeon in a red silk scarf in the pocket of his trousers.

352

As a boy, Picasso liked to draw by candlelight. He had already intuited that the moving shadows cast by the light would instill a feeling of sway in his work.

353

Petit paused on the wire and looked back towards the Old City. Out of the corner of his eye he could see several small exuberant figures leaping from building to building, trying to follow the line of his walk.

He had heard that the fastest way to get anywhere in the Old City of Jerusalem was by cutting across the rooftops.

354

In 1882 a British foundation, the Order of Saint John of Jerusalem, set up an eye hospital overlooking the valley, serving Muslims, Jews and Christians. It was thought to be healing for the patient that his first sight with the bandages removed would be the Holy City, above what were known as the gates of hell.

From the rim of the valley they might then see the Pool of Siloam where archaeologists had uncovered the remains of the Second Temple pool in which Jesus told a blind man to wash in order to restore his vision.

355

Later, Petit would recall that, for no particular reason, he had put the pigeon in the pocket on the Israeli side of his trousers. On the sleeves of his outfit the colors were reversed, so when he put his hand in his pocket it appeared as if one territory was reaching inside the other.

356

Even with his poor eyesight—and long before the surgery to repair his macular degeneration—Moti Richler went along to the walk and stood down in the valley to see if he might catch a glimpse of Philippe Petit.

The cable was longer than the one he had monitored during the '48 war, and went in a slightly different direction, but that hardly mattered: Moti was delighted that the wire was remembered at all.

He waited in the crowd at the bottom of the incline. He could almost hear the throaty sound of his wartime motorbike moving along the valley floor.

357

Forty thousand people were said to have watched Petit's walk across what was once known as No-man's-land.

358

Rami too: he carried three-year-old Smadar on his shoulders.

359

Bassam was in prison.

360

Every Thursday in Manhattan, just as the sun rises, two Hasidic rabbis drive around the perimeter of the city to check if a high-wire fishing line that runs from Harlem to Houston Street, and from the East River to the Hudson, is still intact.

The thin string—found about twenty-five feet in the air—marks the area of eruv, a ritual enclosure that allows Orthodox members of the faith to carry certain objects that would otherwise be banned on the Sabbath.

The men drive slowly, looking upwards—past the United Nations, along the river, crosstown, up the West Side—following the string that loops from building to building, hooks from traffic light to pole, snakes its way around corners.

The eruv creates a private space out of a public one and enables the faithful to carry prayer books and keys or push strollers without breaching religious law.

There are other strings too, all over the city, hundreds of miles of them, marking different areas of eruv. The string is almost invisible in places but the perimeter threads are thicker, sometimes a quarter inch of rope.

A strong storm can bring the wires down. A flock of birds. A parade float. A plastic bag tugging too hard in the wind. If the rabbis find a gap in the perimeter wires they call in a special maintenance crew who repair it as quickly as possible before the Sabbath.

In Harlem, the strings are often brought down by kids tossing sneakers in the air to see if they can make the shoes hang. The eruv can be a particularly sought-after target since the lines are near-invisible from a distance and the sneakers, if they catch, seem to hang, perfectly suspended, in midair.

361

They stood by the Cinematheque, eight- or nine-deep in the crowd. From a distance it was difficult to see what exactly was going on in the valley. The walker seemed to Rami like a stick figure in an ancient painting.

Smadar shifted on his shoulders and tightened her grip on Rami's neck. Her tiny feet bounced against his chest. He kept his hands at her back to support her.

When the walker stopped mid-wire Rami could feel her body tense. Smadar leaned forward, her breath uneven, her small heart thumping against his ear.

362

Rami knew even then that perhaps part of the role of the watcher involved the desire to see the walker fall: matching the walker's need to get to the end of the wire.

The crowd applauded as the walker paused midway. Rami felt the weight of his daughter shift at the back of his neck.

363

From where they watched it looked perfectly choreographed: Petit walked to the middle of the wire, stopped a moment, paused above the valley.

With tremendous skill, he adjusted the balancing bar and held it in one hand. He reached into his right-hand pocket—decorated with the Israeli colors—and felt for the bird. He had wrapped it in a red silk handkerchief, headfirst, wings combed back.

The small heart beat rapidly against his fingers. He slipped the bundle out from his pocket. He allowed the flap of silk to unpeel itself. He had to be careful. He could feel the wings begin to loosen beneath the cloth. Slow going. The more he freed her, the more active the bird became. He could feel the strength of the wings now. No sound. No chirping. He held the wrapped bird in the air, then shook it free.

The bird hovered a moment as the crowd gasped. The red silk fluttered to the valley floor.

Petit waited to hear the flap of wings. He steadied himself, then felt a sharp pinch on the top of his scalp. A piercing pain. A scraping at his skull.

For a split second the Frenchman had no idea what had happened. Roars of delight filtered up from the crowd. A clapping sound went around the valley.

The bird had perched itself on the top of his head. The talons stung his scalp.

He gripped the bar and shook his head slightly, waited for the bird to take off again. The wind blew. The pigeon didn't move. Reaching up behind his head—any sudden move could be fatal—Petit brushed the bird away with his fingers. He heard a frantic flapping around his head—*Go now, go*—took a breath, and refocused. The cheers doubled and redoubled. He could hear the frantic beating of the bird's wings. The crowd clapped again.

Petit felt a slight tug on his balancing bar and when he looked to his right, in the direction of the valley, he saw the bird had now perched on the end of the aluminum bar.

Another gust of wind whipped. The bird remained on the bar. It was so much more than a distraction: the bird, if it moved too quickly, could unbalance him. He rotated the bar in his fingers. The pigeon turned with the rolling bar, its talons gripping. Petit jolted the bar slightly but still the bird did not move. He rotated the bar again, then quickly reversed the move, but the pigeon held.

Petit knelt down on the wire, bowed and swept out his hand in an arc. The crowd roared again. They were sure he had practiced it all: the kneeling, the showboating, the antics of the bird.

He completed his salute, then bashed the side of his balancing bar in order to make the pigeon fly. It flapped frantically and rose slightly. He glanced away. Another roar soared from the crowd. The pigeon was gone.

Petit stood up slowly from his kneeling position, began to walk once more, one foot carefully following the other, his eye fixed on Mount Zion.

Upwards he went again, along the incline. A cadenced clapping had begun to sound out around the Holy City.

After a few steps he heard another roar. He turned his head to glance behind, and saw that the bird had managed to land on the wire. It was walking back in the direction of the Old City, tottering slightly. It looked to Petit as if the rear end of the bird was mocking him as it swayed along the wire: the bird was annoyed, somehow, that it had to go through the process at all.

Petit went forward once more. All concentration, all intent. He made a drama of each step, in tune with the clapping, a perfectly rhythmic sound.

When he looked around, the bird was gone.

364

Once a week, before the Sabbath, Moti brought his brigade's rabbi to bless the cable out in No-man's-land. Moti had already ridden the length of wire to make sure there were no loops or breaks in it, no bombs attached, no traps set.

Like Moti, the rabbi was dressed all in black, his hands, neck and face darkened with shoe polish. He sat on the back of the bike, his hands gripping the bottom of the saddle as they sped on a narrow track across the valley, whispering the ritual prayers as they bumped along.

365

Petit turned on the wire and looked down over the valley. The wire, the trees, a few puffs of white cloud. He bowed. He had walked three hundred meters, all of it at an incline. The crowd applauded from all directions: in his mind he gave them an inner curtsy.

A helicopter broke the sky above him, guided by a pilot who had once captained a crack commando unit. A winch was lowered and Petit snapped his carabiners in place. His final flourish. The soldier had practiced the lift with Petit's brother in the desert near Al Rashidah a few days earlier. The helicopter hovered perfectly.

The high-wire artist and pilot exchanged hand signals. Petit tapped on the winch and gave a final signal.

The walker felt a tug and then he was lifted from the wire up in the air, arms apart, flying away from Mount Zion, out over the hills of Beit Jala.

366

Reminding some of the watchers of Muhammad's night flight from Jerusalem up over Mount Zion and beyond.

367

In Israel, helicopters are sometimes used to capture golden eagles for ringing and research. The pilots track the eagle in the air until the bird lands on the ground and crouches with its head down. The helicopter lands nearby, drops off the biologist, and returns to hover once more, forcing the eagle into submission.

The bird is then hand-grabbed from behind. The biologist is trained to fold back the wings and to avoid the talons and the beak. Sometimes a net gun is used, but the hand-grab is known to be safer for the bird.

368

Large bands are needed to ring the eagles. Their legs can sometimes be three-quarters of an inch thick. If a ring is too tight it will cut off the flow of blood to the bird's feet.

369

Petit's walk on the wire was captured live on Israeli TV. A Bedouin tribe on the edge of the Al Rasari forest eight miles from Jerusalem sat watching television inside their canvas tents.

When Petit rose on the helicopter they stepped from under the large canvas awnings, away from their television sets, to watch the Frenchman fly open-armed in his jester's uniform—one leg in Palestinian colors, one in Israeli—across the sky.

370

The crowd began to part. Smadar leaned forward. Rami held her aloft as he moved through the crowd back toward the Kakao café.

She was pulling back on his neck now, her hands crossed against his Adam's apple.

371

Seven months after Philippe Petit's Walk of Peace, the First Intifada began.

372

The First Intifada begins like this: the Night of the Gliders, 1987. The gliders are made of aluminum bars and sailcloth. They are powered by lawn-mower engines. They take off from the dark of South Lebanon. One glider is blinded by searchlights from Kibbutz Ma'ayan Baruch, but the other operator—and this is where he might variously be called a terrorist or a martyr or a murderer or a guerrilla or a freedom fighter—manages to fly over the land to the Gibor Army camp near Kiryat Shmona.

The glider escapes attention by flying at tree level. The night is stark. Moonless. He flies well, he is agile, he can pilot the craft with one hand, his body extended backwards, his feet resting on the glider bars. He wears a black jumpsuit, black shoes, black gloves, balaclava. The exposed portion of his face is darkened with fire ash. The craft glides. The air sharpens. Below, he sees two pencil-swaths of light. Wings extended, he is not unlike a bat.

He keeps the craft steady, guides it closer to the road, opens fire with a Kalashnikov on the passing truck, a salvo of bullets, killing the driver and wounding the passenger. He flies on two hundred more meters under the whirl of his single propeller. He tops the camp fence and hurls down several grenades at the camp sentry. The sentry panics and runs away. The flying man flings another series of grenades down toward the canvas tents and he sprays the ground with bullets from his AK-47, killing five soldiers and wounding seven. One of the seven— the camp cook—catches a bullet in the leg but manages to take down the hang glider with a couple of shots from his service revolver.

The machine crashes. The lawn-mower engine coughs. A small fire breaks out. Then, silence.

In Lebanon, Gaza and the West Bank, great celebrations take place when the news spreads. The martyrs are sung about in cafés. Boys fly paper hang-gliders off roofs.

In Israel there is consternation about their defenses being so easily breached: lawn-mower engines with sailcloths, Russian-made rifles, Czech grenades.

373

Or it just might be that an Israeli truck collides with a civilian truck in the streets of Gaza, in the Jabalia refugee camp, at two in the afternoon, not stopping, just plowing through, killing four Palestinians and wounding several others.

374

Or it just might be that an Israeli salesman is stabbed to death at the same junction in Jabalia two days beforehand, the knife plunged precisely between his shoulder blades.

375

Or it just might be that Jewish militants wanted to take over the Haram al-Sharif, or the Temple Mount, in East Jerusalem.

376

Or it just might be that it was bound to happen no matter what.

377

The flight of colored stones through the air.

378

He stays to the back of the crowd. His limp makes him slower. The crowd swells around him. Smoke on his tongue, in his throat, in his chest. A dusty hum in his ears. He takes the onion, wraps it in the keffiyeh around his mouth, inhales, moves on again. In his waistband he keeps a brand-new slingshot: Czech-made with a black elastic band and a reinforced leather pouch. In his pocket, several small stones. He is swept along. The flags ripple above his head. The smoke hangs from the underside of the balconies. Older men in keffiyehs, their faces lit by flame. Boys his age and older surging forward. Girls too. A length of limbs and flapping sleeves. The air whistling and concussed. The bloodrush of a dozen shouts. The body heat. He passes a plundered car squatting flat on its axle. A voice erupts over a loudspeaker. Several loud pops sound out. The crowd parts. Four men, their arms entwined to make a chair, carry another boy backwards through the crowd.

The boy stares straight ahead and then, for just an instant, catches eyes with Bassam.

A patch of blood blooms at the boy's groin.

379

To make a proper Molotov cocktail it is important to shake the bottle so that the gasoline or flammable liquid is soaked up by the rag before launching it through the air.

Experienced rioters carry black electrical tape to secure the tongue of the rag to the mouth of the bottle—taping it with a quick circular twist—so the flame doesn't separate mid-flight.

380

During the Winter War of 1939 the Soviet Union dropped hundreds of incendiary bombs over Finland. The bombs—a cluster of loaded devices inside a giant container—were lethal, but the Soviet foreign minister, Vyacheslav Molotov, claimed they were not bombs at all, but food for starving Finns.

The bombs became known, tongue in cheek, as Molotov's bread baskets.

The Finns, in response, said they wanted a drink to go along with the food, so they then invented the Molotov cocktail to wash the Russian bread down.

381

All the way through the First Intifada, the Mayor of Jerusalem, Teddy Kollek, kept a picture of Philippe Petit on his desk, the bird of peace fluttering just above the wire-walker's head.

382

383

For years afterwards Petit wondered exactly why the pigeon would not fly.

Wrapped in the red silk handkerchief and slipped headfirst into his pocket, the bird had stayed upside down while he prepared for the walk, and it remained upside down as he stepped across the wire.

Maybe he had kept it too long in his pocket. Or perhaps the bird had developed a disorientation of the blood, the mind, the body. Then again, its wings might have been clipped by the shop owner in the market—it was known to happen if the birds were to be kept as pets.

Or maybe, he thought, the bird had simply never known how to fly at all.

Anything was possible: he would never finally know.

384

On the day of judgment, in Muslim tradition, it is said that a fine wire rope will be strung from the top of the Haram al-Sharif wall on the west to the summit of the Mount of Olives in the east where Christ and Muhammad will both sit in judgment.

The righteous will be preserved by angels and they will cross quickly, but the wicked will fall headlong into the valley.

385

The Separation Wall. Also known as the Separation Barrier. Also known as the Separation Fence. Also known as the Security Wall, the Security Barrier, the Security Fence. Also known as the Apartheid Wall, the Peace Wall, the Isolation Wall, the Shame Wall, the West Bank Wall, the Administration Wall, the Annexation Wall, the Seam-Zone Wall, the Terrorist Wall, the Infiltrator Wall, the Saboteurs' Wall, the Obstacle Wall, the Demographic Wall, the Territories Wall, the Colonization Wall, the Unification Wall, the Racist Wall, the Sanctuary Wall, the Noose Wall, the Curse Wall, the Reconciliation Wall, the Fear Wall. Also known as the Pen, the Coop, the Trap, the Noose, the Protector and the Cage.

386

Most of the 440-mile barrier is not concrete at all, but a series of ditches, mounds, patrol roads, sand strips, exclusion zones, movement sensors and razor wire coils.

387

When drawing the ceasefire line on a map in 1949—the Green Line that became, until 1967, the boundary—the commanders, Abdullah el-Tell and Moshe Dayan, used thick colored pencils, leaning over, smudging the lines, often not knowing that the border went right through the middle of villages, splitting streets, houses, gardens.

It was possible that a woman might love her husband in Palestine before midnight, and roll across the bed to find herself in Israel for the rest of her life.

In several small villages—separated by a ravine or a creek or a line of soldiers—a trade was set up among pigeon carriers to bring notes back and forth: contracts, land deeds, notices of birth, ownership disputes, and, more often than people were willing to admit, love letters.

Little shots of grey crossed back and forth over the heads of the Jordanian soldiers who patrolled the line and, on occasion, blasted the birds out of the sky.

388

In the beginning of Jerzy Kosiński's Holocaust novel, *The Painted Bird*, he describes a sport practiced by hunters to trap and disguise birds with paint. The hunters release the painted birds into the air as the rest of the flock—unable to recognize their fellow—begin to attack and brutalize the supposed intruder from all angles.

The book was lauded by critics and published in dozens of languages. Kosiński originally suggested that the novel was based on his own boyhood experiences in Poland, but once it was published he refrained from the claim, and later still was accused of plagiarism.

The book was banned in Poland until 1989, when the Berlin Wall fell. Shortly afterwards an artist in Warsaw created several paper birds from the book's pages and released them, in various disguises and colors, from the rooftop of the Palace of Culture and Science, where they were filmed soaring on the wind.

389

NOW THAT HELL HAS FROZEN OVER ANYTHING CAN HAPPEN. CONTROL + ALT + DELETE. HANDALA LIVES. *ONE HAND CLAPPING. This ain't no green line.* FUCK BIBI. (Uh, no thanks.) *JESUS DIED FOR HER SINS.* NIETZSCHE GETS THE LAST WORD. BANKSY, STOP MAKING IT BEAUTIFUL! ARRIGONI IS ALIVE! *ALL ALONG THE WATCHTOWER.* JESUS WAS A WATER SKIER. By the time you read this I'll be gone. UNITY. *PEACE NOW!* ↑ARAFAT. JAMES MILLER, RIP. *HOW LIKE AN ACTUAL PERSON YOU ARE.* REMEMBER '48. BERLIN WAS ONLY THIS TALL. *Fixed fortifications are monuments to man's stupidity:* General George S. Patton. MAKE HUMMUS NOT WALLS. Patriae quis exsul se quoque fugit? TIME IS PAIN, BROTHER. *GOD WAS AN ISRAELI—NIETZSCHE.* Do you hear me, Banksy? This Wall Doesn't Care. Another JANCFU. ICH BIN EIN BERLINER. RESOLUTION 194. ERADICATE CENSORSHIP! CHE SERA, SERA. *RAGE AGAINST THE MACHINE. I>R>A. We will remember you forever, Jimmy Sands! ESCAPE HATCH. Wiser Than Violence!* NOT EVEN MY SENTENCES HAVE A RIGHT TO RETURN. Speak the truth, Sister. STOP SPRAYING SHIT—SKUNK SUCKS. Raed Zeiter Crosses Here. RACHEL CORRIE, RIP. This IS Rachel's Tomb. BOYCOTT DIVESTMENT (and/or) SANCTIONS. (Certainly not.) *Art The Shit Outa This People!* NUDE BATHING PROHIBITED: PALESTINIANS HAVE SUFFERED ENOUGH. THE ANC LIVES! *WHAT'S SO FUNNY 'BOUT PEACE LOVE AND UNDERSTANDIN'?* UBINTIFADA. *RIP Trayvon.* PARKOUR THIS BITCH. Keep it Spotless, Banksy. *Visual Pollution.* SAID THE JOKER TO THE THIEF. I am, because of You, Ubuntu. What Rough Beast. Wagah, Wagah, Wagah. ELVIS PRESLEY, RIP. POLE VAULTERS UNITE. IGNORE FEAR. *And the Wall of the City Will Fall Down Flat.* ABU AMMAR LIVES. REMEMBER THE GLIDERS, 6–1. Sameh Will Make It Seven. Maraabah scores! Get Your Ramadan (Sobhi) On. You are Not in Disneyland Anymore.

Existence is Resistance. The Plough is Slow but the Earth is Patient. STOP AND LET US WEEP FOR THE BELOVED AND THE HOME. *Kiss my Diaspora.* IS THERE LIFE BEFORE DEATH? Be Realistic—Demand the Impossible. *LEILA KHALED WE LOVE YOU.* FREE MARWAN BARGHOUTI! *(with every pack of Cornflakes). WE (in)SHALL(ah) BI(BI) RELEASED.* IF BATMAN KNEW ABOUT THIS YOU WOULD BE IN SO MUCH TROUBLE.

390

Rami's favorite: END THE PREOCCUPATION.

391

One afternoon when driving back through Bethlehem with a Welsh reporter from the *Daily Mail*, Rami thought he saw Abir's face painted high on the Palestinian side of the Wall. A shrapnel of cold sprayed through him. The girl in the portrait wore a tight hijab but her face was identical to Abir's. It was as if someone had taken Bassam's daughter's photograph and copied it exactly: the eyes, the round cheeks, the sweet oboe of the mouth. Rami's heart jabbed in the otherwise silence.

He swung around from the passenger seat to look again, but the road turned quickly, and they followed the Wall, past Rachel's Tomb, near Checkpoint 300, where the Welshman was interested in seeing a piece of Banksy's graffiti.

Rami didn't say anything to anyone, even lying next to Nurit that night. He felt as if he had a roof over his head but no floor beneath him. If he got out of bed, he would simply disappear. He harbored a feeling of living on the lip of silence: there was a meaning here he could not quite utter. If Abir had not gone, she would not need to be remembered. Her absence, then, was her presence.

He didn't sleep, he couldn't. Salt taste of sorrow in his mouth. He remembered, suddenly, the weight of Smadar's wrist when she was a very young child sleeping upon his chest.

Something sounded out in the small hours of morning. He rose. He took his flashlight, stepped onto the wooden deck at the back of the house. He trained the light along the trees. He saw a glint, perhaps even of eyes, random in the night. They quickly disappeared. Animal or human, he did not know.

Rami knew full well that they might watch him from time to time. His phone was probably tapped. He didn't care anymore. He had lost so much more than they could monitor.

392

He rode his motorbike out from Jerusalem later the next day. The graffiti was still there, high on the Wall. It was, he now realized, the image of a different Palestinian girl, about ten years old, yes, and similar in so many ways to Abir, but not, when he stood looking at her for a long time, exactly her: the eyes were a little bigger, the cheekbones a little too angular, a dimple in the chin shadowed too deeply.

393

On one side of the Wall the *Cinnyris osea* has long been known as the Palestinian sunbird, the national bird of Palestine. On the other side—in more recent years—it has begun to be called the Israeli sunbird.

394

In his first-century B.C. treatise *De Architectura*, Vitruvius Pollio said that all walls which require a deep foundation—from barriers to huge wooden defense towers—should be joined together with charred olive ties.

Olive wood does not decay even if buried in the earth or placed deep in water.

395

In 2006 an order was issued within the Israeli government to complete the Wall through the heart of the Cremisan vineyard, dividing the monastery from the nuns' convent.

The convent would be on the Palestinian side of the Wall, the monastery on the Israeli side. The nuns would need permits to meet with the monks.

Six years later, when the order was reissued, Sister Lucretia, a Brazilian nun, gave an interview outside the convent gates: God gave us a lot of things, she said, but unfortunately not grappling hooks.

The following day a large FedEx package arrived at the convent addressed specifically to her.

Sister Lucretia decided not to open it. She scrawled a note on it—*Use If/When Needed*—and brought the package down to Checkpoint 300, deposited it at the foot of the Wall.

396

The watchtowers of Checkpoint 300 are air-conditioned. Soldiers sit at the top of a spiral staircase in a rotating chair—pneumatic and padded—with a 360-degree view over the landscape of Bethlehem, the Seam Zone, all the way back to Jerusalem. The barrels of their guns stick out through shooting holes.

The ceiling has an armored exit in case the soldiers need to be helicoptered off. Inside, they have a folding ladder to allow them to reach the roof of the tower.

The soldiers can fire live rounds or rubber bullets or send out directions to the ground units, or to the water cannons, or to the Skunk trucks, directing them to a series of special trapdoors built into the Wall.

397

The Humanitarian lane at Qalandia checkpoint—for women, children, the elderly and the sick—is a prefab hut with a bathroom and a watercooler.

At one end of the hut there is a fold-out wooden table on which to change babies, and over it a sign in English, Hebrew and Arabic: *The Hope of Us All*. On the opposite wall is a photograph of the Old City of Jerusalem, the rim of the walls covered in snow.

The gate is open for forty-five minutes a day.

398

So many of Rami's acquaintances had never been to the West Bank. They refused even to go to Area B for fear they might be kidnapped, imprisoned, beaten up.

But the Wall, he knew now, was easy to get beyond. Just about any Israeli could make it into Bethlehem. All they had to do was drive to Area B, park the car at the Mount Everest Hotel, get a cab down to the markets in Bethlehem. Dress sensibly. Pass for a tourist. Keep your mouth shut. Or speak English. Say you're Danish. Walk around. Go to the churches. Breathe it in. Dismantle the fear.

They could even drive their own cars through: there were enough yellow plates around Bethlehem to get by.

Getting home was just as easy. Simply drive to a settlement, roll down the window, flash the I.D. card, riff in Hebrew, drive back on the empty road.

It was all in the branding, Rami told them. Everything was built on fear. Operation Security, he called it. Operation Spoonfeed. Operation Hoodwink.

399

Bassam had seen them simply climb over in the places where the Wall was lower, hoisting themselves by hand and foot. Others used ladders of wood, steel, hemp. Others dug secret crawl holes and tunnels or chiseled out spaces in the Wall where they passed items through. He had heard of boys using rock-climbing gear and one young acrobat in Bethlehem who was known for her stilts: when she got to the top of the Wall, she hoisted the wooden stilts over using rope, then hid them in a nearby warehouse while she went to work in a falafel joint on the Hebron Road.

400

401

Rise up, little girl, rise up.

402

Abir's face was soft, tender, dark. Her cheekbones arched. Her eyes were large and sloe-colored. She parted her hair in the middle of her forehead and drew it back some of the time in a ponytail. Her eyebrows were thin and straight. She wore a smile that looked like she was in the middle of a permanent question.

403

Smadar inhabited any camera that was pointed in her direction. She had the manner of a girl who was in control of what could be seen, her brown eyes flitting about, charged through with a petitioning electricity.

404

On the night before Abir was shot, several prefabricated sections of the Wall arrived on articulated trucks from the Akerstein factory in the Negev. The fortified pieces were delivered to the rear of the schoolyard. The huge concrete slabs were eased off by cranes, swung through the air, stacked on the ground.

The path of the Wall had originally been designed to cut off the entire school: the route through the center of the yard was a compromise.

The work was to begin later that night under floodlight: it had been decreed that the noise of the work should not disturb the schoolkids.

Bassam never knew if Abir had seen the prefab pieces arriving or not, but the border guard who shot his daughter testified that among his orders that morning was to protect the workers delivering pieces of the Wall to the schoolyard.

405

The border guard remained unnamed in all the court documents, although Bassam got to know him by the initials Y.A.

406

The Wall workers were mostly Palestinian. They guided the jackhammers. Drove the bulldozers. Looped the cables. Unfurled their measuring tapes. Chalked the marks in the sections of wall. Three or four times a day their prayer mats were unfurled in front of the Wall where they sought a clean place to pray.

407

For five years it was the best-paying construction job in the area: the workers called it the Shekel Wall.

408

A plastic shopping bag animated itself above the walls: it popped in the wind and sounded momentarily like a rifle shot. Nobody flinched.

The Peace Walls were still up in Belfast even years after the Good Friday agreement. They stretched high into the grey of the city, topped, here and there, with razor wire.

Bassam paused at a portrait of Arafat with Martin Luther King. Nearby was a painting of the Black September fighters. *Smash Zionism. Irish Solidarity with the Palestinian People. Arafat, 1993. No Peace Without Justice.*

At the far end of the street, on a gable wall, were the murals of the other side, a portrait of Churchill sitting inside a map of Greater Israel, a painting of Golda Meir. Further along: *Golda, we Love You. Bal-Four, Palestine Nil. Rule Britannia: We Support the People of Zion. Chaim Herzog, President of Israel, born Belfast, 1918.*

Further along, one of Picasso's doves of peace with an Armalite, not an olive branch, in its mouth.

409

In my case, a picture is a sum of destructions. I do a picture—then I destroy it. In the end, though, nothing is lost: the red I took away from one place turns up somewhere else.

~ PICASSO ~

410

The buildings sat grey. The rain seemed to drizzle with intent. Belfast, to him, was a city of vast surprise. He was taken for a tour. The Crown. The Titanic Museum. The Botanic Gardens. Milltown Cemetery. The Shankill. The Falls.

Late one night he walked around what the locals called the Holyland. Bassam was taken by the names of the streets: Palestine, Cairo, Jerusalem, Damascus. He scoured a map. Delphi Avenue. Balaklava Street. Unity Flats. Kashmir Road.

He had arrived from Bradford for a three-day peace conference. He curled into the hood of a borrowed blue anorak, lit cigarette after cigarette, kept walking late into the night.

Palestine Street was a row of redbrick houses, dark gates, tiny gardens. Jerusalem Street ran into a cul-de-sac. There had, he heard, been many shootings here. Short streets, long memories.

He marveled at the sight of the flags fluttering over the rooftops. Parts of the city flew the Star of David. Others flew the Palestinian colors. *White our deeds, black our battles, green our fields, red our swords.* On light poles, bridges, in shop windows.

Still, there was something buoyant about the town too, something cheeky and hopeful. It seemed like the sort of place where he could have grown up. He wanted to whisper to it, to announce his recognition. It was a city with a memory of curfew, a mistscape of ghosts.

He walked to the edge of the dockyards, saw the first of the sun rising over the shipyard, Harland and Wolff. Sitting on a dockside bollard, he listened to the blare of foghorns. Along the shoreline, he strolled alone.

At the hotel, the other conference attendees were finishing break-fast. He slipped in amongst them. Bassam was good at disappearing into crowds. He could make of himself a shadow.

His presentation was at noon. He waited backstage, drinking tea. No matter how many times he told his story, the nerves still cut him raw. Before his presentation he went through a half packet of Silk Cut. He walked onstage, coughed lightly into the microphone, stepped back, put his hand to his forehead to shield his eyes from the light, paused. *I am Bassam Aramin, from Palestine.* A ripple went around the theater.

Afterwards, most of the crowd gave him a standing ovation. The ones who didn't made a point of crossing their arms in their seats. He could already see them gathering together in groups.

Offstage, he was slapped on the back. The Irish accents were even harder to understand than the English. He found himself hanging his head, nodding. His greatest wish was not to offend. He did not want to ask them to repeat themselves. Most of all he wanted to talk to those who had kept their arms crossed, but they did not appear.

The conference was abuzz. He was added to panels. *Theory and Practice. Conflict Analysis. Reconciliation Studies. The Mercy of Dialogue.* He recognized the relative ease of being Palestinian here. He was listened to. He was authentic. He had suffered. It might even be easier, he thought, to be a Palestinian abroad than at home. The notion tugged at him. What might it be if he decided not to return? What might happen if he worked from abroad? Would he have anything to say? It was, he knew, exactly what so many wanted: one less Arab. He knew, too, that if he stayed away three years they might revoke his right to go home. Bassam wanted to take a flight back, that very afternoon, to Jordan, then drive to the West Bank, just to reassure himself.

At night, the participants gathered in groups in the hotel bar and foyer. They sang and drank. There were factions here too. Bassam was called over to meet a group of Norwegian scholars. They had heard he had been a singer in prison. He sat among them, sang an Abu Arab song. Someone put a pint of Guinness in his hand.

—No, no, he said, I never drink.

A minute later a whiskey was put in front of him. He sat back in his chair, laughed and passed the whiskey along the table.

He couldn't sleep, but found solace in walking. He liked moving through the drizzle. It helped him shape his thoughts. He was a quarter way through his thesis now. He thought of himself as a man traveling in several different directions.

At times he stopped to scribble small phrases in his notebook. *Peace without reconciliation. To forgive but not excuse. To colonize the mind.*

411

He established due east and backed down an alleyway to quietly unfold a mat, to say his prayers.

412

In the early 1990s, at least twice a month, Senator George Mitchell bid goodbye to his wife, Heather, and his son, Andrew, a toddler, in New York.

A day later he would land in the Aldergrove airport on the outskirts of Belfast, in order to chair the Northern Irish peace talks. Most of the time he traveled alone with a briefcase and a small bag. In the airport corridors he went largely unrecognized.

At the airport, a car waited to take him to the city. In the back seat he took a nap, one of the few times he could find silence.

Mitchell was known affectionately as Iron Pants because of his uncanny ability to sit for a long time and listen to the stories of opposing factions. The leaders of the parliamentary parties came to his office to sit down and tell him exactly where they stood. He listened quietly, called on himself for patience. The stories seemed, at times, endless. He wondered if he might ever be able to find a language to describe it all.

Eight hundred years of history here. Thirty-five years of oppression there. A treaty here, a massacre there, a siege elsewhere. What happened in '68. What supermarket was torched in '74. What went on last week on the Shankill Road. The bombings in Birmingham. The shootings in Gibraltar. The links with Libya. The Battle of the Boyne.

The march of Cromwell. The cutting down of trees. The removal of nails from the fingers of harpists so they could not play the catgut strings.

Every morning the Senator's driver slid a mirror on rollers under the car to check for bombs. They drove through the streets to the plenaries where he sat once again, listening. Meeting after meeting. Lunch after lunch. Dinner after dinner. Phone call after phone call. Often he had to fight to keep himself awake. There were times he would press a ballpoint pen into his fingertip: at the end of the day the tip of his forefinger was often studded with blue.

Loyalists, Republicans, Sinn Féin, the moderates, the socialists, the Women's Coalition, the vast slalom of acronyms: DUP, UVF, IRA, UFF, RIHA, ABD, RSF, UDA, INLA.

413

In the 1980s the greatest sale of Israeli flags—outside of Israel itself— was in Northern Ireland, where the Loyalists flew them in defiance of Irish Republicans who had adopted the Palestinian flag: whole housing estates shrouded in either blue and white, or black red white and green.

414

Israeli Defense Force Order 101, Regarding Prohibition of Incitement and Hostile Propaganda Actions, was put into effect in 1967. It forbade Palestinians to use the word *Palestine* in official documents, to depict or raise or fly their flag, or to make any sort of art that combined the colors of the traditional flag.

415

On Friday afternoons Bassam and his friends hung the flag from the school gates and waited until the soldiers came to tear it down. Then they pelted the soldiers with rocks and stones.

In return the soldiers fired gas canisters and rubber bullets which bounced off the tin-sided shack at the back of the school. Sometimes the soldiers continued shooting long after the boys were gone.

From a distance, hidden in an alleyway, he listened to the canisters popping off the rusted tin roof, ping after ping, not at all like raindrops.

416

When, in 2009, Mitchell was appointed as special envoy to the Middle East, he had a sudden feeling that he was walking into the middle of another smashed jigsaw—PLO, JDL, DFLP, LEHI, PFLP, ALA, PIJ, CPT, IWPS, ICAHD, AIC, AATW, EIJ, JTJ, ISM, AEI, NIF, ACRI, RHR, BDS, PACBI, BNC—only this time it was so much more difficult to find a straight edge with which to begin.

417

A countably infinite number of sides.

418

Rami finishes his coffee, thanks the waiter in Arabic, leaves the Everest Hotel with fifteen minutes still to spare. Outside, he adjusts his helmet, rocks the bike off its stand, backs the machine out from its parking space. The caffeine has jolted him awake. He would like to rev the machine and push it hard for a while.

419

So many West Bank potholes. To swerve left, he gently pushes the right handlebar. To ease right, he applies pressure to the left.

420

He glides through the streets on the western edge of Beit Jala, the wind whipping the laundry into gymnastics on the third and fourth floors of the blocky white apartment buildings, the breeze animating one white shirt into arms-up surrender.

On past the downhill curve of Salaam Street—rooftops and balustrades and sandbagged upper balconies. Some of the windowpanes are blacked out.

A small group of men hang outside a garage under their faithful clouds of cigarette smoke. Further along, a low house in the row of apartments, beautiful stained glass in the upper windows.

He rounds a curve and eases past the single olive tree in the middle of the street, past the old villas.

He can sense the ancient architecture of these homes: their vaulting ceilings, their whiteness, the mosaic tiles, the thin candles in the tall entryways.

421

Above Nablus—on top of Mount Gerizim, the Mountain of Mercy— is a sprawling mansion owned by Munib al-Masri, the richest man in Palestine.

He built the house on the coveted hilltop in the style of Palladio's Rotonda in Vicenza, Italy. The tiled cupola—which resembles the roof of the Al-Aqsa mosque—can be seen shining in the sunlight from many miles away.

The gate of the mansion comes from a seventeenth-century French estate. Gravel crunches underfoot. Goldfish ponds line the laneways. The granite steps are polished. A marble statue of Hercules stands in the foyer underneath a high dome. A cruciform central hall has four identical doors, each facing in the cardinal directions. The house is chock-full of precious art and antiquities, including paintings by Picasso and Modigliani, Flemish Renaissance tapestries, Biblical portraits, mirrors from Versailles, manuscripts from ancient Iranian mathematicians, as well as a number of sixth-century Arabic scrolls that originally hung in marketplaces.

Stone steps lead to a glass winter garden once belonging to the mistress of Napoleon III. Nearby sits a Roman amphitheater. Two triumphal arches—one from the city of Poitiers, the other commissioned in honor of al-Masri's friend Yasser Arafat—stand guard near a grove of cypress trees. A carefully clipped maze with ten-foot-high walls completes the garden.

Al-Masri—a chronic insomniac—built the mansion as a riddle, a mosaic, a metaphor for his country: he called it Beit Falasteen, the House of Palestine. He wanted to build an ark, a scavenge-ship of everything beautiful, a jigsaw of provocative excess. It stunned those who came to visit.

Al-Masri—who made his money through oil and water speculation—poured tens of millions of dollars into the house.

In the process of excavation, his builders uncovered thin beams of olive wood, charred ties, chisel marks, a tiny piece of porcelain, a step, then a stone that seemed shaped like an altar. A mosaic floor. Colored stones. Blue Roman glass. He halted all work on the house, brought in archaeologists from around the world who meticulously sifted the ruins. They uncovered pillars, dug up a stone altar, sorted through shards of pottery: what they had found was an ancient monastery.

They mapped out the monastery as it would have been sixteen hundred years ago, replicated it, and then al-Masri rebuilt the mansion on top—lifting it twenty feet in the air—so that the structure in the basement was perfectly preserved and made accessible to visitors.

422

The other mountain that can be seen from Beit Falasteen is called Mount Ebal, the Mountain of Curse.

423

In 2011, al-Masri's grandson, also named Munib, was shot while marching along the Lebanese border to commemorate the Nakba of 1948. He was hit in the back as he walked toward a bus. The high-velocity bullet penetrated his kidney and spleen, then rested near his spine, paralyzing him.

He was taken to hospital in Beirut where he begged the doctors to let him die, but eventually he was air-lifted out to the United States for treatment where the doctors in San Diego put him through years of rigorous rehabilitation.

424

Munib still sometimes visits his grandfather's mansion from his home in Georgia. He guides himself around in his wheelchair, bringing visitors downstairs to show them a large mural where, among scenes of historical carnage, there are several portraits of doves of peace.

425

The Nakba. Or the Catastrophe. Or the Hejira. Also known as the Exodus, the Rape, the Cataclysm, the Forcing, the Night We Black-ened Our Faces and Left.

426

Strewn along the roads in 1948: cigarette cases, letters, locks of hair, silk ties, tarbushes, rag dolls, photographs, reels of film, walking sticks, tennis rackets, crystal decanters, headscarves, prayer shawls, medwakh pipes, lira coins, cricket balls, brass coffeepots, shoes, socks.

Most of the three-quarters of a million Palestinians who were dis-placed didn't carry anything too heavy because they were sure they were going to return to their homes in a matter of days: there were legends of soup left boiling on their stoves.

427

One of Borges's favorite stories, overheard in a café in Jerusalem, was about an earthenware pot of soup left simmering for centuries without ever evaporating or changing its taste, a soup that had become an elixir of life for some although when tasted by others it was bitter and sour and often resulted in an agonizing illness.

428

Set me, if ever I return, in your oven as fuel to help you cook.

~ DARWISH ~

429

The statue of Hercules arrived at al-Masri's house from Paris in 2002 in a giant wooden crate. The piece had been carved from a single block of white Italian marble.

A special crane was required to lift the box up the steps to the entrance of the house. The driver miscalculated and released the crate a foot up in the air. The crate wobbled a moment, then toppled over on the steps and smashed wide open in front of al-Masri. The body of Hercules—his left hand gripping a club, his right hand cradling stones—spilled out. The head hit the top stair and separated from the body, then rolled partway down the hill. It had been a time of heavy rains and it took al-Masri's workers two hours to find the head amongst the mud and bushes.

Al-Masri had the head expertly reattached. He placed the tall statue under a giant dome, the light spreading in a wide nimbus around it.

Only on close examination could a visitor see that the head had been reattached.

430

What disturbed al-Masri was the faces of those who, when they saw him in his immaculate suits, were surprised that he was Palestinian. The perfect creases. The cuff links. The pocket squares. The mono-grammed shirtfronts. They wanted some sort of scruffiness from him, a keffiyeh, a holster, a battle dress, a polyester hood.

They looked at him as if he had made a mistake about himself.

431

The front door of Munib al-Masri's mansion is four hundred years old, made of oak and steel, and designed to withstand the force of a massive battering ram.

432

The house was completely surrounded by Area C, but built in Area A, located up a jackknifed road overlooking the flat roofs and minarets of Nablus.

From his height, al-Masri had a clear view of the Balata refugee camp. In the distance lay the village of Assira al-Shamaliya.

433

434

Walk by the fields and watch the women carrying bundles of wheat on their backs. See the boys out threshing in the hard bright light. It is all so very yellow and white.

The women return to the village, past the ancient well, along the cobblestones, under the walls topped with barbed wire, and then they disperse among the shadows of the steep stone staircases.

You can follow their trail by the wheat chaff that falls from their dresses.

435

The village was raided one week after the Ben Yehuda Street bombings. The streets were sealed off. Helicopters hovered. Families were taken outside at gunpoint. The men were arrested and their hands were zip-tied. Women and children were made to kneel on the ground, facing the houses.

The first squad went in to throw out the belongings: photos, books, bedding, knickknacks, shisha pipes, furniture, ancient clocks, ovens, fridges, saucepans, documents, clothes. A second group loaded the smashed items in an army dumpster and crushed them in front of the watchers.

When the houses were bare, the women and children were moved away and another group of soldiers—the construction squad—moved in.

The doors were sealed off, the windows crisscrossed with rebar, the front and back balconies studded with metal spikes. The large spikes were driven in pneumatically. Barrels full of concrete were sealed to the floor so nobody could ever dwell inside again.

New steel doors were welded tight and reinforced with more metal bars strong enough to withstand a battering ram.

The soldiers spray-painted Stars of David on the walls, but immediately after the operation was complete, Youssef Shouli's nephew, Sabri, an eight-year-old gymnast, managed to crawl through the windows where his first job was to scrub the paint away.

436

On the walls the kids later scrawled the names of the men who once lived in the houses: Bashar Sawalha, 1973–97, Youssef Shouli, 1974–97, Tawfiq Yassine, 1974–97. Then the children crawled around on the concrete barrels, close to the ceiling, playing war games: *Kill the Jew, Kidnap, Bombs in Baghdad.*

437

A decade later, in Algiers, Sabri Shouli represented the Palestinian gymnastics team in the Pan Arab Games: he came fifth on the parallel bars.

438

A medieval battering ram consisted of a wooden beam, often over twenty feet long, to be thrust against the wall of a city, or a tunnel door, or a gate. Some were built with a sharp metal head which could be jammed fiercely between stones and levered back and forth to dislodge the brick. Others were capped with a piece of flat metal to batter over and over again.

More advanced rams were equipped with wheels and dragged in wagons by large teams of men or oxen—guarded by slingmen and archers—to the place of attack.

Often a moat had to be bridged or drained before the battering ram could do its work. For the final part of the assault, an improvised track of wooden planks was laid down to make the ram easier to push. The wagon was braked with giant rocks to prevent it from rolling backwards down the steep slopes.

The forward part of the wagon was open to allow the wooden beam to be swung. The ram was hung from the ceiling of the wagon with a thick rope so that it could become a pendulum. When swung back and forth, it gathered momentum until it was released, slamming forward into the wall, dislodging the bricks or shattering the hinges of the gate.

Fire rained down upon the attackers, burning oil, arrows, stones, snakes, even rotting bodies.

439

As part of a deal to return the corpse of an Israeli soldier, the bodies of the three Ben Yehuda Street bombers were eventually returned to their families. It had taken seven years. The IDF left the plastic blue containers on the steps of the original houses.

It was a stealth operation, four jeeps running quietly through the steep streets of the village in the dark. No lights in the windows. No patrols on the streets.

They sped past the Cemetery of Martyrs, beyond the small square, along past School Street.

A spotlight picked out the steps. The blue coolers were hustled out of the vehicles, each one carted by two soldiers. The bodies were placed near the barricaded doors.

In the town, lights had begun to flicker on. Dogs began barking. The sound of doors slamming. Some shouting rose in the distance as the jeeps sped away.

440

The soldiers nicknamed it Operation Jigsaw.

441

The eyeball blown onto the awning of the Atara café had belonged to Youssef Shouli.

442

Normally when the string on a suicide vest is pulled, the bomber's upper body takes the brunt of the explosive force and becomes pure mist. The head and feet are shorn away, yet often still left recognizable as head or foot.

Because Shouli's eyeball was found separated from the rest of his head, forensic experts suggested that he probably bent his head toward his chest at the very moment he pulled the string, perhaps to check on a malfunctioning string, or maybe to crouch down in fear from a nearby fellow bomber's blast, or perhaps even to pray.

443

A few experts in the field prefer to call them *homicide vests*.

444

The new houses for the families of the bombers, built on the outskirts of the village, were said to have come as gifts from the Iranian government.

The payments were funneled through a complicated maze that ended with the local political offices in Nablus, but they had been rumored to be channeled through Ramallah, from Damascus, from Geneva, through another Swiss bank account, all the way back to Tehran.

The money was earmarked for building as a direct military response to the IDF's smashing up and sealing off of the old houses. A video was shot and posted on a radical Islamic website: *What you make fall, we will rebuild.*

445

Rami saw inside the new houses in the raw documentary footage. The parents were interviewed sitting on their sofas with an array of knick-knacks in the background: teapots, flowers, small glass animals, a pendant, a Qur'an, souvenirs from Mecca.

The mother of Bashar Sawalha held a framed photo in her lap. She wept into a white handkerchief. She rose from the couch mid-sentence and then sat down again, exhausted.

The father of Youssef Shouli stared directly into the lens. His wife sat silently beside him. His son had seen the face of God, he said, may Allah have mercy on his soul. When he reached for his water glass the father's hand trembled. He said he had not slept in peace in many years. He couldn't understand it. Their sons had been radicalized while in prison, Allah protect them, but they were put in prison for slinging stones.

—Only this, he said to the camera. Slinging stones. What is this world but stones?

He stood up and went to the back wall, then walked out of the range of the camera, refused to return.

Outside—under an eerily blue sky—the footage showed the village minaret, the tiled roofs on the skyline, a gulp of swallows above the graveyard.

Locals were interviewed in a neon-lit café. They praised the great martyrs of '97 who, they said, had given their lives for jihad. The cousin of Youssef Shouli said he wished he could have taken the place of his blood-kin. He would gladly walk down Ben Yehuda Street again and again and again, blow himself up just to have his cousin back for one more day.

Rami watched without translation but his Arabic was good enough for him to catch most of it.

What surprised him most of all, though he did not know why, was that Youssef—the bomber most likely to have blown up Smadar—had studied graphic art.

446

At Bethlehem University Youssef Shouli had begun a project using found war items—rubber bullets, gas canisters, ammunition cartridges—as birdcages, door chimes, feeders. He told a professor that he was also interested in making a Star of Bethlehem out of tear gas canisters.

Two years into his degree, Shouli was arrested outside the Jacir Palace Hotel where he had gone with several other students to collect riot paraphernalia for their artwork. In military court he was charged with inciting protests and throwing stones.

He refused to recognize the court, making the statement that he had never thrown a stone, not once in his life, but he would now, in the future, whenever and wherever he could.

Shouli was given a four-year sentence.

447

Smadar had cut her hair close and pierced her nose. Thirteen years old, she was just beginning to rebel. She wanted to look like Sinéad

O'Connor, dancing around the house, among the flowerpots, singing *Nothing Compares 2 U.*

448

Afterwards Rami would tell people that he didn't mind the piercing, but the shaving of the hair gave him pause.

449

Many elderly Jews had signed *Heimeinkaufsvertrag* contracts agreeing to pay 80,000 Reichsmarks for the right of residence in Theresienstadt. They were told it was a pleasant Bohemian resort with gardens, fountains, villas, promenades. A perfect setting for retirement. They carried in their luggage all manner of mementos, not least precious mirrors, hair combs, clips and brushes.

450

The shaved hair was used to line the boots of U-boat crew members. Also to make rough work clothes. It is also said to have been used to create the long manes on wooden rocking horses, some of which can still be found for sale in the black markets of Kraków in Poland.

451

When they slid Smadar out on the metal tray, Rami noticed her grandfather's watch on her wrist: it was still running.

452

After Smadar was born, her grandfather, Matti Peled, sat with her in the garden and taught her English and Arabic both. The General liked the role of grandfather. It softened something in him. He brought her to meetings of community boards, activists, human rights groups.

Until she was eight, he carried her around on his shoulders.

453

On the wall of his office Peled hung Rami's poster: *What will life in Israel be like when Smadar reaches fifteen?*

454

They worked on their cars together, Rami and his father-in-law. Peled was tall, taciturn, silver-haired. He talked more when he leaned in over an engine block: it was as if he found it easier to address something ordered and logical.

He fumbled around under the hood. His fingers were thick and clumsy. He cursed as he unscrewed the carburetor.

Peled said to Rami that he was not one to suffer fools gladly, least of all himself.

He had been an architect of the Six-Day War. Lightning strikes. Bombing raids. The aura of surprise. He had become a general, revered all over the country—one of the original Jewish idealists: socialist, Zionist, democratic, but after '68 he grew almost immediately wary of the Occupation. It jeopardized, he said, the moral weight of the cause. It took away from the sense that Israel was a guiding global light. He went to meetings at the Knesset wearing a pin showcasing a Star of David alongside a Palestinian flag. His pale blue shirts showed large oval stains of sweat at his armpits. He was volcanic, temperamental, with a single-minded toughness. His voice seemed to come from his solar plexus. He spoke out on behalf of moderation, toleration, inclusivity, nuance. He was no *lamed vavnik,* he did not want to carry the sorrows of his country. He had fought for Israel, he said, from '48 onwards, and he knew a thing or two about military might. He had met with Dayan, with Herzog, with Rabin, with Golda Meir, with others too. Holding on to the Territories was a mistake, contrary to a secure Jewish democracy. They needed to disengage. Get out.

Rami enjoyed the diatribes: there was something maverick about them. He sat on the bumper and listened while Peled tinkered with the engine.

The General had fought in Palestine, had witnessed the Nakba, had seen the disintegration of what he called the Arab glue. He had been stationed in Gaza and studied Arabic as a soldier. After the war he launched himself into his studies again. Wrote his dissertation on Naguib Mahfouz, the Egyptian novelist. Went to the plays of Ghassan Kanafani. Triumphed the work of Fadwa Tuqan. Translated Salim Barakat. Learned the lines of Khalil as-Sakakini. Went to symposiums on language and politics. Took a secret trip to Cairo to meet Mahfouz. Wrote impassioned editorials for the newspapers. Talked with Nurit and her brothers about the primacy of peace.

He was aware, he said, that humiliation was a deep wound. We are Semitic, both of us, Israelis and Palestinians together. Your generation is in jeopardy, he said to Rami. There was a time for war, I admit it, he said, but no more. He himself carried the burden. He had created so much of it. The Occupation, he said, was a corruption. And the aid from the United States for military equipment had become a plague. Freedom, he said, begins between the ears.

Peled took a job at the Arab language department at Tel Aviv University, teaching Palestinian poetry. His lectures, like those of Nurit, were packed to the rafters. He drove to the Knesset. On several occasions he went to meet Arafat. The two men tried to broker a deal. The talks sometimes went on for days on end. Arafat hugged him, kissed him on both cheeks, bid him goodbye. In Israel the rancor grew. The right wing, the conservatives, the settlers. His home phone rang. Death threats. He was a false prophet, a pig-eater, a PLO henchman, an Arab lover. He chided the callers, said he would meet them anywhere they wanted, talk with them reasonably, he didn't care, he wanted only to talk. They slammed down the phones. He went to synagogue with the two-flag pin in his lapel. He toured Europe, Asia, the United States. He was outraged by the Palestinian bombings too, the hijackings, the kidnappings, the moral cowardice, the rhetoric that came from the most radical elements, but nobody should keep his foot on another man's neck, he said. Peace was a moral inevitability. Neither side could keep the other from it.

The afternoons drifted.

Peled raised himself up from the engine of the car. He banged his head on the raised hood.

—Go ahead, Peled told Rami, crank the engine.

455

Matti Peled died of natural causes eighteen months before his granddaughter. It was the only thing, in either death, that Rami and Nurit were thankful for.

456

Yasser Arafat sent a personal representative to Smadar's funeral. The PLO leader had, on occasion, referred to Smadar's grandfather as Abu Salaam: father of peace.

Arafat himself could not go: he was barred by the Israeli army from entering Jerusalem.

From the top floor of his Ramallah compound, Arafat could look out the window, over the rubble, at the Fat Boy Two blimp hovering over the city.

457

When traveling in America and lecturing to Jewish organizations and in synagogues about peace and its possibilities, Matti Peled carried a rubber bullet in his jacket pocket.

Onstage, under lights, he would hold the bullet up, then peel the rubber back to show the shine of the steel underneath.

458

The bullet hit the back of Abir's skull, fell to the pavement, and was reshaped.

459

Lazarus pills: when possible, they can be picked up and used again.

460

Upon hearing of the death of Lazarus of Bethany, Jesus of Nazareth is said to have ordered the burial stone to be rolled away from the cave. Lazarus was already four days dead.

When the stone was rolled away, Jesus approached the cave and stood outside with Martha and Mary. He cried out in a loud voice: *Lazarus, come forth.*

Lazarus stepped out, still bound in the wrappings of the dead. Jesus said that he should be unbound and allowed to go.

The resurrected man was said to have lived on for another thirty years, long after the death of Jesus. Those around him wondered what Lazarus had seen in the underworld, but it was said that he did not talk when he walked through the streets of Bethany, nor smile anymore, and he never mentioned anything of what he had seen during those four days of death.

461

On Peled's seventieth birthday—in a green Jerusalem garden—Smadar was videotaped in a light purple flowered dress and white headband reading a toast to her grandfather.

—*L'chaim, l'chaim,* she says in Hebrew, brushing back a strand of hair from her neck.

Then, in Arabic, she says *Ahlan wa sahlan,* glancing up at the camera with an impish grin. Her front teeth are prominent, her eyes pellucid.

—Grandpa, she says, nine years you have raised me, fourteen years Guy, sixteen years Elik, and ten months Yigal. You have raised all of us with warmth and love and we grew up with warmth and love.

She then smiles again.

—You have taught us all chess, except for Yigal! Thanks to you we know more about politics, about Israel and about all the wars you fought. I am proud of you that you struggle for peace, she says, and that you are the leader, I think.

Here, in the video, the listeners, including Peled, erupt in laughter. The *I think* hangs in the air as Smadar plays with her hair and smiles.

—I am proud of you that you write in the newspapers. You were always handsome. And don't say you were not, because I saw pictures!

She tucks her hair behind her ears again, before Peled leans down to kiss her cheek in the last frame.

—Till you are one hundred and twenty years old. From Guy, me, Yigal and Elik.

462

Smadar and her grandfather were buried side by side under a grove of knotted carob trees. The wall along the back side of the graveyard was made of limestone but had been reinforced with steel rebars, some of which were hollow. Gliding over the wall, the wind echoed as it caught in the lip of steel.

463

The last article Peled wrote for the newspapers, in 1994, was on what he thought was the devastating nature of the accords, titled *Requiem to Oslo*.

464

The Czech composer and pianist Rafael Schächter was held at the camp in Theresienstadt where he managed to smuggle in a legless upright piano. It was kept, at first, in a basement.

Schächter conducted a chorus of Jewish musicians in sixteen performances of Giuseppe Verdi's *Requiem*. The musicians learned the intricate music from a single vocal score. Schächter was interested in keeping the camp morale high.

The performances were attended by senior Nazis and guards who, at the end, gave standing ovations.

The final performance came during Operation Embellishment when excerpts of the *Requiem* were played for the Danish government officials and the Red Cross, after which Schächter was loaded in a railroad cattle car and shipped off to Auschwitz where he, like the filmmaker Kurt Gerron, heard the pellets dropping down through the grates in the ceiling.

465

The dominant movement of Verdi's *Requiem* is from crushing loss to outright terror, splitting off in several different directions, trumpet fanfares and flute solos, but always returning to the bass drum and the orchestra in forceful flow.

466

The *Requiem* was first performed in Milan in 1874 in a Catholic church where no applause was allowed.

467

After Schächter's final performance, Eichmann is reported to have said: Those crazy Jews, singing their own requiem.

468

The avant-garde theater director Peter Brook once suggested that a standing ovation was surely a sign of an audience applauding itself.

469

In December of 1972, Brook led a troupe of actors and a transportation crew from Paris to Algeria and then into the Sahara desert.

The motorcade of five Land Rovers and a truck carried two hundred gallons of water and seven hundred gallons of fuel. It also carried tents and stoves and water filters and medicines and buckets and crowbars and axes and bamboo sticks and kettles and fold-up tables and aluminum chairs. Drums, gongs, tambourines, xylophones, whistles, flutes, harmonicas, gamelans, cymbals, cowbells and conches. Also thousands of cans of food and can openers and chopping boards and cutlery. Also, dried noodles and plates and cups and saucers, and over eight thousand tea bags.

The troupe journeyed through the desert, stopping in the evenings in the smallest and most isolated villages they could find. They unfurled a large carpet and set up a series of corrugated boxes while one of the actors sounded out a drum call. An audience formed, and the troupe began their performance of an adaptation of *The Conference of the Birds*, based on an allegorical poem by Farid ud-Din Attar, using hand puppets to illustrate the story of a gathering of the world's birds trying to decide who should be their king.

In the play, each bird represents a human fault which prevents man from attaining enlightenment. The wisest bird among them, the hoopoe, suggests that together they try to find the legendary Persian Simorgh to gain enlightenment for themselves.

The script, adapted by Brook and Jean-Claude Carrière, made use of random sounds and movement. During the performance the actors—among them Helen Mirren and Yoshi Oida—made exotic birdcalls and jumped in and out of empty cardboard boxes scattered around the carpet: a dust dance.

The village crowds reacted variously—some cheered, others laughed, while a few stayed silent.

Brook felt that theater was bound to be born in empty spaces. He was in search for what he thought of as the universal theater, an attempt to find the widest human emotion possible among people who were not yet hampered by convention, a new way of communicating without language.

In the evening the crew rolled up the carpet, unfurled their tents in the open desert, and by early morning were driving once more through the Sahara under the nailheaded stars.

470

The Conference of the Birds was written in Persian at the end of the twelfth century.

When the last birds—thirty of them—finally get to the home of the Simorgh, exhausted, they gaze into a lake and, instead of meeting the mythical creature they've been searching for, they find only their own reflections.

471

On the sixtieth anniversary of the founding of Israel, the hoopoe—loquacious, dappled, with a long beak and slicked-back tuft of hair—was chosen as the national bird.

During the vote, Shimon Peres, the Israeli president, said he was only sorry that the most Zionist of birds, the dove, had not made the final cut.

It was, said Nurit, one of the most perverse lines she had heard in her life, although it was, she added, apt that the name *Peres* in Hebrew meant bearded vulture.

472

On the day of the Israeli army's departure from Jenin, in 1996, in the wake of the Oslo Accords, Bassam stood in the central square amid the waving flags and the songs and the loudspeakers and the dancing and the celebratory wailing. He watched young Palestinian men handing out olive branches to the Israeli soldiers.

The day amazed him. No stones. No slingshots. Strangers embraced one another in the streets. The jeeps turned corners. The blimp disappeared from the sky.

Bassam went back to the square that evening and helped sweep up the refuse from the day's festivities with a broom he had borrowed from a local mosque: Coke cans, plastic bottles, streamers, confetti, a raft of olive branches that had been left on the ground.

473

Bassam was two years out of prison and one year away from the birth of Abir.

474

I repeat: Do not let the olive branch fall from my hand.

475

In July of 1994 a young Israeli soldier, Arik Frankenthal, a student of theology and poetry, stuck out his thumb to hitchhike from his military base near Ramallah. He was given a lift by three men wearing yarmulkes. He greeted them in Hebrew and settled in the back seat where he was immediately overpowered.

As a teenager Arik had been interested in the peace movement and maintained that under his interpretation of halacha, or Jewish law, Israelis were required to compromise with the Palestinians.

Arik's battered body was later found in Ramallah. He had been shot and stabbed several times.

476

Three months later, Yasser Arafat, Yitzhak Rabin and Shimon Peres were awarded the Nobel Peace Prize.

477

Arik's father, Yitzhak Frankenthal, journeyed to the public library in Tel Aviv almost every single day. He examined the newspaper archive—so many ringed faces—to find the names of loved ones who had been lost in attacks since 1948, Palestinian and Israeli both.

Frankenthal took down their names in a large spiral notebook and combed through public records to find their families' phone numbers and addresses.

Frankenthal sold everything he could to support himself so

he could devote his time to the search. He finally found forty-four families who were willing to come together to talk. He gathered them in small groups, in libraries, cafés, sometimes his own home.

Many of the relatives were put off at first by Frankenthal's kippah, his fierce stare, his Orthodox ways, but they accepted his invitation. He organized conferences in Jaffa, Hebron, Beit Jala. He phoned reporters, distributed flyers, visited the Knesset. He appeared on TV to say that his son's killers needed to be understood as men born into an appalling occupation. He was not interested in absolving the attackers, but he had to admit if he had been born under the same circumstances he would undoubtedly have become a fighter himself, maybe even the same sort of man who had murdered his son.

Frankethal was, he said, an Israeli patriot. He quoted from the Torah and the Qur'an too. He liked to say that there was no black-and-white in ethics, only white.

The death threats beeped through on his answering machine, but every now and then there was a message from yet someone else who had lost a child.

478

Bassam was twenty-four years old when he was released after seven years in prison.

479

From the prison gates he took a bus. He was dropped off in East Jerusalem in a cloud of grey fumes. In a café on Al-Zahra Street he told his cousin Ibrahim that it was time to find himself a wife.

480

He had never even held a girl's hand.

Her mother was there, her aunts, her cousins, her brothers. Her father was in the back bedroom. A cassette of Abu Arab was playing on a portable stereo. He was given a glass of Fanta. He sat on the couch. It was small talk at first, then her father came out of the room, shook his hand, and gestured to the food on the table. Stuffed grape leaves, chicken dishes, rice, zucchini, sesame bread, maqluba. Bassam piled up his plate. It was, he said, the best maqluba he'd ever tasted. Her mother laughed and fanned herself theatrically. Salwa poured another glass of Fanta. Soon the room cleared. He did not know how: one moment it was full, the next it was empty. Salwa was sitting on an armchair, opposite him. She had one slightly crooked tooth. Her right eyebrow arched. A dimple on her neck. He noticed a tiny stray thread of white on her sleeve. He wanted to pluck it off. He remained with his arms folded. She rose, went to the kitchen and brought back a tray of thyme cakes. They're delicious, he said. My mother made them too, she said. He smiled and took another. Did he want something more to drink? No, he said, he was so full, he couldn't eat another thing, he might burst, did she mind if he smoked? Of course not, she smoked an arghil herself, but she never smoked at home, her father disapproved. Bassam put his Marlboro out. No, no, she said, please smoke, I like it, it doesn't bother me, my brothers all do. He lit a second. They sat in silence. The light outside dimmed. He extinguished the cigarette in the belted ashtray strapped to the side of the sofa. Where did you grow up? Here. Did you like it? Of course, yes. I grew up near al-Khalil. Oh, she said, I knew. How did you know? Ibrahim told my mother. Ibrahim's a snitch, he laughed. How were the caves? They were perfect, he said, there was nothing to worry about, life was easy but we got evicted when I was twelve. What happened? They tucked a note under a rock, we didn't find it until it was too late, it wouldn't have mattered. Why not? They wanted to get rid of us anyway, that's how they evict you, they hide notes under rocks so you can't find them, they give you twenty days to respond, it's just the way it is, you don't find it, it's your own fault, then you're gone. She stood up to pour more Fanta even though his glass was nearly full. They blew the cave up, he said. She paused a moment, then came to sit on the far end of the couch. She was no more than two feet away. How was prison? He shrugged. I heard you were commander. He's a dirty snitch, that Ibrahim, I was general commander yes, just for the prison. He said you're a singer too, that you like Abu Arab. Abu Arab, yes, I adore Abu Arab, I could listen all day long. Ibrahim said they nicknamed you after him, in prison. I could not even tie Abu Arab's shoelaces, but I sang, yes, I sang, it passed the time for me, I sat in my cell and thought about a lot of things. What things? Different things, peace and guns and Coca-Cola, and Allah of course. I heard you went on hunger strike. He nodded, stubbed out his cigarette. Could you sleep? After four days the hunger passed, after twelve it returned, a terrible pain right here, after fifteen it left again. What did you miss the most? I missed your mother's maqluba. You didn't even know my mother. She chuckled, pulled a small pillow to her stomach. I thought you would be taller, she said. He rose from the couch and stood on his tiptoes. I am, he said. She laughed again into her wide sleeve, then glanced away. Her eyes shone. She offered him more to drink. No thank you. They fell silent a moment. She turned the small pillow over and over in her hands, pulled it closer to her stomach. He tapped the bottom of a pack of cigarettes, opened the wrapper, twisted the cellophane. How old are you? he asked. Twenty-two. You look younger. You've a golden tongue, don't you? Not really, I'm shy, I've always been shy, I was a shy kid. Me too, she said. He smoked fiercely and said quietly: I've been waiting for this day for a long time. Salwa blushed and rose, removed some dishes from the table. Are you devoted? he asked when she returned. Somewhat, she said. They were silent once more. Is that a bad answer? Nothing is a bad answer. That's good, she said. He reached forward to pick the thread off her sleeve. She drew back. Oh, she said, and she rose, flustered, moved past him. She lifted the belted ashtray from the arm of the sofa. She went to the kitchen to dump the contents. When she returned she moved once again to the couch. She had, he noticed, removed the thread from her sleeve herself.

482

They were married thirty-four days later. Bassam had talked to her for a total of two hours.

483

Ten months after the wedding, they had their first child, Araab, named after the singer Ibrahim Muhammad Saleh, who went by the stage name Abu Arab.

Bassam himself became Abu Araab, *abu* meaning *the father of*.

He held the child between his elbow and the crook of his hand: What can I tell you? he said aloud to the sleeping boy.

484

The phone call came from the director of the school. Araab had run out the school gates with three other boys. They had gone to throw stones. He had been seen in the area. Bassam, said the director, should hurry and find him.

He found Araab behind a warehouse near the school. The boys had built themselves a barricade of tires. Inside the ring of the tires they had stored stones.

Araab had a primitive slingshot made from the Y of a tree branch, a black eyepatch, and an elastic band.

—Get in the car.

—No.

—Get in the car, ya. Now. You're twelve years old.

—No.

—You do what I say. Now!

Bassam raised the windows, locked the doors, drove through the rutted streets of Anata. Araab played with the handle of the door. On a steep hill, Bassam pulled the hand brake, rolled down his window, put his head to the steering wheel.

—Don't move.

He could sense the rage in the boy, the clenched heart, the distant stare.

—Listen to me.

Bassam had never told his son the whole story: the flags first, then the stones, then the grenades, the lookout from the hilltop, then the arrest, then the prison, then the beatings and then more beatings.

—Do you hear me? They pick you up and they beat you. And then you get out and you throw another stone. Then they beat you again. And you keep throwing stones.

Araab shrugged.

—Do you see how it finishes?

Araab stared out the window.

—It means that they've won.

He shrugged again.

—Do you want them to win?

—No.

Bassam released the hand brake and drove on a moment. He could see the fidget in the boy's knee.

—Out of the car, said Bassam. Now.

He leaned across his son's lap and pushed the car door open. Araab unfastened his seat belt, stepped out into the dust. Bassam rounded the front of the car and picked up a stone from near the wheel. He placed the rock in Araab's hand, folded the boy's fingers across it.

—What I'm going to do is walk over there, said Bassam. And then I'm going to close my eyes. And then I want you to throw it at me. As hard as you can. And I want you to hit me.

—No.

—If you don't, I will go back to your barricade. I will stand there and I will wait for a jeep. When it comes I will throw a stone at it for you. Do you understand?

—Yes.

—If you don't hit me with a stone, I am going to go and throw one myself. And then you know exactly what will happen to me. Is this understood?

Bassam stood not ten paces away, his eyes shut firmly: Throw it, he said. Throw it now.

He heard the stone whistle far past him.

—You're supposed to hit me with it, ya.

He could hear the boy weeping.

—Do it again, he said.

—No.

—We don't leave here until you hit me.

485

What the British might call a knee-knocker.

486

What he feared most of all was that Araab would end up in prison. When they got home that night Bassam made his son put his hand on the Qur'an and promise that he would never again take part in any sort of riot.

487

Riot, from the Old French, *rioter*: to dispute, to quarrel, to engage in argument. *Riote:* noise, debate, disorder, rash action. Also, perhaps, from the Latin *rugire*, meaning to roar.

488

In the early 1990s Palestinian riot paraphernalia became popular among a small clique of Japanese teenagers. They collected rubber bullets, gas canisters, batons, kneepads, helmets, groin protectors, shin guards, tactical goggles, masks and especially the painted stones flung by the shebab during the First Intifada.

A stone in Palestinian colors, if properly documented and tagged, could sell for over one hundred dollars. A used plexiglas shield with an IDF insignia could command one hundred and fifty if signed and verified by a soldier.

A pop-up shop, The Spoils of War, appeared in the Shinjuku neighborhood, a tiny little store with a battered shutter and lopsided shelves, but it went bust shortly after the Second Intifada began, and the riot gear fell out of fashion.

489

The first time they spoke in a Parents Circle meeting, it was difficult for Rami to understand Bassam's accent. Bassam's English was rapid-fire and the stresses came from Arabic. He began to talk about his friends throwing two hand grenades at a jeep but it sounded, in his Hebron accent—*two han-d-eh-gre-nay-des*—like two hundred.

It became one of their jokes: Hey brother, go ahead and throw two hundred grenades.

490

In a letter to Rami, Bassam wrote that one of the principal qualities of pain is that it demands to be defeated first, then understood.

491

Rami pauses for a moment at the top of the monastery road. He opens his visor, removes his glasses, takes off his helmet, shakes his head free, wipes the glasses on the end of his scarf.

To the left, the monastery. To the right, the road down toward the center of town. He glances at his watch.

The sun out now, over Bethlehem. The flocks of birds in their vaulting overhead arcs.

492

While in flight, birds position themselves in order to gain lift from the bird in front. As it flies, the leading bird pushes down the air with its wings. The air is then squeezed around the outer edge of the wings so that, at the tip of the wing, the air moves and an upwash is created.

By flying at the wing tip of the bird in front, the follower rides the upwash and preserves energy. The birds time their wingbeats carefully, resulting sometimes in a V-shape, or a J, or an inversion of one or the other.

In storms and crosswinds the birds adapt and create new shapes—power curves and S-formations and even figure eights.

493

On the hour, he catches sight of a black Kia climbing the hill. At first he is not sure if it is Bassam or not, the wintry light hard and bright on the front windshield.

Then there is the quick beep of the car horn and the shape of a waving arm in the front seat.

Bassam stops next to Rami, pulls the hand brake, powers down the tinted window. The inevitable cigarette in Bassam's mouth.

—Brother.

—Hey.

—How long you been here?

—I mucked up. I forgot about daylight saving time.

—What do you mean?

—We have different daylight savings, brother.

Bassam shakes his head and half-grins: Ah, Israeli time, he says. He pulls hard on his cigarette, taps the ash out the window and a small rush of smoke fills the air.

—I drove around, says Rami, got a coffee in the Everest.

—How many have we got today?

—Seven or eight.

—From all over?

—Think so, yeah.

—Why the monastery?

—No idea. They rented it, I suppose.

—How far down the road?

—Quarter of a mile or so.

—Ever been here before?

—Not inside.

—One hundred and fifty years old.

—Right. Go ahead.

—No, no. You. Go.

—You first.

—Hey, haven't we suffered enough?

Rami smiles at their familiar joke, beeps his motorbike horn and tucks in behind the Kia. He passes a hedge of rhododendrons. A few wild rosebushes. A row of apricot trees.

On one side of the road a wire mesh fence stretches and he can briefly see all the way down to the valley floor, the roofs of houses, the terraces moving in quick succession, Jerusalem in the distance.

494

At the closed wooden gate of the convent Rami pauses the bike. Hard to fathom that one day the Wall may appear between here and the monastery. A watchtower here. A farmer's gate there. A rim of barbed wire just beyond.

495

End the Preoccupation.

496

It doesn't matter to them where they speak. Most of the time they meet in hotel conference rooms. Or in the auditoriums of schools. Or the back rooms of community centers. Every now and then in vast theaters. It is always the same story, heard differently in each place. Finite words on an infinite plane. It is this, they know, which keeps them going.

497

The gate is swung open and Bassam's car nudges through. Rami hits the throttle and catches up, parks, removes his helmet. In the shadow of the monastery the two men approach each other and embrace.

498

In Constantin Brâncuși's bird sculptures—considered by some to be among the most beautiful works of art of the twentieth century—the wings and the feathers are eliminated, the body of the bird is elongated and the head becomes a smooth oval plane.

The Romanian artist cast sixteen examples of the *Bird in Space*, nine in bronze and seven in marble.

In 1926 one of the bronze sculptures was stopped by U.S. Customs officers who refused to believe that the piece of metal amounted to art. The sculpture, along with nineteen other Brâncuși pieces, was due to appear in galleries in New York and Chicago. Instead, the customs officials imposed a tariff for manufactured objects. A court battle ensued. At first the U.S. Customs agreed to rethink their classification and released the sculptures on bond under the heading of *Kitchen Utensils and Hospital Supplies.*

The art world was delighted until a customs appraiser backtracked and confirmed the official classification. The appraiser, F.J.H. Kracke, a key figure of the Republican party in Brooklyn, claimed that he had sent photos and descriptions of the sculptures out to several well-known people high in the art world.

The responses he got suggested that Brâncuși's sculptures were little more than dots and dashes that could have been dreamed up by a simple bricklayer. As such, said Kracke, they left far too much to the imagination.

499

They are greeted in the vestibule by an older monk. He is, he says, honored to meet them. He has heard much about their work.

The monk bows slightly, guides them through the corridor, towards the chapel. The ceilings are vaulted. The woodwork, intricate. The floors are stone.

He speaks in Arabic with a South American accent. He is from a family that once lived in Haifa. They left, he says, like so many others, in '48. Exiled.

It feels to Rami as if his breath operates differently here. The air is cool. The light filters through the stained-glass windows and falls in slanted rows among the pews.

The monk genuflects near the altar and then guides them into a room at the rear of the chapel. On a wooden table sits a jar of water with slices of lemon and two empty glasses.

—The green room, says the monk with a half-smile.

On the wall is the painting of a saint in a carved wooden frame. Alongside it, several photos of the monastery in decades gone by.

The monk turns on his heel. His cassock swishes. They follow him down a high corridor, the emptiness brimming with echo. The walls, he tells them, are several meters thick. The local stone is known as royal stone. The meleke is so soft, he says, that it can be sliced from a quarry with a small knife. It hardens, then, upon contact with the air. Like so much else, he says over his shoulder.

—Many generations have, he says, scrubbed this floor clean. If it could sing it would.

It feels to Rami that they are walking through a watery candlelight. They pass several small rooms. The doors are built of oak with dark iron brackets. Small windows in the doors, chapel-shaped with a cross of white wood between the panes. The rooms themselves each have a table and a bed.

They reach the end of the corridor where the ceiling vaults upwards again. The air is again cooler here. The monk turns slowly and looks along the length of yet another corridor.

—Come, says the monk, your group is waiting, we have a table set for ten.

My name is Rami Elhanan. I am the father of Smadar. I am a sixty-seven-year-old graphic designer, an Israeli, a Jew, a seventh-generation Jerusalemite. Also what you might call a graduate of the Holocaust. My mother was born in the Old City of Jerusalem, to an ultra-Orthodox family. My father came here in 1946. What he saw in the camps he seldom spoke about, except to my daughter Smadar when she was ten or eleven. I was a kid from a straightforward background—we weren't wealthy but we weren't poor. I got in some trouble at school, nothing big, I ended up in industrial school, then studied art, more or less an ordinary life.

The story I want to tell you starts and ends on one particular day of the Jewish calendar, Yom Kippur. For Jews this is the day when we ask forgiveness for our sins, the holiest day of our calendar. I was a young soldier fighting the October '73 war in Sinai, a horrible war, everyone knows this, it's no revelation. We started it with a company of eleven tanks and finished it with three. My job included bringing in ammunition and taking out the dead and wounded. I lost some of my very close friends, carried them out on stretchers. I emerged from the war bitter, angry, disappointed, with just one thing on my mind—to detach myself from any kind of involvement or commitment, to block myself off from anything official at all. I was a sort of anarchist, not really an anarchist even, I had no political involvement, I just wasn't interested at all, the West Bank, Gaza, Sinai, Timbuktu, I didn't care, I didn't think about them, I just wanted a normal quiet life.

I got out of the army and finished my studies at Bezalel Academy of Arts and Design. I got married to Nurit, and we had four kids. One of these children was my daughter, Smadar. She was born on the eve of Yom Kippur, in September 1983, in a hospital in Jerusalem. Her name is taken from the Bible, from the Song of Solomon, grape of the vine. She was sparkling, vivid, joyful, just very beautiful. An excellent student, a swimmer, a dancer too, she played the piano and loved jazz. We used to call her Princess, a cliché of course, but that's exactly what she was to me, a princess, every father knows this feeling, things aren't such a cliché when you're living them.

My three boys and this little princess, we lived what seemed to be a perfect, sheltered life in Jerusalem in our secure house in the Rehavia neighborhood at the time. Nurit taught in the Hebrew University. She was radical, left-wing, stunning, brilliant. She went to the best schools. She was the daughter of a general. The Israeli elite, really. In a way, you could say that we lived inside a bubble, completely detached from the outside world. In this tiny country, smaller than New Jersey, you could drive from one end to the other in a day. It had its problems of course but what place doesn't? I was doing graphic design—posters and ads—for the right wing, for the left wing, whoever paid money. Life was good. We were happy, complacent. To be honest it suited me.

On and on and on this went, month after month, year after year, until the fourth of September, 1997, just a few days before Yom Kippur, when this incredible bubble of ours burst in midair into a million pieces. It was the beginning of a long cold dark night that is still long and cold and dark and will always be long and cold and dark, until the end when it will still be cold and dark.

I have told this story so many times, but there is always something new to be said. Memories hit you all the time. A book that is opened. A door that is closed, a beeping sound, a window opened. Anything at all. A butterfly.

That day, in 1997, three suicide bombers blew themselves up in the middle of Ben Yehuda Street in the center of Jerusalem, three bombs one after another. They killed eight people—themselves and five others, including three little girls. One of these girls was our Smadari. It was a Thursday, three o'clock in the afternoon. She was out buying books for school and later she was going to sign up for jazz dance lessons. A nice quiet day. She was walking down the street with her friends, listening to music.

I was driving to Ben Gurion airport and I heard about the bombings on the radio. At first when you hear about an explosion, any explosion, anywhere, you keep hoping that maybe this time the finger of fate will not turn toward you. Every Israeli knows this. You get used to hearing about them, but it doesn't alter the skip in your chest. You just wait and you listen and you hope that it isn't you. And then you hear nothing. And then your heart starts to pound. And you make a few phone calls. And then you make a few more. You ask and you ask and you ask for your girl. You dial and you dial. But nobody has heard anything. Nobody has seen her. Then you hear something else. The last anyone saw her, she was near Ben Yehuda Street, downtown. And your heart, you can hear it thump in your ears now. You and your wife, you drive into town. You drive so fast, you think no, it can't be happening this way, no no no. You leave the car and you find yourself running in the streets, in and out of shops, the café, the ice cream store, trying to find your daughter, your child, your Princess—but she has vanished. You shout her name. You run back to your car. You drive even faster. You go from hospital to hospital, police station to police station. You lean over the desk. You plead. You say her name over and over. And you know, you just know, deep in your heart, by the way the nurses look at you, by the way the policemen shake their heads, by their hesitance, by the silences, you know, but you won't admit it. You do this for many long hours until eventually, very late at night, you and your wife find yourselves in the morgue.

This finger of fate, it points at you. Right between your eyes. The morgue staff guide you through. They bring you to a room. You hear the slide of the tray. The metal rollers, the rubber wheels. And you see this sight which you will never be able to forget for the rest of your life. Your daughter. On a steel tray. And you will never be the same.

Her funeral was held in Kibbutz Nachshon, on a green hill on the way to Jerusalem. Smadar was buried next to her grandfather, General Matti Peled, a true fighter for peace, a professor, a Knesset member. He was much loved on both sides and people came from everywhere in this mosaic of a country, Jews and Muslims and Christians, representatives of the settlers, representatives from the parliament, representatives of Arafat, from abroad, everywhere. And then she was buried beside him.

You come back home, the house is filled with hundreds and hundreds of people coming to pay respect, offering condolences. These are the seven days of shiva. You are enveloped by these hundreds of people, thousands actually—they lined the pavement, they had to put up orange cones to close the street off. Traffic cops for your daughter. But on the eighth day, everybody goes back to their normal, everyday business, and you're left alone. Without your daughter.

You wander the house. You say her name, you whisper it, and when you're alone you shout it. Smadar. Smadari. You touch things. Her books on her shelf. Her music tapes. You listen for her. She's not there.

Time doesn't wait for you. You want it to wait, to freeze, to paralyze itself, to go backwards, but it just doesn't. You need to wake up, to stand up and face yourself. She is gone. Her chair at the table is empty. Her room is empty. Her coat is on the doorknob. You have to make a decision. What are you going to do now, with this new, unbearable burden on your shoulders? What are you going to do with this incredible anger that eats you alive? What are you going to do with this new you, this father without a daughter, this man who you never thought could have existed?

The first choice is obvious: revenge. When someone kills your daughter you want to get even. You want to go out and kill an Arab, any Arab, all Arabs, and then you want to try to kill his family and anyone else around him, it's expected, it's demanded. Every Arab you see, you want him dead. Of course you don't always do this in a real sense, but you do this by asking other people to kill this Arab for you, your politicians, your so-called leaders. You ask them to slam a missile into his house, to poison him, to take his land, to steal his water, to arrest his son, to beat him up at the checkpoints. If you kill one of mine, I will kill ten of yours. And the dead one, naturally, has an uncle or a brother or a cousin or a wife who wants to kill you back and then you want to kill them back again, another ten times over. Revenge. It's the simplest way. And then you get monuments to that revenge, with mourners' tents, songs, placards on the walls, another riot, another checkpoint, another piece of land stolen. A stone leads to a bullet. And another suicide bomber leads to another air strike. And it goes on and on. And on.

Look, I have a bad temper. I know it. I have an ability to blow up. Long ago, I killed people in the war. Distantly, like in a video game. I held a gun. I drove tanks. I fought in three wars. I survived. And the truth is, the awful truth, the Arabs were just a thing to me, remote and abstract and meaningless. I didn't see them as anything real or tangible. They weren't even visible. I didn't think about them, they were not really part of my life, good or bad. The Palestinians in Jerusalem, well, they mowed the lawns, they collected the garbage, they built the houses, cleared the plates from the table. Like every Israeli, I knew they were there, and I pretended I knew them, even pretended I liked some of them, the safe ones—we talked about them like that, the safe ones, the dangerous ones—and I never would have admitted it, not even to myself, but they might as well have been lawn mowers, dish-washing machines, taxis, trucks. They were there to fix our fridges on a Saturday. That was the old joke: every town needed at least one good Arab, how else could you get the fridge fixed on Saturday? And if they were ever anything other than objects, they were objects to be feared, because, if you didn't fear them then they would become real people. And we didn't want them to be real people, we couldn't handle that. A real Palestinian was a man on the dark side of the moon. This is my shame. I understand it as my shame. I know that now. I didn't know it then. I don't excuse myself. Please understand, I don't excuse myself at all.

Foolishly, at the beginning, I thought I could go on with my life, pretending as if nothing had happened. I got up, brushed my teeth, I tried to lead a normal life, went back to my studio, to draw, to make posters, to create slogans, to forget. But it didn't work. Nothing was normal anymore. I wasn't the same person. I had no idea how to get up in the morning.

Then after a while you start asking yourself questions, you know, we're not animals, we can use our brains, we use our imaginations, we have to find a way to get out of bed in the morning. And you ask yourself, Will killing anyone bring my daughter back? Will killing every other Arab bring her back? Will causing pain to someone else ease the unbearable pain that you are suffering? Well, the answer comes to you in the middle of that long dark night, and you think, dust returns to dust, ashes return to ashes, that's all. She is not coming back, your Smadari. And you have to get used to this new reality. So in a very gradual, complicated way you come over to the other side: you start asking what happened to her, and why? It's difficult, it's frightening, it's exhausting. How could such a thing take place? What could cause someone to be that angry, that mad, that desperate, that hopeless, that stupid, that pathetic, that he is willing to blow himself up alongside a girl, not even fourteen years old? How can you possibly understand that instinct? To tear his own body apart? To walk down a busy street and pull the cord on a belt that rips him asunder? How can he think that way? What made him? Where in the world was he created? How did he get that way? Where did he come from? Who taught him this? Did I teach him this? Did his government teach him this? Did my government?

Then about a year after Smadar was killed, I met a man who changed my life. His name was Yitzhak Frankenthal, a religious Jew, Orthodox, with a kippah on his head. And, you know, we tend to put people into drawers, stigmatize people? We tend to judge people by the way they dress, and I was certain that this guy was a right-winger, a fascist, that he eats Arabs for breakfast. But we started talking and he told me about his son Arik, a soldier who was kidnapped and murdered by Hamas in 1994. And then he told me about this organization, the Parents Circle, that he had created—people who lost their loved ones, Palestinian and Israeli, but still wanted peace. And I remembered that Yitzhak had been among those thousands and thousands of people that came to my house a year before during those seven days of shiva for Smadar, and I was so angry with him, so confused, I asked him, How could you do it? Seriously, how could you step into someone's house who just lost a loved one, and then talk about peace? How dare you? You came to my house after Smadar was killed? You took for granted that I would feel the same way as you, just because I was Matti Peled's son-in-law, or Nurit Peled's husband, you thought you could take my grief for granted? Is that what you thought?

And he, being a great man, was not insulted. He understood my rage. He invited me over to a meeting in Jerusalem of these crazy people, they had all lost a loved one, and I was curious. I said okay, I'll give it a try, I have nothing to lose, I have already lost so much, but they're crazy, they have to be crazy. I got on the bike and I went to see. I stood outside where people were coming for the meeting, very detached, very cynical. And I watched those people arriving. The first group were, for me—as an Israeli—living legends. People I used to look up to, admire. I'd read about them in the newspapers, saw them on television. Yaakov Guterman, a Holocaust survivor, he lost his son Raz in the Lebanon war. And Roni Hirshenson, who lost his two sons, Amir and Elad.

To be bereaved in Israel is to be part of a tradition, something really terrible but holy at the same time. And I never thought that one day I would be one of them.

On and on they came, so many of them. But then I saw something else, something completely new to me, to my eyes, my mind, my heart, my brain. I was standing there, and I saw a few Palestinians passing by in a bus. Listen, this flabbergasted me. I knew it was going to happen, but still I had to do a double take. Arabs? Really? Going into the same meeting as these Israelis? How could that be? A thinking, feeling, breathing Palestinian? And I remember seeing this lady in this black, traditional Palestinian dress, with a headscarf—you know, the sort of woman who I might have thought could be the mother of one of the bombers who took my child. She was slow and elegant, stepping down from the bus, walking in my direction. And then I saw it, she had a picture of her daughter clutched to her chest. She walked past me. I couldn't move. And this was like an earthquake inside me: this woman had lost her child. It maybe sounds simple, but it was not. I had been in a sort of coffin. This lifted the lid from my eyes. My grief and her grief, the same grief.

I went inside to meet these people. And here they were, and they were shaking my hand, hugging me, crying with me. I was so deeply touched, so deeply moved. It was like a hammer on my head cracking me open. An organization of the bereaved. Israeli and Palestinian, Jew, Christian, Muslim, atheist, you name it. Together. In one room. Sharing their sorrow. Not using it, or celebrating it, but sharing it, saying that it is not a decree of faith that we should live forever with a sword in our hands. I cannot tell you what sort of madness it seemed. And I was completely cleaved open. It was like a nuclear event. Truly, it seemed mad.

You see, I was forty-seven, forty-eight years old at that time, and I had to learn to admit it was the first time in my life, to that point—

I can say this now, I could never even think it then—it was the first time that I'd met Palestinians as human beings. Not just workers in the streets, not just caricatures in the newspapers, not just transparencies, terrorists, objects, but—how do I say this?—human beings— *human beings*, I can't believe I'm saying that, it sounds so wrong, but it was a revelation—yes, *human beings* who carry the same burden that I carry, people who suffer exactly as I suffer. An equality of pain. And like Bassam says, we are running from our pain to our pain. I'm not a religious person, far from it—I have no way of explaining what happened to me back then. If you had told me years ago that I would say this I would have said you were crazy.

Some people have an interest in keeping the silence. Others have an interest in sowing hatred based on fear. Fear makes money, and it makes laws, and it takes land, and it builds settlements, and fear likes to keep everyone silent. And, let's face it, in Israel we're very good at fear, it occupies us. Our politicians like to scare us. We like to scare each other. We use the word *security* to silence others. But it's not about that, it's about occupying someone else's life, someone else's land, someone else's head. It's about control. Which is power. And I realized this with the force of an ax, that it's true, this notion of speaking truth against power. Power already knows the truth. It tries to hide it. So you have to speak out against power. And I began, back then, to understand the duty we have to try to understand what's going on. Once you know what's going on then you begin to think: What can we do about it? We could not continue to disavow the possibility of living alongside each other. I'm not necessarily asking for everyone to get along, or anything corny or airy-fairy, but I am asking for them to be *allowed* to get along. And, as I began to think about this, I began to think that I had stumbled upon the most important question of them all: What can you do, personally, in order to try to help prevent this unbearable pain for others? All I can tell you is that from that moment until today, I've devoted my time, my life to going everywhere possible, to talk to anyone possible, people who want to listen—even to people who will not listen—to convey this very basic and very simple message, which says: We are not doomed, but we have to try to smash the forces that have an interest in keeping us silent.

It may sound strange but in Israel we don't really know what the Occupation actually is. We sit in our coffee shops and we have a good time and we don't have to deal with it. We have no idea what it's like to walk through a checkpoint every day. Or to have our family land taken away. Or to wake up with a gun in our faces. We have two sets of laws, two sets of roads, two sets of values. To most Israelis this seems impossible, some sort of weird distortion of reality, but it is not. Because we just don't know. Our lives are good. The cappuccino is tasty. The beach is open. The airport is right there. We have no access to what it's like for people in the West Bank or Gaza. Nobody talks about it. You're not allowed into Bethlehem unless you're a soldier. We drive on our Israeli-only roads. We bypass the Arab villages. We build roads above them and below them, but only to make them faceless. Maybe we saw the West Bank once, when we were on military service, or maybe we watch a TV show every now and then, our hearts bleed for thirty minutes, but we don't really, truly, know what's going on. Not until the worst happens. And then the world is turned inside out.

Truth is, you can't have a humane occupation. It just doesn't exist. It can't. It's about control. Maybe we have to wait until the price of peace is so high that people begin to understand this. Maybe it won't end until the price outweighs the benefits. Economic price. Lack of jobs. No sleep at night. Shame. Maybe even death. The price I paid. This is not a call for violence. Violence is weak. Hatred is weak. But today we have one side, the Palestinians, who are completely thrown to the side of the road. They don't have any power. What they do is out of incredible anger and frustration and humiliation. Their land is taken. They want it back. And this leads to all sorts of questions, not least: What, then, to do about the settlers? Repatriation? Land swaps? Generous compensation for the Palestinians who had their land stolen? Maybe a mixture of all these things. And then those settlers who wanted to stay could stay and become citizens of Palestine under the rule of Palestinian sovereignty like the Arabs in Israel. Equal rights. Equal rights to the letter. Then after a period of trying to make it work we create a Europe of the Middle East, a United States. Both sides make sacrifices. Redefine what we kill and die for. Now we kill and die for simplicities. Why not die for something more complex? There can be no way that one side has more rights than the other—more political power, more land, more water, more anything. Equality. Why not? Is it as insane as theft? As murder?

Nobody can listen to me and stay the same. Maybe you will get angry, or offended, or even humiliated, but at least you will not stay the same. And in the end despair is not a plan of action. It's a Sisyphean task to create any sort of hope. And that's what keeps me going. I tell the story over and over again. We must end the Occupation and then sit down together to figure it out. One state, two states, it doesn't matter at this stage—just end the Occupation, and then begin the process of rebuilding the possibility of dignity for all of us. It's as clear to me as the noonday sun. There are times, sure, when I would like to be wrong. It would be so much easier. If I had found another path I would have taken it—I don't know, revenge, cynicism, hatred, murder. But I am a Jew. I have great love for my culture and my people and I know that ruling and oppressing and occupying is not Jewish. Being Jewish means that you respect justice and fairness. No people can rule another people and obtain security or peace for themselves. The Occupation is neither just nor sustainable. And being against the Occupation is, in no way, a form of anti-Semitism.

Others know all this too, they just don't want to hear it. Sometimes they're angry to hear it, sometimes they're sad, and sometimes they turn their world around completely. That's the truth. It is not any great bravery, it's just ordinary, it's natural, it's what I have to do.

I have been called many things, an insect, an Arab lover, a self-hating Jew. I walk into some places and it's like walking into a volcano. They say I am naïve, self-righteous, that I exploit my grief. Do I exploit my grief? Yes, I do. They're right. Yes—but I'm doing it in order to help try to prevent pain. Is that ridiculous? Okay, even if it's ridiculous, it doesn't mean it's not true.

Somebody, a fellow Israeli, told me once that they wish I had been blown up with my daughter on Ben Yehuda Street. I thought about that for a long time—should I have been blown up? And, after a while, the answer was clear: yes. Yes. Because I *had been* blown up. It had already happened. And it has happened with so many others since. And we are still being blown up, in Gaza, the West Bank, Jerusalem, Tel

Aviv. And we're still looking around and collecting the pieces. Every day my mind begs the question, Why?

You never heal, don't let anyone tell you that you ever fully heal—it's the living who have to bury the dead. I pay the price, sometimes I despair, but what else is there to be, in the end, but hopeful? What else are we going to do? Walk away, kill ourselves, kill each other? That's already happened, it didn't achieve much. I know that it will not be over until we talk to each other—that's what it says on the sticker on the front of my bike. Joining with others saved my life. We cannot imagine the harm we're doing by not listening to one another and I mean this on every level. It is immeasurable. We may have built up our wall, but the wall is really in our minds, and every day I try to put a crack in it. I know that the deeper the story goes, the deeper the engagement, the greater the disappointment when nothing happens, when there is no change. And so I go deeper again. And get even more disappointed. Maybe disappointment is my fate. So what? I will embrace it so tightly that I kill it. My name is Rami Elhanan, I am the father of Smadar. I repeat it every day, and every day it becomes something new because somebody else hears it. I will tell it until the day I die, and it will never change, but it will keep on putting a tiny crack in the wall until the day I die.

Who knows where things finish? Things go on. That is what the world is. Do you understand what I mean? I'm not sure I can tell you exactly what I mean. We have words but sometimes they're not enough.

Once upon a time, and not so long ago, and not so far away, Rami Elhanan, an Israeli, a Jew, a graphic artist, husband of Nurit, father of Elik and Guy and Yigal, father too of the late Smadar, traveled on his motorbike from the suburbs of Jerusalem to the Cremisan monastery in the mainly Christian town of Beit Jala, near Bethlehem, in the Judean hills, to meet with Bassam Aramin, a Palestinian, a Muslim, a former prisoner, an activist, born near Hebron, husband of Salwa, father of Araab and Areen and Muhammad and Ahmed and Hiba, father too of the late Abir, ten years old, shot dead by an unnamed Israeli border guard in East Jerusalem, almost a decade after Rami's daughter, Smadar, two weeks away from fourteen, was killed in the western part of the city by three Palestinian suicide bombers, Bashar Sawalha, Youssef Shouli, and Tawfiq Yassine, from the village of Assira al-Shamaliya near Nablus in the West Bank, in the Mountains of the Beloved, a place of intrigue to the listeners gathered in the red-brick monastery perched on the hillside, by the terraced vineyard, in the shadow of the Wall, having come from as far apart as Belfast and Kyushu, Paris and North Carolina, Santiago and Brooklyn, Copenhagen and Terezín, on an ordinary day at the end of October, foggy, tinged with cold, to listen to the stories of Bassam and Rami, and to find within their stories another story, a song of songs, discovering themselves—you and me—in the stone-tiled chapel where we sit for hours, eager, hopeless, buoyed, confused, cynical, complicit, silent, our memories imploding, our synapses skipping, in the gathering dark, remembering, while listening, all of those stories that are yet to be told.

My name is Bassam Aramin, I am the father of Abir. I'm a Palestinian, a Muslim, an Arab. I'm forty-eight years old. I've lived many places—a cave near Hebron, seven years in prison, then an apartment in Anata, and these days in a house with a garden in Jericho near the Dead Sea. My father raised goats and other animals in the hills, my mother looked after fifteen brothers and sisters. They were both born near Sa'ir, a village close to Hebron, their parents, and their parents before them too. I lived in a cave but not a cave as you might think of it—we had shelves full of books, carpets on the walls, it was cool in summer, warm in winter, always alive with voices and good cooking, we were happy there, we had what we wanted.

When I was a boy, my friends and I raised the Palestinian flag in our school playground. We did it because it was our flag, and it was illegal to fly it, and because we knew it would drive the Israeli soldiers crazy when they saw it up there. We watched them arrive and we threw stones at them. In return they fired tear gas, rubber bullets, live rounds. Then they tore the flag down and we threw more stones and then we put the flag back up again. Putting up a flag could mean a year in jail. We were always ducking and running and jumping walls. We were kids, we didn't really understand what was going on. People come to your village, people you don't recognize, people speaking a language you don't know, who are they? Like aliens. They come in their jeeps and armored carriers and they patrol the streets and they say show me your I.D., get up against the wall, shut your mouth, turn around, get on the ground. They invade your home in the hills, block it off, smash it up. They hide eviction orders under rocks. They tuck them away so you won't find them. They arrest your father, your brothers, your uncles. They stop you on the way to school. They arrest your teacher outside the school gates. Soon enough they arrest you too. They make you stand in the sun at the checkpoints during Ramadan, but they are experts at finding deck chairs for themselves, it's a sandy beach for some of them, they have coolers of soda at their feet, they snap open the cans, they sleep with their hands behind their heads while your brain boils in the heat and you wait.

I had polio, but I still ran to school, avoiding the jeeps. It was like an

Olympic sport. Children I knew were beaten and killed. This is just the way it was, no exaggeration, everyone knew at least one child who was killed, and most of us knew several. You get so used to it, sometimes you think it's normal. At the age of twelve I joined a demonstration and I saw it happen in front of my eyes. I was at the back of the crowd. A boy's arms went up in the sky, he took his last breath, he'd been shot in the groin, he keeled over a few yards from me, they carried him through. From that moment on I developed a deep need for revenge except I didn't think of it then as revenge, I thought of it as justice, for a long time they were the same thing to me, justice and revenge.

At first we just threw stones and empty bottles, but one day my friends and I came across some discarded hand grenades in a cave and we decided to throw them at the Israeli jeeps. Two of them exploded, not even exploded, they just fizzled out. Luckily, no one was injured because we didn't know how to use them properly. We were chased in the hills, caught, arrested, and in 1985, at the age of seventeen, the prison latch slid closed in front of my eyes, a long story, a long seven years.

We had a mission in jail and the Israelis had a mission too. Our mission was to survive as humans. Theirs was to rob us of our humanity. Often, we would be waiting to go into the dining room when the alarms suddenly went off. Then the soldiers appeared and ordered us to strip naked. This was the IDF, the army, not the prison guards. They were on a training mission. Of course they deny it, but it happened. A very embarrassing thing—a group of teenagers to be stripped of everything, first our clothes, then our voices, and then everything else, our dignity. They were heavily armed with guns, batons, helmets. They beat us until we couldn't stand. You realize eventually that you have to preserve your humanity—your right to laugh and cry—in order to save yourself. So I started screaming out at them: "Murderers! Nazis! Oppressors!" They kept beating us, but what struck me most was that these young soldiers, not much older than me, were doing it without hatred, without emotions even, because for them this was just a training exercise. Lesson A, hit the object. Lesson B, kick the object. Lesson C, drag the object by the hair. I don't think they even realized what they were doing, they were so happy with their efficiency, doing such a good job. Let's face it, they are very good at irony—they call it the Defense Forces, but I swear to you those who hold guns are captured by those guns. They would never have beaten their dogs in the same way. And as the leader—I eventually became commander—I was always beaten right until the end. I woke up under hospital lights and then another beating came.

Luckily for me they say you have a hard head when you are born near al-Khalil, or Hebron. In prison, one evening, I saw a TV documentary about the Holocaust. At the time I was happy to think of the fate of six million Jews. Go ahead and die, go ahead, please, make it more, make it seven million, eight, oh nine million, please! For us, growing up, the Shoah was a pure lie, I wasn't interested in made-up history. My enemy was that: my enemy. He could have no pain, he could have no feelings. Not after what he had done to me and my family. Let what happened once happen again. And again. And again. Make it ten million. But after a few minutes of this I began to feel something along my spine, a shiver. I tried to shake it off, to convince myself that it was just a feeling, nothing real, and this was just a movie, nothing real—there are no human beings that would do this to other humans. Impossible, who would do this to anyone? How is that even part of human? And the longer it went on the more barbaric it became. I couldn't understand it. Here they were, herded into gas chambers without fighting back. If they knew they were going to die, why didn't they scream out, push back, fight or try to run? I was turned inside out. I didn't know what to think. I sat in my cell. Trust me, I was not soft, but that night I turned to the wall, pulled the blanket up and began shivering. I tried to hide it from my fellow prisoners but something in me changed—or maybe it hadn't, but something was coming from a new direction, maybe I had just found something that was there all along.

When I was a kid, I thought it was a punishment from God to be a Palestinian, a Muslim, an Arab. I carried it around, a big heavy weight around my neck. When you're a kid you always ask why, but adults forget to ask why anymore. You just accept it. They smashed up our homes. Accepted. They herded us through checkpoints. Accepted. They told us to get permits for things they got for free. Accepted. But in prison I began to think about our lives, our identity, being Arab, and that led me to think about the Jews too. And I knew now this Holocaust was real—it had happened. And I began to think, reluctantly first, that so much of the Israeli mind must have stemmed from that, and then I decided to try to understand who these people really were, how they suffered, and why it was that in '48 they had turned their oppression back on us again and again, stole our houses, took away our land, gave us our Nakba, our catastrophe. We, the Palestinians, became the victims of the victims. I wanted to understand more. Where was all this coming from? In prison I began to pick up a few more words of Hebrew and even Yiddish. And soon I had a conversation with a guard. He asked me, "How can someone like you become a terrorist?" And then he tried to tell me that I was a settler on his land, not him on mine. He really believed that we, the Palestinians, were the settlers, that *we* had taken *their* land. I said, "If you can convince me that we are the settlers, then I'll declare this in front of all my fellow prisoners." He said he never met anyone like me before. It was the start of a dialogue and a friendship. From then on he treated me with respect. He allowed me to drink tea from a glass, he brought me a prayer mat. It was illegal but he did it anyway.

In prison we made belt buckles from coffee cans. One of the other guards, Meir, was very simple. He was told not to talk to anyone, especially me, who they called the Cripple. I was considered dangerous. The authorities were wary of me. The quiet one is forever dangerous. I was always being put in solitary. But Meir wanted a belt for his sweetheart that said *Meir Loves Maya* in Hebrew. I ordered my fellow prisoners to make a nice one—they were astounded to be making a belt for an Israeli, in Hebrew too, but they did it because they trusted me and I was commander. Meir loved it and he said, "What do you want me to bring you in return?" And I said, "Nothing, just a very small gun, please." He laughed and said, "Seriously, what do you want?" "Just a small gun," I said, "oh, and lots of bullets." He laughed again. So I asked my fellow prisoners what they wanted. They were all young and they said they really wanted Coca-Cola, can you imagine? A bottle of Coca-Cola. That was all. And so I told Meir and he brought two large bottles and hid them in a water tank. I made sure everyone got a taste. That day, one hundred and twenty prisoners got to sip a tiny little bit of Coca-Cola. They never forgot it, one of their best days in prison. We all used the same cup. It tastes better in glass—Hertzl, the other guard, had given me the glass. Every single one got a drink, so there could be no collaborators, no snitches.

I also got some cassettes of Ibrahim Muhammad Saleh—Abu Arab—singing mawals about the return of the refugees, about the freedom of political prisoners. Listening to him was like a revolution going off in my head. I sang them out the cell door, it was hard to shut me up, I also sang some of the old fellahin work songs, the wedding ballads too. The best music forgets that it is being sung. It comes naturally. After a while Abu Arab became my nickname in prison.

In jail there was a collaborator on our side, helping the Israelis. I was the leader, so they asked me to deal with him. It was too much for me not to kick him. And I did. I kicked him when he was down. Kicked and kicked and kicked him. But then, as I'm doing it, I said to myself, Why, why, why am I kicking this man? Am I a robot? Do I just want to repeat what the Israelis do to me?

And in prison I was reading more and more. Listening too. I was taking classes, expanding my mind. Gandhi. Mirza Ghulam Ahmad, I didn't like him so much. Martin Luther King, I liked him. No wisdom in the gun. There will come a time. I have a dream. Mubarak Awad. So many people. And so I began to think that maybe they were right and the only way to achieve peace was through nonviolence and resistance.

I got released in October 1992. I got married right away. Out of prison and into marriage, go figure. But seriously, it was the happiest time of my life. In 1994, we had our first child, we called him Araab. I was a father now, I had a duty to think about things differently. Not because I became a coward, but sometimes you sacrifice yourself in a different way. It was the time of the Oslo Accords and there was a great feeling of hope for a two-state solution. When I saw the Israeli jeeps leaving Jenin and the kids threw olive branches at them, I asked myself: "Why did I spend seven years in jail when it might have been achieved another way?" But then Oslo disintegrated. The politicians said we weren't ready for it—they only seem to know what is best for lining their pockets, Arabs and Jews, we're the same, it doesn't matter, there are crooks on all sides, Israeli, Palestinian, Jordanian, they knew what they were doing. I was completely distraught. Another chance gone. And then the bombings started—these were the biggest political, strategic and moral mistake that we ever made during the Second Intifada. I started to get even more active, saying that we needed to change our ways. I read more and more about nonviolence and political engagement. I began to realize that violence is exactly what our opponents wanted us to use. They prefer violence because they can deal with it. They are vastly more sophisticated with violence. It's nonviolence that is hard to deal with, whether coming from Israelis or Palestinians or both. It's confusing to them.

Don't get me wrong, I didn't turn my back on what I believed. It was the same goal I always had and will always have until the day it happens—to end the Israeli Occupation. You see, the Occupation exists in every aspect of your life, an exhaustion and a bitterness that nobody outside it really understands. It deprives you of tomorrow. It stops you from going to the market, to the hospital, to the beach, to the sea. You can't walk, you can't drive, you can't pick an olive from your own tree which is on the other side of the barbed wire. You can't even look up in the sky. They have their planes up there. They own the air above and the ground below. You need a permit to sow your land. Your door is kicked in, your house is taken over, they put their feet on your chairs. Your seven-year-old is picked up and interrogated. You can't imagine it. Seven years old. Be a father for a minute and think of your seven-year-old being picked up in front of your eyes. Blindfolded. Zip ties put on his wrists. Taken to military court in Ofer. Most Israelis don't even know this happens. It's not that they're blind. They just don't know what is being done in their name. They're not allowed to see. Their newspapers, their televisions, they don't tell them these things. They can't travel in the West Bank. They have no idea how we are living. But it happens every day. Every single day. We will never accept it. Even after one thousand years we'll never accept it. The Qur'an says: *Look at the signs around you, do you not see?* The Occupation knocks us down and we get up. We are steadfast. We won't give in. Even if they hang me with my own veins. You see, ending the Occupation is our only real hope for everyone's security, Israeli, Palestinian, Christian, Jewish, Muslim, Druze, Bedouin, it doesn't matter. The Occupation corrupts us all from the inside out. But how do we go about ending it? I knew back then—and even more so now—that we have to do things differently. I tried to make sure my son would never go to the Israeli jails, that he wouldn't end up throwing stones. Look, I understand stones, stones are not bullets, but the Israelis took the stone out of our stone, and made the stones into something else. I wanted to say to them: Just don't be here and then we don't have to throw stones at you. But they're here. Uninvited. What are we left with when they take the stone from the stone? We had to learn to use the force of our humanity. To be violently nonviolent. To bow our heads to the things that we need to tell one another. That is not soft, that's not weak, on the contrary, it's human.

It's a tragedy that we need to continually prove that we are human beings. Not only to the Israelis, but also for other Arabs, our brothers and sisters, to the Americans, to the Chinese, the Europeans. Why is that? Do I not look human? Do I not bleed human? We are not special. We are a people, just like any other.

It wasn't until 2005 that some of us started meeting in secret with former Israeli soldiers. I was among the first four Palestinians. You can't imagine the first meeting. Up in the Everest Hotel. For us they were criminals, killers, enemies, assassins. And for them, we were the same. One of them was Rami's son, Elik. This is how our two families met. We were meeting as enemies who now wanted to speak. These young Israelis were refusing to fight in the West Bank and Gaza, not for the sake of the Palestinian people, but for their own people. We were not acting to save Israeli lives either, but to prevent Palestinians from suffering. We were being selfish, both sides, and that is natural, why wouldn't you be? At first I didn't care about them. Okay, they were different, but so what? It was only later that we both came to feel a responsibility for each other's people. It took more than a year. We started Combatants for Peace. There, in the Everest Hotel, up the road, near the settlement, by the Wall, two minutes away.

Rumi, the poet, the Sufi, said something that I will never forget: *Beyond right and wrong there is a field, I'll meet you there.* We were right and we were wrong and we met in a field. We realized that we wanted to kill each other to achieve the same thing, peace and security. Imagine that, what an irony, it's crazy. We sat in the Everest Hotel and talked about ending the Occupation. Even that word *occupation* makes most Israelis tremble. Of course, each one had a different point of view—they are the occupiers and we are the ones under occupation, so it looks different to them. But in the end we were all dying, we were killing each other, over and over and over. We needed to know each other instead. This is the center of gravity, this is where it all comes down. There will be security for everyone when we have justice for everyone. As I have always said, it's a disaster to discover the humanity of your enemy, his nobility, because then he is not your enemy any-more, he just can't be.

Maybe the story could have ended there. I wish it could have. I wish I could walk out of here now, back to Jericho, to my garden, and not have to tell you any more, story finished, good night, I hope the morning comes with peace.

But on January 16, 2007—two years after Combatants for Peace was founded—my ten-year-old daughter, Abir, walked out from her school early in the morning. It was a quiet day, my Black Tuesday, not much was going on. She was just by the school gates when she was shot by a member of the Israeli border police. With a rubber bullet. An American-made rubber bullet. An American-made M-16. From an American-made jeep. There was no violence or Intifada going on. She was shot. In the back of the head. She had just gone to the store. She had just bought herself some candy.

There were so many lies, everyone was scrambling to tell their version of the truth, the Commander said they weren't in the area, he claimed there was no such operation, then they swore on oath she was hit with a Palestinian rock even though a rubber bullet was found right beside her body, then they tried to suggest she was throwing stones. But there was one simple truth: a ten-year-old girl was shot in the back of the head from a distance of a few meters by an eighteen-year-old border guard who stuck his gun out of the jeep and fired directly at her. She never regained consciousness. The ambulance was delayed for hours because they said there was rioting. Soon the rest of the world was appalled by the details of what happened, not least that Abir had just bought that candy at the store. Some details are heartbreaking because they are so simple, sometimes I think that she hadn't had time to eat it. I often wake thinking about that, the most expensive candy on earth.

So here I was, a man whose daughter is murdered by those he wants peace with. There is an Arabic saying, *As-sallāmu 'alaykum*, peace be on you. We say it all the time. Well, it was not on us, nowhere near us. There was no criminal investigation. There never is when one of us is shot. They never say "killed" with a rubber bullet. They say "caused the death of." That is their language, but it is not everyone's. Most of the time nothing is ever said or done when a Palestinian child is killed, but many hundreds of my Israeli brothers and Jewish brothers around the world supported me in bringing the soldier to trial. Amazing. But the Supreme Court decided there was no evidence, so they closed the file for the fourth time. We had fourteen eyewitnesses but they still said there was no evidence, how is it that twenty-eight eyes can see nothing? My child was not a fighter. She was not a member of Fatah or Hamas. She was sunshine. She was good weather. She told me once that she wanted to be an engineer. Can you imagine what sort of bridges she could have built?

I didn't crave a gun. I didn't want a grenade. For me, there was no return from nonviolence. Not for a split second. At the funeral I said that I would not seek revenge, even though some of the Israelis I knew—Israelis, yes—said that they would seek it for me, they were so angry on my behalf. I wasn't interested. I knew that what happened next was up to me. I needed to do something. People needed to know what was going on. So I joined the Parents Circle just days after Abir passed away. My life became my message. I flung myself into it. It made perfect sense to me. I began traveling with Rami, all over, Jerusalem, Tel Aviv, Beit Jala, talking, talking, talking. We had a mission. The force of our grief. We would not use our memories to take revenge. I used to say: *The year Smadar was murdered, Abir was born*. It was true. But what I didn't know when Abir was killed is that she and Smadar would keep on living. And we will not let other people steal their futures. Try shutting us up, it won't work. Say anything you want. Call me a traitor, a collaborator, a coward, call me anything you want, I don't care, I know who I am. Stand at the school gate, shout, "Death to Arabs," it won't get to me. It has nothing to do with collaboration, nothing to do with normalization, it is just pure grief, the power of it, and, like Rami says, it is atomic. To live on in the memory of others means that you do not die.

It eventually pushed me to try to finish my master's degree on the Holocaust in a program in England. I had to think differently. I had to put my brain in new places. After all, it was one Israeli soldier who shot my daughter, but one hundred former Israeli soldiers came to Anata to build a playground for her. You have to understand how dangerous it was for them to come to Anata. I had to make sure they would be safe. They built a playground with her name at the school where she was murdered. They dug the ground. They put up the plaque. They put the slides in, a sandpit. It took a couple of weekends to do.

Nobody got charged with Abir's murder but I decided to fight it in the civil courts. You can call it madness, and it was, but it took me four more years to prove in the civil court that Abir had been killed with a rubber bullet. Four years. Palestinians have the patience of Job. It was a shock around Israel when I won. When I got the compensation one Israeli said to me: "So, how much did you get?" And I said that it did not matter, the word *compensate* means nothing to me, no amount of money would ever suffice. But he asked again, he insisted on an answer, so I told him the truth. Four hundred thousand dollars. He had this look on his face. "So, we're all paid up," he said, and I said, "What do you mean?" and he said, "Just forget about it," and I asked him again and he said, "Forget about it." The very bone of my heart was rattling. And so I asked him, in Hebrew, if he had a child. And he stared at me and said, "Yes, I have a son." So I said to him that I would give him four hundred thousand dollars and all he had to do was give me his son. "Why?" he said. And I said: "So I can kill him and forget about it." His face, you should have seen it. "No," he said, "what you don't understand is that your child was killed by mistake by the Israeli government, we are all paid up, it was a mistake, we admitted it, there's a difference, so move on, forget about it, man." And I said, "Okay, I will give you four hundred thousand and four hundred thousand more and four hundred thousand on top of that, and four hundred thousand more just for blessing, and I will have the government kill your son—and it will be entirely by mistake." His face went completely white. He was confused. He walked away and then turned around and looked at me from the corner of the room. I think in that moment he was changed too. He was blinking very hard. In the end he threw his hand up in the air and left.

I try to understand it too. It's so difficult to explain. I still sit in that ambulance every day. I keep waiting for it to move. Every day she gets killed again and every day I sit in the ambulance, willing it to move, please move, please please please, just go, why are you staying here, let's just go. Rami was in the hospital, waiting for us. He put his arms to my shoulders. We had no idea what was in store for us.

Afterwards I would sit in my car and weep against the steering wheel. You remember everything, every little thing. Abir liked to draw. She liked bears and she liked the sea. She would hold a crayon in the corner of her mouth. In my dream I bring her to the sea and she runs along the pier. Show me one father in the world who does not want to bring his child to the sea. I couldn't do it then, I couldn't get a permit.

But I refuse to be a victim. I decided that a long time ago. There is one living victim and that is the man who killed my daughter. He was a teenager when he shot her. He had no idea why he killed her. He wasn't some hero, some champion. Who shoots a girl in the back? I saw him in court. I said to him, "You are the victim, not me. You had no idea why you killed her, you were following orders, you did it without conscience. I want to wish you a long life because I hope your conscience will wake you up."

The thing is, we Palestinians don't exist as humans for many people. I am officially stateless. At your airport. At your consulate. Where do I exist? It's an absurd question. Maybe one place—in your prison I exist. Or maybe in your imagination I exist as a terrorist, but nowhere else. I have a travel document, a laissez-passer, yes, but they can take that away anytime. I have been many places. I went to Germany, South Africa, Ireland, all of your countries, I went to the White House, I talked with Senator Kerry, I accused him of murder, but he knew exactly what I was talking about, he understood, and he put a picture of Abir in his office.

We keep on going. We have to. Rami and me, our sons, Araab and

Yigal, are together on this. And we prepare our grandchildren now, Yishai and Judeh. We don't want to have to prepare them. We don't want this for them. We would rather they could live in peace and comfort. Once I thought we could never solve our conflict, we would continue hating each other forever, but it is not written anywhere that we have to go on killing each other. The hero makes a friend of his enemy. That's my duty. Don't thank me for doing it. That's all it is, my duty. When they killed my daughter they killed my fear. I have no fear. I can do anything now. Judeh will, one day, live in peace, it has to happen. Sometimes it feels like we're trying to draw water from the ocean with a spoon. But peace is a fact. A matter of time. Look at South Africa, Northern Ireland, Germany, France, Japan, even Egypt. Who would have believed it possible? Did the Palestinians kill six million Israelis? Did the Israelis kill six million Palestinians? But the Germans killed six million Jews and look, now we have an Israeli diplomat in Berlin and we have a German ambassador in Tel Aviv. You see, nothing is impossible. As long as I am not occupied, as long as I have my rights, so long as you allow me to move around, to vote, to be human, then anything is possible.

I don't have time for hate anymore. We need to learn how to use our pain. Invest in our peace, not in our blood, that's what we say.

Rami went to Germany with me a few years ago, but that's a long story, I had to convince him to go, he hated the Germans. He never thought he could go. But he went. And he saw a different place from what he imagined.

In Palestine we say ignorance is a terrible acquaintance. We do not talk to the Israelis. We are not allowed to talk to them—the Palestinians don't want it and the Israelis don't want it. We have no clue what the other one is like. That's where the madness lies. Put up a wall, put up a checkpoint, write the Nakba out of the books, do what you want. But here's the key—we are not voiceless, no matter how much silence there is. We need to learn how to share this land, otherwise we will be sharing it in our graves. And we know it's not possible to clap with one hand. We will, eventually, make a sound, trust me, it has to happen. Darwish said: *It is time for you to be gone.*

You can hate me all you want, that is fine. You can build all the walls you want, that is fine. If you think a wall gives you security go ahead, but make it in your garden, not mine.

I'm a gardener, I love water. In England I was the only one who loved the weather. The janitors laughed at me when I said how much I loved the rain. I used to stand outside and let it fall on my face. I came home to Palestine. It was all I could do. Tonight I will stop my car and stand for a while under the stars. Have you ever seen Jericho at night? If you see it you will know that you will never see anything like it again.

The engine takes a moment to catch. The evening has grown cold and dark. The windshield fogs with his breath.

Bassam reaches to turn on the heater, glances out at Rami in the dark, standing next to his motorbike, zipping the side-vents in his riding pants. The lights from the monastery cast Rami's shadow long across the parking lot.

He presses the cigarette lighter into place, waits for the coils to catch. The anticipation of the cigarette is sometimes as good as the first pull. Forty years of smoking and still it never changes. He taps the pack into the heel of his hand to tamp down the tobacco, flips the lid, removes one. There were—long ago—so many prison rituals with cigarettes, the careful roll, the rescue of every grain, the twist of the filter, the smoothing of the paper. Sometimes he would pause over an unlit rollie for hours. Later he would keep his eyes closed while he held the smoke in his lungs. It felt to him then like putting on a clean thobe. Always two drags: the second to relax the first. He could feel it re-coating his lungs.

There are times he wishes he could isolate the inhalation. It begins in the throat and then vaults back into the mouth and down again into the lungs where it seems to pause awhile before it moves around his body. He promised himself three years ago to give them up; so be it, he never did. No alcohol, no other excesses. Avoid that which requires an apology.

The air from the vents has begun to warm. He cracks the window, blows the smoke out. Next to him, Rami has already put on his helmet and swung his leg across the motorbike.

The two exchange a nod. The cigarette smoke filters up against the dark.

In reverse, the dashcam flips into life. The guiding red and yellow lines appear on the small screen. Bassam hits his brakes and the light flares against the red brick of the monastery wall. He takes another drag and allows Rami's motorbike to pull out in front of him.

A few stray raindrops slant in the lights above the empty guard-house at the gate. Nothing more than a light drizzle, but it will slow their journeys home: Rami to Jerusalem, Bassam to Jericho.

He watches as his friend raises one hand in the air, and together they pass on through into the dark.

498

It is often a surprise to travelers that the River Jordan is, in so many places, not much more than a trickle.

497

The pools, the crevices, the fissures, the brooks, the streams, the aquifers, the rivulets, the wadis, the creeks, the channels, the canals, the runnels, the brooks, the rills, the puddles, the wells, the spouts, the springs, the sluices, the ponds, the lakes, the dams, the pipes, the drains, the cisterns, the lagoons, the marshes, the surf, the tide, the living seas, the dead seas, the rain itself: water here is everything.

496

Parts of the Atacama desert in Chile have never had any recorded rainfall. It is one of the driest places on earth, but the local farmers have learned to harvest water from the air by suspending large nets to catch cloud banks rolling in from the Pacific coast.

When the fog touches the tall nets, it forms drops of moisture. The water rolls down along the plastic strands and moves through small gutters, collecting at the bottom of the net, where the trickle is funneled into a pipe that leads to a cistern.

All across the landscape, high metal poles hold the dark nets against the pale sky. The fog is captured early in the morning before the sun burns the clouds off.

Out of nothing, something.

495

The farmers call the nets fog catchers.

494

Because of irrigation schemes and dams along the length of the Jordan, the river runs at about ten percent of its natural strength. A large part of the flow is made up of sewage. In summertime, without the effluent and the saline discharge, there would be hardly any river at all.

The trickle barely makes it to the Dead Sea which, as a result, drops up to three feet every year.

493

So that, from above—from the view of a pilot, say, or a bird—the dry, cracked land around the shore looks like a shattered windshield.

492

Once, when he was flying back from a trip to Finland, Rami's plane got caught in a holding pattern over Ben Gurion. A beautiful clear day. He gazed out from his window seat on the landscape below. The West Bank was scattershot with construction, apartment blocks halfway built, warehouses dotted in increments of exhausted grey, roads that seemed to taper off into abandonment.

The plane tilted. The shadow flicked on the landscape, shortened and disappeared from view as the plane circled in a wide loop.

Rami could tell exactly where Israel began and ended: it was more ordered and controlled, logical, highways and flyways and byways.

When the plane curved around in the direction of Jerusalem, he could pick out the settlements with ease: the red roofs, the glimmering solar panels, the cerulean blue of the swimming pools, the perfect rectangles of green lawn.

491

An average swimming pool takes about 20,000 gallons of water to fill.

490

In the high summer of 1835, a Maltese sailor—a vagabond, a sometime servant—happened upon a young English-speaking traveler in the market of Akka, on the coast of the Mediterranean Sea. The sailor, eager for work, had just come off a ship carrying spices from Beirut.

From what the sailor could gather, the traveler was seeking to make a journey by boat from the Sea of Galilee to the Sea of Salt, from where he would, among other things, search out the lost Biblical towns.

The traveler appeared to be in his late twenties. He was tall and slim and wore wire-rimmed glasses. His light-colored hair was thinning. A Christian cross hung at his neck. His bearing was pious, his voice soft.

The prospect of the journey confounded the sailor. The length of the River Jordan had seldom been explored by foreign travelers. Lore had it that anybody who ventured upon the Sea of Salt—known to some as the Dead Sea—would never survive. It was the end of July, almost August, the hottest time of the year. The river would be low but swift and wild, and in certain places unnavigable. The boat itself would require the agility of a canoe and the sturdiness of a sailing vessel. The journey between the lakes was, by his calculations, a little short of seventy miles: not only would the traveler have to deal with curious villagers and roving gangs of thieves, but it was likely that they would be set upon by jackals, eagles, scorpions, snakes and all manner of insects.

The Maltese sailor had spent thirty years on the water, as far adrift as Africa and China. The proposed journey struck him as one of inordinate folly, but the traveler said he would pay handsomely up front for an experienced servant and reward him substantially after the journey was finished. There would also be great reward, said the traveler, in the heavenly sphere.

The Maltese sailor strode forward and agreed, with a handshake, to join the journey.

The pair slept that evening in a boardinghouse near the pier in Akka. The traveler gave the Maltese sailor the only bed while he himself slept on the floor. In the morning they prayed together at the foot of the window as the light rose hard and yellow over the Mediterranean. They packed the traveler's steamer trunk and the sailor's leather bags, then made their way down to the harbor where they haggled a good price for a sturdy wooden boat with copper trimmings and a tall sail. In the market they bought a few weeks' worth of supplies.

The mast was temporarily removed and the hull of the boat was strapped to a camel. Two Bedouin tribesmen accompanied the men on their inland walk. It was their job to look after the boat-carrying camel and to protect the traveling party from thieves. The supplies—water, food, maps, provisions and books—were carried down the road from Akka to the Sea of Galilee.

In the evening, when the sailor and the traveler camped, village children came to sit inside the wooden boat: they rowed in the sand and giggled until they were shooed away by the Bedouin.

The sailor prepared breakfast before sunrise and together the men strapped the boat to the camel and continued their journey.

On the evening of the third day, the Sea of Galilee rose in front of them. A strong wind combed the surface of the lake, long scribbles of white under soaring flocks of egrets. The trees along the water were in full bloom: oranges, apricots, palms. The light lay red on the western sky. To the Christian traveler it looked Edenic: he went to his knees and began to pray.

In the morning the dark lifted generously. The sky seemed to begin at their feet. The traveler settled his account with the Bedouin, dragged the small boat into the water and stepped into the hull. He wanted to get a start before the day's heat rose. He would, he told the sailor, take the helm for the first part of the journey. He fumbled with the oarlock and it tumbled into the shallows. When he retrieved it, he seemed not quite sure how the oar would fit into the lock.

The Maltese sailor was astonished to learn that the traveler had never plied the oars of a small boat before.

489

It was only the fifth boat the traveler had ever been in. The first had brought him from Kingstown, Ireland, to Southampton, England; the second to Port Said in Egypt; the third from Egypt to Beirut; the fourth from Beirut to Akka on the Mediterranean Sea.

488

Known to Israelis as the city of Akko. Known to Palestinians still as Akka. Known beyond Israel and Palestine as Acre: a mosaic town with a low skyline of mosque and flat roof and synagogue, a town of bells and loudspeakers and muezzin calls, where the warm-water wind retreats the tongue and sneaks multiple sounds into the throat: Acre, Akko, Akka.

487

Christopher Costigin was twenty-five years old. He had grown up on Thomas Street in Dublin. His father, Sylvester, was a distiller. His mother, Catherine, a bookkeeper. He was studying theology in Maynooth College in the hope of joining the priesthood.

Costigin had read about the Levant in secondary school. He wanted to see for himself the river that Moses had seen from the heights of Mount Nebo, where Jesus had been baptized by John, and where the Israelites had crossed over into the Promised Land. He had a special interest in the Biblical stories that took place in and around the Dead

Sea, not least the tale of Sodom and Gomorrah, the visiting angels, and Lot's wife who had been turned into a pillar of salt.

As an amateur geographer, he also wanted to draw maps and to make a series of depth soundings of the lake. Costigin hoped to bring back whatever evidence he could: scrolls, rocks, manuscripts, paintings, stories.

The source of God was, he was sure, to be found at the Dead Sea.

486

The Sea—the lowest point of land on earth—is full of salt floes, some of which can be thrown onshore haphazardly by surging waves, calcified and rock-like, hard white surprises.

485

Costigin became known as *Costigan* in the history books. The misspelling stuck when—in the 1840s—a headland on the Dead Sea was named after him.

484

The name of the Maltese sailor went forever unknown.

483

The sailor plied the boat easily across the Sea of Galilee as Costigin took notes in his leather-bound journal. The sun was high but they had taken the precaution, along with the traditional robes and keffiyehs, of bringing two white umbrellas to shade them. A slight breeze came off the shore. The boat moved easily, following the line of the River Jordan through the lake. Both men were in high spirits. Costigin dropped a weighted rope in the water and took measurements, then filled several small glass jars with water specimens.

When they arrived at the far side—where the Jordan once again took up its natural course—they made camp. Darkness fell. They listened to the howl of wild dogs and the dull thrum of distant rapids.

The next day, on the river, the heat began to rise. They moved through a white rock canyon. They kept to the shadowed side of the water and negotiated the first of the rapids. The river was lower than the sailor had expected. The rocks ran high. They bounced the wooden vessel through some of the faster stretches. The copper band that had been fastened around the side of the boat was already dented and broken.

Costigin seemed buoyed by the early difficulty. It suited him. He wanted to stop the boat to explore some caves, but the Maltese sailor told him to strap the provisions down and keep balance in the boat, that there would be plenty of ruins further downriver.

When they looked behind, after the first major rapid, they saw they had lost a white umbrella: it spun daintily in a whirlpool.

The river grew faster, choppier. By noon the next day, they had to portage the boat around several areas of river rock. They unloaded and reloaded the boat, only to have to unload it again. The Maltese sailor implored a return to Galilee, but Costigin wouldn't hear of it. They had enough fresh water and food, he said. The river would change. They had to trust in God: they would reach the Dead Sea and the water would bring release.

The men stopped once again to portage out of the river. They had lost their only telescope and a thermometer too. Exhausted, they camped on the riverside, but they ate well and restocked their freshwater supplies.

They began once again at first break of light. Above the river—beyond the bushes and high grasses—they saw bands of Arab horsemen appear and then disappear into the desert. Costigin wanted to scramble up the cliffs to talk with them, but the Maltese sailor begged him to stay on the river. The figures reappeared along the cliff, but they made no contact.

On several occasions the sailor had to prevent Costigin from clambering out of the boat to explore. On the boat Costigin began to recite Biblical verses, every now and then rocking back and forth, back and forth, with the book clutched to his chest.

The river narrowed and the rapids rose. Costigin's journals were lost overboard. The copper banding around the boat loosened. The heat hammered down. The men dipped their headscarves in the river to cool their boiling skulls. They huddled together under the cloth sail they had rigged above the vessel. The boat was caught against rocks. They used ropes to dislodge it. Costigin's hands were ripped to shreds.

The sailor said they should abandon the river as soon as possible. Costigin said they would go on no matter what. It was God's will. They would be given release. It was a holy river. What they needed was a leap of faith.

No animals or humans were apparent on the riverbanks anymore: no insects even, until dusk, when they were enveloped by mosquitoes and flies. Huge dark swarms. In their eyes, their ears, their mouths.

The sailor watched as Costigin snorted a sleeve of dead flies from his nose.

On the fourth day, within minutes of embarking on the river, they were forced to portage yet again. They hauled the boat out of the river and dragged it over the riverbank, through the thick band of riverside bulrushes and palm trees, and began the overland journey towards the Dead Sea.

482

Taking the only safe route they knew. North in the direction of Nablus. West towards Jerusalem. South, then, to Jericho. The boat once again strapped onto a camel.

481

The suicide bombers camped out for weeks in caves near Nablus. They were brought provisions by kids on horseback: tinned food, water purifiers, clothing, newspapers, matches, kerosene, spices. They had access to a satellite phone but were not allowed to use it unless they walked at least a mile from their camp, disguised as shepherds.

During the day they remained in the caves. There were, they knew, Israeli listening posts all over the landscape, and planes streaking across the sky during the day, taking photographs from above.

480

In his night walks from the cave in order to use the phone, the lead bomber, Youssef Shouli, inserted sheets of aluminum foil and silver thermal blankets beneath his clothing in the belief that it would deceive any heat-seeking sensors that might be set up in the hills.

Shouli returned from his satellite calls soaked in sweat, his body baking inside the silver foil.

479

Imagine this: Shouli's hands and face exposed to a heat-seeking camera as he bobs along through the dark.

478

The Allenby Bridge, also known as the al-Karameh Bridge, also known as the King Hussein Bridge, spans the Jordan River near Jericho. Barbed wire, security cameras and trigger alarms extend for hundreds of yards along both sides of the riverbank.

For years, when the area around the bridge was less built up, it was a tradition to throw small coins from the banks of the river for good luck when traveling across.

The Jordan was deep enough that the local children could dive for the coins.

477

When Smadar was nine she wrote a school report on the most polluted rivers in the world: the Yellow, the Ganges, the Sarno, the Mississippi, the Jordan.

For her section on the Jordan she used a photograph of herself floating on her back at Ein Bokek at the Dead Sea. The caption read: *Where the Jordan ends.*

In the photo Smadar, four years of age, wears a pale blue swimsuit and a white cap with a plastic yellow flower on the front. She leans forward, surprised, it seems, by the sight of her toes.

476

At the swim competitions in Jerusalem, Smadar patrolled the edges of the pool. Her body looked as if it had been set on springs, always fidgeting, moving, on the go. Before a race she had a habit of placing her finger in the rear of the swimming cap, snapping the latex tight against her neck. It became her signature gesture: a loud popping sound echoing around the pool.

Her best stroke was the butterfly. Rami watched her as she plowed through the pool, arms moving symmetrically, her legs scissoring in and out of the water.

When the race was finished Smadar ripped the swimming cap off and shook her hair out. She had heard a rumor that the chlorine would turn her hair a shade of green.

At home she doused her head in vinegar: she dubbed it the Jordan Treatment.

475

After the death of Matti Peled, Smadar got in the habit of winding his watch at bedtime. She didn't want it to stop while she was asleep lest it signal that her other grandfather, Yitzak, had died during the night too.

474

Once she climbed into the pool still wearing the timepiece on her wrist. The second hand froze. She insisted that Rami take her to a jewelry store to get it fixed. He bundled her in the car to a clockmaker's house, an elderly Armenian woman who lived in the Meah Shearim district.

Rami had heard about the Jewish woman from a colleague in the advertising industry.

While the clockmaker dried out the inside of the watch, Smadar walked around the house amongst the hundreds of working clocks.

Before they left, she nudged up against Rami and tugged his sleeve. Why, she asked, were all the clocks in the back rooms of the house exactly one hour off?

It bothered Rami too until he remembered that there was a one-hour time difference between Israel and Armenia.

Perhaps, he told her, the clockmaker wanted to dwell in her original time. Or maybe the clocks just reminded her of her homeland. Or maybe—he thought later—the clockmaker didn't want to dwell in that time at all, and she was, in the back of her house, always an hour ahead, so that the things that had happened there might not, yet, have happened here.

473

Peled had worn the Timex all through the '48 war, his days in the Knesset, the Six-Day War, the Yom Kippur War, the agreement with Sadat, the withdrawal from Sinai, the invasion of Lebanon, and the First Intifada. The timepiece was a talisman of sorts. In his personal diary, in the summer of 1994, he wrote that the only time he wanted not to wear it or consult it at all was at the conclusion of the Oslo negotiations.

The agreement, he wrote, was like a piece of chamber music disguised as a symphony, a temporary salve for the Palestinian ear but designed, in the end, only for the Israeli violin.

472

After he left the morgue, Rami had to go to his father's house to tell him what had happened to Smadar. His father was in the small living room, watching the news. Yitzak did not yet know: none of the names of the dead had yet been announced.

Rami switched off the television, pulled a chair close. His father, almost eighty years old—a thin blanket across his knees—stared at a point beyond Rami's shoulder. He moved his mouth but didn't say a word. It was as if he needed to figure out what new taste this might be.

Yitzak put his hand to the bridge of his nose, then rose slowly and said: I'm awfully tired, son, I have to go to bed now.

471

As if things that had happened there might not, yet, have happened here.

470

From the monastery, Rami's motorbike goes out in front, trailing its red brake light between potholes.

To Bassam's left, down in the valley, the landscape is already lit up. The highway—for Israeli cars only—runs through the valley, a blur of yellow on one side, red on the other, some towards Hebron, some towards Jerusalem, some towards the Dead Sea.

469

Bassam cracks the window of the car an inch to allow the smoke out.

In prison a single cigarette could be shared among two or three cells. At night, he could look along the length of the corridors and see the pulse of red ash as it swung from one cell to the next. The hands of the prisoners stuck out through the holes in their doors to catch the contraband as it swung. The cigarettes were tied on long pieces of dental floss and in the dark they looked like small universes pulsing.

468

The shore around the Dead Sea is pocked with sinkholes. As the salt water recedes, the freshwater aquifers along the perimeter begin to penetrate. The water encounters huge boulders of salt anywhere from five to sixty meters below the surface.

Slowly the salt dissolves and the boulders disappear until all that remains is a giant cavity. The cavities rise to the surface, like air bubbles, until the ground below collapses without warning.

Thousands of sinkholes have formed along the Dead Sea shore in recent years: huge, gaping craters appearing out of nowhere.

Whole buildings have fallen into the holes. Fences. Groves of date palms. Horses. Cars. Portions of road. Bedouin goats.

467

One instant there, the next gone. Whisked out of midair.

466

Water dissolves more substances than any other liquid, even acid.

465

It disrupts the forces of attraction that hold molecules together.

464

In many West Bank houses you fill basins, you line up jugs, you top up bottles by the kitchen sink. You brush your teeth with the tap off. You step quickly from the shower. You put a plastic stopper above the drain in the bathroom. You soak sponges in the standing water. You put aerators on the faucets to reduce the flow. You use a broom to clean the steps, no mops. You wipe your car with a dry cloth. You dust the windows of your house. You know the water can be turned off for weeks at a time and then you will have to buy it at four times the price charged to those across the valley. You climb the stairs to the flat concrete roof and you check the black tanks for leaks. You lift the lid to check the level. You pray for rain even if the tank is almost full.

463

One of the games played by Israeli soldiers is Shoot the Water Tank: the lower the bullet on the tank, the finer the marksman.

462

Sometimes a vindictive Palestinian Authority soldier takes aim too.

461

At the end of the Second World War a young Bedouin shepherd of the Ta'amirah tribe went searching for a lost goat in the sandstone cliffs near the Dead Sea.

Clambering up on the rocks, Muhammad al-Dhib came upon a cistern-shaped cave with an opening. The missing goat might, he thought, have fallen into the cave, or was perhaps foraging somewhere in the dark.

Muhammad tossed several pebbles into the hole and thought he heard an odd sound.

When he lowered himself into the cave, Muhammad took a thin tallow candle from his pocket and lit it. Several jars of ancient pottery sat in a row on the ground. He stepped forward and broke a jar open with his wooden staff. The jar shattered into pieces. He smashed the second, then a third. All empty.

The tenth was sealed with red clay. Inside he found several strips of rolled leather. The writing on the leather was illegible to Muhammad, but it struck him that he might be able to use the leather as a strap for his sandals.

Muhammad wrapped the parchment in his cloak and took it back to his camp. The leather turned out to be too brittle for sandal straps, so he hung it in a goatskin bag in the corner of his hut.

He later told interviewers that the sack remained there, hanging from a cedar pole, for at least another year.

460

In 1947, Muhammad's uncle noticed the leather scrolls hanging in the hut. Curious, he took them to a market in Bethlehem. The first trader, thinking they were stolen from a Jewish synagogue, said they were worthless. They were taken to a nearby market where they were examined by a local sheikh and a store owner who enlisted the help of a shoemaker and a part-time antiques dealer.

Together the men returned with Muhammad's uncle to the caves where the scrolls had been found. They searched the broken jars and found more fragments of scroll.

Eventually a deal was struck: they bought three of the scrolls for seven Jordanian pounds.

459

In the spring of 1948 John C. Trever, a Biblical scholar and archaeologist, heard about the scrolls and sent photographs to a colleague of his, William F. Albright, who said the scrolls were the greatest manuscript discovery of modern times.

458

Seven Jordanian pounds: at the time, twenty-eight dollars.

457

In Jewish tradition it is forbidden to throw away writings invoking the name of God. Prayer books. Scrolls. Encyclopedias. Garments. Tefillin straps. Even pamphlets or cartoon books. Instead of being destroyed, the texts are interred in a genizah, a burial place for the written word.

456

The Dead Sea scrolls were originally hidden in clay pots and placed in caves to protect them. If they were not to be found again, the writing would decay naturally. In the sealed jars—with no light and no rain—the scrolls could slowly molder away.

455

The modern-day genizah is often found in the attic or basement of a synagogue, or even in a sanctioned dumpster on the street outside.

454

One night, driving through a settlement outside Jerusalem, Rami saw a group of Orthodox men and boys gathered by a genizah near a synagogue. They were chatting and laughing, pushing each other around. Two of them wore machine guns strapped across their shoulders.

An elderly man drove up and threw the contents of his trunk into the blue container. The car drove off. The young men lifted the lid of the genizah. Rami saw one of the smaller boys take his hat off. He was hoisted in the air, like a gymnast. The other men dangled him inside the container by the ankles. He appeared to be swallowed whole.

Rami was taken aback: they were dumpster diving.

After a moment they dragged the suited boy up with an armful of books. It happened several times over until the group sat around and spread the books on the ground, flicked through them.

Rami opened his car door and walked along the side of the road. He nodded to the young men but they didn't nod back. Their guns sat on the ground beside them.

He turned back at the corner and passed the group again.

It intrigued Rami. The heritage. The belonging. The things that were passed along. Their black hats. Their suits. Their white shirtfronts. Their payot. Their guns. It struck him that he must have appeared as foreign to them as they were to him. Men of another country. It wasn't so much that they frightened him, it was more that they just did not seem to live on quite the same earth.

Rami gestured good night, but they did not move until he had closed the door of his car. He caught sight of them in the rearview mirror. They were leaning towards each other, laughing. The books were ranged in a circle around them.

He found out later that the men had dangled their friend in the dumpster rather than just climbing inside because it was forbidden to tread with your feet on the name of G-d.

453

On the Sabbath: No sowing, plowing, reaping, binding sheaves, threshing, winnowing, selecting, grinding, sifting, kneading, baking, shearing
wool, washing wool, beating wool, dyeing wool, spinning, weaving, making two loops, weaving two threads, separating two threads, tying, unty-
ing, sewing two stitches, tearing, trapping, slaughtering, flaying, salting
meat, curing hide, scraping hide, cutting hide, writing two letters, eras-
ing two letters, building, tearing a building down, extinguishing a fire,
kindling a fire, hitting with a hammer, taking an object from the private
domain to the public or transporting an object in the public sphere.

452

The custom of substituting the word G-d for God is based on the traditional practice in Jewish law of revering God's Hebrew name. The name
most often used in the Hebrew Bible is the Tetragrammaton, YHWH,
considered too sacred to be uttered aloud, and frequently anglicized as
Yahweh or Jehovah. The other names of God that, once written, cannot
be erased are El, Eloah, Elohim, Elohai, El Shaddai and Tzevaot.

In prayers the pronunciation Adonai is used, and in discussion it is
usually said as HaShem, meaning The Name.

451

In Islam there are ninety-nine names for God— ʾasmāʾu llāhi l-ḥusnā,
meaning the Beautiful Names of Allah.

450

In 1995, the shepherd Muhammad—who had, since 1947, made a living
searching for scrolls in the caves around Qumran—gave an interview
in an antiquities shop in the Old City of Jerusalem.

Some of the scrolls that he had left hanging in his hut, he said, had been discovered by children who used them as kite strips until they disintegrated and blew away on the wind.

449

Four of the Dead Sea scrolls were taken to the Waldorf Astoria hotel in New York in 1954, where they were sold at auction for a quarter of a million dollars.

448

Muhammad said that one of the things he regretted now, as an old man, was that he had never found the body of his lost goat.

447

And we think the myths are startling.

446

Abir would sometimes draw her name in the dust on her father's car. Her writing was tight and controlled. She wrote in naskh and was just beginning to learn the ruq'ah. She flourished the initial arc and moved seamlessly into the underlying line. She joined the dots above the third arc. Her work was fine and decorative. She would write it in one patch at a time, on the passenger door, the trunk, the front bumper.

She liked the notion of her name traveling down the road at fifty kilometers an hour.

445

After the shooting, Bassam walked around the car and tried to find a patch where her writing remained. He found a faint imprint on the rear window.

444

Sometimes Rami would step into Smadar's room and think of it as a sort of genizah too.

443

Costigin and the sailor hauled the wooden boat over the cliffs by rope. For hours they picked their way through the rocks and stones, searching for a path away from the river so they could join the larger road.

Their bodies were so ripped up by desert thorns that they were forced to improvise arm and leg coverings from the spare white canvas they carried for repair of the sail. They secured the wrappings with twine, then dragged the boat behind them, trying not to damage the hull.

Costigin told the sailor that he was sure they would come to no harm. They were, after all, walking in the original footsteps.

When the sun was at its highest they stopped and took shade in the cool of isolated caves. They removed their coverings, bathed their wounds. The moon moved across the mouth of the cave. The silence was immense.

Early the next day—in the still-dark, after rewrapping their wounds—they came across a small group of Bedouin tribesmen. The Bedouin were amazed at the appearance of the travelers, wrapped in canvas, dragging a boat behind them.

They put Costigin and the sailor on horseback and brought them to their camp, where they applied a special poultice made from the pulp of cactus. When they had recovered, Costigin once again hired camels to carry the boat and the remaining provisions.

442

When Bassam went to lecture in the United States in 2014, he was invited to a number of churches where they sang about the Jordan— *Roll, Jordan, roll, I want to go to heaven when I die; Oh the Jordan stream will never run dry, never run dry, never run dry; I'll meet you in the morning when you reach the promised land, on the other side of the Jordan where I'm bound.*

In the pews he sat and listened. He told his hosts later that the music brought him home.

441

The pair arrived in Jericho by the Dead Sea in tatters. They took a couple of days to reorient themselves at a rooming house. Costigin took long baths to bring his body temperature down. A thermometer in the shade read over a hundred degrees Fahrenheit. In the market Costigin restocked on water, coffee, food, clothing, then bought the thermometer from the owner of the rooming house.

They set out for the final part of their journey in August of 1835. When they got to the shore of the lake, Costigin measured the heat at 105 degrees. He knelt in the sand, put his palm upon the bow of the boat, and prayed. He dipped his finger in the lake and ran the salt across his lips. Later, when the sun fell, he ate a meal of guinea fowl while floating on his back.

They launched onto the Dead Sea near the mouth of the Jordan. The sky was blue upon blue. The wind was laden with heat. Nothing else stirred. No fish, no birds.

The lake was bounded on either side by high mountain ranges. The mountains appeared purple in the heat. Costigin was surprised by the size of the waves across the water: he had studied the salt lake in books, but he had not reckoned on its enormity. The boat, he noticed, rode a full hand's-width higher here than anywhere else, buoyed by the salt. He knelt on the wooden slats and began to take soundings, using the rope which went to a depth of one hundred and seventy-five fathoms.

They spent two days crisscrossing the lake. Costigin ventured onshore into the clay hills to see if he could find forgotten ruins or remnants of towns. He returned to the boat, after hours of walking, in an ecstatic fever.

He might, he told the Maltese sailor, have found the sulfur springs where Herod had once bathed.

They docked the boat and slept in their tent. A fierce north wind blew. The thermometer read eighty-five degrees. They hoisted the sail and were on the lake before sunrise. Within minutes it was over a hundred degrees again. The Maltese sailor said he could go no more, but Costigin was convinced that he would find the ruins of Sodom and Gomorrah.

The ruins would, he thought, be somewhere near Ein Bokek. They would fight their way through the heat.

By the fourth day, their skulls had begun to burn. Costigin dipped his keffiyeh in the lake over and over. Even the surface of the water seemed to be boiling. Blisters and sores appeared on his face. He dipped his clothes again. The sun baked him dry. He realized he was making a terrible mistake: the sun was burning the salt through his skin. His eyes were large and inflamed. The blisters had begun to ooze. He rinsed his headscarf in the small supply of fresh water, collected the runoff.

They struck out into the lake once more. The thermometer was stuck at 102 degrees.

By the fifth day the Maltese sailor had fallen silent. He stared straight ahead as he rowed. He no longer joined in Costigin's prayers. The thermometer had vanished. They still had food but their supply of fresh water was rapidly dwindling. In the daytime they tried to shield the water bucket from the heat to prevent evaporation. Costigin could not sleep. His face and his body were ravaged with sores. He had begun to repeat himself, Biblical verses over and over. He accused the sailor of drinking all the water and throwing the thermometer overboard.

The sailor told him that if they didn't leave now they would surely die.

Their fresh water was completely gone after seven days, but there was still a small amount of coffee left. Costigin thought the coffee medicinal. It would propel him forward, give him strength, they would find spring water soon.

He dipped the pan in the sea and boiled whatever coffee he could in the salt water. Within hours he was writhing in agony.

440

On her wedding day, Salwa—as was her family custom—took platefuls of used coffee grounds and spread them on the doorstep of her house.

She scrunched her bare feet into the grounds, darkening her soles, and then walked in a circle in front of her house, leaving the print of the coffee on the steps as she walked.

The ritual had been passed through her family for generations: it signified that she and Bassam would be happy to return after the wedding.

439

A group of rescuers brought Costigin back through Bethlehem to Jerusalem strapped on horseback. A large cushion was attached to the neck of the horse so that Costigin could lie along its length.

The rescuers had been sent out by an Anglican missionary, the Reverend John Nicolayson, who had heard of Costigin's plight. They had journeyed at night to avoid the terrible heat, reaching Jerusalem just as the morning stars faded.

On the fifth of September, 1835, Nicolayson found Costigin a bed in a Franciscan hospice, the Casa Nuova.

Costigin was diagnosed with severe hyperpyrexia. A doctor administered emetics and wet his lips with lemonade made with fresh fruit from the hospice garden.

The young novitiate wavered in and out of consciousness. He lay in the bed under a thin sheet. His fever soaked the pillow. He wanted to be wheeled out into the garden one final time, but it was too warm outside, he would have to wait for night.

He was sorry, he told the doctor, that he had not been properly prepared for his journey to the Dead Sea, but now he was ready to meet his God.

438

On the morning of Monday, September 7, 1835, Christopher Costigin was buried in a cemetery in the shade of Mount Zion overlooking the Kidron Valley, sloping down towards the Dead Sea where he had traveled.

The Reverend Nicolayson oversaw the funeral. He wrote in his diary that for a moment, just as Costigin's coffin was lowered in the ground, a single cloud appeared and gave a brief relief from the heat.

437

Point Costigan was named in 1848 when another expedition—led by the explorer William Lynch, heavily funded and equipped by the United States Navy—managed to make the first complete modern map of the Dead Sea.

Lynch named the northern extremity of the El-Lisan peninsula after the young theologian. The American fired a three-gun salute into the air in Costigin's memory.

436

The Ben Yehuda Street bombs went off in three-second intervals.

435

Closed-circuit cameras later pinpointed the bombers approaching Ben Yehuda Street from at least two different directions: Bashar Sawalha came from Mesilat Yesharim Street, Youssef Shouli from Mordechai A'liash.

They arrived disguised as women. In their hands they carried shopping bags although it was never fully determined what was inside the bags: the explosives were wrapped around their bodies.

The third bomber, Tawfiq Yassine, was not caught on any footage, although investigators suggested that he had come from the area of HaMatmid Alley, past the building which housed the Israeli Ministry of Immigration and Absorption.

434

The women's clothes had been given to them a week before, but none of the men tried them on until just hours before the operation.

For their video, filmed on the morning of the bombings by the Martyr's Brigade for the Freedom of Prisoners, they made sure they were dressed in appropriate male attire—keffiyeh and agal—and spoke their lines looking straight into the camera.

Afterwards they shaved their beards and donned the clothing.

433

The patterns the bombers wore were simple and bare and black. The firing buttons were threaded into their pockets.

432

Witnesses said that the bombers made eye contact with each other from under their veils when they reached the area around Hillel Street.

431

The apartments above. The store awnings below. The fruit stalls, the juice joints, the fashion stores. The cash registers. The loudspeakers. The jangle. The September throb. The flick of a lighter. The opened clasp of a purse. The girls swaying arm in arm down the street. The laughter from a café. The pneumatic door hiss. A car door closing. The plimp of the bombers' soft-soled shoes. The swish of their dresses. The rub of the wide cloth sleeves.

430

Youssef Shouli's was the last bomb to go off. He had gone deepest into the crowd of pedestrians.

429

On the door of their apartment Nurit had put up a sticker: *End the Occupation*. Rami thrust his key in the door. She was standing there, waiting. He felt her shudder. He kissed her hair.

—Hurry, she said.

Rami moved quickly through the house. In his office he picked up the spare battery for his phone. The red light of the message machine was blinking. He hit it. The messages were a day old. The voices seemed to come from afar. He shoved the battery in his pocket, checked himself again for car keys and wallet.

In the kitchen the babysitter—a neighbor—was playing with Yigal. A train set was arranged on the floor. Interlocking pieces. Rami stepped across the room and took the five-year-old in his arms, kissed him, then hurried to the front door.

Nurit had tucked a small Polaroid of Smadar in her handbag. Rami knew better than to ask why.

428

The photograph was taken at a jazz class, her white earphones on.

427

By the time they arrived near Ben Yehuda Street an eerie calm had fallen over the area. The sirens had subsided. No screaming, no shouting. All forms of uniform were moving about: police, army, paramedic, the ZAKA.

Rami and Nurit were stopped at the red tape. They could see the distant floodlights. The shapes moving through the dark. They went to the edge of the tape, leaned over.

—I'm sorry but no one's allowed. We're under strict instructions.

Nurit showed the guard the photo.

—I'm sorry, no, he said.

She held it out further. He considered the photo, shook his head again.

There were groups on the street: parents, teenagers, soldiers. The darkness buzzed. Rami and Nurit split in different directions. They moved among the clusters, met up again on Shamai Street.

—They're saying two people—

—Men or women?

—Forty or fifty injured.

—Have you called home?

—Yes.

—The boys?

—They haven't heard anything.

—Let's try the hospital.

They hurried past the shuttered shops. Rami wanted to call Smadar's name along the street. Perhaps, he thought, they would still find her around here, shivering in a café, or maybe she was dazed and had gone to a friend's house, or she hadn't been in the area at all, and she hadn't even heard about the bombing, and she was blithely sitting in some bedroom somewhere, her and four other girls, on a pillowed bed, sharing lip gloss, giggling over magazines.

He clicked the key from far away and the car horn beeped and the hazards lit up.

They had parked by the Music Museum. When he turned the key in the ignition the radio flared. A talk show. He clicked it off. He turned onto Shamai Street.

Nurit punched a series of numbers into her phone. He could hear every intake of breath.

—Oh, she said into the phone. Yes. Okay. Yes.

He accelerated. The city was bathed in light from the streetlamps. The September air seemed yellow.

—She was seen downtown, said Nurit.

—Where?

—With Daniella and a group of girls.

—What time?

—I don't know. On Hillel Street.

—Who said?

—Elik heard it from Daniella's parents.

—Where's Daniella?

—They're looking for her. Sivan too.

Several cars were parked haphazardly outside the hospital. They pulled in against the curb. Together they ran up towards the circular driveway. Volunteers stood out in front of the emergency bay. They wore makeshift name badges and held clipboards. There was, they said, no access to the emergency room except for the gravely injured. They called on everyone to be calm, said they were there to answer questions.

A man with a clipboard said: Her name, please?

426

A girl emerged from a white door wearing a white bandage on her head: Smadar's height, Smadar's weight, Smadar's hair. Not Smadar. A gurney was wheeled along the corridor with the shape of a living girl underneath the sheet. Not Smadar. There was news of a teenager in an operating room. They begged the nurses to get her name. Not Smadar. They made phone calls to the other hospitals. There was a Smadar, yes, she was lightly injured, released early—she was twenty, blond, with her fiancé. They called the police station. No Smadar. No Elhanan either. Wait a moment, wait. There was a Sam, but sorry, no, no Smadar. They saw Daniella's parents in the hallway. They hugged. Daniella was injured, severely, she was in the operating theater. They had not heard about Smadar, no, they were sorry, but if Daniella was alive then Smadar surely would be too. They ran to the front desk again. The nurse's finger went along the list. Samantha, Sarel, Simona.

—Sorry, no, she said, no Smadar.

425

From the Song of Solomon. The grapevine. The opening of the flower.

424

Under the carob trees, where the crowd stood, Rami read from the Kaddish and later from the Song of Solomon.

423

Also known as the Song of Songs. Also known as Canticle of Canticles. Considered one of the most mysterious and beautiful books in the Bible.

422

The light flared. An officer moved from one corner of the dark to the next. He came to the glass and glanced out, then turned and moved back into the watery dark.

They waited. There were dozens of them now: parents, boyfriends, girlfriends, daughters, middle-aged sons.

—Please, said the desk clerk, we're doing everything we can.

An officer came out. Tall, fair-haired. He leaned over and whispered in the ear of the clerk. She glanced up at him and scrawled something on a sheet of paper. He leaned back in again. She nodded and wrote a second time. The officer tapped the front of the desk twice. They had some sort of code going between them.

They called someone else's name. A woman sprang up from her seat. A half-door was opened up and she was brought back, behind the glass.

Nurit held tight to Rami's hand.

There were others in the police station too. A boy from a street brawl. A woman who had locked herself out of her apartment. A man came in carrying a lost cat, white with a black stripe. He left it on the floor of the station and walked straight out. The cat hissed from underneath the furthest bench. Strange to think that there was another world out there too, an ordinary, functioning world.

Another name was called. Then another. And another.

One couple came out of the offices, arms wrapped around each other, laughing. They had found their uncle, they said. He had been drunk in a restaurant. He had been detained, that's all, wasn't that wonderful?

They paused, then, in the middle of the station: I'm so sorry, said the woman.

The couple left, heads down.

—Try the boys again, said Nurit.

—My phone's running out.

—We could try the police. Jaffa Street.

The cat came from beneath the bench and sidled up against a young man on the far side of the room. It arched its back and rubbed against the boy's calves.

421

She would arrive home jaunty and bright-eyed and jangly. She would stand in the kitchen and let out a patented sigh and say, What's the big deal, Aba? We were miles away, I'm fourteen for crying out loud. She would make herself a Hashachar sandwich, chocolate spread, and then she would go off to her room, turn up the stereo, begin to dance.

420

Or she would arrive back late at night, in a taxi, saying, Sorry, sorry, sorry, Daniella was close to the blast, we had to go get her eardrums checked, I couldn't leave her side, I know, I know, I should have called, I will next time, I promise.

419

Or there would be a bandage around her leg where she fell while running away, and she would come home and she would sit at the kitchen table, and they would comfort her and it would all be fine, and Rami would say that it was time for everyone to go to bed, it had been a long day, she needed her beauty sleep.

418

The station was still full when their name was called. They were brought back behind the glass panel. It was strangely bright when they sat down at the officer's desk. The officer checked Smadar's name again, spelled it out.

He shook his head and tapped the pencil against the edge of his ledger.

The news was neither good nor bad, he said. She was not to be found anywhere. He wished there was more he could say or do. This was no indication of anything at all, but perhaps, as a last ditch, he hated to say this, it was just a precaution, they had to understand, he wasn't being definitive, he was very sorry, it was just, maybe, to clear their minds, they should try the morgue.

417

Morgue: the name of a building in early-nineteenth-century Paris where the bodies of those drowned in the Seine were laid out on an inclined platform and subjected to public view, sometimes for a fee.

416

The only interesting thing, said François Mitterrand, is to live.

415

On hunger strike Bassam allowed himself salt tablets and water. The tablets came in 100 milligram doses. He broke them in half and took a piece every hour. The longer the strike went on, the more difficult it was to swallow. Dizziness. Disorientation. Fatigue. By the seventeenth day his vision had begun to blur.

414

On March 12, 1930, Mahatma Gandhi set out from his ashram near Ahmedabad in India on a trek to the Arabian Sea in order to protest the British salt tax.

Several dozen followers walked alongside him. They walked twelve miles or more a day on winding dirt roads, stopping to have meetings and make speeches along the way.

Once, at a well of the untouchables—those deemed impure under the Indian caste system—he stunned onlookers by bathing with them.

By the time he reached the coastal town of Dandi—241 miles away—tens of thousands of people had joined the salt satyagraha.

Gandhi planned to work the salt flats on the beach at high tide, but the local police had crushed the deposits into the mud. Still he managed to defy British law by reaching down and picking up a small lump of natural salt from the mud flats.

—With this, he said, I am shaking the foundations of the British empire.

413

Satyagraha: the revelation of truth and the confrontation of injustice through nonviolent means.

412

The lectures took place in the rear of the canteen. The prisoners gathered in a semicircle. The fluorescents flickered. Bassam introduced the scholar. A student of philosophy at Birzeit. He was young, clean-shaven, tall. He had been given six months for chaining himself to the gates of the Knesset. He spoke in short sharp sentences. The way forward, he said, was nonviolence, a template for action and counteraction.

Gandhi's idea of civil disobedience was to be broken into its original elements. It took great discipline. The only way to understand it was to take it apart and lay the elements out, rebuild from there.

The civil element, he said, was just as important as the disobedience itself. They had to be considered separately at first in order to put them back together. What it meant to be *uncivil*. What it meant to be *obedient*. What it meant to be *just*. How to achieve the grace of the opposite. The contradictions had to be dismantled and jigsawed back together again. The language of the oppressor, too, had to be taken apart. The civility of the disobedience was part of its power.

The guards hustled them back to their cells. Bassam spent the afternoon reconstructing the talks in his mind. He took notes on sheets, folded them in tiny pieces, secreted them in the pockets of his uniform, the hem of his trousers, the tongue of his shoes, just in case he got sent to solitary again.

411

The phone call came from the principal of the school. Bassam knew her well: always calm, measured. Something had happened to Abir, she said. She had fallen. She had to be taken to the local hospital. He was on his way to work, he replied, he would call Salwa and tell her to pick Abir up. No, said the principal, he himself should probably go now. Was Abir going to be all right? Oh, she was, inshallah, yes.

410

Behind him, the first car horn of the day.

409

He was sure that she had fallen from the top of the school wall. Even from a young age she liked to walk along the length of it. Ten years old. He was afraid that she might have a scar.

408

The apartment was on the fourth floor. No elevator. Bassam took the stairs two at a time. Bare electrical wires hung down from the ceiling of the stairwell. He reached the fourth floor. He stood a moment, hands on his knees, caught his breath.

Further along two very young children pushed a plastic dump truck.

They looked up at him, went back to playing with their truck. He stepped along the corridor.

The door was latched with a chain. He knew how to loop it off with a pen: he slipped the chain off and swung open the door.

Inside, the television was on. A Spanish soap opera. Salwa was by the sink, chatting on the phone with her mother.

407

Trauma to the back of the skull. Contusions on the front of her head. A weak pulse, a fluttering of the eyelids, no lucidity. Watch for bradycardia and respiratory collapse.

406

The sort of hospital that needed a hospital.

405

We're going to switch her to Hadassah, said Bassam.

404

At first she was sure the nurses had made a mistake. No, she said, no. My daughter came by ambulance, from another hospital, she's already here. They glanced up at her. They spoke to her in Arabic. Not yet, they said. I came by taxi, she said, I know she's here, she has to be, they left a long time ago. She called Bassam's mobile. No answer. The nurses checked their computers, made phone calls, went down the corridor to the operating rooms, consulted the doctors. No, they said, there was no child of that name or description. Could you try again? They scrolled through the records. Maybe, said Salwa, they brought her to another hospital, isn't there another Hadassah at Mount Scopus? Yes, said the nurse, but she wouldn't be brought there. Can you try? We already did. They handed her a small pack of tissues, then came out from behind the desk and guided her by the elbow to the waiting room. They brought her a hot tea, spooned sugar in it. Calls went out over the intercom. Salwa strained to hear. She tried calling Bassam again. No answer. A man came along to mop the floor. He gestured at her to move her feet. She felt the top of the mop touch her toes. Sorry, he said. Her sister arrived. Together they went back to the desk. There has to be some mistake, they said. Trust us, said the nurses, we're doing everything we can. Bassam's brother turned the corner. He had not heard from Bassam, no. He was in his business suit, his tie open. He too went to the desk. Trust us, the nurses pleaded. The crowd swelled. Her aunt. Her cousins. Bassam's friends from his peace work. Surely there was a mistake. Maybe Abir had woken. Maybe they had taken her back to the clinic. Everything would be all right. A doctor came, a Palestinian from Nazareth. He sat between her and her sister. He had put out a special call, he said. The ambulance was on its way. It's been nearly two hours, she said. There had been some technical problems, he said, but she was not to worry. Salwa went into a room and knelt to pray. Her sister prayed alongside her. They returned to the corridor. Each time the hospital doors opened, her heart leapt. Another cup of tea came. She cradled it in her hands. Yet more people arrived. There was a buzz in the hallways. Bassam's Israeli friends were making a fuss at the desk. One of them was shouting. He was standing beside a woman with bright red hair and a young man with a beard. The older man was gesticulating. Who's that? asked Salwa. Her brother peered over her shoulder. That's Rami, he said. Rami? She had heard of him, but she had not yet met him. She turned to meet him, shake his hand, but her phone rang. It was a number she didn't recognize. Where are you, she said, I've been calling and calling. We're coming, said Bassam, my battery died, I'm on the paramedic's phone, don't worry. Is Abir okay? We're five minutes away. Tell me, husband, is Abir okay? Don't worry, he said again, we're on our way.

403

It was the fifth-year anniversary of Combatants for Peace.

402

The tenth-year anniversary of Smadar's death.

401

The eight-year anniversary of Rami joining the Parents Circle.

400

The ancient Greeks used sundials to tell the time during the day and clepsydras, or water clocks, at night.

Stone bowls were fashioned with holes in the bottom so that the water fell through to a vessel below. The vessel filled, drip by drip, and marked the passage of short amounts of time.

A steady water pressure had to be maintained and care taken in order to ensure there was no spillage or evaporation.

399

Rami and his son Elik ran into the emergency bay. The red and blue siren was still spinning. They could hear voices over the radio. The paramedics were hustling the gurney down from the ambulance.

—Out of my way, sir, said one of the medics.

They stepped back, allowed the gurney past.

Rami saw Bassam step down from the back of the ambulance. Right foot first. He was pale and drawn. Rami reached for his elbow and helped him down from the height.

—Where's Salwa? he asked.

398

Rami would always remember Bassam's right foot coming first: as if in a ritual, stepping into a holy place.

397

What froze Rami in place was the sight of three border guards, all women, walking along the corridor of the hospital, past the room where Abir lay unconscious. The guards were in the hospital for no obvious reason, but they were in full uniform, guns strapped across their shoulders. They were the same age as Smadar might have been by then, medium height, slim-shouldered, ponytailed.

396

Abir was carried along the streets of Anata, laid out on a stretcher. A flag was draped over her midriff. A wreath of pink carnations was placed by her head. She was carried shoulder-height, passed from man to man, man to boy, boy to man. Black flags fluttered from balconies. Horns blared. Bassam was jockeyed along, shoulder to shoulder with his brothers, his sons, his colleagues. The streets narrowed. Mourners put their heads to the asphalt. Boys climbed up the light poles. A wail went up. The crowd dragged him forward. In his jacket pocket Bassam could feel the bracelet of candy, the hard round stones slipped onto string.

395

When carrying a bier, even in a thronging crowd, attempts are made to keep the head in the direction of Mecca.

394

The bus rattled. Bassam was traveling alone. He leaned his head against the window. He had memorized the geography of Mecca since he was a boy, the soaring minarets, the geometrical streets, the distant hills. Salwa had insisted that he go, even on his own. It was too expensive to take the whole family anyway. She would, she said, return with him someday.

Above the highway at the entrance to Mecca were giant green signs directing drivers toward Muslim roads and non-Muslim roads.

He entered Masjid-al-Haraam, circled the Kabaa seven times in the pale light. I am here, he thought. His ihram was made from two white unhemmed sheets of rough toweled material. He cast his stones at the pillars of rock, went to the cave at Hira, saw the mountain of Uhud from afar.

He was the quiet one who sat in the back of the bus. He stepped forward when they approached a stop: he wanted to have a smoke.

393

Further along, he spotted rows of checkpoints.

392

391

At a conference in Glasgow, Abir's image was blown up to five feet by three so that she loomed over the stage. When Bassam was finished speaking, he couldn't bear to leave her there, so he asked the organizers to take the poster down. They didn't have a cardboard tube to fit it in, so they rolled it up, tied shoelaces around either end.

Bassam carried his daughter's image with him on the train back to Bradford.

At the station he hailed a taxi. The rolled poster was so large that he had to open the car window and prop it on the edge of the seat.

390

The water clocks were used in courtrooms to gauge the length of the lawyers' arguments and the speeches of witnesses. The timbre of the drip changed as time went on until, at last, there was no more.

389

In the written score for John Cage's experimental work titled *4'33"*, the musicians are told to remain tacet for four minutes and thirty-three seconds.

388

Tacet: that is, not to play their instruments at all.

387

Cage conceived of the composition in 1948. He had recently been in an anechoic chamber designed to maintain absolute silence, and had been studying some new paintings by his friend Robert Rauschenberg: huge canvases of white—only white—the surfaces of which varied mostly by their refraction of the light.

Everything coalesced for Cage—the blankness, the chamber, his thoughts on the nature of sound—while he stood in an Albany elevator listening to a piece of canned music filtered over the speakers.

His original intention was to replicate the length of a typical piece of canned music and to call his composition *Silent Prayer*.

386

On car trips, Smadar's game was to take a breath and hold on to it for as long as possible while passing any graveyard. She undid the seat belt and leaned forward and tapped Rami on the shoulder, held her nose with thumb and forefinger, whirled her other hand in the air, made circles, gesturing them to move faster, faster, faster, her face growing redder until she could hold it no more.

385

Years later, Bassam told Rami that Abir had played the exact same game.

384

When you divide death by life you find a circle.

383

Cage's piece was not just about the nature of silence, but also about all the sounds that could be heard within the silence: the foot shuffle, the sigh, the cough, the scuttle of the mouse beneath the stage floor, the raindrops on the roof, the slamming door, the car horn, the boom of a plane outside the concert hall.

What interested Cage was the idea of the aleatoric, in which the course of music may be determined in a general direction, but the details rely on associations discovered by the performer or the audience or even the sounds themselves.

These chance moments then become the core of a process where each note, each freestanding particle, or even non-note, confers on the next the character of mystery.

382

In the ambulance several different voices came through all at once. Then a single dispatcher: Roger that, we're still waiting.

The static crackled and fizzed.

—Permission to move?

381

On the night of the premiere of *4′33″*, in a converted barn on the outskirts of Woodstock, New York, the crowd waited for the pianist, David Tudor, to strike a note on the piano.

The piece consisted of three movements—the first for thirty-three seconds, the next for two minutes forty seconds, and the third for one minute twenty seconds.

Tudor marked the beginning and end of each movement by opening and closing the keyboard lid.

At the end of the four and a half minutes—without once touching the keys—Tudor stood up from his piano stool and took a bow.

The audience laughed, a little nervously at first. After a moment one or two began clapping until the applause gathered pace and began to sound around the barn.

380

Cage said afterwards that he wanted to make the opening thirty-three seconds as seductive as the shape and fragrance of a flower.

379

Abir, from the ancient Arabic, fragrance of the flower.

378

At the first court case, the Commander of the border guard unit testified that the reason Abir's ambulance had been delayed should have been obvious to anybody with an ounce of experience with the Second Intifada. Everybody knew that ambulances were being manipulated by terror groups to bring not only murder and mayhem across the border into Israel, he said, but there was a running trade in weaponry too, and it was not unusual to hear of shipments of guns being tucked under gurneys, and grenades concealed in emergency coolers designed to hold transplantable body parts, and ammunition stuffed between layers of towels, and explosives hidden among plasma bags and other medical paraphernalia. In addition to this, it was generally known that during those days—and here the Commander used the Hebrew word *matzav,* meaning situation—ambulances were constantly being delayed by rioters who were willing to put their own people, yes, even ten-year-olds, in severe jeopardy. The lives of the first responders had to be protected at all costs. He wanted to make clear that he felt great sadness for the subject even though it was obvious to him that she should not have been in the street in the first place and perhaps the school authorities should shoulder the blame. He was under the impression that nothing in the subject's condition had changed during the delay and that at all times she was given proper medical care. There were riots: of that there was an absolute certainty. The fact of the matter was that he himself had felt the startling thud of rocks against his jeep that very day, it was akin to being inside a drum, just imagine what it might have been like to be in an ambulance if it were to come under siege. It might even be more accurate to point out that the supposed delay had actually protected the child and the father from coming under siege in the ambulance. Such were the terrifying conditions of war.

377

The judge had to slam the gavel several times in order to get the court to calm down.

376

In response, Bassam's lawyers said that there was absolutely no evidence of rioting near the school on the morning of the shooting. Construction of the Wall was taking place at the rear of the secondary school a couple of hundred meters up the road, and while it was true that the border guards were sometimes subjected to sporadic rock-throwing, it generally happened much later in the afternoon, after school, and Abir's death had occurred just after nine o'clock in the morning. Abir was outside the school gates at the time because school was in recess and students were allowed to cross the road to go to the local shop. There was adequate supervision from a crossing guard who had also testified that there were no disturbances in the vicinity except that of the army jeep itself. It was true that there were known incidents of rock-throwing that had occurred *after* the death of Abir, but they had taken place at a significant distance from the hospital and the various locations where the ambulance had been halted. As for the assertion that ambulances were regularly used to ferry weaponry, it had indeed been documented, though never proven, during the Lebanon War, and was suggested on several other occasions in relation to incidents in Gaza and the West Bank, but the assertion that an ambulance might be running guns, or gunmen, from East to West

Jerusalem was patently absurd since there would have to be a crew in the Hadassah hospital to process and hide the contraband. The idea that grenades might be held in emergency coolers was so fanciful and indeed imaginative that perhaps the Commander—who had, incidentally, been promoted just six months after the incident—should follow a new career in fiction, though he should be perhaps a little more attentive to his metaphors. There was no doubt that the Commander was likely at times to have been present in a jeep when it was being stoned, and it was noted that he had said, rather flamboyantly, that it was akin to being inside a drum, but it should be pointed out that it was probably safer to be *inside* the drum than *outside* the drum and certainly that was the case for Abir Aramin, who really wasn't so much a *subject*, as the Commander had asserted, but more likely, in his eyes, an *object*.

375

Each day, after the hearings, Rami met with Bassam to go over the day's events. They drank coffee and combed meticulously through the documents and petitions. They tried to figure out the angle at which the jeep came around the corner. They matched the autopsy and the X-rays, created time charts, pored over photographs and maps.

The information came to them, drip by drip. The next morning they met with lawyers and spread the sheets out on the table.

The jeep was here, they said. It came around this corner just here. It went down along the graveyard there. That had to be a couple of minutes before nine, because recess was at nine. And here, see here, that's the entrance to the school. It takes about two minutes to get from the classroom to the gates, here. She might have walked, she might have been running, who knows. But we do know that she had been in Niesha's shop. The crossing guard saw her too. And Areen, of course. Abir stepped out of the shop after a minute or two, which is exactly the time the jeep would have come from the graveyard considering they would have had to turn here. There were no cameras, no time stamps, but the other girls were waiting outside, remember. The jeep turns the corner here, at the asterisk. See here, there's a clear sight line to the shop. The angle and the distance match with the autopsy report. If you look at the photographs here, the X is exactly where she fell.

374

Rise up, little girl, rise up.

373

Years later—after the court case was settled—Bassam and Rami were delivering a lecture in the Jerusalem Gate Hotel. The room was cramped. Twelve Swedes from a visiting advocacy group had come to hear them lecture. The guide, an Israeli, remained at the back, behind the row of chairs. He paced up and down during Rami's talk, then froze when Bassam started speaking. He let out a low guttural sound.

It was not unusual for one or two of the listeners to begin crying, even openly weeping, during the talks, but Bassam was surprised to see the guide choke up and leave the room.

When the question-and-answer session was over, Bassam stepped out into the hallway and shook the guide's hand. There was something familiar about him: compact, clear-cut, dark-eyed.

—Sorry, said the guide and then stepped away.

372

A few days later a one-thousand-shekel check arrived at the offices of the Parents Circle with a note at the bottom: *Michael Sharia (former ambulance driver).*

371

At the top of the monastery road Bassam sees the single brake light flicker.

370

He watches as Rami pulls the motorbike to a dirt patch at the side of the road. A thin stream of raindrops shines in the red flare. He eases himself off the bike and rocks it onto the kickstand, walks back towards the car. Bassam powers down his passenger window.

—You've a headlight out, says Rami.

Bassam cups his hand to his ear.

—Your headlight's broken, brother.

Bassam moves through the dark, his cigarette flaring. He hunkers down to the front grill and taps on the light with his knuckles, raps on the side panel as if this might somehow spark it. He rounds the car again, scrunching the cigarette on the ground as he goes. A damp chill in the air. He leans in the open window and flicks the lever for the high beams.

—Must be the bulb, says Rami.

Bassam reaches around the steering wheel and turns the keys in the ignition, then slips into the seat, puts his foot on the brake, starts the engine again in the vague hope that the light might somehow flare back into life.

—You could park it here, says Rami. Come back with me. We can pick it up in the morning. I have an extra helmet.

Bassam clicks his tongue and half-smiles. A familiar and hopeless gesture: they can travel together anywhere in the world, but not these few miles.

—I have to get home.

They glance back at the burned-out light.

—At least, says Rami, it's on the passenger side.

369

The men part ways at the top of the monastery road, Rami pulsing his brake light three quick times, their own form of morse.

368

Bassam's one headlight shining small and votive in the dark.

367

This, then, is his nighttime route home: from the monastery through Beit Jala, through Bethlehem, down the hill to Beit Sahour, out the road to the Wadi al-Nar, the Valley of Fire, to the Container Checkpoint. Only Palestinian I.D. holders in Palestinian plated cars. Diving down into the valley, from eight hundred meters above sea level to four hundred meters below.

A drop of over a kilometer, down, down, down, over the stunned landscape.

A drive like a gasp.

366

The tires drum out a quiet meter on the road as he passes through the twists of Bethlehem: University Street, New Street, Mahmoud Abbas Road. He has memorized all the speed bumps. Even in the dark, with one headlight, he knows where and when to brake.

365

On my way, he texts Salwa when he slows and pulls over for a large pothole. *An hour or so, I hope. A good day. x B.*

364

There was fresh falafel and sea salt and virgin olive oil and hummus and romaine lettuce and tomato and cucumber and garlic and yogurt and pomegranate and parsley and mint and maftoul and there were beans and sprigs of rosemary and several cheeses and jars of water with slices of lemon, all laid out on the wooden table.

363

It is a tradition in both Israel and Palestine—*hachnasset orchim* in Hebrew, *marhabaan fi algharib* in Arabic—to give gifts of fresh bread and sea salt to newly arrived strangers.

362

This, thought Bassam, was pure Palestine.

361

There was still no news, the South American monk said, about the construction of the Wall across the valley. The plans were in place but they hadn't yet been carried out. There were several reasons why, he said—the first being optics, the second being politics, and the third being military of course, but let's not talk of this just yet, he said, come along, let us first break bread while we have time.

360

End the Preoccupation.

359

The monks made their wine in cedarwood barrels. The staves were cut from blocks of wood. They followed the grain of the tree. The pieces were sanded, and then cut at an angle, wide in the middle, narrower at the end. The monks used more staves than traditional coopers: thirty-three in all, one for each year of Jesus's life. They placed the staves inside a hooped metal ring in the shape of a flower, a *mise en rose*. The hoop was tightened and the staves brushed with water, then bent in the heat of a fire.

The staves were tightened with a vise and then the monks toasted the interior with lit straw and leaves to lightly singe the inside of the barrel.

Tiny pieces of straw were inserted between the staves to make the barrel watertight. The monks sanded it, drilled a hole in the side, and created panels for the top and bottom. The Cremisan stamp was imprinted on the top panel.

A blessing of the wine took place when the barrel was filled and stored. The monks aged their wine for up to five years. Then the barrels were put on donkey carts and rolled into Bethlehem. It was sold primarily to holy places, including the Church of the Nativity where Jesus was said to have been born.

358

Modern-day scholars say that the cross Jesus carried through Jerusalem was possibly not full-size at all. It was more likely that he would have carried only the crossbeam. The beam alone—five feet long—would have weighed about seventy or eighty pounds. Jesus, who had already been flayed and crowned with thorns, would have hauled the weight toward the hillside at Golgotha, the Place of the Skull, helped out by Simon of Cyrene. At Golgotha, the Romans would have already erected a series of permanent upright stakes in their execution zone. Jesus would have been stripped naked and forced to lie down on the ground with the crossbeam beneath him. His stretched arms would have been bound to the beam with henna rope. The executioner would have taken out two six-inch nails with square heads, three-eighths of an inch wide. He would then have wielded a large mallet to precisely hammer the nails into Jesus's forearm, near the radius and straight through the median nerve. First the left, then the right. The nails would have penetrated his wrists, deep into the crossbeam. The henna rope would then have been undone while Jesus still lay on the ground, his arms stretched and nailed to the beam. The Roman soldiers would then have lifted him up from the ground. They would most likely have used a pulley system and a wooden ladder. Jesus's full weight would have been on the nails as he was hauled upwards. The thick wooden stake would already have been notched and the crossbeam would have been hefted upwards and slotted into place so that he could hang there, suspended on the nails, his arms wide. His hanging feet would have been grabbed by one of the soldiers and pressed together into a U-shaped wooden block attached to the standing stake. His ankles would have been forcibly turned sideways and his knee would have been bent to the side so that his feet aligned. The executioner could then drive another long nail through both of the heels at once, through the flesh, beyond the bone, into the wood. In order to breathe Jesus would have had to force himself to haul his body weight upwards every few seconds until he no longer had the strength to do so anymore and at that point, just a few minutes after three o'clock in the afternoon—*Eloi, Eloi, lama sabachthani*—he would have dropped his head to his chest and suffocated.

357

The tightening, then, of his lungs.

356

The crown of thorns was possibly made of natsch thistle interwoven with other vines. The Roman soldiers would have bent the stems in a circle and braided the pieces together so that they would pierce his scalp as he carried his cross down the Via Dolorosa.

355

In the nineteenth century the Christian women of Bethlehem wore padded hats with heavy coins sewn on. The more coins, the wealthier the family. Their long dresses were stitched with gold and silver thread to create fabulous floral designs, while poorer women embroidered just the breast panels and sleeves.

In the market the shop owners could tell a woman's history as she approached. An entire life could be glimpsed in a matter of yards: if the woman was married, where she lived, her husband's lineage, how many children she had, how many brothers and sisters.

A colorful collision of cross-stitching and couching techniques identified a maiden. A blue thread running at the bottom of the dress indicated a widow. If the widow wanted to marry again, she would weave a line of red through the blue. The dresses incorporated amulets in the shape of triangles to ward off the evil eye.

354

During the First Intifada the women of the West Bank began to weave other symbols into their handmade dresses: maps, rifles, political slogans. The beads they used to ward off the evil eye were green with a black rim and a white dot in the center.

353

In the first century, the most extreme sect of Jewish zealots, the Sicarii, used stealth tactics against the Romans and Herodians. The Sicarii wore long dark cloaks and carried sharp daggers hidden in their flowing robes. They blended in among the crowds at public gatherings in Jerusalem.

As they walked along, they chose their targets, a Roman soldier or an official, even a woman or a child.

The neck was their favorite target, followed by the heart and then the groin and lastly the stomach. They plunged the knife in, snapped it across with a flick of the wrist, hid the blade in the folds of their cloaks, and then dissolved into the crowd, pulled along by the scattering tide.

352

The term *sicario* was adopted by South American drug cartels to describe their hit men in the 1980s and '90s. One of Pablo Escobar's most notorious killers, Jhon Jairo Arias Tascón, alias Pinina, who was accused of being responsible for hundreds of murders in Colombia, is rumored to have had the Latin term *sicarius,* or daggerman, tattooed elaborately in prison ink all down the length of his spine.

351

The cloak was more than decorative: swordmasters taught their pupils how to use it to combat the movement of their opponents' weapons through the agile use of cloth.

350

In the spring of 2014, Sigalit Landau, an artist from Jerusalem, placed a long black dress in the waters of the Dead Sea, suspending the gown in a wooden cage at a depth of fifteen feet.

Landau and her husband left the dress in the water for two months. They took underwater photographs at intervals.

After a week, the jet-black cloth began to attract salt crystals; after two weeks the crystals had begun to cling and accumulate; after three, the cloth appeared silver and grey in the water; after four, the buttons and collar had turned a shining white.

The dress—a replica of one worn for a 1920s theater production about a Hasidic woman who is possessed by the spirit of her dead lover—remained suspended for another four weeks until it sparkled with white crystals like a wedding gown.

When the artist's team went to lift it out of the water, the dress had grown so heavy with salt that they were unable to bring all of it to the surface: pieces of cloth sheared off at the seams and drifted to the sea floor.

349

A smaller version of the dress—what the artist called a princess version—was made as a museum piece, so that when, around the anniversary of Smadar's death, Rami saw a photograph of it in the Bezalel Academy journal, he was so taken aback that he went to his daughter's room where he sat in silence.

348

She would have been thirty years old, a few days from thirty-one.

347

One afternoon, from the second-floor window of his apartment in Anata, Bassam saw Abir out rolling a car tire along the street. A simple child's game. With four other girls her age.

They were happily rolling the black tire from one end of the street to the concrete barricade at the other. It had rained and water had collected in the well of the rubber. Abir was wearing a new dress, blue with a fringed white lace. The tire was small but unwieldy for girls their age. It wobbled so that the standing water in the bottom sloshed around as it was rolled.

Every few seconds Abir and the girls jumped back from the tire to avoid the splashes. When one of the girls got hit with a drop she disappeared for a minute or two, then returned again.

One end of the street to the next. Over and over again. Every few minutes Bassam heard his apartment door open. He listened as Abir went to the basin in the kitchen.

Gradually it dawned on Bassam that she was coming home, time and again, to clean the splotches of dirty water off her dress. Within moments she went out again and joined the game once more, laughing, rolling the tire to the end of the street.

The longer the game went on the less rainwater remained in the well of the tire, so the braver the girls became, leaning in closer and closer, pushing it back and forth, daring each other to see who would get splashed.

When the dirty rainwater was finally gone, they filled the well of the tire again, but the water was cleaner this time and the game fizzled out.

Bassam watched her as she sat on the barricade, in her pale blue dress, swinging her legs back and forth.

346

They came in cars of four or five. Bassam met the convoy at the checkpoint outside Anata. Together they moved through town, a large van at the rear. It was early Sunday and the streets were quiet.

Most of them had never been in Anata before, or if they had, it was only as soldiers. They drove around the back of the graveyard to the school, got out of their cars. Bassam counted them out: thirty-three men and women. A nervous hum rippled among them. They had dressed conservatively—long-sleeved shirts, jeans, hats. No bare arms, no bare legs. No kippahs of course. They gathered in small groups. They avoided Hebrew, spoke in English. They were within breathing distance of the Wall. They chalked the area and drove stakes into the ground. The men worked the jackhammers. The women worked the shovels. Buckets of dirt went back and forth. They put up a mesh wire fence. Laid down the irrigation pipe. They shared bottles of water in the heat. They lifted their heads at the sound of the muezzin. More cars arrived. Bricks were stacked. Mortar was mixed. Post holes were dug.

By the middle of the afternoon the sun had disappeared behind the Wall and the convoy was escorted out of Anata. At the checkpoint the on-duty soldiers stared at them as they left.

The following weekend they returned. The concrete had hardened and the bricks had set. A soft prefabricated rubber flooring emerged from the back of the truck. It was unfurled and carefully cut, spread on the ground. A dump truck arrived with sand. A cheer went amongst them when the pit was filled. Their numbers had swollen to one hundred now: there was so little work now that most of them just watched. The basketball hoop was put in place. The small red slide was bolted down. The spinning cage was tested. A small area of garden, one meter square, was cultivated in order to plant a tree in the rear of the school. Tins of paint were passed back and forth. The plaque was screwed in place: *Abir's Garden*. Another cheer went up. They put their arms around one another. They took photos. They came back the third weekend for the dedication.

All the time a small weather balloon hovered above them about a thousand feet in the air.

345

344

It was the only playground in the town of Anata.

343

After he stopped using the candy bracelet as a prop in lectures anymore, Bassam placed it in a bedside drawer beside a small leather Qur'an and a blue pencil Abir had used for her drawings.

When, years later, he bought the house in Jericho, he noticed that he still had the book and the pencil, but somehow the bracelet had disappeared. He rummaged through the moving boxes, his clothes, his papers, his office materials, but after a while he had to give up searching.

He never found the bracelet: there were times he wondered if it had been swept away or maybe even eaten by one of the other children by mistake.

342

In the mosque near his home in Jericho, where he prays most days, Bassam volunteers to help clean the outside steps. He uses a broom made from natsch thistles. A simple and rhythmic job, the woven strands rake over the coarse stone steps.

As he sweeps, he looks out to the dry land over which the warm wind undulates.

341

The presence of natsch on a plot of land is sometimes thought of as a sign that the soil is not being tilled or used properly.

In Israeli courts, under an interpretation of the Ottoman land law of 1858, the existence of the thistle in rural areas is often used as an argument that the land is not being cultivated and therefore can be declared state land and turned over to settlers.

340

Your Oasis Awaits.

339

The Valley of Fire Road. The Wadi al-Nar Road. The Kidron Valley Road. The Road of the Burning Brakes. The Road of the Boiling Radiator. Hell Road. Tar Road. Dusk Road.

338

After the Nakba of '48, hundreds of Palestinian refugees, many of them from Beit Jala, boarded steamships bound for South America. They landed in Buenos Aires, crossed the mountains by mule and donkey, carrying what they owned across the border into Chile.

Many families settled in Santiago and Valparaíso and found work in the copper mines and the shipyards, but some continued their travels on to the remote areas of the desert.

Over mountains, through canyon lands, along dry riverbeds. A long, arduous journey, with the dead buried along the way. The bodies were often interred in shallow graves beneath piles of rock. Decades later—after General Augusto Pinochet's regime went on its massive killing spree, dumping thousands of bodies all over the country—the mothers of the disappeared, out combing the desert for their own sons and daughters, would come upon random piles of bones.

Sometimes the women were perplexed to find that a key—with Arabic letters scratched on it—still remained on a string at the skeleton's neck or wrist.

337

The key belonging to the door of a house back in what had become, now, Israel.

336

Scrawled in Arabic on a rock on the outskirts of the ghost town of Santa Laura in Chile: *8,276 miles to go.*

335

After the second century Hebrew was deemed to be a holy language and was not spoken as a conversational mother tongue again until Eliezer Ben-Yehuda and others began, in the 1880s, to use it with their families and friends. A pidgin Hebrew was in use in the markets of Jerusalem, but among the Jewish community in Palestine the dominant language was Arabic, along with Ladino, French, Yiddish, and a small scattering of English.

334

333

Ben-Yehuda, like Einstein, said that Jews and Arabs were *mishpacha*, a family, that they should share the land and live together. Many of the new Hebrew words that he helped coin were derived from Arabic roots. The two were, he said, sister languages which, like the people, could live with and alongside one another.

332

The bombs went off near the conjunction of Ben Yehuda and Ben Hilel Streets, also known as Hillel Street, named after Hillel the Elder, author, in the first century before Christ, of the ethic of reciprocity: *That which is hateful to you, do not do to your fellow.*

331

Once, in a fever, Rami dreamed himself installing a microphone in the ground so he could hear all the answers to the questions he had not yet asked Smadar.

330

Smadar liked to play Simon, an electronic game in which four colors light up in bright sequences. Green, red, yellow, blue. The lights were accompanied by a high beeping sound. She practiced it at night in her room in the dark—green, green, red, green, yellow, red, red, blue, green—sometimes bringing the sequence all the way up to twenty or more, so that from outside the house Rami and Nurit, coming home from a walk, were reminded of a small pulsing discotheque.

Smadar was so good at the game that she was able to play two different machines at once.

From her room came a cacophony of beeps.

329

During Christmas of 2009 the music students at the university in Bethlehem wheeled a piano down to the central square where hundreds of people had gathered by the Church of the Nativity to sing Christmas carols.

The piano had been prepared with shell casings, tear gas canisters and stun grenades strategically placed between the strings to alter the sound. On the hammers they had placed thin pieces of metal which gave out a high ping.

The students had learned all the traditional carols. *O Come All Ye Faithful. Silent Night. I Saw Three Ships. Angels We Have Heard on High.* Most of these were sung in Arabic, with occasional English versions.

When the caroling was finished, they wheeled the piano down the hill to the checkpoint near the Wall where they stopped and sang again before being scattered by a cannon firing a yellow mist of foul-smelling Skunk water.

The piano, an old Polish-made Irmler, was abandoned overnight. In the morning the students came to retrieve it. They stuffed their noses with cotton wool as they wheeled the Irmler back up the Hebron Road.

The sound of the trundling piano was recorded by a tall, twenty-six-year-old Palestinian doctoral student, Dalia el-Fahum, who hoped to incorporate it into her dissertation.

328

Among the protesters, the Skunk water acquired the simple nickname of Shit. The smell of Shit was known to linger on the body for at least three days. On clothes it could remain for weeks, even months on end.

One of the few ways to get rid of the smell—something close to a cocktail of rancid meat, raw sewage, and full-blown decomposition—was to take an immediate shower and then bathe with tomato juice to mask the stench.

Some of the demonstrators took to shaving their hair, their beards, their eyebrows. Others bought rain-repellent gear and wore black plastic bags over their shirts, jeans and shoes. They smeared mint vapor rub beneath their noses.

327

In 2012, in the village of Ni'lin, seven young Canadian women—volunteers on a nearby water well project—gathered to protest the use of Skunk. The women wore multicolored rainboots and unfurled white umbrellas with black lettering that read, when lined up together, FUCK YOU.

When they saw the water cannons approaching, they got into position, each on one knee, their faces scarved, the umbrellas held above their heads, glistening lines of vapor rub above their lips.

In images taken at the protest the Canadians were photographed running away, drenched, still under their umbrellas, the letters mixed up so that they read YUCKOFU for a moment and then COKFUYU seconds later.

The photos rocketed around the Internet for days.

326

In the following weeks, outside the Israeli consulate on Bloor Street in Toronto, several young protesters—Israelis and Palestinians both—were seen wearing pink T-shirts with variations scrawled across their chests, YOFUCKU, FUCUKOY. The most popular version, which some suggested was anti-Semitic, read OY U FUCK.

325

The curators of the museum in the Walled Off Hotel tried to purchase one of the original umbrellas to exhibit alongside other artifacts of the Occupation.

The hotel contacted the Canadians only to find out that the umbrellas had been confiscated at Ben Gurion airport where the women were interrogated for three hours before their return to Toronto.

The Canadians had no plans to return to the West Bank—the water project they had been working on had been shut down due to lack of permits.

Other items confiscated from their luggage included a keffiyeh, a Fodor's guide, four bottles of olive oil from the Cremisan monastery, a Palestine-shaped key ring, an empty tear gas canister, an Arabic phrasebook, and numerous perishable food items including a shrink-wrapped tray of kanafeh pastry.

324

The Walled Off, an art hotel set within slingshot distance of Checkpoint 300, was opened by the graffiti artist Banksy in 2017. It stands within yards of the high concrete barriers.

Even the most expensive rooms only get a few minutes of direct winter sunlight each day: the shadow of the Wall is cast down into the rooms and can be tracked as it crosses the carpet.

The maids can tell the time of day by how much of the carpet is shadowed.

323

There were times Bassam would drive past the settlements, and from a distance he would swear they had swollen overnight. He could envision them in time-lapse: they grew redder and wider each time, with roofs and the apartment blocks spreading out, gnawing at the hills, coaxing the desert into form. They were fishlike, swimming.

At night the lights were so extraordinarily bright that it looked as if the towns were breaching upwards. He tried looking away or blocking them with his visor, but there were other settlements on the far side of the road too, smaller ones, feeding, he thought, on the plankton of every small stone.

322

The curators in the Walled Off museum once toyed with the idea of including an olfactory exhibit: visitors would lift a flap marked with a warning and then inhale the scent of Skunk. The staff tested the exhibit and quickly realized it would cause most visitors to the museum to vomit.

321

The manufacturing company Odortec advertises Skunk as the most innovative, effective and non-lethal riot control material available, designed in consultation with the Israeli armed forces and the police. It is made, they say, using local water and food-grade ingredients and it is one hundred percent eco-friendly—harmless to both nature and people.

320

At a major gun show in Tulsa, Oklahoma, in 2015, Irina Cantor, a top executive from Odortec, stood onstage, packed her nose with cotton wool and demonstrated the harmless properties of Skunk by drinking a shot of it.

She raised the shot glass, toasted the crowd and downed the contents without flinching.

—L'chaim, she said before moving backstage to remove the cotton wool from her nose and vomit.

319

Harmless to both nature and people.

318

The door of the Walled Off was swung open by a man in a red bow tie. Bassam stood stunned a moment by the sight of a plastic chimp carrying a suitcase. What was it? he wondered. Some sort of ruse? Some sort of colonial joke?

He bent his head and walked into the dark swell of shadow. His eyes took a moment to adjust. The accents behind the desk were Palestinian. He nodded in their direction. They greeted him back. They wore red waistcoats and starched collars. Some of the waiters were women, he noticed. He heard laughter from afar. Trays of drinks were being carted across the hotel foyer. Music came from the piano but there was no player. Bassam could hardly move. He felt as if his feet were rooted in tar.

Everything rattled him. The cameras on the walls, the slingshots, the paintings, the large sofa with a snakehead insignia. He wasn't sure which way he should turn. It struck him as more Beirut than Bethlehem. He fumbled for his phone. No messages. He peered around the foyer. White teapots on the table. China cups. Ice in tall glasses. Small groups of three and four. Men in shorts, women in low-cut dresses. Sunglasses. Some sounded English, some German, but no Italians: he was here to meet a crew from Naples, it had been arranged for weeks.

Moments like these, they froze him: he always preferred the periphery. So many years in a jail cell had taught him that.

Bassam interrogated himself for cigarettes, patted his shirt, removed the box from his breast pocket.

He could smell smoke drifting from outside. At least there was that: he could smoke. He moved through the room. Perhaps he had the time wrong? He flicked a look again at the mobile phone. Three in the afternoon. On time.

A waiter asked in English if he needed help. He replied in Arabic that he was just fine.

The lobby seemed to him like some sort of preposterous movie set. Cherubs hung from the ceiling, plastic gas masks attached to them. He stood under one and observed it. From the corner of his eye he caught a small red light, a camera perhaps. He tapped the bottom of his cigarette pack. A curtain billowed. There were tables outside. Two of them were full, but the third—no more than a few yards from the Wall—was empty.

Bassam shifted the chair, sat in the shadow of the Wall. He lit up, waited, checked his phone again, caught sight of another red light moving inside the foyer. He tried to recall what had been here before. He had driven past many times. A bakery, perhaps. Or a pottery shop. He wasn't sure how to feel about the hotel—on one hand it seemed ludicrous, on the other so necessary. At the core of it all was the need to draw attention. There were rumors of settlers trying to move into nearby houses and buildings.

The waiter arrived and spoke, this time, in Arabic. It surprised Bassam, the new politeness, the smile.

—Have you seen a film crew? he asked.

—No.

—Italians. They're supposed to be here at three.

—They're all Italians, said the waiter.

—Pardon me?

—They're all Italians. Especially the English.

Bassam laughed, sat back, lit a new cigarette.

—The Swedish too, said the waiter.

Bassam was halfway through his Fanta when a curtain of hair fell over the table. The woman was tall, dark-haired, clear-eyed. Her teeth were slightly lipsticked. She pointed from the ground-floor balcony into the hotel. Another small red light emerged from the shadows. So, he realized, they had been filming him all along. No matter. What should he expect? He had grown accustomed to it, the constant positioning, the jockeying, the angles. He was a creature, now, of the camera, whether he liked it or not.

They had already set up in a room upstairs. A huge portrait of a pillow fight was drawn on the wall: an Israeli, a Palestinian, hitting each other with feathers flying. He had seen the work before: he was repulsed by it. But it was exactly the repulsion, he knew, that made it work. The simplicity, the absurdity, the brazen surprise. To hold these opposite things.

—We'll have you sit under the painting, she suggested.

Bassam shook his head, went across to the window, opened it, sat on the window ledge. He knew that the angle worked for them: a Palestinian sitting in a window of a hotel overlooking the Wall.

The interview lasted twenty-five minutes: he felt sure they would cut it down to a matter of seconds. So be it. It didn't bother him. He wanted, quite simply, to tell the story. *My name is Bassam Aramin. I am the father of Abir.* They went walking afterwards, five of them together, along the Wall. The crew were eager to get Bassam to pass alongside a portrait of the Italian activist Vittorio Arrigoni. It was so often this way: they wanted Bassam to fit into their box of ideas. And yet he had agreed to meet them. He had arrived on time. His story was his duty and his curse.

Still, what he really wanted to do now was to disappear, unfilmed, back to his car, go home, close the windows, be silent alongside Salwa.

He shook the hand of the interviewer, thanked the crew. He knew that they were filming him as he walked away. He put his hands deep in his pockets, kept his head raised: he hoped they wouldn't showcase the limp.

He passed the portrait of the young girl that Rami had once mistaken for Abir. He glanced at it from the corner of his eye. The likeness was remarkably close.

He didn't linger.

317

316

He saw her one afternoon walking home alone from school. She played a child's game, trying to move in and out of her own shadow. Normally he would have picked her up and given her a lift, but there was something about her that day, the flick of the foot, the arc of the head, that made him hold back and just watch. He kept the car in first gear and remained close to the curb. Her schoolbag swung.

She ran the final portion of the hill up the broken staircase toward the apartment block until he saw her uniform disappearing behind the grey wall.

315

Anata School for Girls, Anata. Spring Report 2006.
Abir Aramin.
Age: 9. Grade 4.

Arabic: Excellent.
Writing: Very Good.
Mathematics: Excellent.
Music Studies: Excellent.
Physical Education: Very Good.
Religious Studies: Excellent.
English Language: Very excellent.

General Comments: Abir does excellently all across the board. She is a model student in all classes.

Participation: Excellent.

Appearance: Clean, tidy, dress neat, fingernails good.
Attention to detail, excellent.

Lateness: 1 (excused)
Absences: 0

314

Afterwards neither he nor Salwa could recall the one lateness: if anything, Abir was perpetually early. They wondered if she had come upon an army patrol on her way to school and was stopped, but, if so, they would most likely have heard about it from Areen: they nearly always walked to school together.

Areen too could not recall any morning when her younger sister had been delayed. On Areen's card there were no latenesses. Perhaps it was just a simple mistake?

They should ask her teacher, said Salwa. But there was something about the question that Bassam wanted to hold on to, the small mystery that he could return to again and again, some form of her, at nine years of age, standing outside the school gates, perhaps to help another student, or to pet a stray dog, or to be intrigued by a cloud, or some other question that would keep her dawdling along the road.

313

When they finally moved to the house in Jericho, they packed up their car, hefted their belongings down the steps, and filled a trailer with clothes and furniture. On the way out they avoided the road where Abir had been shot.

312

Always for Bassam there was the thought of the near-miss: the bullet just one foot higher in the air and Abir would have been running down the street, the candy bracelet in her bag, the missile skittering on the ground far ahead of her, the multiplication tables still rattling around in her head.

311

The tiny swimming pool at the back of Bassam's house in Jericho holds one thousand two hundred gallons. He fills it only twice a year: once at the start of school holidays, again towards the middle of summer.

310

In his lectures Rami told the audience that there wasn't a minute of his waking life—not a single minute—that he did not dwell on Smadar. He knew the idea must have sounded exaggerated to his listeners— nineteen years, every minute of the day—but every now and then another parent would come along, or a brother, or an aunt, and he would look at them and recognize the grief carried within them like clocks.

309

308

She seemed to forget her body for hours at a time. After her dance classes she would lie in the living room, reading, the book on the floor, her head hanging over the edge of the couch, abandoning herself to gravity. As if she were contemplating some abstract problem.

The longer she read, the more she shifted and the less her body relied on the couch, until she was practically upside down, almost perpendicular to the furniture.

Rami took a photo of her one afternoon when she was twelve years old, her hair still long so that it splayed in a fan on the floor, obscuring the book in front of her. She had propped herself on her elbows and her feet were extended in the air. Only her hips and thighs were reliant on the couch.

When Rami clicked the shutter button she mischievously arched her head and her hair—soon to be cut short—flipped acrobatically in a dolphin move which later would surface and resurface in his mind.

307

One afternoon, home from her swimming lessons, Rami tried to get Smadar to towel her hair, and she said to him: I'm not some little kid, you know, I'm eleven.

306

At thirteen, she had just begun to take a shine to boys. Rami noticed it first at the swimming pool. He could see it in the way she held herself at the back of the diving boards. She stayed a little closer to the wall, consulted her flip-flops. A little more shy, self-aware.

She flicked her eyes across the pool to where the boys were stretching.

In bed at night he and Nurit read together, chatted. Nurit had spotted a love heart scrawled inside the back of one of Smadar's notebooks. At the bottom of the heart Smadar had written out a poem or a lyric in Hebrew that she didn't recognize.

—What was it?

—Can't remember.

—You're useless, he chuckled.

He crawled out of bed, tucked his feet into his slippers, stood. He came back moments later with the notebook in his hand, stood at the end of the bed and flourished it.

He leafed through the notebook: it was regular schoolwork. Her handwriting was large and spidery. In the inside back cover he found the small love heart drawn with red marker. Inside the heart it said: *Smadar and Zev.*

—Who's Zev?

—He's in the school jazz club.

—What's he like?

—A nice kid I think.

At the bottom of the heart, where it dipped to a point, Smadar had written: *All the flowers you planted in the backyard died when you went away.*

—That's cute, said Nurit.

—Cute?

—What's wrong with it?

—Shotgun time.

—Oh shut up, she laughed.

Rami flipped the notebook to the end of the bed, kicked his feet out of the slippers.

—Put the book back in her bag, said Nurit, and come here.

305

Prince recorded the first version of *Nothing Compares 2 U* in Flying Cloud Drive Warehouse, a makeshift rehearsal space just off a two-lane highway in Eden Prairie, Minnesota. The studio was small, wood-paneled, badly insulated. The sound of traffic could be heard from outside.

304

Prince sprinkled lines from the Song of Solomon on various tracks on his fifteenth album, *Come*. The lines, originally written for the song *Poem*, took bits and pieces of the original, shaped them and reshaped them on tracks like *Pheromone* where he sings about his left hand under a lover's head while his right embraces time.

303

That afternoon, on Ben Yehuda Street, she wore a pair of black jeans, a Blondie T-shirt, Doc Martens, and a simple gold necklace.

302

English: 89, Good/Very Good. Cheery demeanor, a pleasure to have in class. Needs to work on punctuality. Still grasping contents of conditional tense, though shows mastery in others. Displays aptitude for Literature Seminar next semester.

Religious Knowledge: 59, Poor/Fair. Often distracted in class. Needs encouragement at home, particularly with Torah studies.

Social Studies: 80, Good. River/pollution report excellent (needs to understand principles of annotation). Is inquisitive and logical. Cheerful. Could focus more. Might benefit from being separated from her friends in classroom. Homework assignments occasionally late. Smadar is not afraid of expressing her opinion in class.

Mathematics: 68, Fair. Strong aptitude for high concepts but sorely lacking in principles of organization and discipline (is often seen fiddling with her Walkman).

Geography: 82, Very Good. An unusual sense of history gives Smadar's geographic endeavors a twist, especially in relation to Greater Israel. Her paper on natural geographic features was the best in class.

Hebrew: 96, Excellent. Engages quickly. High aspirations. Exemplary paper on Elisha Porat.

Physical Education: 95, Excellent. Distractible, but excels in dance, particularly jazz and freestyle. (Credit also given for outside swim team participation.)

301

Smadar's face was left perfectly intact. The shrapnel sprayed the lower part of her body, mostly her back and shoulders and legs. In forensic analysis it was determined that she was relatively close to the bomber when she was hit. Most likely, said the scientists, she had her back turned and she did not see his face, though it was also possible that she was already running away with her head bowed.

300

Bamboo shoots surrounded by gunpowder, known as thunderclap bombs, were developed in the eleventh century during the Song dynasty. The heated air inside the bamboo exploded and caused a thunderous racket.

Two hundred years later the Chinese began loading their bombs with tiny shards of broken porcelain and pieces of scrap iron, hooks and caltrops, that shot out in every direction: they were known as thundercrash bombs.

The technique was rediscovered in 1784 by Henry Shrapnel, a lieutenant in the British Royal Artillery, who filled a hollow cannonball with spheres of lead to wreak maximum damage.

The shrapnel method has been used down through the years with glass shards, razors, marbles, arrowheads, nails, screws, chain links, staples, pins, rivets, ball bearings and other sundry items.

During the Second Intifada, claims were made that Palestinian bombers laced their shrapnel with rat poison, or warfarin, to make the victims bleed out quicker, though the claim was ridiculed and later dismissed since, firstly, the amount of poison needed would be enormous; secondly, its effects would not be instantaneous; and lastly it would be rendered mostly ineffective by the tremendous heat of the blast.

299

After the bombing Rami took long and frequent showers so Nurit couldn't hear the sound of his sobbing.

298

He was sure that Smadar would have been a member of the Machsom Watch, the Israeli women who monitored the checkpoints. She would have gone every Friday. To Qalandia. Or Checkpoint 300. Or Atara. He could imagine her walking around, hair in a short bob, black blouse, black jeans, black boots with deep red laces.

297

Women in Black, an Israeli human rights group, was founded in Jerusalem in 1988—nine years before Smadar was killed—following the outbreak of the First Intifada. The women stood at intersections and traffic lights and in central squares, wearing dark clothing head to toe, carrying signs with the image of a black hand with white lettering: *Stop the Occupation.*

296

Chromesthesia is a perceptual phenomenon in which sounds automatically evoke the experience of a color. For those with the condition, music is seen as much as it is heard. A high-pitched sound suggests brightness. A low-pitched sound suggests something of a darker tone.

The first recorded instance of chromesthesia comes from the English philosopher John Locke, who, in his *Essay Concerning Human Understanding*, wrote about a blind man. When asked what the color scarlet was, the blind man replied that it was akin to the sound of a trumpet.

295

Abir tried to learn to play the oud when she was eight. She had found the instrument propped up against a garbage can near her school in Anata. She carried it home and brought it straight to her room. The neck of the oud was cracked and it gave out a low-pitched whine, but Bassam repaired it as best he could with glue and wood filler.

He installed his old record player in her room and gave her a 45-rpm record by Farid al-Atrash. When Abir first heard it she turned up her nose and said to him: Baba, that sounds like old people music.

294

Flower of my imagination, I guarded her in my heart.

293

Women in White, Las Damas de Blanco, were formed in 2003 to protest the imprisonment in Cuba of lawyers, students, journalists and intellectuals. The women met each Sunday at the Santa Rita de Casia church in Havana, with photographs of their jailed loved ones pinned to their chests. They were inspired, they said, by the mothers of the disappeared in Chile and the Mothers of the Plaza de Mayo in Argentina too.

The Damas de Blanco group was awarded the Sakharov Prize for Freedom of Thought, given by the European parliament, in 2005, although their government prohibited them from attending the ceremony.

292

Smadar went to Paris Square in Jerusalem with Nurit to join the protesting women. Nine years old, she had no proper black shoes and wore, instead, a pair of ballet slippers which she darkened with polish. She stood at the intersection, alongside Judy Blanc, an older activist. Together they held a sign aloft: *End the Occupation*. Neither flinched when a car full of dark-hatted settlers threw a carton of popcorn at their feet.

291

Nurit was awarded the Sakharov Prize in 2001. She and Rami traveled to Strasbourg to receive the award for her writing. She wore a purple satin dress and carried, in her handbag, a picture of Smadar.

She was given the award alongside Izzat Ghazzawi, a Palestinian writer and teacher. Ghazzawi's son—also named Rami—had been shot dead in his schoolyard by Israeli snipers at the age of sixteen.

290

On the eighth anniversary of his son's death, Ghazzawi wrote in his diary: *Only madness drove us to celebrate your 24th birthday. The cake was as big as the man who will not come. Nobody ate from it. As though it were a gift to silence.*

289

When Nurit stood at the podium she asked them please not to applaud.

288

After winning the Sakharov Prize, Ghazzawi went about his teaching duties at Birzeit University, but was arrested numerous times for political incitement.

He was stopped several mornings a week at the Atara checkpoint where he underwent strip searches in front of his college students.

Two years after the award, Nurit heard that he had died of a broken spirit.

287

Forgive us our longing, Ghazzawi wrote, *if it intensifies.*

286

When Checkpoint 300 first went up, in 1994, it was a simple wooden hut with a couple of orange barrels placed in the middle of the road. The barrels were filled with stones. A radio played. A flag fluttered. A few soldiers stood guard.

Bassam could recall when a flock of birds could easily shadow the whole area.

After a year, the barrels were replaced with concrete blocks. A road barrier was added, then some fences, then some barbed wire, then a temporary structure, then a large steel tower.

In 2005 the area was incorporated into the Separation Barrier and the checkpoint became one of the largest in the West Bank, topped along its length with glass and razor wire.

285

In the winter of 2008, Dalia el-Fahum began cycling from Bethlehem to parts of the Kidron Valley, collecting sounds of the natural environment for her ongoing dissertation.

Dalia was an unusual sight in Bethlehem—six foot two, her dark hair drawn back in a tight chignon, a silver badger streak at her brow.

She traveled, in a headscarf and modest Western clothes, out from the edges of the city into the dry hills beyond the valley, often cycling twenty or more miles in a single day.

Dalia was sometimes stopped by patrols. When chatting with the police, she slightly bent her knees and stooped over so as not to appear too tall or intimidating. She explained she was taping sounds in the hills for a music project. The soldiers asked her to hit the play button. A rush of water, the bark of a wild dog, the sound of wind through the natsch, the applause of birds flying overhead.

Twice the police dismantled her recorder and once it was taken from her altogether by an officer who sheepishly returned it to her father's village home later that night, minus its batteries.

284

283

Dalia's project concerned the work of the composer Olivier Messiaen, a Parisian organist and friend of John Cage's, who had incorporated birdsong into much of his music. In particular Dalia wanted to take Messiaen's *Catalogue d'Oiseaux* for solo piano and meld her own West Bank sounds with it, creating an electronic version that she would then extend into a slow eight-hour piece that she wanted to call *Migration*.

One morning, towards the middle of her project, in a village eight miles outside Bethlehem, Dalia heard pre-dawn bulldozers interrupting the quiet. She had noticed the machinery before, and had seen the strobe lights down near the main road, but never quite so close.

Through the bushes she could see the army plowing up a grove of olive trees. The sun caught the silvery sheen of the branches. They flashed as they were yanked from the ground.

Dalia crawled on her belly, moved closer to the sounds and—from a distance of fifty meters—held out the microphone of her Sony digital recorder, and began to tape.

282

Using laser-powered microphones, scientists in Germany determined that plants and trees release gases when they perceive themselves to be under attack. These gases, in turn, produce sound waves that register on a level inaudible to anything but the most sensitive machines.

The scientists, at the Institute of Applied Physics at the University of Bonn, suggested that flowers emit a whine when their leaves are cut, and that trees can warn each other of approaching swarms of insects, and that the scent of fresh-cut grass comes from a secretion system within the grass blades.

The team built on previous research findings that neurotransmitters such as dopamine and serotonin can be found in plants, though there was no evidence of neurons or synapses within their sensory systems.

281

In the jargon of radio operators in the Israeli army, a *flower* is someone who has been seriously wounded in battle.

280

In a 1940 essay G. H. Hardy wrote: *The mathematician's patterns, like the painter's or the poet's, must be beautiful; the ideas, like the colors or the words, must fit together in a harmonious way. Beauty is the first test: there is no permanent place in the world for ugly mathematics.*

279

At a conference in Greece, Bassam told the audience that they had to understand that the olive tree was everything to the Palestinian mind. Uprooting an ancient tree, he said to them, was tantamount to smashing a precious artifact in a museum. Take a Cézanne and put your fist through it. Allow a Brâncuși to melt under tremendous heat. Lift a Grecian urn and poke it full of holes.

278

His father had operated an olive press in a barn on the edge of the village of Sa'ir, near the cave where Bassam grew up. Inside, a white horse circled around and around by the light of an oil lamp. The horse—blindfolded so as not to grow dizzy—turned the wooden beam, causing a circular stone to grind against another stone, crushing the olives, releasing the oil.

What Bassam couldn't understand, as a child, was how the horse could keep circling all day without falling down, exhausted. It wasn't until he was six years old that he realized that there were three identical white horses rotating through.

Two years later, an electric press was introduced and the horses were put out into the stony field where they spent the rest of their days moving, still, in endless circles.

277

One of his favorite prison songs: *Give my greetings to the olive and the family that brought me up.*

276

When Dalia listened to her tapes later, alone in the recording studio at the university, she thought it a much softer sound than she recalled from the hillside. An animal purr to it, filtering upwards along the slope, nothing mechanical.

She was disappointed by its neutrality, having hoped that there would be something more brutal there, the rip of the earth, the tear of roots, the flop of the dirt: as if she might have been able to hear a ghostly groan from the trees themselves.

She went back and forth on the mixer controls, trying to isolate the harshest spots where the engines grew throatier. She tried to isolate the shout of a soldier, the wail of a siren, the beeping of the reversing bulldozers, but isolating the sounds made them particular, even comic. The music, when she tried to mix it, struck her as pathetic.

She went back to her raw recordings. The interlaced call of a cuckoo. The noise of a mouse in the underbrush. The sound, too, of her own movement through the grass.

Some music existed here, she felt. Perhaps she could use the sounds, punctuate them with some of the older birdsong she had taped, but the more she thought about it, the more convinced she was that the sound was something to leave alone, that it was not the bulldozers nor the olive trees nor the buzzing strobe lights that needed attention, but the quietness itself.

275

She was also drawn to the sound of the rain clicking upon the olive leaves.

274

One of the things Rami's son, Elik, learned early on in his training as a paratrooper was the special discipline needed to carry water. On long desert marches not even the slightest noise was permitted. His water canteen had to be filled to the very brim and covered with a small piece of plastic wrap before being sealed. If his canteen was even partly empty, the water would slosh around and possibly alert a nearby enemy.

When opened, the water had to be drunk in its entirety to prevent any further sound. Choosing the right moment to drink was key to avoiding dehydration. Elik knew that one early sign of dehydration was a very slight blurring of the vision.

The soldiers worked in tandem, but sometimes they were sent out alone on training exercises with just a single canteen for an eighteen-mile march.

Elik's commander also insisted that food be taken with the water in case the liquid began to bounce against the walls of the stomach.

273

In times of drought it was the practice of the ancient water carriers to travel to distant sources and fill large containers made out of buffalo hide. They carried the supplies from the oases by ox-drawn cart.

Upon visiting a village or a town they went to the wealthy residents first, and filled the barrels in their basements and courtyards. Afterwards the poorer villagers lined up to fill up their clay jars.

The business was brisk and the carriers often became quite wealthy.

272

The Greek word *clepsydra*, given to ancient water clocks, comes from the amalgamation of the Greek words for *water* and *to steal*.

271

In the West Bank an arrangement was made by Mekorot, the Israeli national water company, to make the price for settlers as cheap as possible.

Palestinians paid up to four times the price. Privately the water executives called the deal the Swimming Pool Clause.

270

One afternoon on a visit to her publishers in Tel Aviv, Nurit had a fender bender at a traffic light on King George Street, near Meir Garden.

She had leaned across to adjust a briefcase full of papers in the passenger seat. She popped the clutch by mistake. Her car lurched forward and dented the bumper of a metallic blue Mercedes in front of her.

A tall middle-aged man stepped casually out. He wore a crisp white open-neck shirt and a slim blue suit. A curl of unlikely hair flopped down over his eyes.

He surprised her with a smile: Don't worry about it, he said, I'll take care of it.

—Not at all, it's my fault.

—I can get it fixed, he said, don't worry, seriously, here's my card.

—No, no, that's—

—Nothing to worry about, I'll pay for it.

He bowed slightly. Nurit flipped the card over in her hand. She recognized the logo right away, the blue circle, the white background, the water tower: he was a vice president of Mekorot.

She watched him climb back into his car. He adjusted his rearview mirror and pulled out quickly into the traffic. Nurit stood there a moment until the other cars behind her blared their horns.

The following morning she wrote a check for six hundred shekels for the damage, then wrapped a copy of her book in plain paper, and sent both by messenger to his office.

269

Palestine in Israeli School Books: Ideology and Propaganda in Education, by Nurit Peled-Elhanan (I.B. Tauris & Co. Ltd., London, New York, 2012). Introduction: A Jewish Ethnocracy in the Middle East. 1: The Representation of Palestinians in Israeli School Books. 2: The Geography of Hostility and Inclusion: A Multimodal Analysis. 3: Layout as Carrier of Meaning: Explicit and Implicit Messages Transmitted Through Layout. 4: Processes of Legitimation in Reports about Massacres. ISBN #: 978 1 78076 505 1. Reprinted 2013, 2015.

268

Mekorot: meaning the sources.

267

Two weeks later Rami found her at home at the kitchen table, chin on her hand, her bank statement in front of her: Well, she laughed, you won't believe it, but the asshole actually cashed the check.

266

Nurit got hate mail at the university. Some of it arrived on notes neatly folded in tiny phylactery boxes. Others were messages on her answering machine. The worst of it called her a Jewrab, a traitor, a whore, a mother of refuseniks. She kept the mail in an untidy stack on the shelf behind her office desk. She read it once and only once.

265

She wanted to write back and say that her grandfather was a signatory of Israel's Declaration of Independence, that her father had fought as a general in the Six-Day War, that her husband had fought in three of Israel's wars, that her sons had made their own decisions about military service, that her own daughter could have served too if she had been given a chance, which she wasn't, through no fault of her own, or maybe if the truth be told it was the fault of the Israeli government leaders who were the actual murderers, and while these things did not necessarily make her proud—in fact she felt sure that her daughter might have refused service or would, at the very least, have joined a medical unit—they had occurred in the unfolding of her country's history, a future for which she no longer held out much hope, though once when young she had dreamed she could be part of a vast mosaic, Jew Christian Muslim Atheist Other Buddhist, call it what you will, a country that would be complicated, nuanced, democratic, visionary, a place where the idea of hate letters, like those which continued to arrive on her desk, would be anathema to the patriotic imagination, the idea of patriotism applying not necessarily to a country or a nation, but to a state of being which could only rightfully be called human, although she was prepared to acknowledge, given history in general, but especially that of the modern Israeli state, that the desire itself had almost become preposterous, and yet the only way to fight against the inanity was to speak out against it in the vain hope that one might be heard, most especially at learning institutions where minds were still pliable and the poison had not, or at least not yet, penetrated the consciousness.

264

Her classes at Hebrew University were among the most popular, filling up seconds after registration. They were also the most reviled, especially amongst those who did not attend.

263

Dalia el-Fahum's album, *Migrations*, was due for release by a small music company in Ramallah in 2009. It was to consist entirely of natural sounds. In her diary she wrote that she had decided not to include the sound of the trundling piano, or the bulldozers in the olive grove, or any other moment that might have suggested anything urban or machine-related.

She acknowledged the irony of using a machine to capture the sounds, but she said she wanted to find a place within the sounds where nobody could find her.

262

Her last known location was her office in the university. Surveillance footage tracked her, in headscarf and jeans, to the steps of the Science building where she had parked her bicycle, an old Mandate-era Raleigh.

She cycled out of frame, wearing a light backpack. It was early evening but she used both front and back dynamo lights on her bicycle. It was not determined where she went from there but it was assumed that, since she did not go home, she may have traveled past the outskirts of the city in order to tape a series of night sounds.

Dalia had written in her diary that she was still missing a nocturnal element to her album. She was especially interested in capturing the noise of hyenas and wild dogs: for her they represented a note which she hadn't yet caught. She could have captured these sounds during the day, but there was something about the way they carried at night that fascinated her.

Her father reported her missing that very evening, but the Palestinian police didn't begin searching for three days by which time a number of rumors had begun swirling around her: she had been arrested and taken by the IDF, she had run away to pursue a romantic relationship with an Israeli music engineer, she was part of a secret underground terror ring, she had been seen on a bus to Ramallah.

The rumors gathered pace, most especially the idea that she had been picked up by the military and was being questioned at a secret location in the Negev. She had, after all, some students said, taped the destruction of the olive grove and it was possible that someone had informed on her.

Two weeks later, a cousin of Dalia's, out exploring in the desert, came home with a shattered headlamp from an old bicycle. He had found it, he said, in an isolated spot near a wadi. From its shape and size it was determined to be part of an old Raleigh.

Several search groups were sent out to look for other parts of the bike, the frame of which was eventually found half a mile further into the desert, with one wheel stuck in a mudbank. A shoe was found nearby.

The search intensified. Lacking helicopters, the Palestinian Authority police joined with the Israeli army in an effort to locate the body which they now assumed had been caught in a flash flood.

The searchers used unmanned aircraft and infrared equipment and even sent out a team of elite Bedouin trackers. Caves were explored and fresh mudbanks dug. Another shoe was found almost two miles further down the Kidron Valley. It was impossible to determine what had happened to her body in the rushing water.

A concert was held on the bank of the wadi, all of Dalia's friends from university, gathered around, performing on various instruments, including the oud.

260

Dalia's *Migration* album was never finished or released. Several students in Bethlehem University, along with two music producers, said they would be happy to help try to complete the project, but Dalia's mother—convinced that her daughter would still come home, that she was out wandering the desert somewhere, lost or concussed—refused to let anyone near her daughter's room. Her father, too, refused access to her computer files.

They were convinced Dalia would walk through the door, her backpack on, her dark hair pulled back in a chignon, a bicycle pump in her hand.

259

Dalia's body was never found.

258

Rami followed a water truck one afternoon with a Dutch film crew. He had volunteered to help them out. They had picked up the truck in Beit Sahour as it went from house to house. They stayed behind the vehicle as it labored up the hill between houses, unfurling a thick black hose at each stop.

Within twenty minutes they heard the screech of tires behind them on the steep laneways. Two jeeps. Palestinian Authority forces. Four policemen in blue shirts stepped out.

Rami's heart vaulted. Perhaps he had made a mistake this time around. He was in Area A. He was without Bassam. He had his Israeli I.D. They would find it if they searched him. They could turn him over to the Israeli forces. They could make a spectacle of him. Even jail him if they wanted to.

There were three others in the car: a producer, a soundman, a cameraman. Rami sat in the back seat.

The smallest policeman came to the front window with a lazy disdain. He leaned in, more menacing for his smallness. He spoke in perfect English. Who were they? What did they want? Did they have a permit to film?

—Out of the car, said the policeman.

Rami tugged the door handle, stepped out onto the cobbles.

Some children had gathered to watch. It was something Rami had noticed about the West Bank. Most of the men stayed away or hovered at a distance. The younger women too. But the children sidled right up to them.

He made his hands as visible as possible. He had learned this from Bassam. They went to the producer first, quizzed him, lazed over his passport. The cameraman. The soundman.

A tremble lay at the pit of Rami's stomach.

Was there anything that made him stand out as Israeli? He hadn't even thought of it that morning. Here he was, in long trousers and an open-neck shirt. He should have worn shorts like the cameraman. Only foreigners in the West Bank wore shorts. It could have been a form of disguise. He had grown too complacent. His vanity. The need to be seen. The need to dispute. Perhaps he could fake a Dutch accent, he thought. Something sharp, guttural.

—Passport please.

—I'm from Amsterdam, he said in Arabic, I came here from Amsterdam.

He had been learning the language for years now, sometimes listening to it on his earphones while he rode the motorbike.

The policeman wheeled around to his colleagues: This one thinks he speaks Arabic.

They gathered in a small ring of dark blue. Rami could hear them laugh.

They remained twenty minutes in the street until the policeman flicked his hand and told them they were free to go, any direction they wanted. Just no more filming of the water truck: they should know better than that. Go. If they wanted to know something about water, he said, they should ask the sky.

257

The only line of Rami's that made it into the eventual documentary was that Smadar was, like the rest of us, sixty percent water: an offhand comment he had given as they drove through the streets of Bethlehem.

256

As much as possible Bassam always travels with a clean car, making it easier at the checkpoints if he is stopped: his jacket neatly folded in the front seat, no large bags in the trunk, no plastic containers, everything arranged so that a soldier can quickly glance inside and send him on his way.

255

Just beyond the traffic circle, a series of red lights flare in the dark.

254

The Container Checkpoint—named for a small grocery store that was once housed in a shipping container at the side of the road—is an internal checkpoint, separating one area of the West Bank from the other, so that when it is closed down, the West Bank is sliced in two.

253

He scrunches through the gears. Only seven or eight cars ahead of him. He immediately cuts the headlights. Parking lights only. Both hands high on the steering wheel. Perhaps they will not have noticed the blown lamp. He must, he thinks, have looked like a motorbike approaching. He leaves enough distance between himself and the car in front. Always a good idea not to nudge too close.

He powers down the window with his elbow and reaches deliberately for the cigarettes on the dash, places the box on the rim of the steering wheel. All part of the intricacy. He flips the lid with his thumb, making sure both hands are still visible. He mouths the cigarette out of the package. The little flash of flame might give them pause, but he has heard somewhere that a smoking man is seldom guilty.

Around the watchtower, the shadows of the soldiers stretch back and forth.

He blows the smoke sideways out the window, waits for the slow and painful theater to play out. The front car moves and then the second jolts forward. Sometimes he thinks he can tell the age of the driver just by the way they pull into position. He has seen it all: the furious forward jump, the slow roll, the humiliated pause, the Fred Flintstone move on an incline with the foot out the open door.

In its dashboard holder the cellphone flashes. A message from Rami: *Home, brother. See you tomorrow.*

No response yet from Salwa.

Six cars. Five. Four. The faces of the soldiers come into clearer focus as he inches along. He guides the car over the spike strips into the laneway. They are always so startlingly young: seventeen, eighteen, nineteen years old.

He drops the cigarette perfectly into the open ashtray, nudges it shut with his knee. Best not to throw the cigarette out the window. They might take that as some sort of provocation.

Three guards circle the lead car now: two boys, one girl, her ponytail jumping behind her.

The hood of the front car springs open. With the barrel of her gun, the young girl waves the driver out. He is mid-twenties, thin, white T-shirt, gold chain, his hair shining. The two male soldiers spread-eagle him against the car. Legs wide, hands against the windows. The men run the barrels of their guns up along the inside of his legs with one final flick at the crotch. The driver flinches, turns his shoulder, coils his body. The soldier presses a palm hard between the driver's shoulder blades and thrusts him up against the window of the car, spreads the man's legs a little wider.

This will take a while now, thinks Bassam. He considers a second cigarette, decides against it.

It is late enough now that Salwa will be getting ready for bed. He should message her again. *All is well. Go to bed. I'll be back soon.*

The driver looks from one soldier to the other, waits for a nod, then reaches into the trunk. The three guns are trained on him now. The driver pulls out a large blue plastic bottle. Mistake number one: having anything at all in the trunk. Mistake number two: the writing is in Arabic. Slowly the driver unscrews the lid, then holds the bottle out to the tallest soldier as if to get him to verify the fragrance.

Anything can happen now: they can knock the bottle from his hands, they can spill the contents at his feet, they can take him in for questioning, close the checkpoint, freeze all movement for the next few hours. Or they can affirm the smell of the detergent, rescrew the cap, let him go.

The driver flicks a far-off look towards the line of cars: he appears for a moment like an angry sailor looking out to sea.

The soldiers consult the driver's I.D., and then with a simple nod of the girl's head, the driver's day is ruined. His shoulders slump. No point in protest. He screws the cap on the bottle, shuffles forward, climbs into his car.

A gate is opened to the side of the laneway, and the driver—with two guns trained on him—is guided into the bay for a further search.

252

There will, habibi, be no laundering of clothes tonight.

251

In 2004, revolving turnstiles were installed at the pedestrian checkpoints of the West Bank so that sequenced lines of people would be able to get through.

Soldiers—perched in offices behind darkened glass—regulate the speed of passage using electronic controls. Every few seconds the turnstiles are stopped and the pedestrians remain caged in long metal chutes, barred at the top, for as long as the soldiers deem necessary.

The technology used at checkpoints is so sensitive that even the faintest of whispers can be recorded. Cameras are set to look along the length of the chutes.

After the installation of the turnstiles, the contractors found that if they changed the length between the metal arms from the standard 75–90 centimeters down to 55 centimeters, the turnstiles could press against the pedestrian's body to ensure that there was nothing hidden underneath their clothing.

The narrow spaces proved to be especially difficult for pregnant women trying to get to the other side.

250

In the winter of 2012 a young Israeli soldier from Unit 8200, a crack computer unit, downloaded a whole day of conversations from Checkpoint 300.

She wasn't quite sure what to do with the recordings but she put them on a flash drive and gave them to her boyfriend, an aspiring rap artist from Tel Aviv.

Her boyfriend brought the recordings to a studio and sampled them, tried to make them into a protest song, *Lift Your Fucking Shirt Asshole*, looping the vocal samples and using a snare drum, until his girlfriend realized that if the song were released she might be liable for stealing government material.

She destroyed the file, but a year later, after they broke up, he sent a duplicate set of the recordings to a Palestinian DJ in the student radio station at Birzeit University.

249

What's your problem? Step behind the line, please. Not my decision. Whose wedding is it? Her fever's one hundred and three. I came through an hour ago. I promise I won't. Speak up, I can't hear you. Lift it. Your undershirt too, asshole. How long have you been working there? Step behind the line. Not without a permit. My classes start at nine. Back please back. Take off your veil. Door on the left. Next on line. It's out of date, sorry. Next on line. [Unintelligible] watermelon. Next on line, hurry up. Turn the handle. God preserve us. Go to the office over there. You're trying to tell me you work there? What am I, a goat? The funeral's at ten. Am I your problem solver? I was there for three hours. What do you mean, you don't know? Spell it for me. He took the jeep across. I am begging you in the name of God, just let the boy through. Feet behind the line. Every knot can be untied. He's sixty-seven, what's he going to do? It's not my call, ask my supervisor. I'm not shouting, you're shouting. Open the zip. I put it in the dryer by mistake. What did you say his name was? A leopard doesn't change its spots. A permit is a permit. I never saw her before in my life. I'm telling you, she's a twin. I don't care if she lives in Outer Mongolia. In the next world too. I won't tell you again, take it out of the plastic please. Just doing my job. Who packed your case? I won't repeat my question. I need the original. It's not a [unintelligible] dishtowel. I cut myself shaving. My son-in-law works there. Be sure to send a lazy man. What curfew? It says it right there. My father borrowed it by mistake.

248

The song was played a few times on the student radio station until callers complained that they recognized the voices of loved ones in the looping lyrics.

247

Most of the hackers in Unit 8200 are under twenty-three years of age. They search through phone calls, emails, satellite messages and sift through the vast debris of data that comes their way, mining for any suspicious patterns. They use satellites to track cars and trucks. Information from jets and weather balloons. They intercept communications from universities and hospitals. They employ facial recognition software. Search for mathematical flashpoints in the data. Look in every available electronic corner, creating algorithms to bring the new information together in a nugget. A repeated word, a code, a series of numbers, a phone call at the same time from the same place every day. Even a strange hiccup among the patterns can alert them to an operation or a rally or a protest. Most coveted of all is material of a sexual nature—an affair, a homosexual encounter, a lurid photograph, a suggestion of an illicit relationship—to bribe the hacked subject into becoming a collaborator.

246

Combing the signals like moisture from the air.

245

Bassam nudges the car forward. Only one soldier left, but he is soon joined by another, a tall young man in spectacles, Ethiopian perhaps, maybe Somalian. They glance down at Bassam's license plate and wave him through without even looking at his identification card.

244

A one-cigarette checkpoint. A tiny slice of good luck. Always then the little private joy, the trivial victory, of driving away, switching off the roof light as he goes.

243

He has seen it before, the flying checkpoint, the extra jeep waiting a half mile beyond. It's a numbers game. Maybe every fourth car tonight. Or every blue car. Or every car with a woman in it.

His single headlight makes him a likely candidate but in the chill and the dark, he feels calm.

A mile past the checkpoint he presses down a little further on the accelerator. Nothing in the rearview mirror. Nothing up ahead. Even the light rain has stopped.

242

Permission to resume my life again.

241

Out now, through Bethany, towards the roundabout, with Jerusalem at his back and Maale Adumim on the other side. Turning, then, onto the modern highway where he is, for the first time since Beit Jala, allowed to accompany Israeli-plated cars on their way back and forth to the settlements.

On the back of a street sign, in thick red marker: *Bye bye, Apartheid Road.*

240

The walls of the valley are vertiginous. The caves in the cliff faces have for centuries been a perfect hiding place for archers, lookouts, gunners, marksmen, snipers.

239

The military bow evolved to incorporate several natural materials—wood, animal horn, tendons, sinews and glue—into the powerful composite bow. The skeleton was not made from a single block of wood but combined pieces of different trees with varying degrees of pliability to maximize draw distance and strength.

The back of the bow was covered with bands of sinews. The belly of the bow was reinforced with sections of animal horn.

The composite bows had an effective range of around four hundred yards. For the first time in history it was possible to surprise the enemy and attack from beyond the range of retaliation.

238

The arrow was composed of three parts. The arrowhead was made of the hardest available material—metal, bone or flint. The slender body was harvested from wood or reed. The tail, designed to keep the arrow in straight flight, was made from the feathers of eagles, vultures, kites or sea fowl.

237

The feathers were known as the messengers of death.

236

The Yom Kippur War struck Rami out of nowhere. He was twenty-three years old. He felt pushed suddenly onto a ledge. He tottered there. In a sketchbook he drew a pencil portrait of a soldier dragging a tank behind him on a piece of string.

235

He went to war in his civilian clothes. They didn't have enough uniforms for those who had been called up. A green khaki shirt, a pair of old trousers and worn boots. He was given a long-barreled rifle, an FN Herstal. The tip of the barrel was flaky with rust. The firing pin was unoiled. It was the only weapon around. Others in his reserve unit carried nothing but old revolvers.

He was in a tank repair unit. There were no transporters around. No spare parts either. The warehouses in Jerusalem were empty.

They began their drive out into the Negev. On top of the tank they had a machine gun, a .50 caliber. The darkness clamped down. They were due to go all the way to Suez. He knew that the tracks would get ripped to bits on the road, but there was nothing he could do: they were under instructions. They drove through the night. His jaw shook. His cranium shook. His collarbone shook. They consulted their maps. At least fifty miles still to go. Halfway through the night the caterpillar tracks on the left-hand side of the tank snapped. They pulled to the edge of the road and stumbled out into the dark. The tracks lay in the dirt. The sprockets were torn. They tried a quick repair but it was useless. The tank couldn't move. All the supply trucks had already gone ahead. He almost laughed. The war was inside out: the tank repair unit couldn't repair its own tank.

Distant tracer fire went across the night. Other tanks rumbled past, jeeps, military cars. Rami shouted out for spare parts. There were none. The radio, too, was jammed. They would have to wait until morning. He crawled under the tank and laid out his bedroll. Yom Kippur. The last of the ten days of penitence. He couldn't sleep. He walked a short way into the land. He crouched in the hard dirt. Twenty-three years old. He had just met Nurit. The stars shone their shrapnel above him.

In the morning a small red aspirin of sun rose. Reports were coming from the front. A surprise attack. They were being decimated. The Arabs had made huge gains. The Bar-Lev line was broken. Israel was in danger of being overrun. He could hear booms further up ahead. The road was jammed with army vehicles. A supply truck came shortly after dawn. The faces of the drivers were hollow, pitted, drawn. They set to work immediately. The tank was fixed within an hour. A transport came. They loaded the tank. He sat by the turret. Ambulances went in the other direction, sirens spinning. Close to the border, smoldering vehicles began to appear. Shattered jeeps. Tanks. Oil trucks. Makeshift hospital tents. Nurses ran to and fro. Soldiers walked about in a havoc of white bandages.

He knew right away that if not for the breakdown the night before, he would have been killed: the snapped tread had saved his life.

They stopped at a village to gather themselves. He was given a uniform, but no new rifle. He had to hold on to the FN Herstal. A young nurse handed him a plastic glass of cold lemonade. He held the cool empty plastic against his forehead. A shout went out from his commander. Time to move on. He climbed back onto the tank, his feet dangling over the side, his rifle placed across his lap. The heat bore down upon his skull. They pushed on. He sketched the sky in a notebook, a picture of a few birds wheeling in the emptiness.

Instructions were given. Dozens of tanks had already been lost. Their job would be to hold the line. The whole of Israel was dependent on this. God would protect them.

They reached the front late in the afternoon. The foul odor of war: cordite and flesh. He knew these smells from '67. They joined the rear of the front line. It was his job to go forward and repair the tanks, bring in ammunition and then to take out the dead and injured. He hefted the weight of the stretchers. Boys younger than himself grasped his arm. Blood ran from their mouths. He gathered them up.

The war was turning. They could hear it in the reports. Israeli planes streaked the sky. The Hatikvah played on the radio. There were rumors that they would cross the canal soon. Rami's unit moved backwards and forwards, backwards and forwards. The nights bled into days. The days bled into nights. Supplies came. Boots, shirts, American-issue MREs. Still no new rifle.

They huddled and spread maps at the rear of the tank. They would attack here, here and here. Reinforcements would come from there, there and there. They would be supported from the air. He blackened his face with soot from a saucepan. He wrote Nurit a letter. He couldn't finish it. It was stupid, pathetic. He tried to sketch, but it too was useless. He tucked the letter into his breast pocket. He tightened his new uniform, opened the tank hatch, climbed in. His team took the rear of the line, behind the other tanks. Soon they approached the canal. It was one o'clock in the morning. There was no such thing as darkness here. The far side of the canal was encased in smoke. The outside of the tank pinged. He was in a shooting box. A shell exploded in front of them. The driver panicked, the tank swerved, hit a guardrail. The tank stopped on the precipice. A shout went up. Out, out, out. He jumped from the turret to the bridge, crouched behind the tank. He aimed his FN at the other side. Save me. Where's the radio, grab the radio. Incoming, incoming. Tracer fire arced above. They called for the engineers to pull the tank back from the precipice. Other jeeps and tanks flowed past. The night quietened. Israel was crossing the Suez. The bridge was theirs. The dark was lit with bombsmoke. He had a momentary thought of just walking back home through the fog of it all, the war, the filth, the stench. The engineers pulled up. Quick, brusque, efficient. They attached a chain to the rear of the tank. More bullets. Keep your helmet on. Watch for planes. They pulled the tank back from the precipice. He was on his way again, inside the tank, over the Suez, enemy territory, pushing up to the front of the line.

They crushed a roll of barbed wire, reached a massive berm. Nowhere else to go. They turned the tank sideways. Rami opened the hatch again, jumped out, hit the sand, crouched, ran, found cover. The FN Herstal bounced at his chest. He lay on the ground. This fucking rifle. My death warrant.

He could see movement in the distance. Lights. Flares. He shot into the dark. The radio ordered another advance. He followed the coordinates, ran in a crouch. They moved forward, dozens of them together. Still the bullets came.

A large rock rolled against his boot. He looked down. Not a rock, but a helmet. Further along, he found a scrap of bloody clothing.

And then the bodies. He could see them on the ground, isolated at first and then in clumps, jigsaws of men, arms bent, legs blown off, torsos severed. He leaned down to pick up a discarded Kalashnikov. It was cold to the touch. It had not been used in hours. Ammunition too. He picked up clips, dropped them into the pockets of his trousers.

He threw the FN away and moved forward. He would not need it anymore.

234

Rami fought the rest of the war with the enemy's gun.

233

It was, he would say years later, like being inside a video game. He was walking forward with the Kalashnikov. He had burned his hand on the hot barrel. He could hear shouts and screams in the distance. And then, in an instant, one shout was isolated. He turned toward it, pulled the trigger, held it down. He saw the shape disintegrate: it crumpled, dissolved, fell.

232

He never told Smadar that he had killed at least one person, probably more, perhaps several. He told the boys about it, individually, at different times: but it was clear to him that they already knew. There was always the sickening feeling when he wondered if they too knew that moment of nothingness that exists between the bullet and the fall.

231

In science, the *hard problem of consciousness* is the question of how physical processes in the brain give rise to our subjective experience of the mind and the world.

From a purely objective point of view we can seem to scientists to be akin to robots governed by the elemental triggering of synapses in our brains. Our minds register the experience. The neurons fire. The brain receives a form of documentary cinema which rolls onward.

In war, for example, we can shoot bullets as we move forward over the dunes in the dark of night. We move on. We crouch. We take aim. We fire again.

From a subjective point of view, however, it becomes a matter of how we *feel*. We see colors, we see the shape of bodies in the air, we apprehend the dead in their hideous contortions as we step along with the rifle in our hands.

In these moments we are moved to consciousness in the dimensions of sight, of sound, of touch, of taste, of odor, of thought, in order to create a pattern that we will remember in any number of ways, be it glorious or terrifying or humiliating or just a matter of simple survival.

230

On his deathbed Mikhail Timofeyevich Kalashnikov asked the patriarch of the Russian Orthodox Church if he was responsible for the deaths of those who had been shot as a result of the design of his AK-47.

Kalashnikov was worried about his legacy: he had wanted to be remembered as a poet, not a gunmaker.

The patriarch wrote back to say that the Church's position was well known and if a weapon was used in defense of the Motherland, the Church would support its creators and those who used it.

229

When the British took control of Mandatory Palestine they used the Russian compound in Jerusalem as a prison for members of the underground resistance.

The Jewish prisoners were paramilitaries who used bombings, assassinations and lightning raids to fight the British and the local Arab population. The aim of the Irgun and the Lehi was to evict the British from Palestine and to create a Jewish state. They were known to the British as terrorists.

The cells were cold and spartan. Rag mats covered the floor. Punishment beatings took place in solitary confinement. In the execution room a single noose hung down from the wooden platform.

In 1947 two Jewish fighters, Moshe Barazani and Meir Feinstein, were scheduled to be executed in the prison. Barazani was charged with conspiracy to murder. Feinstein had been arrested for planting three suitcases filled with explosives in a Jerusalem train station.

The two men refused to acknowledge the authority of the British court. Hours before they were due to be executed, a basket of oranges was delivered to the prison. Inside the hollowed-out oranges were pieces of a grenade to be assembled.

Feinstein and Barazani requested a private moment of prayer with no rabbi or military presence.

Alone, they assembled the grenade, stood close together, lodged it between themselves, lit the fuse, put their heads on one another's shoulders, embraced, prayed and waited.

228

With a rubber bullet, kinetic energy is converted to elastic energy, then converted back to kinetic energy, whereas with an explosion it is an inelastic collision: momentum is conserved, but the kinetic energy is not.

227

Feinstein wrote in a letter before his death: *There is life worse than death, and there is death greater than life.*

226

On the morning after the bombing, Netanyahu called. The shrill ring of the phone seemed louder than other calls somehow. Nurit picked it up. She knew Netanyahu from school. They had been college friends.

A journalist in the house overheard the conversation. No, Nurit said, he was not welcome in her house. Not now, not for shiva, no, please do not show your face. She put the phone down, then tipped the receiver over so it was off the hook. The next day the conversation was news. She was interviewed again later in the week. The killing was not the fault of the bombers, she said. The bombers were victims too. Israel was culpable. The blood was on its hands. On Netanyahu's hands. On her own hands too, she said. She was not immune, everyone was complicit. Oppression. Tyranny. Megalomania. She was shown on national TV. Pundits said she was just in shock. It wasn't shock at all, she replied. The only shock was that the Palestinian bombings didn't happen more often. Israel was inviting its own children to be slaughtered, she said. They might as well put Semtex in their schoolbags. It would never be at peace until it recognized this. Cartoons were drawn in the conservative newspapers: Nurit in a university classroom, wearing a general's uniform, a keffiyah wrapped around her head. On the right-wing radio stations it was said that she wasn't properly Jewish at all, she had been brainwashed, her father had become a peacenik after all, he had betrayed Israel, he was a friend of Arafat's. She turned the dial on the radio. It broke her heart to hear Sinéad O'Connor.

Days passed, weeks, months. They were inundated with phone calls. Reporters from all over the world. Europeans mostly, French, Estonian, Swedish. They wanted to make documentaries featuring her. It disturbed her how fond many of them were of her point of view: she feared becoming a mouthpiece, a pawn. She didn't want to talk about it anymore. No more television, no more newspapers, no more prodding of the wound.

She took a sabbatical and went to London for eleven months. She wanted to be as far from Israel as she could get, to cleanse herself of the noise, the rancor, the pity. Invitations to speak still came from all over the world but she didn't want to talk publicly about Smadar anymore, she was done with that for now—she would talk about racism, apartheid, prejudice, yes, but not what had happened to her daughter. It simply hurt too much. She took Yigal with her. Rami and the two older boys stayed behind. There were whispers of course, but she and Rami didn't care: it was what she needed to do. The open sky of London buoyed her. The city had an order to it, a natural flow. She and Yigal stayed with a family in Hampstead—the bottom flat of a three-story Tudor, yellow roses out the back, the branches of the trees gently scraping the windowpane. She read books, wrote articles, took long walks. Translated Memmi and Duras into Hebrew. On Saturday afternoons the smell of freshly cut grass drifted from nearby gardens. Yigal was five. He guided a football at his feet. Nurit walked alongside him, afraid that the ball would roll out into the middle of the street. She didn't want to let him out of her sight. He was the youngest. She doted on him. They dialed Rami from a telephone box in the village. There was something reassuring about the red phone box: ancient, glass-paneled, a gold crown above the door. They had a phone at home, but the visit to the box became a Sunday ritual. She allowed Yigal to roll his small fingers in the rotary dial. Hi, Aba, it's me. After a moment she eased the phone away from Yigal, bent down and held her arm around his waist as she spoke. She didn't want news of Jerusalem, or Israel, or anything else, she simply wanted to hear that her boys were all right. Will Elik be home next weekend? Did Guy get the book I sent? Did you water the petunias? Did you see what Miko wrote? Did the university papers come?

Sometimes at night she would steal out from the house, alone, and call Rami again, in the dark, in the rain. She tried not to mention Smadar: the name alone twisted her core. She fed the phone slot with a pocketful of fifty-pence pieces. The coins tumbled in the space between minutes. She bid him good night and walked home again in the dark. In the morning she woke before Yigal, sat at her desk and wrote her academic treatises. She railed against the Occupation, military service, racism, myopia. She wanted to plow through the anger, to turn it into language. The translations were easier. There had always been something about Hebrew that released her. It brought her back to herself. But there were times she wondered if even Hebrew was failing her: it took a moment to remember certain words. It was odd to walk through London and see no script, no aleph, no tav. No home without language. She loved her job, her husband, her children, even her Israel, or what was left of it, that original idea, that smoldering mess, her father's heartbreak. There were times she thought she mightn't return at all, but she knew it was chimerical, she would have to go back, where else was there to live, where else could she survive, what else could she possibly know?

225

ISRAELI GOVT. KILLED MY DAUGHTER, Haaretz, September 8, 1997. **General's Daughter Accuses Israel of Murder,** Yedioth Ahronoth, September 9, 1997. <u>Family of Bombing Victim says Israel Breeds Terrorists,</u> Associated Press Newswire, September 9, 1997. Israel Bomb Victim's **Mother Blames Leaders,** Chicago Tribune, September 10, 1997. **Bereaved Mother Rips Government,** Jerusalem Post, September 11, 1997. **MOTHER BLAMES ISRAELI POLICIES FOR CHILD'S DEATH,** L.A. Times, September 11 1997. **Bereft Mum Blames Israel,** Courier Mail, Queensland, September 11, 1997. **BIBI KILLED MY GIRL,** The Sun, England, September 11, 1997. **Oppression Drives Arab Extremists to Violence, Grieving Mother Says,** Moscow News, Sept 12, 1997. *Mother Blames Israel for Daughter's Horror Death,* People's Daily, China, September 13, 1997. Israel's Uneasy State, The New York Times, September 14, 1997. OCCUPATION AT FAULT FOR MY DEAD CHILD, Paris Match, September 14–21, 1997. "Out of Lebanon!": Mother's Cry Rouses Israelis, Tel Aviv Journal, September 19, 1997. **"BIBI, WHAT HAVE YOU DONE?"** Le Monde Diplomatique, October 1, 1997.

224

Abir's sister, Areen, was in the habit of scissoring out the newspaper clippings. Most of the time the newspapers used the same photograph: her sister at the age of nine. She kept the clippings in a shoebox under her bed, even when they went to Bradford. Sometimes at night, when she couldn't sleep, she reached in under the bed for the box, woke in the morning with her sister scattered all around her.

223

Abir was hurtled through the air with such force that the shoe skidded on the road and came to a rest, perched on its emptiness.

222

Bassam disappeared into the coal shed for hours at a time. Wind whistled through the slats in the door. Giant cobwebs hung from the corners of the ceiling. He rustled through the items the previous renter had left on the shelves: bags of coal, a broken weed whacker, gloves, a *Garden News* jacket, pruning shears, fly killer, fertilizer, a handsaw, jam jars full of old screws, a plastic bottle stained red with petrol: it struck him that all the ingredients of a bomb were here, in this suburban English house.

When he lifted the old tins of paint a strange universe of bugs appeared in the damp: earwigs, slugs, daddy longlegs. He tidied the shed but left the cobwebs on the ceiling.

He stepped outside with the small pitchfork under his arm and began to perforate the patch of lawn, turning the soil at the bottom wall, made a row for planting.

—An English garden, he told Salwa.

He planned out what he would grow: courgettes, cucumbers, scallions, rhubarb, lettuce, parsley. He contemplated a small fountain, decided against it. He found a cherub statue in a flea market, painted it white.

At the edge of the shed he planted two roses, one named Sally Mac, the other Red Devil.

He loved to work the garden on Saturday afternoons in particular: the neighbors were out listening to football games on their radios. He could always tell how the local team was doing by standing in the middle of his garden and listening to the shouts from the fathers and their sons in their own gardens.

221

Sally Mac: an apricot-pink floribunda, yellow at the base with a gentle fragrance. Red Devil: medium-red hybrid tea, with a high centered bloom, dark at the base with a deep perfumed fragrance.

When they bloomed he cut them for Salwa and put them in a vase on the windowsill.

220

I repeat: Amicable numbers are two different numbers related in the sense that when you add all their proper divisors together—not including the original number itself—the sums of their divisors equal each other.

The numbers—esteemed by mathematicians—are considered amicable because the proper divisors of 220 are 1, 2, 4, 5, 10, 11, 20, 22, 44, 55 and 110 which, when added together, reach 284. And the proper divisors of 284 are 1, 2, 4, 71 and 142, of which the sum is 220.

They are the only amicable numbers under 1,000.

219

Do not let the olive branch fall from my hands.

218

Salwa didn't open the newspapers. She stepped away from the television. She didn't ask where Bassam had gone that day, or what he had seen, or with whom he had talked. It wasn't isolation, and it wasn't exhaustion, and it wasn't bitterness, though she knew it could have been a little of all of these, wrapped in the desire to remain intact. She didn't go to the Parents Circle. She didn't attend women's groups. It was not that she disagreed with them, but it was, she knew, her silence that spoke. It was part of her Du'aa. She was not called upon to tell her story. It lived, instead, in the aspects of her devotion. The path to understanding came from supplication. It was not anything the interviewers were able to understand. They were nearly all Western, mostly European. They wanted to tell the story, to write their reports. They were good people, she liked them, she invited them into her home, cooked for them, poured tea, emptied the ashtrays, but she stopped short of letting them interview her. She knew that they wanted to get a picture of her in her hijab. She understood it, but she also understood that it would be misunderstood. Once she was filmed carrying her youngest, Hiba, through the apartment. She had stopped to look at a photograph of Abir and the cameraman caught her crying. If they could have understood her anger, if they could some- how have captured it without making a spectacle of it, she would have talked with them, but she knew, she just knew: a Muslim woman, a Palestinian, the crime of her geography. She supported what Bassam did, Rami too, Nurit as well, but she wanted only to pursue the ordinary. She would find blessing there. In the late morning, after prayers, when Bassam and the children were gone, she went down to the marketplace. She wore long patterned dresses and a veil. Some- times she had sunglasses propped on her head. Her name rang out among the stalls. She laughed and waved. Yalla, yalla, yalla. She answered questions about her children, about their school, the scout troop, the kindergarten food drive, but mostly she stayed quiet about Abir. Even years after Abir's death, the sellers in the market still dropped a little extra in her shopping bag: a pear, a pinch more spice, some dates. She left the market with her bags overflowing. She drove fast, a habit she had picked up from Bassam. There was no recklessness in it, just a thrill. She had liked the narrow streets of Anata, but the wide boulevards of Jericho were better. She sped past the palm trees and the abandoned casino, her window open, the warm breeze playing at her hijab. She slowed down near the mosque. After noon prayer she would gather with the other women. They were gossipy: who might get divorced, who was sick, who left the country, whose son was lifted during the night. They asked her about Bradford. She told them about the five-bedroom house, the garden out back, the walks in the park, the English lessons, the mosque in Horton Park. It was like recalling someone else's life: she wasn't quite sure it had happened to her. No checkpoints. No strip searches. But she had been homesick. Her family, her friends. There was something about the light of Palestine that she missed, its sharp yellowness, the way it clarified shape. The air too. The dust even. She was glad to return. She had become so adept at packing boxes that—on the week of the move—she sharpened both thumbnails so that they would easily slice through the tape. Coming back through the airport they strip-searched her again. Her youngest two were kept in the same room as she took off her clothes. She had them turn away. She could hear them weeping as she stepped out of her dress. She stayed stoic. Then they strip-searched the children too. In front of her. She knelt down by their sides, whispered to them as the clothes came off. Down to their underwear. She dressed them, then, slowly, button after button. She told them never to give in. Remain steadfast. Trust in Allah. Things would change. It was bound to happen. There was so much to deal with—Araab's anger, Areen's guilt, Hiba's confusion—but she would deal with it, she had to, it was her lot in life. So many other mothers had it much worse. She looked after her own, made sure they came home safe: that was what mattered. She counted them home—one two three four five pairs of shoes by the door. It was only then that she could breathe. In the evening when the children had gone to bed she waited for Bassam to return. She lit the coals and arranged the hookah outside on the porch beside the small card table. She spread the cards out and watched for the pinpoints of car light coming up the road.

217

The house in Jericho was extraordinary. It lay on the outskirts of the city, down a rutted dirt road lined with orange and apricot and palm trees, with a view to the open desert.

Four bedrooms. Tall ceilings. Thick walls. Vaulting archways. Latticework windows. Intricate tilework in the kitchen. Pine floors.

The waste systems were reliable. The heating pipes. The electricity too. There was even a small concrete swimming pool at the back.

When Salwa first saw the house she walked up and down the staircase, touching the surface of things, skimming over them with her fingers. She switched the lights on and off. In the kitchen she stood under the air from the circling fan, paused for a moment by the stove, wiped the dampness from her cheeks.

Bassam climbed the stairs and looked out from the second-floor windows. The neighbors' houses were well kept too: whitewashed walls, intercoms, satellite dishes, electronic gates.

Around the house, three dunams of land: enough to plant a small orchard.

216

The architecture of well-appointed houses in Jericho is such that they are considered introverted—many of their rooms point their gaze towards the inner courtyard rather than out into the street: they gather into themselves.

Some of the houses are crowned by malqaf or windcatcher towers: a tall tower which faces, on one or more sides, the prevailing wind. The windcatcher scoops the high-density cool air and funnels it down into the belly of the house, where it acts like an air conditioner. Water vessels are sometimes placed inside the shaft, or damp towels are hung across the bottom vents, to increase the cooling effect.

In certain homes one can feel the immediate cool nudge up against the curtain of heat.

215

In the nineteenth century, imported ice—packed tightly in sawdust and transported in wooden boxes from the east and north—could remain cool in the basements of the towers.

The ice was taken in giant straight-edged blocks hauled by oxen from frozen lakes in Turkey, Iran, Iraq, moved at first by train and then, when the stations were reached, hauled by camel. The boxes, then, were lowered underground by rope and pulley.

To have a glass of tea with ice and a sprig of mint was the height of Palestinian luxury.

214

A week later, on her birthday, Bassam handed her a sheaf of papers, rolled up and fastened with a ribbon: the deed to the house.

Outside, the tiny concrete pool. Bassam stepped into the back courtyard, uncurled a hose and began to fill it with water from the outside tap. He had already nicknamed it the Puddle.

One by one the children clambered in and splashed around.

213

All, of course, except Abir.

212

Late in the evening he woke to hear Salwa tidying up the living room. He sat on the top of the stairs, looked down past the wooden railing.

She didn't notice him. She moved quietly, picking up towels, T-shirts, a small beach ball that sagged in the corner. She leaned down to the coffee table, brought a plate and a glass to the kitchen.

When she shut off the water from the tap he could hear her breathing. She turned off the kitchen lights and stopped once again in the living room.

A single lamp remained lit. Salwa reached to turn it off. She noticed something hidden in the folds of the couch. She lifted the cushion. Underneath lay an orange plastic swimming armband, crumpled and deflated.

She pulled up the adjacent cushions, searching the folds for the second armband, found nothing.

He watched as she moved to the bookshelf and stood by the photo of Abir. She popped out the small plastic nipple of the armband, put it to her lips and blew. She pinched the top and sealed the air inside, slipped the armband above her wrist.

She remained there a moment, then stepped towards the cupboard, deflating the armband on the way.

211

Rami didn't like seeing the casually thrown uniforms when the boys came home for the weekend. A green jacket slung on the coat rack. Brown boots askew at the door. He could almost tell what area of the country they had been in by looking at the soles. The dust from the Negev. The salt marks of the Dead Sea. The worn-down heels of Hebron.

210

Elik served from 1995 until 1998: first sergeant in the Maglan unit. Guy served from 1997 until 2000: lieutenant in a tank regiment. Yigal entered a noncombat educational unit and served from 2010 until 2013.

209

Salwa kept Abir's clothing for Hiba to wear. She brought it out in increments over the years: a shirt here, a scarf there. The only thing she didn't use was the school uniform or the patent leather shoes. She couldn't bear the thought of her youngest going off to school a close mirror of Abir.

208

When Nurit came home from London she laundered everything except the military uniforms.

207

A week after shiva, Elik was back with his unit. His commanding officer found him in the control room at base. The officer had seen footage of Smadar's funeral on television. He put his hand on Elik's shoulder. It was all about action now, the officer said. It was psychological. Something had to be done. Elik had to get back in the field. There was an operation coming up in Lebanon in a few days. They were going to take out some Hizbollah. Elik should get ready for it. Someone was going to pay for his sister's death. He would feel better. Trust me, said the officer. He could score a bit. Hit some Hiz.

Elik sat, silent. His commanding officer hadn't yet seen any of the comments that his mother had made in the newspapers.

Two days later his commanding officer said that there had been a change of plans. Elik was transferred to an intelligence unit where he would not be allowed out on field operations.

Elik knew that the decision had been made for fear of a public relations disaster.

206

Salwa drove the English roads: it was the only way to get Hiba to sleep in the daytime. She tucked her into a child seat and drove round and round the neighborhood. After a couple of weeks, she ventured further. To the outskirts of town and then beyond.

No military barriers. No checkpoints. Out through Shipley, Bingley, Keighley. It didn't bother her to be driving on the other side of the road.

She took small back roads through the Yorkshire countryside. Stone

walls and curves. Mills and church spires. The car flashed underneath
the green trees. Sunlight shot through the overhead branches. The
tarmac hummed. There was not a single pothole in the road.

She found a horse farm outside Keighley where Arabian horses
stood, sleek and muscled against the green. She leaned on the door of
the car.

When Hiba woke, she propped the child up on the edge of the
fence, and together they watched the horses prancing high-legged in
the field.

205

The Arabian horse has a short, straight back, usually by virtue of having one less vertebra than other horses. Her natural line is revered, and
she is famous for her floating trot, a spectacle of beauty and symmetry,
all the sinews moving together.

204

The Dead Sea is known to terrify horses—if they step into the buoyant
water their legs can disappear from underneath them and they get
turned over on their sides and sometimes drown.

203

In the nineteenth century, Bedouin tribes used Arabian mares for
raiding parties. The raids—to capture sheep, camels or goats—
depended on surprise and speed. Unlike the male horses, the females,
or war mares, did not nicker or neigh when they approached an enemy
camp. This silence was venerated.

Among the Bedouin, no greater gift could be given to an outsider
than an Arabian war mare.

202

*In the hospitality of war, we left them their dead as a gift to remember
us by.*

~ ARCHILOCHUS ~

201

The packages unhinged Rami and Nurit. They arrived from the
Ministry every Memorial Day. Neatly wrapped in sky-blue paper with
white ribbons, and sealed with a silver Star of David. They were left on
the doorstep along with a note from the Minister of Defense: *Dear
Elhanan family.*

A different item every year: a cut-glass bowl with names of the
fallen engraved around the rim, a pewter vase with Biblical quotes, a
porcelain flag, a pair of silver Shabbat candlesticks.

Rami unwrapped a book one Memorial Day—*Trails: Fall in Love
with Israel Again.* The book had a different trail for every day of the
year: fifty of them were located in the West Bank. The book suggested that Israelis should carry a gun if hiking a trail near an Arab
village.

The note—a special message to the bereaved—was florid. *On this
momentous Memorial Day we wish to honor Smadar's memory and the
special sacrifice you and your family have made for the eternal State of
Israel.*

Nurit was livid: it was not just the vulgarity of the gifts or the
saccharine letters, but how they co-opted Smadar as their own, as if
the child had been somehow complicit, as if she had stepped selflessly
down Ben Yehuda Street into the arms of the bomb.

She and Rami took a hammer and a wedge to the glass bowl and
smashed it to pieces, a small rubble of death and memory.

They put the pieces in the box, re-ribboned it, and shipped it to
Netanyahu with her own note: *Dearest Bibi, something is broken.*

200

She would see Netanyahu sometimes at the swimming pool at Hebrew University, a thin man with a pale blue swimming cap and a little surprise of white flab jiggling above his hips.

They would nod to each other and pass by in separate lanes.

199

He waited for the delivery. On the doorstep. Outside the house. Amid the blooming flowers. Just before noon a young soldier in uniform pulled up in an army car: white, with black plates. He was open-faced, jovial. The box was blue again, the white ribbon neatly tied.

Rami walked along the garden path, silently took the package. The soldier wished him well, turned and walked back to his car in the hard sunlight.

On the doorstep, Rami unwrapped the package. A metal globe with a map of Greater Israel raised in bas-relief. It was burnished bronze, hollow, lightweight.

He dropped the box and called out to the soldier who had just opened the door of his car.

—You see this?

The young man turned, startled.

Rami could feel the heat shoot through him. The globe was slippery in his hands.

—You think we want it?

—Sir?

—This?

—What about it, sir?

—You think we actually want it?

The globe sailed through the air, over the top of the car, bounced on the pavement, rolled and settled in the middle of the road.

The soldier stared at Rami for a half-minute, then strolled around the front of the car, bent and picked up the globe, wiped it free of dirt, got in his front seat, closed the door, took off slowly.

The following year, the gifts stopped arriving.

198

Still, he and Nurit always stood at attention when the memorial sirens went off.

197

The sirens sound out every year in memory of fallen Israeli soldiers and the victims of terrorism. Work stops. Traffic stops. Keyboards stop. Elevators stop. Citizens step from their cars in the middle of the highway. Television and radio stations go silent. All theaters, cinemas, nightclubs and bars are closed. There is no construction noise. Flags are flown at half-mast.

The sirens blare for one minute at sundown and for two minutes on the following day.

196

After his service, Elik threw away his beret and drove on the main road from Jerusalem to the Dead Sea where he camped overnight in an abandoned water park near Ein Gedi. He drank a fifth of vodka, smoked half a joint, wandered among the abandoned lifeguard chairs and the dusty sunshades, then walked alone up and down the dry waterslides for most of the evening.

In the morning he awoke on the concrete floor of an empty pool.

195

194

Rami threw the arguments around in his head, day after day. Point and counterpoint. Affirmative constructive. Negative rebuttal. Resolution. Refutation. How many times had he gone through this with the other two boys as well? Now here he was with Yigal. Rami woke in the middle of the night, tossing and turning. So, what are you going to say, son, when you're standing there in the middle of the road and along comes a black Kia and you flag it down, and it's Bassam inside? I'll let him go. And what about your buddies? They can make their own decisions. And what if your commander says, Arrest him? I'll refuse. And what if they arrest you for refusing? Then they can arrest me. And go to prison for it? Yes. So why not do it now and refuse altogether? It's my duty, my obligation. Tell me this, if you let Bassam go through do you let the next guy through as well? Depends. And what about Araab or Areen or Hiba or Muhammad or Ahmed, are you going to shake them down too? I'll do the right thing. And what if you're told to do something you don't want to do? Like what? Like commandeer a house, shoot a water tank, break a bone. I won't do it. Everyone says that. I'll make my choice when it comes. And what if it's the wrong one? Then I'll pay for it. Is your mind made up? I don't know. Sooner or later you've got to make a choice, son. If I don't serve, I have no voice. Your voice is louder if you don't go. I'm not scared of prison if that's what you think. I know that, son. You served, you went, you got to do it. Those were different times. That's what everyone says. Well, it's true. Why should I rot in prison when I could change things now? Because you won't be able to change things. That's what you say. You can't ignore reality, son. We need protection too, it concerns me to protect my country, we need good people in there. Yes, we do. So what should I do, emigrate? Of course not. I'm not ashamed of my flag, we need a democratic army. You'll eventually find out that there can be no such thing. A place has got to defend itself. I understand. They're not all Bassams you know. I know that. There are other people out there. Yes, there are. They blew up my sister.

193

There were some things, Rami knew, to which there were no responses, not even to himself.

192

The evenings of waiting seemed to occur in geological time. Every air raid siren, every beep on Rami's telephone, every news alert on the television. Another day of not knowing. He couldn't shake the dread from his mind. Waiting for the measured knock on the door. The long slow steps from the living room into the foyer. I'll get it, honey. The pull of the side curtains. The glance out the window. The edge of a shoulder. The shape of a hat. The relief of seeing the postman or a canvasser or a neighbor. He had his response carved out in his mind, like every father did: he would stand there quite still, he would refuse the messenger entry, he would hold the gaze, he would nod, he might even smile, he would reach for the letter, he would slip it in his shirt pocket, close to his skin. He would hold up his hand, his only language, then he would shake his head, close the door, wait for the footsteps to travel along the driveway until the car door was gently closed and the messenger was gone. What to do with light then? What to do with sound? What to do with all the color in the room? He would be calm and measured. He would be in control. He would turn in the foyer and walk back down through the kitchen and reach in the cupboard and run the tap and pour her a glass of water and bring it to the table for her because she, of course, would have already intuited it. And she might lean across and take the letter and gently unfold it and read it and put it back in the envelope and then place it down in the center of the table.

And even though the knock never came, it seemed to them that no knock was a sort of knock anyway.

191

Four years later—after completing his military service—Yigal stood onstage in Tel Aviv in front of seven hundred people, alongside Araab Aramin, in the Alternative Memorial Service, for Palestinians and Israelis both, and together they called out against occupation, segregation and dispossession.

190

My name is Yigal Elhanan. I was five years old in 1997 when I lost my sister Smadar.

189

My name is Araab Aramin. I was fourteen years old when my sister Abir was shot in the back of the head.

188

Seven hundred people heard the boys speak. Rami and Bassam watched from the side of the stage. Bassam stood with his hands locked behind his back. Rami held the edge of the curtain. He said later that what he was hearing was nothing short of nuclear.

The stage manager sat at the control panel. She hardly moved. The boys stood side by side at the high podium, dressed in open-neck shirts. Afterwards, onstage, they embraced. Their fathers emerged, then, from stage left.

Rami went first to Araab. Bassam went to Yigal.

187

Heavy water—deuterium oxide—is used to keep chain reactions going. The water helps to slow down the pace at which the uranium splits apart.

186

The soldier who killed my sister was a victim of an industry of fear. Our leaders speak with terrible smugness: they ask for death and vengeance. The loudspeakers sit atop the carriages of amnesia and denial. But we call on you to remove your weapons from our dreams. We have had enough, I say, enough, enough. Our names have been turned into a curse. The only revenge is making peace. Our families have become one in the unsavory definition of the bereaved. The gun had no choice but the gunman did. We do not talk about peace, we make peace. Uttering their names together, Smadar and Abir, is our simple, unadulterated truth.

185

Araab was twenty-three years old, Yigal twenty-four.

184

Mordechai Vanunu, a nuclear technician whose job it was to produce lithium-6 in the Dimona nuclear plant in the Negev, was sentenced to eighteen years in prison for divulging details of Israel's weapons program. Vanunu smuggled a 35mm camera into Machon 2 and took fifty-nine photographs despite signing a secrecy agreement years earlier. He divulged the details first to a church group in Australia where he fled. Later, in London, where he went to publish the information, he was seduced in a honey-trap operation by a Mossad agent. He met the female agent again in Rome where he was overpowered, drugged, kidnapped, bound to a stretcher, driven by motorboat out to a spy ship, bundled into a cabin. He was interrogated by Mossad agents, whisked back to Israel to a secret prison run by the Shin Bet. Nearly twelve of his years in prison were spent in solitary confinement.

183

Cheryl Hanin Bentov—the honeypot who lured Vanunu to his capture—became a real estate agent in Alaqua, Florida, specializing in gated communities and waterfront properties.

182

Rami saw Vanunu sitting in the back courtyard of the American Colony Hotel in East Jerusalem. He was tall, slim, elegant. The two side-lawns of grey hair accentuated his dark skin. There was something inherently Israeli about him: the way he dressed, an expensive blue shirt, opened two buttons down, a slight crease in the jeans, loafers without socks. Only the thin gold chain at his neck seemed slightly flagrant.

Vanunu was surrounded by half a dozen listeners, four men, two women. A carafe of water sat in the middle of the table along with a bottle of white wine in a silver bucket.

The tables were shaded by tall mulberry trees. Ivy on the limestone walls. A slight breeze ruffled the flowers: hydrangeas, rhododendrons, a flowering mint.

As he walked past, Rami heard a quick volley of Hebrew at the table. It dissolved, then, into English, which surprised him: one of Vanunu's conditions, he knew, was that he was not allowed to talk to foreigners.

Rami chose a table far enough away not to draw attention but close enough that he might hear something. Some laughter and then a brief silence. As far as he knew, Vanunu was still under house arrest, living in the cathedral down the street.

Rami checked his wristwatch. He was ten minutes early for his own meeting. He ordered a beer from the waiter, opened his phone, strained forward to listen to Vanunu's table.

It was only then that Rami noticed the rhythm of the fountain, a thin sheet of noise. All the words were somehow softened by the fall of the waterdrops. He had seen the fountain when he came through the lobby but he had not really listened to the sound. It seemed designed exactly to mute the neighboring tables, falling relentlessly, relentlessly falling.

He thought for a moment about walking over to the table to reach out, introduce himself, shake Vanunu's hand, look him in the eye. Still, there was a part of Rami that became arrhythmic at times like this: he wasn't sure quite what he would say. Vanunu too had been called an Arab lover, a peacenik, a traitor. He had been burned in effigy on the streets. He had gone through more humiliation than Rami could imagine. Had his passport taken away. Was not allowed to talk to reporters unless his words were reviewed by censors first. Lived in a small room in the walled compound. Was arrested and rearrested, again and again—once for talking with tourists in a bookshop, another time for refusing community service in West Jerusalem, demanding to do it instead in the eastern part of the city, the Arab area.

At the table Vanunu had his hand at his mouth, covering his lips. The four men and two women were leaning in intently, listening. What secrets might be filtered there? What ordinary things? What longings?

When Rami stood to leave he caught Vanunu's eye and a quick sliver of recognition went between them.

181

Traitor: one who betrays a country, a friend, a principle.

180

Collaborator: one who cooperates traitorously with an enemy.

179

~~Peacemaker: one who has grown sick of war.~~
~~Peacemaker: one who was sick of war.~~
Peacemaker: one who is sick of war.

178

One of the primary conditions of aid from the United States, under the Economic Support Fund and Foreign Military Financing laws, designed to promote political and economic stability in areas key to U.S. interest, is that Israel is not allowed now or at any other time to produce weapons of mass destruction.

177

I am sorry to tell you this, Senator, but you murdered my daughter.

176

It was Bassam's job, as commander, to punish the prison collaborators. Those who cooperated, those who conspired, those who squealed, those who broke. The stool pigeons. The rats. The reed men.

The Fatah network was tight, but the Israelis always managed to infiltrate. There was always a prisoner willing to bend for a small favor: a shortened sentence, a new cell, a supply of cigarettes. Most of all the prisoners broke for their families on the outside. Perhaps the man's brother had been arrested. Or his son was in trouble. The prison guards came to them—in hospital or in solitary—and whispered a casual deal. It was always a minor thing at first. Find out who toppled the basket of detergent in the laundry room. Identify the prisoner who took salt from the kitchen. Point to the one who was tapping messages on the pipes.

One single snitch was all it took and then they were snared. They would spend the rest of their time in verbal handcuffs.

The easiest ones to identify were those who had already arrived as snitches. They had been co-opted early. Bassam could tell from the way they carried themselves: they feigned fear, but the pretense itself belied them. They would always wait a week or two before beginning to squeal. They were punched and kicked in their cells by the prison guards and then hauled away. Bassam knew it was a faux beating, an excuse to get the prisoner off the cellblock. The screams were too loud, the guards too bellicose. Actors in the game. He watched them being taken away on a stretcher. They seldom returned, but if they did, they seemed to mix their anger with a little plumpness: they had been taken care of in custody.

Bassam found them useful for misdirection. Keep your enemy close. Never let them out of your sight.

The more difficult ones to identify were those who broke while in prison. They were real, they were true, but prison took its toll on them. Often it was late in their sentences. It wasn't possible to tell if prison had broken them, or if it was the prospect of freedom, but something in them was eviscerated. These were the ones to worry about. They knew the cell structure. They knew the names of fighters. They were aware of the operations.

They also knew how to carry their prison bodies: they didn't squeal too loudly, they didn't betray themselves.

Bassam tried to keep spirits up in prison with songs, classes, shared cigarettes, but sometimes a man just broke and there was no way to stop it. At the lowest level they were shunned by the other men.

Sometimes the snitches were snitched upon and left to the mercy of the guards.

At the highest level it was Bassam who had to administer the punishment: whether the snitch was to be isolated, or his family threatened, or whether he was to be beaten into submission.

At the worst of times—when the collaborator was high-level—it was Bassam himself who had to do the kicking.

From the beginning the beatings didn't feel right. He didn't want to become the jailer. Why do to a fellow prisoner what your jailer is doing to you? The beatings went against proper jihad. A man who requires revenge should dig two graves.

Bassam wasn't sure how to turn the tables. It kept him awake at night. He wasn't interested in falling back on the polio or the limp as an excuse not to kick anymore. It was important to remain nonviolent but not to seem weak. He liked the ideas of Doctor King: to find a method to reject revenge, aggression, retaliation. The past is prophetic. Wars are poor chisels. Lightning makes no sound until it strikes.

He turned into the pillow. He tried to sleep. He could not.

175

The reed men: those who bent with the wind.

174

His favorite instrument in the prison was the ney, a long flute played at an angle to the body's axis: there was an Egyptian at the far end of his cellblock corridor who played it beautifully. The neys were fashioned from the legs of chairs or tables, hollowed out and carefully carved.

173

Smadar owned a pair of headphones with adjustable knobs for volume control. She liked to hold her palms to her ears and splay her fingers wide in the air while she danced around the living room, skirting the flowerpots and the chairs. She was able to control the volume with her palms, sometimes turning it all the way up, playacting and laughing with her brothers: *I can't hear you, I can't hear you, I can't hear you.*

172

The piercing cry of the zaghareet is made during weddings and other celebrations, to honor the living and the dead.

The sound is created by darting the tongue to both sides of the mouth in rapid succession while an undulating noise is let out from the throat—*eleleleleleelelel.* The women cover their mouths with their hands and close their eyes while they catch the sound.

The zaghareet lasts approximately the length of one whole breath, although a series of ululations can be pulled together into an ongoing song or keen.

171

The zaghareet was famously captured by the filmmaker David Lean in *Lawrence of Arabia* when the veiled women in black on the clifftop call to the men in the valley below as they head out to battle.

170

169

In 1361—639 years before the third millennium—the first permanent pipe organ was installed in the Saint Burchardi church in Halberstadt, Germany. Local craftsmen spent years perfecting the design for the Blockwerk organ. Master carpenters were brought in to fashion the wood. The most skilled blacksmiths forged a series of perfectly symmetrical pipes. Clergymen gathered to discuss the purpose and placement of the instrument.

The organ, with its twelve-note claviature, became a local treasure, the pride of the town. It was known among some locals as the Voice of God. Musicians from all around Europe came to hear and play it.

Seven centuries later, a John Cage piece was due to be performed at the cathedral. The eight-page score was titled *As Slow as Possible*. The aim of the music was to stretch the notes so they would sound out, uninterrupted, for another 639 years.

The project was conceived by theologians and musicians as a tribute to the late Cage and also as a philosophical examination of the helixes of music and time.

The beginning of the performance was slightly delayed but opened with silence in 2001. At first the only sound that could be heard was the whoosh of the electric bellows filling with air.

The first full chord vibrated through the cathedral in 2003. Seventeen months later a note was added and the tone changed. That tone, then, remained steady: a drone.

A special acrylic glass cage was built around the organ to reduce the volume. The bellows was carefully maintained for a constant supply of air. Another chord sounded in 2006 and went on until 2008. At that stage the weights holding down the organ pedals were adjusted and the sixth chord sounded out.

168

Each movement of *As Slow as Possible* lasts about seventy-one years. The music will last until September 5, 2640, ensuring that everybody who hears any of it will never have heard all of it.

167

The average life expectancy for a Palestinian is 72.65 years. An average Israeli expects to live almost ten years longer.

166

She lay there in a blue smock, the wristwatch on her arm, the blown-apart sections of her discreetly covered. Her face had remained perfectly intact. No cuts, no bruises. For this Rami was grateful. The door closed with a vacuum hiss. Then, silence. He knew even then that all subsequent sounds would derive from this.

165

For her tenth birthday Abir was treated to a visit to the Amigo Pita restaurant on Anata's main street. It was a brightly lit Mexican café with plastic jalapeños dangling from the fluorescent lights and sombreros on the walls. Mariachi music was piped out from the speakers.

In the middle of the party, the owners brought out a piñata in the shape of a donkey.

At first Abir didn't want to hit the donkey, but when she heard that there was candy inside she put on the blindfold, took the stick and slapped the brightly colored toy.

The sweets scattered and bounced on the floor.

164

The sound bomb—also known as the flash grenade or stun bomb or flash bomb or long-range acoustic device—is considered another means of riot control: when thrown into a crowd the tiny canister makes a huge boom.

The Israeli army also uses sound bombs to disable water wells deemed illegal in the West Bank: when they drop a bomb to the bottom, the noise waves are powerful enough to crack the well's sleeve from top to bottom.

163

Most of all, the sound bomb has a percussive effect on the imagination.

162

Imagine one rolling in at your feet.

161

As slow as possible.

160

Current residents near the Saint Burchardi church in the town of Halberstadt complain that the performance of *As Slow as Possible* now emits—and will continue to emit for the next six hundred years—an unending drone not unlike that of an approaching train.

159

Antonin Artaud, the French writer, said that he was interested in liquefying the borders of sound.

158

In Borges's short story *The Aleph*, a manuscript written by Sir Richard Francis Burton is discovered in a library. The story contains a description of a stone pillar in Cairo in which the whole world of sound is reflected and heard. Anybody who puts their ear to the stone can hear a continuous hum that contains all the concurrent noises of the universe.

157

Operation Opera. Operation Inferno. Operation Gift. Operation Wooden Leg. Operation Solomon. Operation Orchard. Operation Noah's Ark. Operation Rainbow. Operation Hot Winter. Operation Just Reward.

Rami knew the designations worked. It was what he had done his whole life as a graphic artist, catching the moment, making it memorable, justifiable, clean. It gave people ownership, like a song title or a poem, a melody for the times.

Operation Days of Penitence. Operation Sharp and Smooth. Operation Summer Rains. Operation Autumn Clouds. Operation Sea Breeze. Operation Returning Echo.

156

In Paris in 1933, Artaud was invited to speak about his essay *The Theatre and the Plague* to a packed house at the Sorbonne University. He spoke quietly at first, but then gathered pace. He began sweating and shivering. His eyes rolled back in his head.

His interviewer, a psychoanalyst, sat paralyzed as Artaud began to contort and twist with anguish. Towards the end of the lecture, Artaud fell off his chair and began to writhe on the floor. The crowd in the amphitheater listened nervously as Artaud's moans grew louder and louder. His eyes were wild, his face was gaunt.

A few audience members—thinking it an act—began to laugh. Soon boos and hisses rose. Programs were thrown onstage. A coin landed at Artaud's feet. A series of slow handclaps went around the theater. Some of the audience began to drift out.

There was nothing his interviewer could do: Artaud was, it seemed, in the grip of a full fever.

Artaud stayed on the floor until the audience was clear of everyone but a handful of watchers, including the writer Anaïs Nin. Artaud collapsed in silence and then got to his feet, stepped down to the front row, kissed the Cuban-American on her hand. The edges of his lips were darkened, probably by laudanum, she thought.

Artaud brought her out through the theater, into the mist of Paris, towards La Coupole where they sat together and drank.

155

Anaïs Nin wrote in her diary that Artaud was shocked the audience hadn't understood his portrait of death. It was his desire to give the audience the actual experience—short of the plague itself—so that they would awaken from their everyday stupors and be terrified.

154

Rami had long learned to embrace the confusion. Chaos was the fuel of Israel. It was a country built on shifting tectonic plates. Things were constantly colliding. Everything led to the edge, the next moment of rupture, but life became most vivid at moments of danger. It was why people drove so fast and so close. It was why they didn't wait in lines at the airport. It was why the cafés throbbed in the mornings. It was why the markets were so loud and raw. People were chaotic in unison. Molecular in their turmoil. But it worked. Even the polar opposites were attracted to one another. Occasionally they would bash together and it made the ground pulse. There was left and there was right, and there was Orthodox and secular, and there was Arab and Jew, and there was gay and straight, there was high-tech and hippie, and there was rich and fiercely poor. Israel was a condensed everywhere. A tiny country bursting at the seams, but they were in this together. Every dream and neurosis under the sun. The psychoses. The passivities. The pretensions. The pride. The electricity of it all. And the fear too. Everyone wore a loud armor. Always in search of a debate over who and what and where they were. Rami could hear it on the radio. On the TV. In the offices. In the supermarkets. Two Israelis in a room, the old joke went, and three arguments would erupt. He soaked up the clamor. It was apparent in the way he moved: his walk was jittery, shot through with energy. He went straight to the heart of a room. He was seldom one to hang back. Yet there was a quietness about him too, he could hold those contradictions, it was something he had always been good at. It was the Mediterranean part of the soul, the sort of Israel that wanted ease and slumber. At Shabbat, the family gathered, the grandchildren arrived, everyone came indoors, the table was arranged, the arguments were put away for a moment or two. There was nothing religious about it for him, but it was still a cherished ritual. It was not something he could truly explain to an outsider. There was a sort of patriotism here that, try as he might, he could not avoid. He was Israeli. A shameful and powerful thing to be. He bristled a little when outsiders criticized it, but he bristled too when the insiders boasted. Their cellphones. Their medicine. Their make-the-desert-bloom bombast. The miracle of Waze. Yet he had to admit that, at the same time, it sent a little frisson of pride along his spine. He knew that he lived in two Israels: a small one which admired him, and another one, a larger one, bursting with disdain. This was the land of Netanyahu, but also the land of Vanunu. The land of Bennett, but also Khenin, Shaffir, Pappe. It didn't murder or kidnap its complications, or at least not yet. So many people considered Rami a traitor, a lackey, a turncoat, but in the end he didn't care: he knew what he was doing, he knew he was getting under their skin, he was peeling it back, exposing the rawness. He was outnumbered, yes, but they would find a tipping point sometime, somewhere, along the way. It was inevitable. He had to keep telling the story. Repeating it again and again and again.

153

Rami underlined a passage in Edward Said's collection of essays *Culture and Imperialism,* where the Palestinian critic wrote: *Survival, in fact, is about the connection between things.*

It was one of Nurit's favorite books and it sat on her bookshelves beside a picture of her father, Matti Peled. In the photo he had his arm draped around Said's shoulders.

152

Bassam knew the corruption. The capitulation. The isolation. The craven talks. The setbacks. The self-pity. The defeats. The resignation. The refusal to acknowledge failure. The false power. The liars, the swindlers, the fakes. The shell jobs. The backhanders. The shame. The riot control of hope. His own leaders applied for permits just to walk into another room. The Palestinian police shot into crowds of their own. Roads were closed to allow the curfews. City planners demolished ancient houses in Ramallah, Jericho, Jenin. The clerks demanded

kickbacks. The humiliation ramped up on all sides. It was a slow strangulation, an endless repetition of defeat. Everyone knew just how
rotten the system was. He was integral to it himself. Locked in the
puzzle. He hated the endless matryoshka-doll boxes his people were
shoved into, even among themselves, but he wasn't going to be reduced
to a single idea, a spectacle of disintegration. He was Palestinian.
Waiting was a matter of spirit. There was perseverance in the refusal of
defeat. He had already lived out his life across a score of slaughters and
he, like his people, had survived. He, like them, had been sentenced to
live. He had spoken out for peace long before he had lost his daughter.
He had decided to resist. He wasn't immune to criticism, but he had
served his time. He was difficult to pick apart: those who criticized
him were forced to criticize themselves too. He looked to some, at
first, like a pushover. In he came, dragging his foot, head down, slightly
smokestale. And he remained that way for a minute or two, until he
knocked them off-kilter. His moves were audacious. He made no
excuses for them. He went to Israeli schools. He talked to Israeli
generals. He even spoke to AIPAC, the lobbying group for Israel. He
was prepared to tell the story anywhere. It was, he said, the force of his
grief. The weapon he had been given. He could stand up onstage and
take the impact. He could smile at them and imagine, at the same
time, the knife slipping between their shoulder blades. He had a habit
of opening his hands wide when he spoke. Take me on. Try anything
at all. The worst has been done to me. Call me names. I have heard
worse. No one knew quite where he stood on the issues. He talked
around corners. It was part of his talent. He quoted poems. He seemed
to wear them as concealment. A rhyme to cover the wounds. *A
pessimist of the intellect, an optimist of the will. What is closer to my heart,
a soldier from my country or one of my enemy's poets?* So many times
people would come up to him after his lectures and say that they
wished there were more like him. What do you mean? he would ask.
Immediately they would realize what they had said and drop their
heads. As if he didn't encounter people like himself every single day, at
every single angle. As if he were the only sort of Palestinian they could
stomach.

151

Said, who was born in Mandatory Palestine in 1935, was fond of T. S. Eliot's idea that reality could not be deprived of the other echoes that inhabit the garden.

150

In the Himalayan highlands a Ladakhi engineer, Sonam Wangchuk, came up with an idea to counteract the acute seasonal water shortages. He proposed capturing the huge outflows of glacial meltwater, redirecting them, and freezing them into simple conical mounds that resembled local religious structures. The artificial ice stupas—two and three stories high—behaved like mini glaciers. They melted slowly and released millions of liters of water over the planting season.

149

It was the fourth day of his hunger strike. It wasn't just the pain in his lower stomach—sharp jabs that shot across his kidneys—but the noise outside too. He could hear the shouts from further along the wing, the slamming of doors, the slap of a billy club against a metal staircase, a jackhammer outside, an irregular siren somewhere in the distance. It felt as if a tiny speaker had been installed in his cranium.

They had given him, without warning, two extra months on his sentence. He went immediately on strike.

Food wasn't a problem. He didn't crave it yet. He rose from his bed. He walked back to the toilet area. He had heard that it was a good idea to keep moving. Not to overdo it, but to be fluid, to keep the body agile. He had the words lined up from the Qur'an. *And surely they will test you with something of fear and hunger.* He lay down again. Covered his ears with the pillow. A guard came in and ripped the pillow off his face. He stared up at the camera. Who was watching? What were they recording? He had heard that it was a good idea to read, it would pass the time. He opened his Qur'an again. *Give good news to the patient ones.* He couldn't focus, his eyes seemed to fall away from the page. The sounds echoed and reechoed.

He went to the prison canteen three days in a row. Each time he took a cup of water and an empty tray, sat in the corner. He slipped half a salt pill into his mouth.

On the fifth day they removed him from his cell. He was installed in no-man's-land: not solitary, not a medical unit, just an isolated cell. He could no longer visit the canteen. He would have an hour's exercise each day, alone in the yard.

The cell was larger than the one he had spent years in. Two cameras hovered in the ceiling. He tried to figure out their angles, where their blind spot might be. There was no television to watch. No way to listen to music. He rose and paced.

They had added the two months for security reasons they said. Bassam knew he could take the chore of extra time. He had already spent seven years, a third of his life, inside. Sixty days hardly mattered. But this was a matter of principle. He knew the hunger strike routine. Other prisoners had gone through it. The body would start to break down after three weeks. After five it would become critical. After six the damage would be irreversible. He had to focus. Concentrate. Burn.

They started heaping his plates with larger portions. Bread, rice, maftoul. They left the food in his cell for hours on end. He draped it with a towel and put it under his bed so he could not see it. The food was ever more fragrant: they had, he was sure, added spices.

He squatted over the toilet. His body purged itself. Seven days now. He kneeled to pray.

More food arrived. The guards were quiet, courteous. They set the plate on the table, turned around, left. He filled his water glass and swallowed half a salt tablet, sat on the bed, made maps out of the brickwork patterns on the wall.

He became meticulous with cigarettes. He inserted a filter, rolled the tobacco with great care. He wondered if putting his tongue to the glue of the rolling papers might constitute breaking the strike. He folded the paper over, sealed it carefully. The smoke filled him, made a small grey universe in his lungs. It expanded inside him. He breathed out. It staved off the pains. He glanced at the clock. Even when he was a child, time had never gone so slowly. He recited songs in his head, over and over. *Certainly we'll be back no matter how long the journey. Give my greetings to the olive and the family that brought me up.* He took another sip of water. He could feel the iron in it, the earth. A clarity of taste. He was back at the well as a boy. He turned the wheel to tighten the rope. The bucket rose. He carried it upward to the cave. His mother took hold of the bucket handle. The ladle dipped. The water fell.

On the ninth day the sounds outside subsided and the hunger began in earnest. It was what he had expected. Rhythmic, rolling pains: a sea of them moving through him. He thought of Akka along the water. He would go there when he got out. Walk along the pier. Watch the waves roll in, white horses on the olive press of the sea.

The hunger tired him out. He didn't pace the cell as much anymore. He tried not to think. The mind, he had heard, could use as much energy as the body. *Pour over my head the penalty of boiling water.*

He found himself sleeping more. The guards came in and shook him awake. A lamb stew. An orange soda, bubbles rising in the see-through plastic cup. A slice of baklava drizzled with honey.

Bassam threw the towel over the tray. One of the guards remained at the door of the cell, looking in on him.

He called for an extra blanket: he had begun to shiver furiously.

A doctor arrived, took his pulse, his blood pressure, his oxygen level. He shone a flashlight into Bassam's eyes and mouth. Look right, look left, look upwards. Bassam rolled up his sleeve, looked away as the doctor took a vial of blood. On the way out the doctor said in Hebrew: *Mazal tov.* He wondered what the doctor had meant. *Mazal tov,* your health is good. Or *Mazal tov,* continue your strike. Or *Mazal tov,* you are a terrorist and you're dying and it is your destiny that it is so.

He noticed the pungent odor that the doctor's aftershave left behind.

On the twelfth day he went to the bathroom again. He could not believe it. He did not think he could have anything more inside him. It rushed from him in a foul torrent.

The odor was sickening. He stood up quickly. He was light-headed. He braced his hand against the wall to steady himself. A dribble of watery shit ran along his legs, staining his uniform.

148

It was always, in later years, Salwa, not him, who got upset when their kids did not finish the food on their plates.

147

Early in a hunger strike, the human body—like that of a bird in flight—begins to use muscle protein in order to create glucose. Potassium levels fall. The body sheds fat and muscle mass. The heart rate lowers. Blood pressure fluctuates. Disorientation sets in. A loss of coordination, a sluggishness, a feeling of drift. After two weeks of hunger strike, low levels of thiamine and other vitamins become a risk to the prisoner, resulting sometimes in severe neurological problems: cognitive dissonance, loss of vision and a reduction in motor skills.

146

While in prison, Vanunu, the whistleblower, spent thirty-three days on hunger strike.

145

A guard arrived early the next morning. Get dressed, he said to Bassam. He was already wearing the only clothes he had. Another guard stood at the door with a folded wheelchair. Bassam waved the chair away. He was fine, he said, he would walk, he could run if they wanted him to, in fact he would run right out the gate, would they mind opening it for him?

He paused at the cell door, chuckled, turned around and picked up his Qur'an. They would use the time away to search his cell, he knew. He did not want them to touch the holy book.

He could hear cheering and banging from the side corridors. His name sounded through the din. He pushed on. His eyes felt heavy. He paused a moment to regain his balance. He made no gestures, no sounds. The metal stairs swam before him.

He wondered if he could ever get down, but he was guided towards the guards' elevator instead. The lights on the buttons pulsed. He was led into a waiting room. A woman brought him a glass of water. She was dressed in civilian clothes. When she turned away her hair swished. A scent of almonds hung in the air.

He kept his Qur'an in his lap.

Bassam tried to stop himself from dozing off, but a large hand shook him awake. He was not sure how long he had been waiting. He was ushered into an office. The chair was deeply cushioned. He could feel how much weight he had lost.

There were books on the shelves, maps on the walls, photographs arranged on the desk. A cup with a small Israeli flag propped inside. A bowl of wrapped candies sat at the side of the desk. Red and white. Wrapped in clear plastic.

He knew the warden, Dobnik. They had sparred many times. Dobnik was thin, grey-haired, blue-eyed. Bassam knew full well how the conversation would go. Dobnik would say that he hoped Bassam was being treated well. Bassam would reply that he only wished to be treated fairly, that was all. Dobnik would tell him that nothing could be done until he came off hunger strike. Bassam would say that he could not come off hunger strike until something was done. Dobnik would tell him to consult his lawyer. Bassam would half-laugh and tell them that access to his lawyer had been blocked. Dobnik would say that they would gladly investigate it. Bassam would reply that he would be glad for it to be investigated. Then Dobnik would say, once more, that nothing could be done until he came off hunger strike. And Bassam would repeat that he would not come off hunger strike until something was done. Dobnik would sigh and say that something surely could be done if Bassam was willing to help them out a little, the world was full of give and take. Bassam would reply that he had been giving and taking for seven years and two more months wasn't going to break him.

After fifteen minutes Dobnik leaned forward in his chair and plucked one of the wrapped candies out of the bowl. He pushed the full bowl toward Bassam. One of the wrapped candies tumbled onto the desk.

Dobnik leaned back in his seat and slowly unwrapped the plastic from his red and white sweet. He made a show of untwisting the plastic and rolled the candy noisily around in his mouth. He pushed his chair even further back and seemed to contemplate one of the maps on the wall. He tapped the sweet against his teeth and sat conspicuously sucking it for a moment, then rose and left the room.

Bassam laid his Qur'an on the table. He wanted to turn around and wave to the cameras in the upper corners of the room, but he sat still, staring straight ahead.

Dobnik returned five minutes later, perched behind his desk and said curtly: We'll inform you of our decision in a couple of days.

Bassam nodded, reached forward and picked his Qur'an off the table. He paused a moment, bent his head. The map on the wall was from 1930. British Mandate Palestine. He had no idea why Dobnik might have put it there. Some things in the world, he thought, just could not be accounted for.

144

Abir's last words.

143

On his way back to the cell, he felt for the tiny wrapped candy in his pocket. The plastic was twisted at both ends. He had scooped it into his fingers as he stood up. Dobnik had not seen him take it.

He hadn't even contemplated taking it at first. It was just there on the desk. Nothing but boiled sugar after all. There was no forethought to lifting it. If he ate it, he would be breaking the strike. Then again, they would not know that he was breaking the strike. And if they did not know, perhaps he was strengthening his strike? Still, he would be destroying his own effort. He would have to live with it. It was thirteen days now.

He stopped at the door of his cell. His evening food was already there, waiting. A chicken dish with a cream sauce. They had put Coca-Cola in a clear plastic cup.

He threw the towel over the tray. When he lay down on the bed, he tucked the candy underneath the mattress. They would find it, he thought, if they did another late-night search. They would use it to discredit him. He knelt to pray. He slipped the candy into his pocket once more. Perhaps he could use it as some sort of talisman? Or perhaps he should just throw it away, smash it up and flush it down the toilet?

He paced the room. Stood in the blind spot where the cameras could not see him. Put his hand to his nose. His hand to his brow. His hand to his lips. He ran his fingers through his long beard. He unwrapped one end of the plastic, twisted it shut again.

He paced some more.

He slipped the candy in his mouth.

The taste was alarmingly minty.

142

After four days Bassam was told that the order had been reversed. He would not be required to spend an extra two months in prison. The condition was that he had to announce that he had given up the hunger strike first and that he would have to spend another full week in recuperation—when he had done that, the prison authorities would release a statement. He replied that he would only do so if they could release simultaneous statements and he added that he would not spend another week in recuperation, the absolute maximum he would do was three days. They said they were willing to grant him a four-day provision, but they were categorically unable to release simultaneous statements. He said that perhaps if the prisoners were told late at night, then he would allow for their statement to be issued first thing in the morning, and he would issue his own official statement, for prison outsiders, at noon, but if and only if his fellow prisoners were told first. They said they were perhaps amenable to that and, in addition, they would make the concession of a three-and-a-half-day recuperation provision. He said that he needed written commitment. They said they could not provide that, but they could provide their word that the statement would be released expeditiously. He said their word was not worth the air on which it was written. They said that at least they had allowed him to breathe. He said it would be three days' recuperation or nothing. They said okay, fine, it's a deal. He said, I will tell the prisoners tonight.

141

To reach a deal between Israelis and Palestinians, said Senator George Mitchell, proposals for the future, intended to help solve the problems of the present, could not be fairly evaluated without some intricate knowledge of the past. And yet he knew that the past could always be construed in several different ways. Therefore the present too. But, said Mitchell, that did not necessarily mean that the future was automatically tainted. A peace would come, he said. Of that he had no doubt. It was important first that everyone, on all sides, desire it. While that was an obvious stipulation, it wasn't always a given. So much of it came down to the historical narrative, but what worried him, always, was the duration of the present, combined with the echo of the past, while trying to negotiate a clearer pathway to the future.

140

Bassam never told the story of the candy to anyone, not even his sons. He had been seventeen full days on hunger strike.

139

On the morning of his scheduled release he was escorted to the lowest floor of the prison. The fluorescent lights hummed. The guards removed the handcuffs and shackles. He was given his old clothes. The jeans were too short and the shirt too big. His feet had grown: he had to stuff his feet into the shoes he had been arrested in.

He felt as if he had stepped back reluctantly into his seventeen-year-old self. He tightened his belt four notches.

He was handed an envelope with three hundred shekels. He tucked the bills in his pocket. His only possessions were a mother-of-pearl key ring, a pair of broken sunglasses and a half-packet of Marlboro cigarettes.

Nobody was waiting outside to meet him. The sky was grey. The trees looked lifeless. A few women in headscarves patrolled the edge of the prison wall.

The cigarettes were so stale that they were brittle to the touch. He bought a fresh packet at a kiosk just outside the prison. He closed his eyes and inhaled, then walked briskly towards the market. He bought a pair of sneakers, white with green swooshes, and haggled for a tracksuit, black with red stripes on the sleeves. A plain white T-shirt. Socks. Underwear.

He stepped into a café to change.

At a phone booth in the bus station he dialed his cousin Ibrahim. The phone rang and rang.

138

Bassam was a little surprised, when he shaved his beard, that his face was not more hollowed out.

137

He left his old clothes hanging on a hook in the bathroom of the café. He laced his spare shoes and threw them in the air where they caught on the telephone wire and dangled.

Bassam looked back towards the prison and saw several cardboard blowguns sticking out from the upper floors. A few notes, like bits of spittle flying, sailed out from the windows to the waiting women below.

136

Rami was attracted to patterns. He sketched them endlessly. His small red notebooks were filled with intersecting lines. It was not a matter of simple crosshatching. It was, he supposed, his form of meditation, a way to think. Bring the pen to the edge of the page. Let it drop.

The sketches seemed to vault off and extend themselves outwards into the void. He seldom used any of them in his advertisements. When it came to corporate ads, he was called upon for bolder images. But there were times he would look back through the sketchbooks, searching for ideas, and be taken by the patterns themselves, their ragged sense of purpose, their forms growing out of necessity.

135

Among scholars of Islam, mathematical numbers are considered to be not just quantities, but qualities too.

134

One of the most beautiful works of Islamic art ever produced was the towering wooden staircase and pulpit that sat for eight hundred years in the Al-Aqsa mosque in Jerusalem.

The pulpit, known as the minbar of Saladin, was built originally in Aleppo in the twelfth century in celebration of the defeat of the Crusaders. It was transported under guard to the mosque in the Holy City, where it was installed and became one of the most revered pieces in the Muslim world.

The minbar was considered a masterpiece of sacred geometry, wood carving, marquetry and calligraphy. Nineteen feet high and thirteen feet deep, the pulpit was fashioned by hundreds of guilded craftsmen who were considered the geniuses of their time.

Sixteen thousand finely carved blocks were joined together in interlocking pieces. The inside was hollow. The whole structure seemed to hang miraculously on itself. The latticework doors led to the staircase which led, in turn, to the upper pulpit. The panels were studded with ivory and ebony. The patterns emerged from a simple six-sided shape, but the resulting geometric effects—spiraling rosettes, honeycombs, circles, squares, triangles, arabesques—were almost unfathomably intricate. The cascading calligraphy featured lengthy quotations from the Qur'an.

Every Friday for centuries the imam climbed the staircase and delivered sermons to the faithful below.

133

When Bassam was six, his father took him and his brothers to Jerusalem. They walked through the grounds of the mosque where their father sat and smoked and told them stories: the night flight of Muhammad, the tale of Saladin, the melting of the gold for the roof of the Dome. He said that there used to be a very beautiful pulpit in the mosque but that it had since been burned down.

132

The German writer Goethe said that the tone of mind produced by architecture approaches the effect of music—that to look upon a thing is to hear it. Music is liquid architecture, he wrote, and architecture is frozen music.

131

The minbar stood for eight hundred years without a single nail or screw or any glue holding it together.

130

In the early morning of August 21, 1969, an Australian tourist, Denis Michael Rohan, passed the early morning guards at the Al-Aqsa mosque, carrying a camera and a backpack. The guards knew the young man: he had been visiting every day for over a month. He had already tipped them extravagantly. He greeted them in Arabic and asked if he could slip in early to take photographs. They allowed him to pass.

Inside the mosque, Rohan opened his backpack, laid a scarf down on the steps, sprinkled kerosene over it, climbed the staircase, doused the pulpit with benzene and then set it all alight. He walked calmly out of the mosque, stopped to chat with the guards, then began to run when the flames were noticed.

Inside, the roof of the mosque caught. By noon only a few charred pieces of the minbar remained.

When word of the fire reached the Islamic world, a state of emergency was declared. King Hussein of Jordan called for a military summit. Saudi Arabia immediately put its troops on standby. A general strike was called in Pakistan. Iraq announced the execution of fifteen foreign spies. Deadly riots erupted in India.

Rohan was arrested two days later by Israeli police. He was, he said, acting on the word of God. The fire would hasten the return of the Messiah. He saw himself as a direct descendant of Abraham—his last name spelled backwards, Nahor, was the same as Abraham's grandfather.

At his trial the Australian said that the fire was the most important event for the world since the trial of Jesus Christ. He pleaded insanity and was sentenced to lifetime confinement in a mental hospital in

Jerusalem, but he was released in 1974 on humanitarian grounds. He died twenty-one years later in Callan Park hospital in Sydney.

129

During his trial, Rohan admitted to Israeli psychiatrists that his first-grade teacher in Australia used to make him crouch in a wicker basket when he misbehaved. His classmates filed past and taunted him, calling him Moses.

128

In the second half of the twentieth century psychiatrists began to notice an increasing number of tourists in Jerusalem suffering from acute psychotic decompensation: delusions and other episodes induced by proximity to the holy places of Jerusalem.

Because of the high incidence of the cases—at least a hundred a year—they were channeled to one central facility, the Kfar Shaul Mental Health Center.

The patients who suffer from the syndrome—some believing they are Jesus, some Mary, some Moses, some Paul—can be found wandering in the streets of the Old City in clothing adapted from towels and hotel bedsheets, wearing crowns of woven thorns on their heads.

Often the syndrome disappears as soon as they leave the city.

127

The Kfar Shaul Mental Health Center was built on the site of Deir Yassin. The village—a series of arches and gateways and narrow stone streets built with local limestone and lined with low palm trees—lay on the outskirts of Jerusalem.

In early 1948 the residents of the village signed a nonaggression pact with the neighboring Jewish village of Giv'at Shaul, but in April rogue elements of the Jewish militia broke the peace and over one hundred Palestinian men, women and children were murdered.

The event helped to set off the Nakba. Fears of another massacre prompted hundreds of thousands of Palestinians to flee their homes, never to return.

On a wall of the village is a slogan in Danish scratched on a rock with a nail. It reads: *True masonry is not held together by mortar, but by time.*

126

Albert Einstein wrote to the American Friends of the Fighters for the Freedom of Israel—known also as the Stern Gang—to say that, after the massacre in Deir Yassin, he would no longer be willing to assist them with aid or help raise money for their cause.

125

Over the years the Saladin pulpit had been photographed and sketched and filmed, but had never been intricately mapped. There were no blueprints. No working drawings. No craftsmen could be found who knew the full secrets to the patterns.

A call from the Hashemite royal family in Saudi Arabia went out to teams of architects, mathematicians, computer experts, calligraphers, biomorphic designers and even theologians, but nobody, even with the aid of advanced computers, was able to decode the secret of the wooden pulpit.

The craft skills, too, had been lost for centuries. Most craftsmen had, over the years, begun using nails or screws or glue and the joinery skills had all but disappeared.

After three rounds of global searches, the job of designing the new minbar, and putting together a team of the world's best craftsmen, was given to a candidate nobody had ever heard of before—a Bedouin civil engineer, Minwer al-Meheid.

He had discovered that the secret to the structure was that the thousands of parts were not hung on a framework at all, but were harmoniously integrated.

124

The raw wood took years to source—the perfect grove of walnut trees was finally found by a Turkish joiner who led the designers to a remote forest on the border of Iran and Iraq. The walnut trees were chopped down in the middle of winter, but the lumbermen had to wait four months for the roads to unfreeze so the trunks could be hauled out.

The wood was tough, hard, beautiful, with a fine grain and a subtle shade. The trees were tall enough to yield long panels and were not given to splitting.

In a warehouse in Amman the craftsmen came together—Indonesians, Turks, Egyptians, Jordanians and Palestinians.

Following al-Meheid's design, they began to cut and piece together the sixteen thousand pieces of wood. The first panel took them two and a half months. The remainder took several years.

When they were finished, art critics from London, Amman, New York, Paris, Baghdad, all said that they had somehow, miraculously, given new life to that which had disappeared.

It had taken, in all, thirty-seven years for the minbar of Saladin to be reconstructed.

123

Philip Glass's experimental opera *Einstein on the Beach* exists without a traditional plot. The libretto uses short bursts of poetry, song, rhythm, solfège syllables, and instances of numerical repetition. In performance, the four acts take five hours or more.

The piece—intended to draw out what Glass thought of as a *discovered* Einstein, perhaps even a more truthful one, from the apparent plotlessness—is kept together by its knee plays, or intermezzos, stretching between the acts.

The knee plays combine a chant-like choral pattern with a pulsing human narration. The effect is a sort of serenity surrounded by the feeling of being constantly disturbed.

122

From the age of eleven Rami knew the difference between a Panther and a Tiger. He could distinguish between the Obersturmbannführer and the Reichsführer SS. He learned the specifications of the Messerschmitt BF 109. He knew the engine sizes of all the Stuka planes. Sneaking up behind him were Eichmann, Goebbels, Koch, Himmler. Anger swelled in him.

He did everything he could to nourish the rage. He studied all the books he could find on the Holocaust, combed through them late at night. Raul Hilberg. Israel Gutman. Chil Rajchman. He knew by heart all the names of the camps. Buchenwald. Flossenbürg. Belzec. Herzogenbusch. Mauthausen. Treblinka. He could rattle off the exact dimensions of the camps at Auschwitz.

Every fact, every figure, haunted him. The uprising at Sobibor. Kristallnacht. Lidice. He studied the backs of products in the supermarket to make sure they weren't German. He had nightmares about being turned into soap. He even abhorred the sound of the accent, found himself attributing it to teachers he disliked.

The very thought of visiting Germany brought a fierce pour of cold along the length of his spine.

121

120

The trains rattled through them. Berlin. Cologne. Munich. Hanover. Frankfurt. Leipzig. Interview after interview. Town hall gatherings. Meetings with philanthropists. They were whisked around from place to place. By the end of the days they were exhausted. It stunned Rami to be there. He tried to explain it to journalists: that he had grown up a child of the Holocaust and had vowed never to visit. He had been sure it would unhinge him. The thought of traveling near the death camps made him bristle. A train station. A loudspeaker announcement. A man in uniform. A belted overcoat. A trolley car. A pair of hands clasped behind a back. A woman hurrying along the street. Anything at all. They were met at the arrival gate by a small group of professors and activists. Rami felt the fear skipping along the walls of his throat. His hands were clammy. He couldn't shake it. The trunk of a Mercedes was lifted. The silver badge shone in the fluorescent light. It appeared like an ironic peace symbol. He eased his way into the back seat. On the drive into the city he stayed silent, allowed Bassam to do all the talking. Out the window, the high glass buildings, the clean architectural lines. The hotel was what he had anticipated—the high columns, the brickwork, the fountain, the grand entrance—but the employees were cheery, the light bright. Somehow he had expected Germany to be darker, lower, more insidious. He took the elevator to his room, locked the door, called Nurit on the phone. She chided him. She had been to Germany many times: there was nothing to worry about. Relax. Enjoy yourself. Call me every day. He stepped into the shower. Even that, even here: the shower. He paused and looked at himself in the mirror. His bright pale skin, his hair newly cut. He shaved carefully, put on a fresh shirt, phoned Bassam's room. They went downstairs together. The restaurant was a mirrorhouse of chandeliers. A table of ten people, at least two of them Jewish, he thought. He knew that Bassam would likely be doing the same mathematics, listening for the Muslim names, looking for the Arab faces. The hosts outlined the trip: the talks they would do, the interviews, the meetings. There was extraordinary interest among the German people, they said. An Israeli and a Palestinian traveling together. More than that. An Israeli, against the Occupation. A Palestinian, studying the Holocaust. How to hold these things together. How to waken the sleep in the audience. The silence was there to be undermined. They were sure that people were ready to listen. Trust us, they said. The restaurant filled. Wine was opened. Bassam stepped outside to smoke. Rami told the hosts about his Hungarian father. He observed every Memorial Day, he said, but he had grown over the years to watch for the manipulation of those times, the nostalgia, the industry of it. The grief. The fear. The way the past now shaped the present. To be powerless against it. Rami poured another glass of wine. Topics swirled, contradicted, returned. The flights over Auschwitz. The delegations at Bergen-Belsen. What it meant to re-member, as opposed to never forgetting. The restaurant felt kaleido-scopic: so many plates spinning. He was surprised when he slept well that night. He walked out into the morning and followed a streetsweeper who sounded as if he was the first man ever to whistle. The light was raw and yellow. He walked by the Main river. The height of the skyline surprised him. It was a country, he thought, that was pushing itself upwards. In the late morning they had the first of their meetings, at a law firm in Innenstadt. A silence settled over the room when their stories were finished. A journalist waited for them in a restaurant on the Goethestrasse. She had a shine to her eyes, fierce and tender. She layered her questions, dug at acute angles. She wanted to know what Bassam thought of the Arab response during World War Two? What did Rami have to say of the Second Intifada? Did they think they were normalizing the conflict? Rami leaned forward. How does grief normalize a conflict? he asked. He could feel himself opening: a perplexing freedom. The interviews piled into one another. In the evening they addressed a crowd of two hundred. Rami could hear a rustle in the audience. A handkerchief being furtively passed along the front row. So many accents, so many languages. Hebrew, Arabic, English, German. He could feel his body loosen. They continued on trains across the country. The stations were neon-lit. Music was piped along the platforms. No flags flew. The carriages were comfortable. They snoozed on one another's shoulders. In the evenings the halls were full. Rami spoke about being a graduate of Auschwitz. The listeners sat up. He could see something travel across their eyes. He might have been a thorn, a reminder, he knew, but afterwards they came up to talk to him, shook his hand, thanked him for coming. He kept looking for a crack in the veneer: a curt dismissal, a misplaced word. None came. They took a plane to Berlin, went to the last remnants of the Wall. End the preoccupation, he whispered to Bassam. They laughed quietly. At the Shalom Rollberg center, Rami said to the audience that all walls were destined to fall, no matter what. He was not so naïve, though, to believe that more would not be built. It was a world of walls. Still, it was his job to insert a crack in the one most visible to him. They traveled south to Leipzig and walked through the gates at Buchenwald. It felt to Rami like an ancient ruin. The sign on the ironwork could only be read from the inside. *Jedem das Seine.* They walked back out together. To Each His Own. In interviews they tried to defer to one another. It became, at times, like a comedy routine. You first. No you first. They were Assi and Guri, Abbott and Costello. Once, at the end of an interview, Bassam touched Rami's elbow, smiled and said: Haven't the Jews suffered enough? Their own private joke. The journalist was mystified. Rami pulled up an Israeli TV clip on his phone and showed her a video from the *Hahamishia Hakamerit* comedy show. For a long time the clip had been Rami and Bassam's way to blow off steam. They knew many of the words off by heart. *On your marks. Get set! It's about the bambino in Lane Six. Come on, finish the job.* The journalist was stone-faced at first, but at the end of the video she allowed herself a small embarrassed chuckle. Rami played it again on the train towards Hanover. Wolfgang, he laughed, get your head off my shoulder, I've suffered enough.

119

Bassam received a note from a professor of theology in Ludwig Maximilian University in Munich: *It is in your image that I would like to enter into the remainder of these days given to me.*

118

SCENE: A running track in Stuttgart, Germany. 1995 World Championships. A German SPORTS OFFICIAL is about to pull the starting gun trigger at the 100-meter hurdle race.

> SPORTS OFFICIAL
> On your marks. Get set!

Lined up at the blocks are several tall, well-built sprinters from all over the world, along with a short skinny ISRAELI ATHLETE. Just as the race is about to begin two APPARATCHIKS make their way across the track, pushing aside the hurdles to get to the SPORTS OFFICIAL.

> APPARATCHIK ONE/TWO
> Excuse me, excuse me, just a moment please!
> Hello and good evening. We are from the
> Israeli delegation and we wanted to ask for a
> favor. Look, I'll be honest with you, it's about
> the bambino in Lane Six. The little one. He is,
> how do you say it? not very fast. Slow even.
> Very. But very talented. Very. And we wanted to
> ask you a little favor. Nothing big. Just to give
> him five or six meters' head start.

The confused Sports Official turns around to look for help and calls on his friend Wolfgang, but nobody replies.

APPARATCHIK ONE

Come on, what do you say? Only six meters!
Anyway he will come last! We just want to
lessen the humiliation! You know, it's not nice,
his mother is in the stadium.

The Israeli Athlete gestures from the starting line, putting his fingers to his lips to quiet them.

APPARATCHIK ONE

Look over there, his mother. Very brave woman.

The German Sports Official guardedly waves the starting gun in the direction the Apparatchik was pointing. The athlete's mother is nowhere to be seen.

APPARATCHIK ONE

After all she's been through—she came back
here to see her son running! It breaks the
heart!!

SPORTS OFFICIAL

Wolfgang?

APPARATCHIK ONE/TWO

Look at them, they are all on steroids. Only
him with the chicken legs, like popsicle sticks.
What are we asking from you? Just a little help
to—to—lessen the historic injustice. What do
you say? Eight meters?

The Sports Official again calls for Wolfgang, but there is no reply.

APPARATCHIK TWO

You gentiles have hearts of stone. You love
humiliating us.

> APPARATCHIK ONE

Calm down, Feldermaus.

> APPARATCHIK TWO

I should calm down? The dog should calm down.
How are you not ashamed? You should be
ashamed. Did you not see *Schindler's List*? All the
televisions of the world watching us! You don't
care! Haven't the Jewish people suffered enough?
Haven't the Jewish people suffered enough?!!!

> APPARATCHIK ONE

Relax, Feldermaus, don't waste your breath.

> APPARATCHIK TWO:

Did we ask for a medal? To win? All we ask for
is nine meters. Why does he enjoy humiliating
us?

He grabs the Sports Official's starting gun and puts it to his neck.

> APPARATCHIK TWO

Come on, finish the work, I'm a Jew too, finish
the work, come on, come on!

> APPARATCHIK ONE

Stop, Feldermaus, stop!

> APPARATCHIK TWO

You technocrat. Eichmann!

The Sports Official takes a deep breath and gestures with his head
for the Israeli Athlete to go forward. The Israeli Athlete in Lane Six
sheepishly picks up his running block.

> ATHLETE
> *(To other runners.)* I'm sorry, guys.

As the Apparatchiks watch the Athlete move forward, they shake the
Sports Official's hand.

APPARATCHIK TWO

The Jewish people thank you very much, you
are a great man.

APPARATCHIK ONE

(To Athlete.) More, more, take more. Stop! Not
too much! *(To Sports Official.)* He's a good boy.
You are a great man, thank you very much,
thank you very much.

APPARATCHIK TWO

I wish you a kosher Passover. Thank you.

APPARATCHIK ONE

After this we will take your details and build a
big tree in your name on the Hasidic Boulevard,
University, in Jerusalem!

SPORTS OFFICIAL

(Speaking for the first time.)
Yes! Thank you. Thank you!

APPARATCHIK ONE

Uh, just a small thing. If it's not too much.
Before you . . . *(about starting gun)* "Boom
boom" . . . just give him a little with the eye. So
he can be prepared.

SPORTS OFFICIAL

With the eye?

APPARATCHIK ONE

He's a good boy.

APPARATCHIK TWO

A hint.

SPORTS OFFICIAL

A hint! Yes. Good.

               APPARATCHIK ONE
He's a good boy.

               SPORTS OFFICIAL
Good, good . . . Shalom!

             APPARATCHIK ONE/TWO
Shalom, shalom, thank you.

              SPORTS OFFICIAL
Shalom, shalom . . . On your marks! Get set!
(Raises starting gun and shoots.)
Go!

117

Their favorite shot in the skit was the final one where the Israeli athlete, given a head start of seven or eight meters, runs to the first hurdle, puts his hand on the crossbar and attempts, very gingerly, to step over.

116

After the segment aired on Channel 2 in the 1990s, the author of the script, Etgar Keret, was labeled a self-hating Jew and an anti-Semite by a well-known Israeli ethics philosopher, Assa Kasher.

    Kasher had—years before—helped develop the IDF's code of ethics, enshrining the idea that it was the Most Moral Army in the World.

115

On the Wall near Qalandia checkpoint: *THE WORLD'S MOST ~~MORAL ARMY~~.*

114

Six weeks before Abir died, Bassam penciled her height on the door of their apartment in Anata: he struck a single dark mark halfway between the doorknob and the keyhole.

Until the day they moved, neither Bassam nor Salwa painted over the mark. Their other children grew up above it.

Bassam darkened the single strike with pencil every year on her birthday.

113

Araab was three years older than Abir; Areen, two years older; Muhammad, one year younger; Ahmed, two years younger. Hiba, the youngest of all, by three years, was most like Abir.

112

Even nowadays, when he passes through the unmarked doorways of his home in Jericho, Bassam feels that the unwritten mark somehow touches him in the midpoint of his chest.

111

He paced the corridor. The officials in the hospital had refused an autopsy. It was not necessary, they said. It was clearly blunt force trauma, a splintering of bone in the posterior casing of the skull, the bone itself penetrating the brain. They had X-rays they could give him. The official reports of the doctors. Blood tests. Cardiograms. The results could be notarized if he liked. They addressed him formally. Even bowed slightly to him. They understood his pain, they said. They wanted to relieve any burden he was feeling. But an autopsy would be complicated. They would need official permission. There were a series of things to consider. These decisions would take time. There were official channels to go through.

Bassam insisted again on an autopsy. The officials stepped away to make phone calls. The clock hands on the wall turned. They came back, their ties more firmly mounted to their chins. Could he explain again why exactly he needed an autopsy? Bassam could feel the blood move to his face. He had thought about it for the previous two days, he said, and he was going to bring criminal charges. Against whom? they asked. Against the State, he said. They paused a moment, tugged the ends of their white coats. They were sterner now in their politeness, and yet there was also something in them that aligned with him. Yes, they said, something has gone astray, there is quite possibly blame to be apportioned, but criminal charges, Mister Aramin, really? Yes, I'm sure, he said. We're just not convinced that's the right path. It's not a path, it's a fact. We apologize, they said, but we haven't got the power to order an autopsy. As a parent, he said, I have the right to demand one. We have made several phone calls to our superiors, they said, and our requests have been denied, but you can still have access to all the records, all the information you might need is there. No, he said, I need an official autopsy. They fidgeted. We're sorry, we have gone through all the channels, we have orders.

He could tell from the way their eyes flicked about that there was something more going on: already the IDF had released a statement claiming that no shots had been fired from the patrol, that there had been rioting in the area, and that Abir had most likely been hit by a stone thrown by Palestinian rioters.

The officials understood perfectly well, they said, but if he wanted an autopsy he would have to pay for it himself. It could not be state-ordered. It would cost many thousands of shekels. He would be better off relying on the records.

—Okay, said Bassam, I'll pay for it.

110

The autopsy cost six thousand eight hundred shekels. It was paid for immediately after a whip-round in the hospital among those waiting alongside him: Rami, Alon, Suleiman, Dina, Muhammad, Robi, Yehuda, Avi and Yitzak.

109

When the autopsy was finished he was given her belongings in a sealed plastic bag. Her nightdress had been carefully folded. Her school clothes, too, were neatly placed. At the bottom of the bag were the two patent leather shoes, one slightly scuffed from where it had skidded on the ground.

108

The criminal case was thrown out almost immediately: lack of sufficient evidence. It didn't surprise him. He had felt all along it would happen this way. The small press corps met outside the courthouse on a sunny Thursday afternoon. Bassam wore a suit and tie.

—I will bring it now to civil court, he said.

107

Six thousand eight hundred shekels in 2007: one thousand five hundred and seventy dollars.

106

Halfway through the case the judge called for a reenactment. She wanted everyone involved to go to Anata to see if they could figure out what had happened, and how.

A hum rose in the court. The defense team immediately lodged an objection: there were issues of safety here, procedure, court jurisdiction, but the judge waved their arguments away.

—We will convene in Anata, she said.

The convoy drove out from West Jerusalem on a Thursday morning. Streets were cordoned off. Several jeeps stood idling. A helicopter hovered above, making a loud dragonfly of itself.

The day was overcast. A blanket of warmth lay over the whole town. The wind was shrapneled with dust.

Bassam arrived early. He watched as the judge got out of her car. She wore a modest dress that covered her arms and knees. She reached in her handbag for a headscarf, tied it deftly in a knot beneath her chin. She shaded her eyes with her hand and looked around. It was possibly the first time she had ever been to Anata: the houses high on the hill, the ramshackle apartments below, the garages, the discarded tires, the two-lane road, the roundabout, the boarded-up shops, the broken concrete barriers, the dented signposts, the kids skipping their way to school, the crossing guard in her hijab.

The judge turned her face from the wind, dug in her handbag for a pair of sunglasses, donned them, then strode to the spot where Abir had fallen. She looked down at the ground and nodded, ordered a photograph, then stepped back to the corner. She told the court clerk to count out the steps and then beckoned the Commander of the Border Police unit.

—Where's the graveyard?

—Excuse me?

—The one you were coming from.

—Sorry?

—In your testimony.

—Just over there, Your Honor.

—Around the corner?

In response, the Commander had no response. The judge gazed up at the apartment building between the graveyard and the death spot. She penciled something in a small red notebook.

—Let me see the graveyard.

—I don't think that's a good idea, Your Honor.

—These are my proceedings, Commander.

His face reddened. He summoned the soldiers. They formed a ring around the judge and walked her to the corner. She halted the group underneath the tall graveyard wall.

—They were throwing stones from here?

—Yes.

—They've come a long way, these Arabs.

—Excuse me? said the Commander.

—Quite a feat. Throwing stones around a corner.

—With all due respect, Your Honor, they could have been firing from several angles.

—I see.

—You have to understand, Your Honor, these are combat conditions. We are constantly under attack. There can be stones coming from anywhere. The top of the roof even. We have to have eyes in the backs of our heads.

—She was ten years old, Commander.

She turned on her heel and walked back towards the corner. The soldiers followed. She strode forward again to the spot where Abir had been shot: Here?

—Yes. I suppose, said the Commander. About here. Maybe.

—I need to see a jeep.

—Your Honor?

—I want to see the inside of a jeep.

—Yes, Your Honor.

A call went over the radio and a jeep pulled up from the roundabout. It was shepherded in by two other jeeps. The judge stepped towards the middle vehicle, hitched her dress, climbed in.

—Around the corner, she said to the driver.

A quick hard wind dusted the side of the jeep. Bassam was sure he could hear every grain of sand hit. The vehicle rounded the corner, then returned and reversed once more. The back flap opened and then it was closed again.

A small gasp went around the watchers when the barrel of a gun emerged from the small square hole.

The door closed and opened again. It seemed to Bassam that everything had to be repeated.

When the judge stepped out of the jeep, her dress rose slightly. She pulled it down tight on her knees, walked once again to the spot where Abir had fallen.

She paused a moment, lifted her sunglasses, and looked down.

—Okay, we will reconvene in Jerusalem.

105

Y.A. appeared early. He was twenty-three years old, but his hair was already beginning to thin, a scattered peninsula on the crown of his head. He wore a grey jacket, a rumpled blue shirt and a yellow tie that seemed much too bright. His eyes were quick, but he kept them low to the floor. He was shadowed by a lawyer who held a briefcase across his midriff as if to protect himself from a blow. Y.A. scrunched against the wall. He looked like a man who would have given anything to disappear into the brickwork. He had said publicly, months before, that he would attend the trial. He could not get out of it now. He would, he said, be vindicated. His lawyer sat next to him and placed the briefcase down. They were joined by two women who sat immediately behind them. It was as if, in some chess game, Y.A. had made himself into the corner rook: he would remain there, he would never be castled. He folded his hands in his lap, gazed forward as the press seats filled.

A half-dozen reporters unfurled their notebooks. A number of law students sat in the back rows. Bassam's supporters filled the other seats: they were mostly Israelis. Some of them held pictures of Abir at their chests. They rose to their feet when the judge came in. She interlocked her fingers, made a pyramid of her hands. She glanced at Bassam, briefly caught his eye. He hadn't expected that. She leaned forward, spoke slowly.

The court is of the opinion. We have come to the decision. We have weighed the varied testimonies. Abir Aramin was a resident of the Jerusalem municipality. We have decided. The responsibility of the State of Israel. It has been determined.

Gasps rose from the press gallery. The state's lawyers remained seated. Bassam's supporters erupted in applause. He turned and bowed his head, pleaded with them to be quiet. He glanced across at Y.A. The soldier stared straight ahead. He might yet have been staring through a small four-inch hole in the rear door of the jeep. Rat tat tat. A teenager still. In a video game.

Bassam noticed that Y.A. had nodded when the verdict came. As if he knew. As if he had expected it. As if he had been forewarned.

The compensation was yet to be determined. Still, the State would have to pay for loss of years, negligence, burial expenses. The gate in the dock was opened. Y.A. was hustled to the back of the court, shadowed by his lawyer. He seemed to pause a moment at the door and then the small coin of his youthful baldness disappeared into the shadows. Shouts and cheers skittered around the court. An officer called for calm. There were handshakes for Bassam, backslaps, smiles. He could hardly stand. He needed to take a breath. The way to the rear of the court was blocked. All around him his supporters carried the photo of his daughter. Here she was again, Abir, multiple versions of her, yet always the same, his gone daughter. Someone touched his elbow. Congratulations, brother. A landmark. Can you believe it? He hung his head. It seemed that the case had happened to someone other than himself, someone out there hovering in a different world. He didn't feel that he had won anything at all. There had been no criminal charges, no official admission of guilt. He pushed his way out of the courtroom. He turned a corner into another, it was all corners, always corners. Around another corner he saw men filing out from the bathroom. He eased his way past. He was not surprised to see Y.A. standing at the mirror, still in a huddle with his lawyer. Y.A. looked up at him. Something penitent and fearful in his eyes. The lawyer tried to move him aside, but Y.A. stayed. Bassam had rehearsed it in his head, in Hebrew, a hundred times.

—You're the victim here. Not me.

104

A decade after the bombing the family of Yael Botvin, the fourteen-year-old blown up alongside Smadar, brought a lawsuit in the Washington, D.C., District Court.

The family sought damages from the Islamic Republic of Iran, the Iranian Ministry of Information and Security, and the Iranian Revolutionary Guard, who they said were collectively responsible for the Hamas attack. The lawsuit alleged that the suicide bombing was approved at the very highest levels of Iranian government, and argued that Yael, as a U.S. citizen, could have her case adjudicated under United States law.

In her testimony Yael's mother, Julie, said that one of the most difficult things of all was watching Yael's friends moving on with their lives, getting married and having babies.

103

In 2012, the Botvin estate was awarded $1.7 million.

102

The Islamic Republic of Iran never paid.

101

Every day, outside the courthouse, Rami gathered with Bassam and his supporters. Each time a vehicle went through the gates they held giant pictures of Abir high in the air.

100

Several newspaper articles were published in Israel and the United States deploring the judge's decision in the aftermath of the Aramin case. No civil proceedings should ever be allowed in such a military situation, they said. The criminal courts had already indicated that there was a lack of sufficient evidence. Why should the State have to shoulder the burden? It had been pointed out in court that it was possible that the child had been hit by a rock thrown by rioters and, even if she had been struck by a stray rubber bullet, an unlikely scenario, the Commander had testified that they were under relentless attack. The legal decision could, in the future, endanger the lives of Israeli soldiers forced to make crucial split-second decisions in the interests of security. If made to hesitate, they could endanger not only themselves but their fellow soldiers and indeed citizens. Furthermore, and most alarming, Bassam Aramin was a convicted terrorist. He had spent seven years in prison for a series of hand grenade attacks. He belonged to the Fatah faction, which he continued to support. One million shekels would, no doubt, go a long way towards another terrorist venture and who could know what he was planning now.

99

The grenades rolled in around the body of the jeep. One, two. They looked to him, from a distance, like small round stones. One grenade stopped by the back wheel. It bucked around and brought up a plume of dust.

98

Other newspapers said the Aramin case was a landmark decision. Despite the lack of an earlier criminal conviction, the defendant had been afforded due process in a civilian court and the judge's decision was a significant step forward in reinforcing the democratic essence of the State. It reiterated the integrity of the judicial system while simultaneously questioning the nature of what was often referred to as the world's most moral army. If indeed the army was to be moral— as it had been designed, decades ago, to be, by the founders of the country—it had to embrace the system of checks and balances. The action of a single soldier or a rogue commander was not necessarily the policy of the army, and it was important for the integrity of the military to acknowledge the nature and extent of its mistakes. The verdict opened up the landscape of possibility for both Israelis and Palestinians and enabled them to properly question the actions of those whose duty it was to protect them. Throughout the process it had to be remembered that the life of Abir Aramin, ten years old, had been lost and nothing, now, would ever bring her back.

97

A second small bang came from under the wheel. He thought he saw the tire shred. He waited for the other to blow. Nothing happened. The jeep lurched forward and then the doors opened. Two, three, four shapes spilled out.

96

Other papers said that the case of Abir Aramin was the single exception that proved the existence of a brutal system. It was a victory, but a Pyrrhic one. The fact that this single case garnered so much attention highlighted the wildly unbalanced nature of the Israeli judicial system and military courts wherein not a single criminal case, including the Aramin case, had ever been successfully brought against an Israeli soldier for the murder of a noncombatant, even a child. A criminal case would have brought into question the true nature of the conflict, but that had been dismissed out of hand. The actions of the civil court judge, while admirable in the specific, were but a minuscule gesture in the wider political context. The Aramin case was diverted into the streams of civil law. The verdict encouraged the illusion that Palestinians were afforded a self-determining series of rights within the wider system. It was an essentially undemocratic system in which children, when not being shot with rubber bullets, could be brought to military courts where there was a 99.74 percent chance of being found guilty. Abir Aramin had suffered the same sort of fate—she had been guilty of being a Palestinian, ten years old, standing outside the school gates, having bought two shekels' worth of candy.

95

Apeirogon: a shape with a countably infinite number of sides.

94

From the Greek, *apeiron:* to be boundless, to be endless. Alongside the Indo-European root of *per:* to try, to risk.

93

As a whole, an apeirogon approaches the shape of a circle, but a magnified view of a small piece appears to be a straight line. One can finally arrive at any point within the whole. Anywhere is reachable. Anything is possible, even the seemingly impossible.

At the same time, one can arrive anywhere within an apeirogon and the entirety of the shape is complicit in the journey, even that which has not yet been imagined.

92

Later—when the compensation was announced—Bassam saw Y.A. again. This time Y.A. wore a kippah on his head. He had made a decision to become a repentant, a *chozer b'teshuva*, to be born again, to go back to his roots.

91

Maimonides, the twelfth-century Jewish philosopher, said that the process of repentance included three stages: confession, regret, and a vow not to repeat the misdeed.

90

In the Qur'an, God is variously called Al-Ghafoor, Al-Afuw, Al-Tawwab, Al-Haleem, Ar-Rahman and Ar-Rahim: the Most Forgiving, the Pardoner, the Clement, the Forbearing, the Most Merciful and the Most Compassionate.

89

At times Bassam would imagine Y.A. not living the life of a *chozer b'teshuva* at all, that it was a ploy, a ruse, and the soldier had turned his back on the idea of repentance altogether, left the army, found himself a job, high tech of course, low on the ladder, but still highly paid, a surprise even to himself, a lucky break for an ordinary border guard, not a repentant at all, no, and he was possibly living, nowadays, in a light-filled apartment in Tel Aviv on the edge of the sea, something he liked showing off, small but impressive, a room so full of mirrors that he would not have to look back.

Artwork on the walls. Brazilian hardwood floors. Handwoven carpets. Lots of fancy white machinery in the kitchen. Modems and television screens and wires neatly tucked behind the walls. Soft rock music coming from hidden speakers.

Y.A. would walk around in his bare feet, marveling at his new life. His white linen trousers rolled to the ankles. His short-sleeve shirt flagrantly open. A number of thin string bracelets displayed on his wrist. He would be carrying a glass of ice water with perfectly square cubes and he would catch a full reflection of himself in the plate glass windows, pause a moment, turn, glance again, cock his head sideways, finish his water, dump the ice in the sink, run his hands along the high silver tap, place the glass in the drying rack, check his mobile phone as he crossed the floor.

At the door of the apartment Y.A. would slip into a pair of white loafers, lean down to pick up a beach bag, flick another look in the mirror, close the door, making sure he locked it.

He would step along the corridor in soft fluorescent light and move towards the elevators. The elevator would come quickly, efficiently. He would nod to a neighbor—someone tall, elegant, smart perhaps—carrying a poodle in her arms. Y.A. would pause on the ground floor to let the woman out, then glide around her to open up the first of two heavy glass doors.

Outside, in the street, the woman would set the poodle gently on the ground and the dog would strain against its leash. Y.A. would lean down and pat the dog goodbye, begin his glide down the street, the sort of walk that would make him seem as if he wore cushions on his feet. He would hear the high beep of a reversing truck. The tinny sounds of a coffee shop. The thrumming engine of a crane. The click of car locks. A bicycle bell from the path along Frishman Beach.

He would walk past orange construction barriers, pause a moment at the lights, pat his beach bag against his leg. The traffic would roar by: taxis, trucks, a plain white police car.

He would cross at a clip towards the promenade, stop at the bicycle path, watch the bare-chested runners go by, the young women in their running bras, the elderly in their purposeful seaside shuffle. Y.A. would slip off his shoes and carry them in his hand, then unbutton his shirt further as he strolled.

On the beach, the dull wooden sounds of the matkot players, their shouts, their laughter, their paddles slapped against their bare thighs. The umbrellas, the coolers, the towels, the oiled bodies, even now, early in the morning. The babies held to chests. The older men with their copies of *Haaretz*, their coffee flasks, their flip phones. The single discarded stiletto. The radio music: a mizrahi rhythm, a rap song, a Degibri jazz riff. The immigrant vendors. The English football shirts. The French football shirts. The Spanish football shirts. Y.A. would find himself a patch of sand and unfurl his towel from his beach bag, tuck his mobile phone in a zip compartment, crack open a bottle of water, and stand there, looking out at the bright kayakers and the three-colored windsurfers and the blue of the Mediterranean and the lines of swimmers churning along the shore, and at the sun climbing in the high and very blue sky. He would stretch his arms wide and pause a moment, and then he would re-cap the water bottle, place it back in his beach bag, before stepping out of his linen trousers to reveal a tight blue swimsuit, and then he would move towards the shore, zigzagging past the last of the matkot players, easing into a slight jog, and making his way blithely along the shoreline, a man known to, and intimate with, the sea.

88

At times like this Bassam would imagine, too, a single rubber bullet in flight along the beach, coming in over the waves, over the sun-bathers, over the deck chairs, over the umbrellas, the bullet pausing a moment, mid-beach, as if to make a decision, spinning in place, defying time, then slamming forward without warning into the back of Y.A.'s head.

87

Splintering, precisely, the back of his skull.

86

You're the victim here, not me.

85

Rami, on the other hand, imagined Y.A. in a low-ceilinged flat. In a town in the Negev maybe. In an apartment block. A little run-down.

Shabby at the edges. On the third floor, maybe the fourth. At the end of a corridor. Several locks on the door. A Likud sticker by the bell. The door slightly ajar. A creak from the hinges. The cramped darkness inside. The smell of cigarette smoke. The shape of Y.A.'s mother at the sink, gently humming over last night's dishes. Her expansive floral dress. Her hair in a net. A radio on in the background, Reshet Gimmel, 97.8 FM. The hanging dishtowels. The Formica counter. The jar of Nestlé. The mismatched crockery. The chipped olive dish. The Armenian ceramic clock ticking just to the side of the stove. The curling linoleum rolling up against the tassled carpet. The Seder plate on the wooden coffee table. The floral motif. The handblown crystal bowl beside it, full of knickknacks. The photographs ranged along the shelves: Y.A. at the Dead Sea, Y.A. with his mother before he went to camp, Y.A. at his bar mitzvah, Y.A. at a skating rink, Y.A. blowing a ram's horn, Y.A. graduating from vocational school, Y.A. in his border guard uniform, Y.A. under the hood of his very first car, Y.A. at a dance hall with an unknown girl, and—at one end of the shelf—in a tiny silver frame, Y.A.'s father when he, too, was young, along the banks of the Lena River outside Yakutsk in northern Siberia, with a pair of homemade skates slung over his shoulder, taken in the year before he emigrated to Israel to work in a munitions factory in Netanya.

84

With Y.A. in his room, stretched out in his bed, one hand holding a cigarette, the other shielding his swollen eyes.

83

No *chozer b'teshuva* at all.

82

What Rami wanted was to take Y.A. out into a large field, no stones, no fences, and push him around, gentle to begin with, just jab him in the shoulder, rock him back on his toes a little bit, to ask him *why* in a logical way, to jab him in the shoulder again, the right shoulder, then the left, with Y.A. stepping quickly backward through the field—moonlit now, a sea of dark grass—with his hands up in the air, in half-surrender, saying it was a mistake, just a mistake, hold on, hold on, not my fault, leave me alone, not my fault brother, and Rami would push Y.A. harder, saying don't call me brother, and Y.A. would stumble in the grass, his hands up, his fingers splayed, hey wasn't my fault man, you've got to believe me, I was just following orders, the Commander told us to shoot, you know what it's like out there, it's a jungle, man, I was just a kid, he told us to fire, we didn't mean to hurt anybody, honest, man, we didn't even look where we were firing, it was a mistake, I had no idea we were near a school, we were being pelted with rocks, you know what that's like, come on man, you served too, come on brother, the stones were pounding off the roof, it was orders, it's terrifying man, how would I know it was a girl anyway, tell me that, and here Rami would punch him for the first time, hard, in the very center of the chest, so that Y.A. would bend over, gasp, his hands closer to his face now, to protect himself, hey leave me alone, you don't know what you're doing, and he would snarl a little now, get away from me, I did nothing wrong, don't blame me, I was just doing my job, I saw her, yeah, she was throwing stones man, she had a rock in her hand, they're a bunch of liars, born to lie, fucking Arabs, all of them, she was there, just like the rest of them, and here Rami would come with a hard flurry of punches, right, left, right, left, so Y.A. would stumble backwards, cowering, fuck you, man, fuck you, you have no idea, leave me alone, she had a rock in her hand, I saw her standing there, she wasn't hit by a rubber bullet at all, she got a rock in the back of the head, that's what happened, it wasn't me at all, fuck you, I didn't fire, she was hit by one of her own, and now Rami's punches would be raining down upon him, a fury of knuckles, hitting the soldier's head, his neck, his ears, and the punching would continue until the soldier fell and lay splayed out beneath him in the dark grass, and Rami would stand above him, and here the soldier would begin to whimper that he was sorry, he didn't mean it, he had no idea what happened really, just listen to me please, it all happened in a flash, the metal flap opened, the gun was sticking out, the truth is man I was scared, I was just scared, I didn't know what the fuck I was doing, you would have done the exact same thing, admit it, man, admit it, you would have.

81

Eighteen years old: there are sometimes no ways out.

80

In prison Bassam would occasionally wonder if the grenades had been planted near the mouth of the cave on purpose. Two explosives sitting on a bed of brittle straw. They thought at first they had come upon a crate of pomegranates.

The grenades were ancient, probably leftovers from '67. It was not beyond possibility that they had already been tampered with, the gunpowder reduced, the pins disengaged.

79

The Hebrew word for pomegranate, *rimon*, is also the word for grenade. It was, according to some Biblical scholars, the forbidden fruit in the Garden of Eden. It is said to consistently have 613 seeds, corresponding to the number of commandments in the Torah.

78

Commandment 598: That those engaged in warfare shall not fear their enemies nor be panic-stricken by them during battle.

77

On the morning of his third meeting with the Parents Circle—twelve days after the death of Abir—Bassam was stopped at a checkpoint in the Walaja valley. He was taken into a side room in a prefab hut and told to strip.

The room was small and cramped. A Beitar Jerusalem poster hung on the wall. He noticed a camera in the corner of the ceiling: it swiveled on its metal arms.

He took his clothes off, down to his underwear and socks. He laid his shoes on the ground, folded his shirt and jacket and trousers on the table. A soldier came and put the clothes in a white plastic bag.

—Wristwatch too.

—Why?

—Testing.

—For what?

The soldier said nothing.

A January wind whistled through the open door. Bassam handed him the watch.

—I need a blanket, said Bassam.

He was surprised when the soldier came back moments later with a small red blanket. Bits of dog hair clung to it. It smelled slightly of a young child.

—How long will I be here?

—As long as it takes.

Bassam pulled the blanket around his shoulders. This was how the Occupation worked: you waited. And you waited. And then you waited to out-wait the waiting. It was always best, he knew, to pretend not to be bothered. You wait standing, you wait sitting, you wait stretching against the wall. You wait for another soldier to come in. You wait for him to leave. You make waiting into an art.

The door opened. The soldier asked him if he wanted a smoke break. It was as if, Bassam thought, he, too, was on a job. Yes, he said, he would have a cigarette.

The soldier lit the cigarette, placed an empty soda can on the table for Bassam to use as an ashtray, then left again.

Bassam inhaled deeply, made the cigarette last as long as possible. He glanced at his wrist for the gone watch.

It almost came as a disappointment when two new soldiers came into the prefab, carrying his clothes.

—One more thing, they said.

They told him to drop his remaining underwear, stand over a mirror and squat.

76

In his book *Pensées,* a collection of fragments of theology and philosophy, the seventeenth-century French philosopher Pascal suggested that all of humanity's problems stem from our inability to sit, alone, in one room.

75

What Salwa hated most of all was when, at the airport, they pulled on plastic gloves and searched through her hair. As if her scalp contained something which would very soon blow apart.

74

On the Henley passport index, the Palestinian Authority passport, a laissez-passer, is consistently among the world's most useless.

73

Lift your fucking shirt, asshole.

72

Among the countries where Rami, by virtue of his Israeli citizenship, was not allowed to go: Malaysia, Bangladesh, Pakistan, Oman, Saudi Arabia, Sudan, Libya, Lebanon, Kuwait, Iraq, Iran, Brunei, Syria, United Arab Emirates and, of course, by order of his own government, anywhere in the West Bank or Gaza.

71

He drove them to the airport: Smadar and his father, Yitzak. She was ten years old. She had just completed her genealogy project. The pair were on their way to Hungary.

It was the first time Yitzak had visited Europe since the war. Smadar's questions had woken something in him.

They sat together in the back seat as if Rami was the chauffeur.

—Excuse me, Sir.

—Yes, Madam?

—Could Sir please drive a little slower?

—Whatever you choose, Madam.

Rami tipped the brim of his hat and increased the speed.

—Slower, she laughed, slower!

At the airport he carried their bags from the car all the way to the check-in desk, bowed ever so slightly, told them to have a wonderful journey, that the chauffeur service would be delighted to meet them upon their return.

—I expect for you to be prompt, said Smadar.

—Absolutely, Madam.

—No dillydallying.

—Whatever you say.

—And please wear a better cap next time, she said.

—Indeed.

He watched them walk off together, his father, his daughter, towards the departures area. Flight announcements came over the public address. The airport was abuzz. They melted into the crowd.

Somehow he expected that Smadar would break character, turn around and jump into his arms.

She never did.

70

When she returned from Hungary, she asked Rami to go to the Blockbuster store to rent the Zarah Leander film *The Great Love*.

He was unable to find a copy anywhere until many years later, in Berlin, he went into a video store and discovered a VHS in a collection of historical classics.

69

For most of his life, Rami's father had not been willing to go back to Gyor. He had worked as a runner. He had been captured at the age of fourteen. He had been put in a camp. He had seen terrible things and had come to Israel to make a life for himself. He felt no compulsion to live on the fumes of the past. He had raised a family. That was enough. There was never any need to say anything more until Smadar asked him to help with her school genealogy project. He took her into his study, sat in the swivel chair and said: Go ahead, bunny, ask whatever you want.

68

What will life in Israel be like when Smadar reaches fifteen?

67

Rami arrived home from the airport exhausted. He walked slowly to the fridge, took out a pint of milk, opened the cardboard container, drank.

He closed the fridge and walked back across the room. Nurit was in her office, typing. He could hear the sound of the keys clacking.

It was strange to think that Smadar was up there, in the air, flying over the sea on her way to Europe, a yerida of sorts, a descent.

He went into his office, sat down, typed up a fax to the hotel: Princess, he wrote, don't forget to take pictures.

66

When he flicked through her passport he lingered at the Hungarian stamp. He had never really thought of himself as someone who came from a country other than Israel. In his lectures Rami said that he was the seventh generation of a family from Jerusalem, but also that he was a graduate of the Holocaust. It was an odd word to use, *graduate*. He knew it rattled people but that it made sense too, that the terror was still there and always would be, but that there was something about moving on, something akin to growing up, leaving a skin behind. Europe was a distant root, far from the branch. He didn't belong to it in any real sense.

He kept the photographs that she had captured on her camera. He put them on his hard drive and every now and then went into his office and clicked through them.

65

64

Bassam had only ever met one of his grandparents, Abu Abdullah from his father's side. He too had lived in the village of Sa'ir. He was a bookkeeper for a wealthy family on the outskirts of Hebron that had made its money from grape sugar.

Abu Abdullah had kept his ledgers, with beautiful penmanship, from his days in the Ottoman empire, through the British rule, through the days of the Egyptians and then the Jordanians until the entries abruptly stopped in 1967.

An inkblot marked the end of the journal. Years later Bassam figured out that the blot was not so much a result of the Six-Day War, as of a severe infestation of vine trunk disease in which the leaves and stems of the grapevines had shriveled and the crop had been wiped out by black measles. The owners of the vineyard sold their stake to another Palestinian family and moved to Sweden where they set up a business importing Hebron glass and olive oil.

The land was lost and eventually legally bought in the 1990s by a family of right-wing settlers from Minneapolis who built a tract of red-roofed houses.

63

Dextrose is one of the primary sugars found in wine grapes. The word stems from the Latin term *dexter*, meaning right. In an aqueous solution of dextrose the plane of polarized light bends toward the right.

62

Frankenthal had told him where the Parents Circle meeting would be: a suburban school in north Jerusalem.

Rami arrived early on purpose, parked the motorbike a block away. He still carried the helmet in the crook of his arm. He leaned against the wall, feigning nonchalance. He stood in the shade where he could not be seen. He had ordered an espresso from a nearby café. He had no newspaper, no phone to look at. He slowly stirred the coffee, sipped it. It was bitter and sharp.

It sounded so corny, so trite. All this talk of justice, of kinship, of reconciliation. Why was the assumption there that he would want to go? Because he was the son-in-law of Matti Peled? Because he was married to Nurit? It was all so patently naïve. He would rather pledge his allegiance to cynicism.

It all felt off-kilter. Frankenthal had come to the shiva. Rami recognized his face from the newspapers. His suit jacket was slightly rumpled. They shook hands. Frankenthal was quiet, soft-spoken, careful with his condolences. He said he had heard that Smadar was a beautiful girl. He was bereft for the loss. It was senseless what was happening. Rami and Nurit would be welcome to visit a meeting, he said.

Rami had felt some sort of immediate distaste. Something oddly intrusive lay in his stomach. He said nothing. He bid farewell to Frankenthal at the door.

He saw Frankenthal again months later in a bookshop on Be'eri Street. Rami felt his teeth clench. The arrogance of it all. The ease too. How could you do it? Rami asked. How could you step in my house just days after she died? What made you think that you had any right to assume anything at all about me?

He was surprised when Frankenthal nodded and held his gaze. He had, thought Rami, an interesting stare. The eyes were a lively blue.

—Come to a meeting some time, Frankenthal said. We have them every week. Stand at the back. See what you think. That's all.

Rami shrugged, turned, but he couldn't block it off, even after he left the bookshop. It gnawed at him. He couldn't sweep it away. Maybe it was the anger itself. He didn't know how he would react if he went. Maybe he would drop all his vitriol in a heap at their feet. Take this, it is all I have. She is gone. You are useless. Your circle means nothing to me.

He spilled the contents of the coffee out on the ground. It slowly trickled at his feet and spilled off the curb.

A few cars had arrived. They passed through the school gates. He heard laughter from the parking lot. It riled him. They arrived in clumps. Some of them he knew. Guterman. Hirshenson. He had read about them in the papers, seen them on television. Strange to be in their vicinity. To be brought together in this way. There was something sentimental here, it wanted to erode him, this little club of self-righteous grief. But he had come this far. He would go to the meeting, he would listen, he would come out, he would go home, job done, never again, no more.

He crushed the coffee cup underfoot, walked towards the school gates.

A bus was pulling in through the narrow gates. The driver had miscalculated and he had to back the coach up. A high beeping sound rang out when the bus reversed, then eased forward again.

Rami stood on the pavement watching the row of faces at the windows. The men were younger than he would have thought. The women too. One of them wore a hijab. Back and forth she went.

Afterwards he wondered how he might have looked to them: a middle-aged man, a silver helmet in one hand, a crushed coffee cup in the other, one foot propped against the wall. He harbored no feeling for them at all: not hatred, not frustration, nothing. He simply wanted the bus to move so he could go inside and get it finished.

61

She stepped off the bus carrying a picture of her daughter clutched to her chest.

60

Deuterium oxide, or D_2O, is colorless, transparent, and non-radioactive.

59

Nothing would ever be the same again.

58

Every once in a while Rami and Bassam found protesters waiting for them outside the school gates or the town hall doors.

Mostly it was middle-aged men. They looked to Rami like cork-screws: coiled, silvery, thin men. A town mayor, a city representative, a council member. He knew full well that they needed the attention. In the beginning he tried to reason with them. Hands out, his voice low, his body open: no helmet, no leather jacket. He strode up, held out his hand. They seldom took it. They waved him away. He watched the anger rise in their faces: the veins in their foreheads shone. It was as if someone had turned up the thermometer in them.

He knew his own capacity for rage, his ability to explode. He had to force the anger down, let it implode. He kept his hands wide as if to say I have no other weapon: Look at me, sixty-seven years old, there is no desire for fight in me.

He made a point of watching their shoes. He could tell so much from the polish, the scuff, the laces, the buckle. Any man with a new pair of shoes had other places to go. Those with worn shoes were a little different, they were more likely to push and shove, there was something already ripped in them.

He was not a true Israeli, they said. He did not know the meaning of history. He was sleeping with the enemy. He was contaminated. A *yafeh nefesh*. He was bringing terrorists in amongst them, poisoning the minds of their young people. Did he have no idea what he was betraying? How could he share the stage with a bomber? Had he no scruples?

He waited a moment, paused, allowed a silence. The more the anger rose, the more he tried to open his body and feign calm. He knew he needed to have the same tenacity as the fanatic. He had learned to breathe: to hold it deep at his core. He had practiced the smile. He unfolded a picture of Smadar, held it chest-high.

Rami watched their eyes dart about. He knew the approaching arguments from the step slightly forward, the shuffle. It was, he knew, their isolation that had made them so vocal. They thrived in the grandeur of their rage. Yet underneath their masks they were riddled with self-doubt. He could sense the fear behind the clenched jaw. He almost knew the coming lines by heart. Once a terrorist always a terrorist. We didn't ask for them to blow up our children. They deny our very existence. They want to wipe us off the map. We gave them freedom, they gave us rockets. They want to push us into the sea. Security. Never forget.

All the time Bassam waited in the car outside. When the time came, Rami gave him the nod.

Bassam walked in through the gates confidently, trying not to draw too much attention to his limp.

57

Sometimes, in the classrooms, there were boos until they were finally allowed to speak.

56

Whenever either he or Nurit gave a newspaper interview he would arrive home to find the light on the answering machine blinking and he would wonder how many friends he had lost today.

55

She emerged from the dark of the shop. Areen waited outside. Twelve times nine. One hundred and eight. Twelve times ten. A small bell on the door rang. The street outside was dusty. The sunlight swung underneath the metal awning. She tucked one bracelet away, handed the other to Areen. Twelve times eleven. Their shadows bobbed into the street. One hundred and thirty-two. The thud of a wheel near the roundabout. Twelve times twelve. Her schoolbag swung as she ran.

54

One afternoon, in the Dheisheh refugee camp south of Bethlehem, Bassam watched four boys in white jeans and white T-shirts carry a single mattress past the low houses. They moved carefully through the narrow alleyways with the mattress propped high on their shoulders. Placed on top of the bed were four red carnations, arranged in a neat row.

It took him a moment to realize that the boys were in rehearsal for carrying a bier.

53

The only interesting thing is to live.

52

He exits the highway at Jericho. No patrols tonight. No need to stop. The traffic light shines high and green in the dark. He passes a series of billboards and a long row of palm trees. The single headlight catches one of the red signs at the side of the road:

DANGEROUS TO YOUR LIVES
AND IS AGAINST THE ISRAELI LAW

He feels an immediate ripple through the steering wheel as the texture of the tarmac changes.

51

Jericho: the oldest walled city in the world.

50

The Oasis Casino Hotel resort in Jericho was, for a short period, at the turn of the twenty-first century, one of the most successful gambling houses in the world.

Built by the Palestinian Authority, the casino was located just off Highway 1. It had over one hundred gaming tables and three hundred slot machines. The casino was open to Israelis and Jordanians and those with international passports. No Palestinians were allowed unless they were working there. There were several back rooms where high-stakes card games took place. Special air filtration systems were put in to combat the cigarette smoke.

It was a place that seemed jaunty with type: it was popular among local settlers who carried large bundles of cash strapped to their stomachs, thin Jordanian businessmen who trailed lines of aides in dark suits behind them, office workers from Tel Aviv who wore their shirts ambitiously open, dark-skinned African women in tight silver skirts.

The casino didn't last long. During the Second Intifada, local mili-tiamen used the space to fire at Israeli soldiers, and the IDF blew a hole in the front facade, but for the short time it was open it was reputed to have made the highest percentage margin for the house per minute of any casino on earth.

49

Your Oasis Awaits.

48

False stars in the casino's ceiling were set in exact constellations, oper-ating as cameras. No windows. No clocks. Music was neutral, mostly American pop, though some Israeli tunes were allowed, but nothing with Arabic lyrics. Drinks were sugary. Alcohol, though freely avail-able, was carefully monitored and consumed mostly by international guests. Pimm's No. 1 was considered the drink of choice among the high rollers and bottles of Veuve Clicquot were kept on ice at the best tables.

47

In the 1930s the British army established three golf clubs in Mandatory Palestine: the Jerusalem Golf Club, the Palestine Police Golf Society, and the Sodom and Gomorrah Golfing Society. The Sodom and Gomorrah course was nine holes long and watered frequently by pumps from the local wells.

Every summer bank holiday the British police played for a marble statuette called Lot's Wife. The statue was presented in the clubhouse early in the evening as a round of chilled Pimm's was served to the men.

Later in the evening a special tongue-in-cheek prize was given for any golfer who claimed a hole in one.

46

When the British left the club in early 1948 the fridges and pantries were ransacked and the clubhouse destroyed, but the menu of drinks was left untouched on a chalkboard on the inside wall: among them were the Holy Moses (one part gin, one part arak, apricot, lime juice and olives), the Virgin Mary (tomato juice, celery, cucumber, baharat), the Jesus Wept (red wine spritzer), the Doubting Thomas (vodka, citrus juice, turmeric, freekeh peppers) and the Adam and Eve (secret recipe, served with a fresh green apple slice).

45

Outside the Oasis, the road is speed-bumped every fifty yards.

44

Bassam taps the steering wheel and guides the car to the side of the road, near the curb, where the bump is less pronounced. A slight sway and then he redirects back into the middle of the road where the tarmac is flat.

43

There were times, not long out of prison, when he drove out into the hills of Hebron. Just to clear his head. He avoided his hometown of Sa'ir, drove further until the landscape yawned in every direction. The stars bulletholed above him. He drove the back roads, uneven and rutted. He could make out the small red glow of lights from the military towers. He never once came upon a patrol. He pulled the car down a dirt track and parked when he could go no further. He turned off the headlights and stepped out of the car. It seemed to take a moment for the car to understand where it was. The engine gently ticked. He paused to take in the moon, the stray clouds. Every now and then he could hear jackals yipping in the distance. He walked around the front of his car, hitched himself up on the bumper and lay on the hood. Palestine. It always took a moment for his eyes to adjust and then the quality of darkness deepened. He could feel the heat from the engine pouring through his shirt.

42

The easternmost point in the Big Dipper, Benetnasch, is known in Arabic as the Daughters of the Bier.

41

Bassam was stunned to hold his first grandchild in his arms. He felt the backspin immediately: the same fragrance, the same eye shape, the same dark scatter of hair. Even the coarse hospital blanket was the same color: off-white with a blue and pink stripe along its edge.

He carried Judeh along the corridor and slipped a tiny white shoe onto his foot.

40

Rami's first thought when he held Guy's youngest, Anna, was that she looked just like Smadar.

39

In the ninth century the Persian mathematician Muhammad ibn Musa al-Khwarizmi wrote *The Compendious Book on Calculation by Completion and Balancing*.

It was the first book to introduce the concept of algebra to European scholars. Al-Khwarizmi developed a unifying theory which allowed rational and irrational numbers to be treated as algebraic objects.

It focused on moving quantities from one side of an equation to the other in order to maintain balance.

38

The word algebra comes from the Arabic *al-jabr,* suggesting the repair of broken bones.

37

Traditional bonesetters rely on the touch of their hands. Most of the time they can tell within seconds whether a bone is fractured or broken.

The most difficult bone to figure out by touch alone is the femur, the strongest bone in the body, deeply set in the thigh.

A rubber bullet in the front of the thigh is more likely to break the bone than one from behind. A gas canister with a downward trajectory—shot from a rooftop, say, or a helicopter—will probably fracture the bone, though one shot from a low angle close to the ground might break it in two.

36

The bullet caught Abir in the back of the head, smashing her skull in a radial manner, so that one of the splinters shot inwards and penetrated her brain.

35

The shrapnel obliterated the back of the Blondie T-shirt that Smadar wore.

34

When Bassam went to the AIPAC conference in Washington, D.C., he was asked how it was possible to be an archivist for a country that doesn't exist.

33

My name is Bassam Aramin and I am from Palestine.

32

In October of 1972, Wael Zuaiter, a poet and translator, was shot dead by agents of the Israeli Mossad. He was heading home to his apartment in Piazza Annibaliano in northern Rome, carrying with him an Arabic-language copy of *One Thousand and One Nights*.

Zuaiter had adored the book since childhood and had, since arriving in Rome from Nablus in 1962, begun to translate it from his native tongue into Italian. He wanted more than anything to capture the original poetry. Few in Italy knew the real beauty of the stories, he thought—their translations had all come through either English or French but never directly from Arabic. The current translations were a bourgeois dilution: they washed out the color and the wit and the charm of the texts, and put manners and meanings on the myths. The true texture and nuance of the language and humor were getting lost, and this amounted, he said, to a form of infantilization of the Arab mind which made it easier to dehumanize and occupy his people.

Zuaiter was thirty-eight years old, from a wealthy family, but had for years scraped by as a poet, a journalist, a singer, an actor and a painter. He could quote, at length, from the works of Voltaire, Montesquieu and Rousseau, and showed an avid interest in the work of Calvino and Borges. He was a regular at the Arab Bar on Via del Vantaggio where he often read poetry aloud. He liked to organize literary salons around the city. He was often seen strolling the streets, humming the partisan ballad *Bella Ciao.*

In the early seventies he joined Fatah and set up a small library, the shelves of which were full of revolutionary literature.

On the night of the murder, Zuaiter took two buses across Rome from the house of his girlfriend, an Australian artist, Janet Venn-Brown, and made his way towards his own apartment. He was tired and hungry. He hunched up into his sports jacket and pulled his keffiyeh around his neck. The night was cool. He carried a notebook, several pencils, two bread rolls, wax candles and volume two of *One Thousand and One Nights.* His phone and electricity had been cut off: unpaid bills. He was readying himself for a long night. In his notebook he had written: *To find living marrow in the ancient bones. To uncover. To make real. Feeling without action will shrink the heart.*

When he passed the vestibule into his staircase a figure stepped out of the dark brandishing a .22 pistol with a silencer. Zuaiter put his hands in the air and was shot thirteen times.

Twelve of the bullets hit him in the head and chest. The thirteenth entered the book still in his pocket, ripped through the stories, and stopped when it hit the spine.

31

30

The bullet passed right through the Tale of the Hunchback, Smadar's favorite.

29

Zuaiter was first in a series of assassinations by the Mossad as revenge for the killing of eleven Israeli athletes in the Munich Olympics a month earlier.

He was, they said, a member of the Black September group that had carried out the killings, but in a press conference in Beirut, Zuaiter's friends testified that he was a pacifist, his capacity for violence was just about nil, he was not interested in revenge and he probably knew more about *The Magic Flute* than he ever did about the PLO Charter.

28

The assassinations—called Operation Wrath of God—took place in cities all over the world and later became the subject of the Spielberg film *Munich*. What struck Spielberg was the literary nature of many of the killings both before and after the Olympics: the murder of playwrights, the targeting of journalists, the poets who had their writing hands riddled with bullets, the bombs placed inside the memoirs of Che Guevara, so that if you opened the book it would explode in your face.

27

In 2006 Emily Jacir, a Palestinian artist, went to a shooting range in Sydney, Australia, to teach herself how to handle a .22 caliber Mauser pistol. When she felt familiar with the weapon—the exact type the

Mossad had used to assassinate Zuaiter, silencer and all—she collected one thousand blank white books and lined them up, one by one, in a shooting gallery. She fired a single bullet into each of them from a distance of fifty yards. The blank books represented, she said, the untold stories of Palestinians around the world.

She displayed the shot-up books in an exhibition at the Sydney Biennial, alongside photographs of Zuaiter's copy of *One Thousand and One Nights*, documenting exactly where in the pages the bullet had traveled until it hit the spine and stopped.

Jacir fired so many bullets that she gave herself a permanent callus on the ring finger of her right hand.

26

To this day an Italian translation of *One Thousand and One Nights* direct from the Arabic does not exist.

25

One Thousand and One Nights: a ruse for life in the face of death.

24

At AIPAC he looked out into all the stunned faces. They were all so very white and round. The men wore button-down shirts. The women sat up straight. They were neat and ironed and combed. He leaned into the lectern. He could hear the murmur around the room when he introduced himself. He counted four who walked out immediately. No matter. He had concentrated his mind. He had dressed carefully. Polished his shoes. Creased his slacks. Worn an open-neck shirt, blue. A dark jacket. His hair was cut short. He had shaved closely before he left the hotel. They expected a beard, or at least its shadow, from Palestinians. He had nicked himself on the neck and wore a tiny pink

Band-Aid low on his throat. He had forgotten it but could feel it now as he spoke. He wondered if he should remove it, just brush it away, or perhaps stoop beneath the lectern and peel it off out of sight. Every move had a meaning. He wanted to ease into his speech. He had, over the years, learned the rhythm of pause, of silence, of modulation. He had said the word gently: Palestine. He knew they expected some sort of qualifier but he wouldn't give it. On a tightrope, he thought, you look into the distance. Not down at your feet.

He lifted his hand to shade his eyes, then touched the Band-Aid with his thumb, pressed it down.

He was a child. In the caves. At school. He raised a flag in the yard. Their silence surprised him. No shifting in the seats. No coughing. The lecture room was three-quarters full. A hundred and twenty people. Maybe more. He had been astounded by the invitation. To risk it. To talk into the dark. The congress of the conservative. The difficulty of it thrilled him. To shift just one mind. It was never enough, but it was worth it anyway. He was seventeen years old. In the hills. A lookout. Prison. When he reached the part about the beatings he could tell that one or two of them had begun to shift in their seats, uneasy, but still no walkouts, no shoutbacks. Maybe it was an American politeness. He thought he heard the sound of a phone. It was quickly turned off. The mention of the Shoah vacuumed all other sound. He knew it would. No movement at all. He paused, closed his eyes a moment. There were times he didn't like his own theater, he was tired of himself, but not today. Even for those things he repeated over and over again. The victims of victims. The quiet one is forever dangerous. Nothing, just a small gun please.

He could hear someone talking, louder now, a sort of buzzing in the back corners of the room, a man and a woman, she was angry, he was calming her down, heads were turning, whispers, shushes. But he had been in much noisier rooms. In Tel Aviv, Haifa, Jerusalem. Wait them out. Stare forward. Stay quiet until they quieten too. That was part of the theater. He went on. Some laughter then. The prison belt. *Meir Loves Maya.*

He leaned further forward. The microphone squawked. A mistake. He leaned back. His jacket was warm. He didn't want to take it off. A pale blue shirt. It would show ovals at the underarms. He gripped the side of the podium. He had notes in front of him, but he hadn't consulted them once.

It was Occupation that got them. Just the word. He wasn't quite sure why it rankled so much, but it did—it was always the word that seemed to slide a little dagger into the rib cage. There was coughing now and someone standing up in the third row, he tried not to look, two people, leaving. Knock us down, we get up. There was another movement at the back. A swing of light from the opening door. Several dark figures were moving about. But perhaps they were coming in? But how could they arrive in the middle of his speech? Security perhaps. Maybe they had come to arrest him. Two hand grenades.

He thought for a moment about the cut on his neck. He reached for the Band-Aid, but it was gone, the cut was dry, he was in control, he had it, he was sure, he didn't mind that people were arriving or leaving, or both. He was close to the microphone now. Beyond right and wrong there is a field, meet us there.

A curious calm came over him when he spoke of Abir. A breath went through him, he felt it seep through his body, a flow all the way down to the back of his calves. She was shot in the back of the head. She had bought herself some candy. The world's most expensive.

A red light at the foot of the stage pulsed. He would not let them off. Invest in our peace, not in bloodshed. Spend ten percent of the money differently, five percent, one percent even. They're your tax dollars, after all. Try it. A half a percent. Why not? The power is yours. Another murmur shot around the room. He stopped and bowed his head slightly. He didn't want them to think that he was soft, a dupe, an easy mark that they would use later to pretend that they knew what life was like in Palestine. He had come here, as always, to knock them sideways. Don't get me wrong, he said. We will never give up. It is not our intention to walk away. He was astounded to see that a few of them had risen to their feet, he was not sure whether it was to applaud or leave. He wanted to uproot them. He wanted them to know how it felt. He was not finished. The sweat dripped in his shirt. The lights were so hot. The red stage light was solid now. He let his hands fall along the side of the lectern. Tonight, he said, and then he held their attention with a cough. Tonight I will walk along the Washington Mall and pass by the Lincoln Memorial and I will look up to the stars like I always do when I go back home to Jericho.

23

I am sorry to tell you this, Senator, but you murdered my daughter.

22

At a reception in Dupont Circle he was surrounded. Handshakes. Business cards. Afterwards he could not remember a single thing that had been said, but he would never forget the woman, small, blond-haired, tight-dressed, in front of all these people, she was smiling, her teeth were white, she leaned towards him, there was flesh, the edge of her dress, a shoulder, her fingernails painted a shade of green, she was reaching, it was not to shake his hand, no, her hand was near his chest, near his shoulder, everything was frozen, reaching, so very blond, so very freckled, she was going to touch his cheek, or his neck, he leaned away, embarrassed, but she was still smiling, this American, and someone else was laughing, the room was full of trays, trays of drinks, trays of food, trays to protect you, smashed trays, prison trays, batons, solitary confinement, people were laughing and her fingers were still reaching out, *Here,* she said, *Let me,* and she touched him then on the collar of his shirt, he could feel the graze of her fingernails against his neck, at the artery where it pulsed, and she drew away swiftly and she was folding something, a piece of fluff from his collar maybe, a hair perhaps, or an eyelash, something, she was wrapping it in a white napkin, she was still smiling, he knew it, she had lifted it with her bare fingers, the Band-Aid had fallen on the rim of his collar during his speech, draped itself there, he could feel the heat shoot through him, what could he do now?

21

He settled the next day in the Senator's office. He had shaved closely again but had been careful this time not to nick himself. He wore a suit and tie and he had re-polished his shoes. He was due to talk for only ten minutes and he had only one thing to say, and when he said it he slid a photograph of Abir across the table, a large glossy, eight by ten, *You murdered my daughter,* and the Senator wasn't even ruffled, he picked up the photo, nodded, laid it down carefully on the sheet of glass above the desk. He knew exactly what Bassam meant, he said. The American rifle. The American jeep. The American training. The American tear gas. The American dollar. He was aware of the arguments on all sides, he said, but the tide was turning, there were agreements in place, everyone wants the same thing, we approach it in myriad ways, I understand your pain, Mister Aramin, I don't mean that in any dismissive sense, trust me, I can feel it, as a father, I am learning every day, tell me more about Abir.

The door opened and an aide came in. The Senator waved her away. He picked up the photo again.

It could, thought Bassam, have worked as political sham but there were no cameras there, no reporters, no tape recorders. The Senator looked at the photo: And you, Mister Aramin? Where did you grow up?

—In a cave.

—I mean, said the Senator with a smile, where really?

20

Smadar was born in Hadassah hospital. Where Abir died.

19

One story becoming another.

18

Still to this day John Kerry keeps the photograph of Abir on the wall in his office.

17

The fences along the roadway were painted white. The driveways of the houses were lined with rosebushes, rhododendrons, bluebells. The cars in the driveway glistened silver and black. Children's toys lay scattered all about. Flags fluttered under the eaves of houses: blue, white and red.

A dread spread through him. Unbidden. There were times this would happen: a hollowness touched him and he would wonder what it all meant, this traveling, these conferences, the infinite repetition, the uselessness of it all. He would go back home. The airport. The interrogation. The strip search. The endless explanations.

He could not shrug off the thought of the woman who had lifted the Band-Aid from his collar.

She had lifted the tiny bandage and had folded it in her fingers, a little round circle of blood.

16

Sound is the preferred form of communication among birds since the noises made—singing, calling, honking, whistling, squeaking, warbling, croaking, clicking, trilling—carry far beyond the places the birds might be able to see.

15

He was on holiday in Tuscany with Nurit when he saw the sign. He was taken aback. The Wael Zuaiter Center. The arrow pointed down a narrow laneway in the town of Massa. The street was thin and cobbled. Laundry hung from the upper windows of the buildings. Children were dragging each other along on flattened cardboard boxes.

It was an old shopfront. The door was locked. They shaded their eyes and peered inside. A few tables with glass boxes. Some bookshelves. Some posters on the wall. They knocked on the window but nobody answered.

Halfway down the street Rami heard someone calling out behind them. A woman waved them down. Her hair was grey, but long and ribboned. She wore an elegant dress a couple of sizes too large. House slippers on her feet. She spoke in English. She had seen them peering in the window, she said, from the vantage of her apartment. The director of the center was away in Sydney but she had been given keys to the center. There hadn't been many tourists around but they were welcome to go inside, she was sorry but she had to go shopping for her son, would they mind taking the key and then locking up after they were finished?

Only in Italy, thought Rami.

She held out the key but then hesitated a moment and asked: Where are you from?

The question startled him. Perhaps she had heard his accent? Perhaps she would wonder why exactly he was there? Did she misunderstand him?

—From Hungary, he said after a moment.

—Hungary?

—Originally.

She smiled and she placed the key in his hand.

14

It was remarkable how little damage the bullet had done to the actual pages. The entrance hole was clean, only a little tear at the edges. It had angled in on the right-hand side of the book and then nosed itself in the center near the spine.

13

Rami touched the bullet. It seemed tiny and warm, like something that was still intent on reaching its destination.

12

In the Theresienstadt camp in 1943 Viktor Ullmann composed a one-act opera called *The Emperor of Atlantis*, using a libretto written by another inmate, the artist Peter Kien.

In the libretto, the Emperor of Atlantis—also called the King of Jerusalem—declares a universal war. *Total all-out Holy War! Each against the other! No survivors!*

Ullmann in his prologue had referred to it as a *kind of* opera. It began with the German anthem set in a minor key. The Emperor was a baritone. Death was to be played by a bass.

The Emperor tries to conscript Death to his cause. But Death, who appears as an old retired soldier, finds himself offended by the mechanization of killing, and the modern way of dying, which has put him out of work. Death goes on strike and, from then on, it becomes impossible for anyone to die.

Under Death's decree, even natural death is declared dead.

At first, the Emperor interprets this as a liberation from Death's tyranny—*Freedom from death! Liberty of the soul!*—but soon the inability of anyone to die, from bombs or bullets or anything else, leads to panic and revolt and paralyzing boredom among the Emperor's people.

The Emperor scrambles to enforce his rule but—since he can't kill anyone—his power has already begun to rapidly fade. So, he begs Death to resume his traditional duties. Death agrees to start killing again, but with a single caveat: only if he can begin with the Emperor as his very first victim.

In 1944 the Nazis saw a dress rehearsal of the opera taking place in the barracks of the camp. Aware of the possible allegorical intent—

following the assassination attempt on Hitler that summer, along with Himmler's call for total war—they quietly closed it down.

Later that year Ullmann was marched out of camp towards the Auschwitz-bound trains, but managed—just before being forced into the cattle car—to secretly slip the score to his friend Emil Utitz, the director of the camp library.

11

Ullmann had once written that the secret of every work of art was the annihilation of matter through form.

10

Borges said that his despair as a writer came when he was unable to translate the limitless nature of the aleph: that point in space which contained all other points. While some fell back on birds and spheres and angels, he himself was unable to find the metaphor for this timeless repository of everything. Language was successive: it could not, by its nature, be frozen in one place and therefore couldn't catch the sheer simultaneity of all things.

Nevertheless, said Borges, he would recollect what he could.

9

Little bitterns, red-throated pipits, blackcaps, yellow wagtails, whitethroats, turtledoves, bee-eaters, Arabian babblers, European rollers, griffon vultures, pied bushchats, storks, flamingos, pelicans, sandpipers, buzzards, cranes, kites, eagles, hawks, gulls, owls, nightjars, sparrows, swifts, sunbirds, plovers, northern wheatears, ruffs, shrikes, starlings, cuckoos, warblers, flycatchers, thrushes, hoopoes.

8

Operation Returning Echo.

7

Swans and ortolans too.

6

He drives slowly along the high garden wall. The flat roof of his house peers from behind the tall brickwork. The road is rutted and pitted but he knows each and every pothole. He angles the car wide, pulls the hand brake, opens the door, steps out to the high metal gate. The gate has been bolted shut. The motor is broken: he must open it by hand.

A stiffness in his bad leg. The pain shoots upwards through his hip. He slides the rusted lever across and the gate gives out a little groan. He pushes it sideways along the high white wall. The pain rests for a moment in the small of his back. The metal runners squeak and clank.

Bassam steps back towards the car through the light from the single headlight. Yet another thing that will have to be fixed.

He leans on the car door and swings himself into the seat once more, drags the bad leg in behind him. He picks up his phone, keys it alive and texts Rami: *Home, brother.* Their simple ritual, how many thousands of times now? He tosses the phone into the passenger seat, eases the car through the gate, brakes, then climbs out once more to close the gate.

By the time the gate has clanked shut, Rami has replied, a simple emoji of a thumbs-up and beneath that, *See you tomorrow.*

Bassam parks in the driveway under a blue cloth canopy. He sits a moment in the driver's seat, leans forward. Another long day. Yet again tomorrow. And again after that.

He pats his pockets to make sure of his cigarettes, his lighter, his phone. All intact. He flips the handle, pushes open the door, steps out.

The night is cool and sharp. No rain here today. He can tell simply by the smell of the garden.

5

Four lemon trees, two fig, two clementine, two Chinese orange, one almond, one persimmon, one pomegranate, one edible cactus, rows of zucchini, eggplant, squash and loofah vines right along the wall to the neighbor's house: in summertime you can smell the garden half a street away.

4

Salwa sits on the porch at the rear of the house, waiting, wrapped in a thin wool blanket. A small universe of smoke above her head. She adjusts the hose, lays the mouth of the hookah pipe on the table, leans across the card table towards him.

—You're late, she says.

He kisses her, once on the forehead, once on the lips. The sweet tang of tobacco. It is her calming ritual every night. She laces the shisha with fruit from the garden. Evens the bowl out with a kebab skewer. Perforates the tinfoil. Lights the coals.

—The restaurant is already closed, she grins, but you might find something on the counter.

He pulls across the folding chair, sits opposite her. Lays out his cigarettes and places his lighter on top. Leans his head back. Takes a long deep breath.

—All present? he asks.

—Of course not.

—Judeh?

—He's already sleeping.

It is rapid-fire between them then, the pulse of the day, the phone calls, the visits, the dramas. She went to the market. He went to Beit Jala. She paid Muhammad's phone bill. Rami was early, he messed up daylight savings time, he drove around for an hour, went to the Everest Hotel, got himself a coffee. She bought an anniversary present for her sister, a new perfume from Oman, it came in a ribboned box, it was a little expensive but it was worth it, she found it in the little stall in the market. The monk showed them around the monastery, you should have seen the thickness of the walls, the paintings, they went downstairs later to look at where the wine was made long ago, he brought her some olive oil, a gift, he left it in the car, he'll get it for her tomorrow. She was asked by the women's committee to figure out the new hiring schedule for the kindergarten, there will be two new teachers, both graduates from Birzeit, they're wonderful, they will make such a difference. He had a meal in a room with a vaulted ceiling, so fresh, delicious, the falafels were almost as good as hers, maybe even as good as her mother's, only kidding. There was an hour on the phone with Areen in Jerusalem, same old story with the permits, is it ever going to end? There were eight people there, they had all sorts of questions, we talked for hours, didn't solve a thing of course, but we tried, there was tea in the late afternoon. Araab came by around three o'clock, he had borrowed a car, he wanted to get that piece of wood to fix the roof of his house. The sound in the chapel was beautiful, the acoustics, even for such a small group, it bounced around and later they went back to the lunchroom, talked some more. She is sure that there will soon be a wedding, Araab has that look in his eye, she hopes that he saves enough money, he needs a car to get around, but he's worried about the insurance. When they left he could see all the lights down in the valley, the construction is incredible, more and more every day, he hates the sight of the cranes. Hiba is staying the evening at Mariam's house, she forgot her toothbrush, maybe you can bring it over to her in the morning. There was no bother on the way home, it was a one-cigarette checkpoint, and oh the headlight went out on the car, he almost forgot, but nobody noticed, they gave him a quick glance at Container but that was it. Funny that, the microwave dish stopped spinning for a while, then it just started again, no reason at all. He will bring the car down to Ibrahim's son tomorrow, see if he can fix it, that thing just eats money. She is due at the food fair at noon, she is in charge of the English table, they all think she knows England so well, she would try to make some scones in the morning, that's the only recipe she can remember. What goes up must come down. Mariam's mother is due for an operation in the next few days, if it doesn't work here they're going to try to take her to America, she has something wrong with her eyes. He has to be, he's not sure where, West Jerusalem, he thinks, by two-thirty, a school this time. He better check the daylight savings then. Did anyone get a chance to look at the plants in the afternoon? No, she didn't think so. Let's face it, the world would stop turning if he wasn't around. Could he please shut up and put another coal on the burner, tap the charcoal in the tray and shuffle the cards? She was really quite funny, did she actually think she was going to win this time?

3

Solitaire. Known as Patience in Britain, Success in France, Secrecy in Poland, Kabal in Norway, Serenity in Palestine.

With variations such as Eagle Wing, Maze, Parallels, Streets and Alleys, Elevens Up, Alhambra, Serpent Poker, Black Widow, Carpet, Three Blind Mice, Sultan, Tower of Hanoi, Ninety-One, Rouge et Noir, Shamrocks, Puss in the Corner, Zodiac, Imaginary Thirteen, Quadrille, Windmill, Tableau, Perpetual Motion, Grandfather's Clock, Osmosis, Sly Fox, Thieves of Egypt, Intrigue, Emperor, and Simplicity.

2

He steps out of the room onto the landing wearing his nighttime thobe. His hip aches. The long white cotton swishes against his bare calves. He moves in his slippers to the top of the stairs and holds on to the steel banister as he edges through the dark. The banister is cool to the touch.

At the rear door he slips off his sandals and puts on a pair of dark sneakers. He leans down to tie the laces. A sharp pain slices through his lower back. He parts the sheet that hangs in front of the rear door, presses the handle open. He reaches for the cigarette behind his ear, decides against it.

Quiet outside. No traffic, no barking, no chirping of insects.

The yellow hose is coiled beneath the kitchen window. He checks to make sure the nozzle is closed, opens the water valve halfway. A tiny drip appears at the base of the valve where the hose attaches. He re-tightens the hose, steps back a moment, waits. Good. No leakage.

He shuffles along the rear of the house, past the empty swimming pool. The stars are out, deeper than their darkness. He leaves three empty buckets on the porch, loops the hose around them.

He has built four steps off the porch down into the garden. He eases himself down, following with the bad leg. The hard dirt crunches under his feet. It is clumped and broken in the areas where he has loosened it with the shovel. He could easily close his eyes and walk the length of orchard without error, past the car, under the canopy, beyond the abandoned fridge where he keeps his fertilizer.

Every few yards he snaps the hose behind him.

Bassam glances back to see an overturned bucket fallen from the porch. No matter. In the morning he will collect the fruit: even in winter the Jericho trees bloom.

He begins with the citrus trees at the far end of the orchard. They overhang the garden wall abundantly. At the foot of the tree he leans over the well of soil he has created, a crater around the base. He opens the nozzle, allows the water to pour, adjusts the pressure as he circles the tree. The ground darkens and drinks.

He reaches for the cigarette behind his ear, takes a lighter from the thobe pocket, snaps it aflame. He takes a deep drag, coughs. Time to give them up, yet again time, always time. Somehow, though, they seem to relieve the pain in his back and legs.

The scarf of smoke rises behind him.

The vegetables. The loofah vines. Not bad, he thinks. Nothing too difficult tonight. A one-cigarette garden.

He moves along the wall to the second tree, fills the well of it, and then tightens the nozzle, stops the flow of water, steps towards the clementines and the Chinese orange trees, their small bursts of color.

1

The hills of Jericho are a bath of dark.

ACKNOWLEDGMENTS

This is a hybrid novel with invention at its core, a work of storytelling which, like all storytelling, weaves together elements of speculation, memory, fact, and imagination. It also gathers from friends and acquaintances all over the world who have helped me in countless ways. These people and their acts of generosity have helped shape the work. They opened their homes to me, gave me access to archives, helped research, provided inspiration, read drafts, chased down sources and permissions, provided refuge, insight, and criticism.

The list of people who have helped me is so long that it feels sometimes that I should just leave well enough alone, for I fear leaving some people out by mistake, and I apologize in advance for any omissions, but I would be remiss not to single out a number of people without whom this novel would not have been possible.

I first went to Israel and Palestine with two nonprofit groups, Narrative 4 and Telos, run by Lisa Consiglio and Greg Khalil, respectively. At every turn they have provided help, advice, insight, inspiration, and grace. They led me to new places. They guided me when I felt sure that it was an impossible task. They inspired me. Without their help and guidance it just couldn't have been done. Simple as that. And I was supported in every possible way by my family, my wife, Allison, and my children, Isabella, Christian, and John Michael. Thank you endlessly. My agent, Sarah Chalfant, believed in the book from the very beginning. Also, my editors all over the world had a huge part in keeping me going, especially Jennifer Hershey, who encouraged and supported me in every instance. Alexandra Pringle enabled the vision. Jaco Groot sent me clippings virtually every week. Caroline Ast and Thomas Uberhoff were inspirational. I had a number of great readers as I went along. These were the ones assigned with the most challenging task, to see the work when it was raw and unformed and messy. John Michael took over the role of my late father, Sean, and read the book for me late in the evenings: his advice was a constant ballast, especially when things were rough. Assaf Gavron, Darragh McKeon, Ray Dolphin, and Emily Jacir put in endless hours and somehow managed to help direct me without throwing me off course, a remarkable act of generosity and friendship. And Martin Quinn came along, amazingly as always, to pull the ties together. Others provided me with precise reading, research, and inspiration: Gideon Stein, Marc Briz, Mickey Madden, Raja Shehadeh, Nathan Englander, Michael Ondaatje, Bob Mooney, Dan Barry, Tyler Cabot, Ishmael Beah, Penny Johnston, Dani Gavron, Elik Elhanan, Ed Caesar, Gabriel Byrne, Tom Kelly, Phil Metres, Nathalie Handal, Liat Elkayam, Lee Keylock, Kelsey Roberts, Joe Lennon, David Scharia, Jack Saba, Dana Czapnik, Steven Hayward, Zaha Hassan, Tamer Nafar, Mariam Bazeed, Barry Lopez, Brad Fox, Susie Lopez, Christopher Booth, Daniel Sokatch, Michal Brimm, Heather Mitchell, Loretta Brennan Glucksman, Bill Whelan, Tim and Kathy Kipp, John Greally and Niall Burgess. To Sting and Joe Henry and Gregory Alan Isakov and Colm Mac Con Iomaire, *go raibh maith agaibh go léir*, this book was written to your music, in fact it became your music. And as always Jim Marion and Ronan McCann. As for those who helped me out with research and sketches and photos, there was Elizabeth Eagle, Lilly Khoury, Taliah Nathanson, Cindy Wu, Ellis Maxwell, Philippe Petit, Kathy O'Donnell, Noah Passavoy, Gary McKendry, Hal Grossman, and all the librarians at Hunter College and the New York Public Library.

Which leads me to the countless books, articles, photographs, films, and websites I encountered along the way. I want to offer my sincere thanks to the many scholars, scientists, historians and mathematicians whose works I have quoted or referred to, but I have not been able to individually acknowledge. In many cases there were several sources. I have begged, borrowed and copied, then begged and borrowed and copied again. Everyone knows that there are many versions of the truth. In some cases the sources were directly contradictory of one another and even the experts are at odds with one another. In the end the mistakes are all mine, alongside the inventions.

At Random House, Erin Kane, Steve Messina, Simon Sullivan and Holly Webber were remarkably helpful. Thanks to Etgar Keret for permission for the *Hahamishia Hakamerit* transcript. Thanks to David Byrne, Brian Eno, Pat Woods, Kevin Wong, and Laurie Fabiano for access to the lyrics. My colleagues at Hunter (most especially Peter Carey, Téa Obreht, and Tom Sleigh) deserve great thanks, as does Jennifer Raab, always. Thanks to everyone in the Irish diplomatic corps both in Tel Aviv and Jerusalem/Ramallah, in particular Deirdre Bourke, Tim Reilly, and Jonathan Conlon. Thanks also to everyone associated with Pal Fest and the Jerusalem Book Fair. We get our voices from others: it is, yes, a community of feeling. I traveled all over the world and so many doors were opened for me. My deepest thanks to Josh Sapan and Anne Foley for the cottage in Milford, Pennsylvania—what a place to work, with great memories of Frank McCourt at every turn. Thanks to Mikela Chartoulari for the wonderful house in Greece. To Valérie and Gaël Patout for the house in France. Yehuda Shaul and friends for the hospitality in Israel. Thanks also to the McCann clan, my mother, Sally, in particular. Also Sean and Freda, Roger and RoseMarie Hawke, Issa Jiries Khalil, Sandy Cooter, Mary Ann Stein, Bill Shipsey, Karen and Bayard Hollins, the good folks in Steamboat Springs, Santa Fe, Bad Gastein and all the other places that allowed me to extend my stay: I looked out so many windows during the course of this book.

And, of course, greatest thanks to Rami and Bassam and their families.

Finally, to those who feel compelled (and please do) to contribute to the nonprofit agencies mentioned here, please send your contributions to the Parents Circle Family Forum (theparentscircle.org): they really deserve all the support we can give. Other charities to keep in mind are Combatants for Peace (cfpeace.org), Telos (telosgroup.org), and Narrative 4 (narrative4.com). And last but not least, please look out for the new initiative The Abir-Smadar Foundation.

APEIROGON

COLUM McCANN

Random House Book Club

Because Stories Are Better Shared ™

A BOOK CLUB GUIDE

A Conversation with Marlon James
and Colum McCann

MARLON JAMES: So, the average person who googles an apeirogon is going to just assume this is some "both sides of the story" kind of novel. How is the novel more than just that? And, by the way, how do you draw an apeirogon?

COLUM McCANN: An apeirogon can't really be drawn, it can only be suggested. But maybe that's like everything in life and art? It would have to be something wild and expansive that folded on over into itself, suggesting an infinity—and yet, within the infinity, there are always places to land. I wanted to suggest that we are all part of this story of Abir and Smadar. What happens to Rami and Bassam must matter to us because it affects us. We are there, we are involved, we are complicit. Rami says that anybody who hears their story is changed. I think that's true. Certainly, I was changed.

Apeirogon is a weird word, I know. And difficult to approach at first. But I loved it from the moment I heard about it. The idea that it had an infinite number of sides was attractive to me because I knew this wasn't a two-sided situation, that it wasn't balanced, and I wanted the reader to experience that for herself. My intention was to throw readers off-balance so they could forget about the facts and the figures and the boundaries and the disputed histories that often seem to handcuff us in this part of the world. Instead I wanted the reader to experience deep down the pain and grief of an honest story. Because that's what Rami and Bassam give us—an honest, heartbreaking story that is somehow, against all the odds, full of hope. Even calling the book *Apeirogon*—which the publishers were brave enough to do—is already asking the reader to step out of the realm of comfort. It's like Michael Ondaatje: *Trust me, this will take time but there is order here, very faint, very human.*

MJ: When did you realize the novel was going to take this structure?

CM: Okay, can I admit it? Novelists aren't anywhere near as intelligent as our readers seem to think we are. It's our readers who bring meaning to a book when they engage with it. We're not as intentional as it seems, we're not as conscious, we're not as aware of the process—or at least I'm not. I embark, I explore, I fail. I fly by the seat of my pants. I get in front of the imaginary orchestra and I say: Okay, play something for me, let me hear the music, and let's shape it together. Then the content finds a structure. The language finds a structure. If you begin with a predetermined structure you're in trouble.

That said, I knew pretty early on that I wanted to find a way of telling that reflected the fragmentation of the contemporary experience. I wanted to take big shotgun leaps in style and time. Originally it was going to be in 100 cantos, then 365, and then, when I began thinking about *One Thousand and One Nights,* I knew I had my structure. But that was about two years into a five-year project. It was a bolt of lightning for me. I suddenly understood that Rami and Bassam were both doing the Scheherazade thing—they were telling their stories in order to keep their daughters alive, so naturally, then, it had to be in 1001 cantos. It turned out to be difficult keeping that many pieces, or notes, in the air, but I was driven onwards by the force of their stories.

Sometimes I think novelists are architects. You create a structure and you hope that it houses the very best of human endeavor. You want it to stand for a long time. And you want people to enter the structure and be changed by it. When I think of how you structured *Book of Night Women,* or *Brief History,* I know that I'm in the presence of a great architect. The structure becomes a container for the human music.

MJ: You know I'm going to ask about voice and appropriation. People are going to ask, What right do you have telling this story? Or are they asking the wrong question? Like Anna Deveare Smith, you have made an art out of writing other voices, so what do you do to prepare? How do you know you've hit the right note, and can there ever really be empathy?

CM: This is such an important question right now. And it's the right question. And there's a lot of necessary noise about it. Firstly, thank you to all the people who have insisted that the question be asked. And, first things first, let's face it, cultural appropriation is very real. For decades—centuries even—writers and artists and others have gone in places and condescended, patronized, plundered, mocked, belittled, taken advantage. We have failed to see past our own shadows. We sometimes even pat ourselves on the back for our supposed bravery when all we're doing is creating a cartoon of ourselves. It's all so patently colonial and cheap and wrong. If our intention is to take away from another culture, we deserve to be called out on it.

At the same time, on the exact same hand, it is possible to go in somewhere with your head bowed. With humility. And an honest intention. With the knowledge that you know so little. With the desire to learn. With the possibility that you might even get humiliated in the process, expose your own failings. To visit with a sense that it might be with apology that you know so little about yourself. To enter with grace. To say, I'm confused, please teach me, I'm willing to be knocked around a little by the complicated truth. So that we can come out at the far end a little wiser and a little more expansive. Or to invite the other person into your own home with the same sense of humility. There's bravery in that. You risk yourself. You change.

That's what I wanted to do with this novel. And that's what Rami and Bassam talk about. It took my breath away when they said to me that it's all very simple—we need to know each other above ground because otherwise we will end up knowing each other six feet below ground. But nothing, of course, is simple. Both men realize this. I had to tell that story. It belongs to all of us. I knew I was taking a risk. But the people who took the real risk were Rami and Bassam in allowing me to tell their stories. They gave it to me. They gave me a chance to listen.

MJ: A lot of bad "otherizing" has come from good writers. What's the difference between embodying a character and the *Heart of Darkness* thing, where you simply project your fears or desires on a character and react to it?

CM: The Conrad debate is really important. You yourself taught me so much about this in our various conversations down through the years. Instead of embodying the Black characters or even just observing them, Conrad projects his fears and desires on top of them. He judges them, then, from his own fantasies and simplicities. This is incredibly problematic, of course. I have used the word *other* wrongly before. I suppose I might prefer *one another*. But I stand by my characters. One of the simple things to do is to get as many reads as possible from people who know the world you're trying to write about. With this book, I showed it to dozens of readers, Palestinians and Israelis alike, to get a read on it, and not just liberal readers, but people across the spectrum. I never worked as hard to get something right. Inevitably certain people will say this is wrong or that it is skewed, but in the end—the deep, honest end—I would like to think that I embodied the characters the best way I possibly could.

MJ: I call you my favorite living Irish writer. What about being Irish helped you with this book?

CM: And you're my favorite living Jamaican! I remember reading *John Crow's Devil* all those years ago, in manuscript, and knowing, just knowing, that I, as a reader, felt suddenly authentic and open to a world I could never experience, except in literature.

As for this book, yes, being Irish helped enormously. I came to the subject as an Irish writer who, by the nature of where I grew up, had experienced colonialism and appropriation of land and checkpoints and national grief and psychological tremors like the famine. So yes, I think my background helped me in understanding what was going on. The passivity. The psychoses. The violence. All the lies and half-lies.

In terms of language, I think it's important to note that if the names were turned and the situation was entirely the same—if the Israelis were Palestinians, and the Palestinians were Israelis—that I would feel the same way about the story. This may sound overly simple, but I find it very affecting. I have no skin in the game in the sense that I'm not Jewish, I'm not Muslim, I'm not Arab, I'm not waving the flag for one side or the other. But I do have skin in the game in the sense that I want to understand what is going on, and I am fundamentally interested in ideas in and around peace. It's always a miracle to me that we have had peace in Ireland now for the past twenty-three years. It's shaky, but it's there.

As for Israel and Palestine, people seem to think that it's naïve to be hopeful, but Bassam puts it very succinctly when he says that it's hard to believe that there is an Israeli embassy in Berlin, and a German embassy in Tel Aviv, just fifty years after the Holocaust. Peace comes dropping slow, as Yeats says, but one of its inevitabilities is that it does arrive, it must arrive. And when it arrives—like it did in Northern Ireland—it was due to the work of extraordinary people taking risks for what other people scoffed at.

MJ: So, about that trick in the center of the book (section 1001) where you actually acknowledge that the reader is the narrator of the book—
CM: Ahh, you're the first one to ask me about that. Yes. That's all I will say. The reader is the narrator. When I discovered that, I felt like I had discovered ice.

MJ: This book came out during the pandemic, which still surrounds us. Where will this pandemic leave literature?
CM: This is a question to avoid like the plague. Seriously, though, who knows? We're slap-bang in the middle of it all and it's so hard to tell. It feels like the recent past is such a distant place and the future, of course, is uncertain, even if it arrives at an exponential pace. I have had simultaneous feelings of meaninglessness—looking down on myself as just a mass of moving molecules—and absolute meaning, where everything I do matters, my mask matters, my six feet distance matters. It seems we are simultaneously epic and tiny. There will be so many stories that will locate time by adjusting a character's mask, for instance. Or talking about the weight of a cough. I tried writing a COVID story last summer (2020), but it felt too early. Journalism must get there immediately. Literature has to pause a moment, adjust that human mask.

MJ: There's a film version in the works. what are you most concerned about when it comes to adaptation?

CM: I trust the people who are adapting it with all my heart. The good thing about it is that the Elhanan and Aramin families both have representatives in the making of the film. That's the most important thing to me. That the experience is valid and authentic and true to the message that both men want to convey about the memory of their daughters.

MJ: We have spent a good deal of our friendship in bars and restaurants. I haven't been to Israel or Palestine. Is there a particular bar or restaurant you would take me to?

CM: Damn, I would love to bring you to Palestine! The hospitality there is really astounding. Honestly, I have never come across such generosity anywhere, not even in the west of Ireland—it's really startling how open the people are. There's a coffee shop, the Singer Café, in Beit Sahour that I really love. Great food. Great beer. A rooftop terrace. I went there once with a group from my nonprofit, Narrative 4, and the Irish musician Colm Mac Con Iomaire played an impromptu concert on the roof. In Israel there's a restaurant in Akko, or Acre, run by a guy called Uri Jeremias who is known as one of the great purveyors of modern Israeli cooking. He's an incredible spirit too. A storyteller.

MJ: Which Palestinian and Israeli authors should we be reading?

CM: It's always difficult to make a list because I am afraid I will leave someone out. I am an enormous fan of Raja Shehadeh's work. He gets to the core of things in Palestine. He's a writer for our times. And Assaf Gavron captures the temperature of contemporary Israel in an extraordinary way. If I began the rest of the list it would extend for pages on end, but I always recommend going to the poets, and Darwish is a great staple.

MJ: What's next?

CM: Oh, I don't know, Marlon. Something simple maybe. A New York love story? But as we suggested earlier, nothing is simple, neither stories nor love itself.

Questions and Topics for Discussion

1. The book takes its name, *Apeirogon,* from a geometric shape with a countably infinite number of sides. Why do you think this title was chosen for the book?

2. Rami Elhanan and Bassam Aramin are real people, and their story of uniting as friends after losing their daughters and beginning a movement for peace is true. Do you think it makes a difference to your reading experience that this novel was based on real people and events as opposed to wholly fictional characters?

3. What did you know about the conflict between Israel and Palestine before you read this book? How have your thoughts about their situation changed after reading *Apeirogon*?

4. This novel is a unique blend of fictional and nonfictional elements and takes on an unusual structure of weaving together 1001 cantos. Why do you think this shape is important to the book?

5. The author ties together seemingly dissimilar topics over the course of the book and shows the reader how these unrelated items are actually connected to one another. Which of these unexpected connections stood out to you the most? Were there any you found superfluous?

6. Birds are used as a powerful piece of imagery throughout this book, from the discussion of Beit Jala as a part of a major migratory highway for five hundred million birds each year, to Philippe Petit's symbolic use of a pigeon during his high-wire performance, to the sketch of the dove that hangs in Smadar's bedroom. What do you think these birds represent in the story?

7. In a moving act, Rami and Bassam decide to use their grief as a weapon for peace. Have you ever experienced a time in your own life when you channeled your sadness or anger toward a more positive goal?

8. At one point in the novel it is said, "If you divide death by life, you will find a circle." What do you think this quote means? How does this concept apply to the story?

9. In the book, Rami and Bassam assert again and again that "it will not be over until we talk." Do you agree with them that talking is the only way to achieve peace?

10. Water is also used as a significant symbol over the course of the novel. We learn about a game called Shoot the Water Tank that the Israeli soldiers play; we hear of the night that Elik, Rami's son, spends in an abandoned water park; and we accompany Christopher Costigin while he travels from the Sea of Galilee to the Dead Sea in search of the lost biblical towns. Why do you think water imagery is so important to the book?

11. In a dramatic scene, Bassam finds out that his son has gone to throw stones at Israelis. In order to teach his son a lesson, Bassam demands that his son throw a stone at him. What do you think Bassam is trying to teach his son through this moment?

12. The concept of being met with roadblocks and checkpoints is a significant theme in *Apeirogon*. How does Bassam learn from the experience of the checkpoints he must navigate? Can the checkpoints, in Rami's case, be metaphorical too?

13. "History repeats itself" is a commonly accepted maxim. How do you think that idea plays out in the book? Do you think the story demonstrates that we are destined to repeat ourselves, or does it suggest that this cycle of repetition can be broken?

14. When Rami attends his first Combatants for Peace meeting, it is a bit of an intimidating experience for him, and he is skeptical as to whether he belongs. However, in the end, the group becomes an important source of support in his life. Have you ever taken a leap of faith that turned out for the best?

15. The act of tracing a consequence back to its source is a pattern that we see repeated throughout *Apeirogon*. Do you think it is important to identify who or what is responsible for a given outcome? Is the search for consequence endless? Might the book be suggesting that the original consequence or consequences belong within us?

COLUM MCCANN is the internationally bestselling author of the novels *TransAtlantic*, *Let the Great World Spin*, *Zoli*, *Dancer*, *This Side of Brightness*, and *Songdogs*, as well as three critically acclaimed story collections and the nonfiction book *Letters to a Young Writer*. His fiction has been published in over forty languages. He has received many international honors, including the National Book Award, the International IMPAC Dublin Literary Award, a Guggenheim fellowship, the Pushcart Prize, and an Oscar nomination for his short film *Everything in This Country Must*. He is a member of the American Academy of Arts and Letters, as well as the Irish association of artists Aosdána, and he has also received a Chevalier des Arts et des Lettres award from the French government. In addition, he has won awards in Italy, Germany, and China. A contributor to *The New Yorker*, *The New York Times*, *The Atlantic*, and *The Paris Review*, he teaches in the Hunter College MFA Creative Writing program. He lives with his family in New York City, where he is the cofounder of the global nonprofit story exchange organization Narrative 4.

colummccann.com
Facebook.com/colummccannauthor

ABOUT THE TYPE

This book was set in Caslon, a typeface first designed in 1722 by William Caslon (1692–1766). Its widespread use by most English printers in the early eighteenth century soon supplanted the Dutch typefaces that had formerly prevailed. The roman is considered a "workhorse" typeface due to its pleasant, open appearance, while the italic is exceedingly decorative.